Understanding language change

Understanding language change

April M. S. McMahon

University Lecturer in Linguistics, University of Cambridge, and Fellow of Selwyn College, Cambridge

CAMBRIDGE
UNIVERSITY PRESS

Published by the Press Syndicate of the University of Cambridge
The Pitt Building, Trumpington Street, Cambridge CB2 1RP
40 West 20th Street, New York, NY 10011–4211, USA
10 Stamford Road, Oakleigh, Melbourne 3166, Australia

First published 1994
Reprinted 1995, 1996, 1999

A catalogue record for this book is available from the British Library

Library of Congress cataloguing in publication data

McMahon, April M. S.
Understanding language change / April M. S. McMahon.
    p.   cm.
Includes bibliographical references and index.
ISBN 0 521 44119 6 (hardback) ISBN 0 521 44665 1 (paperback)
1. Linguistic change   I. Title.
P142.M38   1994
417'.7-dc20   93-8121   CIP

ISBN 0 521 44119 6 hardback
ISBN 0 521 44665 1 paperback

Transferred to digital printing 2002

To Rob

At the still point of the turning world ...
... at the still point, there the dance is

(T. S. Eliot, Burnt Norton)

Contents

Preface and acknowledgements

This book is based on a one-term undergraduate course taught at the University of Cambridge. It is intended to be usable without prior exposure to historical linguistics, and the majority of general linguistic terms will also be defined as we go along. However, readers with no knowledge at all of general linguistics may find it helpful from time to time to consult Crystal (1987), Lyons (1981) and Yule (1988), for general background points; Burton-Roberts (1986) for syntax; Ladefoged (1982) for phonetics; and Katamba (1989) for phonology.

Books may end up with one name on the cover, but are by their nature cooperative enterprises, so that I have a great many people to thank. Members of the Department of Linguistics, and numerous colleagues elsewhere, have provided advice and encouragement. Various Fellows of Selwyn College have cheerfully submitted to tests designed to work out where they put their [r]s, and have enthusiastically gone on neologism hunts for me. Sections of the text have been road-tested on three years' worth of Cambridge undergraduates and research students, and my special thanks go to James Dudley-Smith, Adam Isaacs, Kirsty Watt, Nick Ukiah, Felicity Burbridge, Jackie Hopkins, Toby Mitchell, Rob Findlay, Ishtla Singh and especially Paul Foulkes and Mari Jones. My editor at the Press, Judith Ayling, has been unfailingly helpful; and I am most grateful to Peter Matthews, Jean Aitchison and two readers for Cambridge University Press, whose comments have changed the book immeasurably for the better. Last but not least, very many thanks to Rob, who helped enormously with Chapter 12, coerced the wordprocessor into action, and stopped the cats from starving while I was up to my eyes in what follows. I dedicate this book to him.

1 Introduction

1.1 Linguistic similarities and relationships

> I knew that Magyar belonged to the Ugro-Finnic group, part of the great Ural-Altaic family, 'Just', one of my new friends told me, 'as English belongs to the Indo-European.' He followed this up by saying that the language closest to Hungarian was Finnish.
>
> 'How close?'
>
> 'Oh, very!'
>
> 'What, like Italian and Spanish?'
>
> 'Well no, not quite as close as that ...'
>
> 'How close then?'
>
> Finally, after a thoughtful pause, he said, 'About like English and Persian.' (Leigh Fermor 1986:33)

Although not everyone knows the names for groups of languages, most people will recognise that certain languages share similarities, or resemble one another in particular ways. For instance, any native speaker of English who has ever learned any French or German will have noticed that some items of English vocabulary look and sound more like their translation equivalents in German (as in (1a)), or in French (1b); others share affinities with both (1c), or indeed with neither (1d). I remember being particularly delighted, on beginning German at school, to find how similar *Kuh* [kuː] 'cow' and *Tochter* [tɒxtəʁ] 'daughter' were to the [kʉː] and [dɒxtəɹ] found in my Scots dialect.

(1)	English	French	German
a.	*hand*	*main*	*Hand*
	milk	*lait*	*Milch*
	son	*fils*	*Sohn*
	book	*livre*	*Buch*
b.	*colour*	*couleur*	*Farb*
	flower	*fleur*	*Blume*
	knife	*canif*	*Messer*
	river	*rivière*	*Fluss*
c.	*cat*	*chat*	*Katze*
	mother	*mère*	*Mutter*

three	*trois*	*drei*
night	*nuit*	*Nacht*

d.

horse	*cheval*	*Pferd*
child	*enfant*	*Kind*
black	*noir*	*schwartz*
cloud	*nuage*	*Wolke*

The discipline of comparative linguistics involves the identification, enumeration and evaluation of such cross-linguistic similarities. On the basis of a close inspection of the vocabulary and structures of the languages under inspection, linguists can propose groupings of languages which show close and consistent similarities into families. For instance, we find that Latin, German and English have a large number of words which show regular and repeated correspondences of a particular sound in one language to another sound or sequence of sounds in the others, along with similarity in meaning. These words are cognates, and we hypothesise that they derive from a common ancestor. However, as (2) shows, these similarities do not extend to the Indian language Kannada, which does not have forms cognate with those in the three European languages.

(2)

English	Latin	German	Kannada
mouse	*mūs*	*Maus*	*ili*
father	*pater*	*Vater*	*appa*
three	*trēs*	*drei*	*muru*
fish	*piscis*	*Fisch*	*minu*

However, although Kannada does not belong to the same group as English, German and Latin, it does have a family of its own: this is the Dravidian group, which also includes Tamil, Tulu and Malayalam – their words for 'mouse' are *eli*, *ili* and *eli* respectively, clear cognates of Kannada *ili*.

So far, however, we have only established that one can classify languages into groups on the basis of shared features and common patterns. We have barely touched on the historical relevance of such groupings, or the 'language change' of our title. We can introduce this historical dimension by taking our analysis one step further, and claiming that related languages, which belong to the same group or family, were once the *same* language: that is, they are derived, due to the operation of linguistic change over long periods of time, from a single, earlier ancestor language. To be more specific, English, German, French and Latin all form part of a much larger group known as the Indo-European family, all members of which have a common ancestor known as Proto-Indo-European. The Indo-European family includes many of the languages of Europe and some from areas further east, including India, Turkey and Iran, and has been extensively studied from the historical point of view. Such families of genetically related languages may be represented graphically using family trees like the one in (3), which includes all the branches of Indo-European (IE), but does not list all the constituent languages, since the family is a very large one. Linguistic family trees are, rather confusingly, drawn upside-down; the root of the IE tree in (3) is therefore at the top. Proto-Indo-European is the mother language of the family, from which all the others, its daughters, have diverged. The branches below correspond to language subfamilies like Celtic or Indo-Iranian, and the individual languages, or twigs, appear at the lowest level. It is not at present clear whether the IE family has other, more distant relatives.

(3)   The Indo-European languages

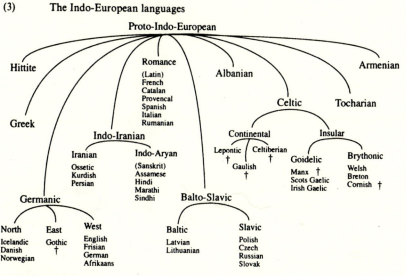

† = no longer spoken

Some rudimentary texts, in the shape of the first line of the Lord's Prayer in languages from seven of the branches of IE, are given in (4), to indicate the range of variation which can be accommodated within one family. These languages have been diverging from their common source for at least 5,000 years, and have become considerably differentiated, so that our methods for uncovering relationships between languages must clearly be rather powerful. However, if there is little apparent resemblance between Celtic and Balto-Slavic, or Germanic and Indo-Iranian, there is clear evidence of relationship within subfamilies, as is shown by a comparison of Scots Gaelic with Irish Gaelic, or of Latin with French; and the word for 'father', for instance, does show some consistency across the whole range of IE languages.

(4)   CELTIC
        Ein Tad, yr hwn wyt yn y nefoedd (Welsh)
        Ár n-atheir, atá ar neamh (Irish Gaelic)
        Ar n-athair a tha air nèamh (Scots Gaelic)

        GERMANIC
        Unser Vater, der Du bist im Himmel (German)
        Fæder ūre, þū þe eart on heofonum (Old English)
        Fadar vår, som är i himmelen (Swedish)

        ROMANCE
        Pater noster, qui es in caelis (Latin)
        Notre père, qui es aux cieux (French)
        Padre nuestro, que estás en los cielos (Spanish)

        ALBANIAN
        Ati ynë që je në qiell

        GREEK
        Páter 'ēmōn, 'o en toîs ouranōis (New Testament)
        Patéra mas, poù eisai stoùs ouranoús (Modern)

        BALTO-SLAVIC
        Otĭče našĭ iže jesi na nebešĭchū (Old Church Slavonic)
        Ótče naš, súščij na nebesách (Russian)
        Ojcze nasz, którys jest w niebiesiech (Polish)

        INDO-ARYAN
        Bho asmākhaṃ svargastha pitaḥ (Sanskrit)
        He hamāre svargbāsī pitā (Hindi)
        He āmār svargat thakā pitri (Assamese)

In spite of the striking nature of some of these similarities, such relationships among languages were only recognised relatively recently. Sir William Jones first suggested that Sanskrit, Latin and Greek might be related in 1786, when he wrote, with the reverence for ancient languages common at the time, that:

The Sanskrit language, whatever be its antiquity, is of a wonderful structure; more perfect than the Greek, more copious than the Latin, and more exquisitely refined than either, yet bearing to both of them a stronger affinity, both in the roots of verbs and in the forms of grammar, than could possibly have been produced by accident; so strong indeed, that no philologer could examine them all three, without believing them to have sprung from some common source, which, perhaps, no longer exists.

Jones' conviction, and subsequent work in historical linguistics, arises from two related facts about language and linguistic change. First, patterns in language are predominantly arbitrary: that is, there is no inevitable and natural connection between, say, the English word *cat* and the small, nominally domesticated, furry feline quadruped which it denotes. This entity might as well be called a *seagull*, or a *pot*, or a *tac*, and the fact that it is not is a matter of convention, not the result of any inalienable and essential connection of sound and meaning. If languages were entirely arbitrary, speakers of each language could invent their own word for each entity or action to which they wished to refer, and we might then expect each language to differ in random ways from every other. When, instead, we find principled and repeated similarities, such as those obtaining among the IE languages, we clearly have something to explain.

Of course, producing an explanation in terms of genetic relationship of languages, and their derivation from a common source, is only one of a number of possibilities. For instance, the sorts of resemblances we have been discussing could be due to chance; for any two languages selected at random, it is likely that there will be at least one fortuitous resemblance, such as those shown in (5).

(5)	English *man*,	Korean *man*	'man'
	German *nass*,	Zuni *nas*	'wet'
	Italian [dɔnna],	Japanese [ɔnna]	'lady'

However, coincidence is always a rather weak explanation, quite apart from the fact that we would have to assume an extraordinarily high accident rate to allow for the number of similarities between Italian and French, for instance.

There are also similarities between languages that result from borrowing: that is, one language originally had a word, and the speakers of another have imitated it and introduced it into their own language. It is certainly true that historical linguists can be misled if they do not consider language contact of this sort as a factor when attempting to explain cross-linguistic resemblances. For instance, English *street* and German *Strasse* are both borrowed from Latin *viā strāta* 'a paved road'; English *wine* and German *Wein* are loans from Latin *vīnum*; English has borrowed *river* from French *rivière*; and conversely, French has borrowed *canif* from English *knife*. However, it is highly unlikely that borrowing should have taken place as frequently, and affected as much vocabulary, as we would have to assume to account for the shared properties of the IE languages. As we shall see in Chapter 8, languages are not often quite such promiscuous borrowers; and furthermore, contact between speakers of some groups of IE languages has been rather sparse, so that it might be difficult to show when so much borrowing could have taken place. Consequently, since the other available explanations are insufficiently strong, we hypothesise that most of the similarities between the IE languages, and the members of other similar groups, are due to genetic relationship and common origin.

The fact that sound-meaning relationships are generally arbitrary also places a natural limit on language change, in that speakers must learn their native language(s) in such a way as to allow communication with the generations above and below them: since language is a vehicle of communication, it would be failing in its primary function if it did not allow parents to be understood by their children, or grandchildren by their grandparents. It follows that change is most unlikely to occur in catastrophic ways, altering the whole structure of a language and rendering inter-generational communication impossible. One theme in this book will be the identification of trends in language change; and one such trend is that change is predominantly gradual, and very frequently regular. Of course, if change were random, arbitrary and unconstrained, we would not be able to recognise languages which came from a common ancestor. The fact that we still can, some thousands of years after their initial divergence, is testament to the fact that linguistic change is often slow and steady. So, paradoxically, the arbitrariness of language ensures the non-arbitrariness of change: because language must be learned, and used for inter-generational communication, there must also be limits on how much can change, how it does so, and how fast it happens.

1.2   Language change and linguistic reconstruction

It is, in fact, possible to study the history of languages in two ways, or in two directions, just as a video may be played forwards or backwards. There exist, in other words, methods for climbing both down and up linguistic trees, or for moving both forwards and backwards in time (always with the proviso that we can go no further forward than the present day – few historical linguists would claim to be able to see, with any degree of reliability, into the future). These two parts of historical linguistics are known as the study of language change and linguistic reconstruction respectively.

In practising reconstruction, linguists begin with the earliest actual data available for the members of a language family, whether written or spoken, and attempt to ascertain what earlier stages of the languages, or ultimately their common ancestor, might have been like. For instance, in (6) some words cognate with English *ewe*, from various IE languages, are given; by the methods of linguistic reconstruction, these can be traced back to a projected ancestral form in Proto-Indo-European, the mother language. This proto-form appears in (6) with a preceding asterisk, to indicate that there is no direct evidence for it; we have no texts and no speakers, and must rely on comparative reconstruction using the daughter forms to hypothesise what the word would have been.

(6)   Proto-Indo-European *owis
     Lithuanian   *awis*   Greek   *ois*
     Luwian   *hawi*   Sanskrit   *avis*
     Latin   *ovis*   English   *ewe*
     Old Irish   *oi*

Although the methodologies of linguistic reconstruction are powerful and sophisticated, and much of interest can be said about them, reconstruction will not be pursued in this book. The speed of current developments in both subfields of historical linguistics makes it impossible to do justice to both in a single volume, and our topic here will be the other subdiscipline, language change. That is, we shall concentrate on the development of earlier stages of languages into later ones, and the mechanisms involved, rather than on the reconstruction of hypothesised past language states from present or recorded ones; we shall be moving from the past closer to the present, rather than extrapolating from the present into the past. We shall therefore be charting developments over time from nearer the top of linguistic trees like that in (7) to nearer the bottom, and attempting to seek patterns which repeat themselves from family to family and period to period, as well as explanations for such repetitions.

(7)

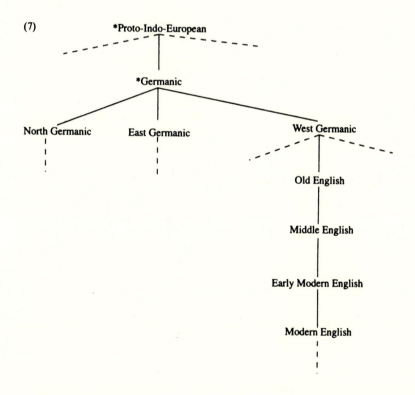

Part of our investigation will focus on *what* in fact changes in the course of linguistic change. It is as well to be clear now that the very notion of 'a language' is an idealisation, a shorthand term for the usage of a group of people, all of whom consider themselves to be speakers of Norwegian, or Welsh, or Quechua. Some people may think of 'Welsh', for instance, as the linguistic units and patterns which all Welsh speakers have in common; or perhaps as the totality of units and patterns which make up the usage of *all* Welsh speakers; others might consider 'Welsh' to mean 'Standard Welsh', and not include dialectal or non-standard usage in their definition. To some extent, therefore, we have to recognise that the notion of a language is not a linguistic one at all, but rather a socio-political matter. However we define language, we must also accept that whole languages do not change wholesale: as discussed above, it is rather the case that only small elements of them alter at any particular time, and that these are changed by speakers. In other words, we should never lose sight of the fact that languages are spoken by people for purposes of communication; consequently, speakers change languages, although that is not to say that they are necessarily conscious of doing so, or that they intend to make changes. Indeed, the history of any language, from a sociolinguistic point of view, is the story of an unbroken chain of generations of speakers, all able to communicate with their parents and children while perhaps noticing minor differences in inter-generational usage, and all believing they speak 'the same language'.

It follows that we should be careful not to see languages as single entities; they are rather amorphous masses made up of accents, dialects and ultimately individual idiolects. On the other hand, linguists often find it useful, convenient, and enlightening to idealise, and to talk about developments in a language – after all, certain changes must ultimately affect all speakers, since there are for instance no English speakers today who natively use Old English, while the rest of us have moved forwards to the Modern variety. It can be profitable to recognise that there is an idealised system which native speakers of a language, or perhaps a dialect, share – so long as we remember that we are abstracting, or idealising. It is clear that there are also norms of behaviour which members of a speech community perceive, although they do not always follow them: for instance, most British English speakers consider it to be 'wrong' not to produce the [h] in words like *hat*, *high* and *heaven*, although many who recognise this overall attitude in the speech community nonetheless drop their own [h]s. If we recognise that there are individual idiolects, shared norms, and an idealised linguistic system, we can in theory study language change in all of these areas, and their possible interrelations: that is, an individual or group of individuals may produce a novel pronunciation or other form of speech, which contributes to variation in the speech community; this may ultimately be adopted by more speakers, and cause a change in the norms of the community; and finally, it may become the expected, or standard usage, being incorporated into the shared linguistic system of native speakers of the language. This sort of interactional approach, which takes account of idealisation and variation, and involves both the individual and the language, informs much recent historical linguistics, and will form the basis for the rest of this book.

1.3   Synchrony and diachrony

Any language, or group of languages, can be approached in two different ways: we can establish the properties of the language(s) at a given point in time, in which case we are making a synchronic study; or we might wish to consider the history and development of the language(s), the domain of diachrony. Of course, our topic of language change is part of diachronic linguistics.

In what follows, I shall be presenting synchronic and diachronic linguistics as inextricably linked, and adopting the view that studying language change involves the examination and comparison of distinct language stages and systems, which may be profitably analysed using models and theories developed in synchronic studies; conversely, these models can be usefully tested against historical data, and cannot be considered complete if they do not allow for the incorporation of change into the grammar. This approach requires a little consideration here, since not all linguists agree that synchronic and historical studies can or should overlap: some, on the contrary, adhere to the absolute distinction of synchrony and diachrony proposed by Saussure, who claimed that 'the opposition between the two viewpoints, the synchronic and the diachronic, is absolute and allows no compromise' (1974: 83). This assertion arose primarily from Saussure's idea that a language should be described from the point of view of its current speakers; these know, or perceive their language only in its synchronic state, and generally have no access to its history. So, if linguists wish to describe a language from the average speaker's-eye view, their goal will necessarily be the description of the single synchronic state. Historical linguistics could then be carried out, but would involve comparison of successive states as established by synchronic study. It follows that many synchronic linguists have seen diachronic work as secondary, and indeed often as an unnecessary extra.

A number of countering observations can be made here. It may, in fact, be the case that neither the synchronic nor the diachronic approach can provide a true picture of a language, but rather that both furnish us with particular types of information, which may then be combined to give a fuller account. To use a technological metaphor, a synchronic analysis is like a still picture, whereas a diachronic one is more like a film. Imagine, for instance, walking into a cinema after the programme has begun, but finding that projector problems mean the picture has frozen. The single image you can see is of a man holding what might be a half-open book, unless of course it is a half-closed one. Now, a synchronic analysis would involve looking intently at this single frame, then formulating more or less elegant, illuminating and helpful hypotheses about it. On the basis of this analysis, we might even predict whether the book is being opened or closed. However, a diachronic analysis would introduce further information which might make our interpretation clearer. If we run the film backwards, then study the sequence of events leading up to the crucial frame, we are likely to glean some insight into the present situation. If previous shots show the character with a closed book, which he then begins to open, we have good evidence that the original image shows a half-open book. Of course, without moving the film forwards, we still cannot be absolutely sure that we are correct, and the problem with being a linguist, rather than a soothsayer or even a cinema projectionist, is that we can only look back and not into the future. Nonetheless, it seems that past events may cast light on present situations, so that we may understand current systems better by considering how they came to be. For these reasons, historical linguists may be able to illuminate synchrony, the study of a single language state, through diachronic work: understanding language change means understanding language better.

Furthermore, it seems that synchrony and diachrony, or the present and the past, cannot in practice be as separate as Saussure's dictum assumes, either in language or elsewhere. We might take the analogy of a tree, which is, as perceived at a particular moment, a synchronic fact. However, if we look at it from the roots up through the trunk to the branches and leaves, we are seeing the way the tree has grown and developed over time, to become the synchronic entity it now is. If we want to force a synchronic analysis, we can rob the tree of part of its diachronic dimension by cutting it down; but although we can eliminate its future in this way, we can't remove its past: in the cut surfaces of the trunk there will be rings, which reflect the age of the tree and the environment in which it has been growing. Languages, in this sense, are rather like trees; they have a past, and the synchronic state is a function of that past development. It is true that native speakers may not be aware of the history of their language, as they may not understand the mechanism by which seeds become plants, but that has never stopped botanists from developing diachronic theories, and arguably should not stop linguists either.

To pursue a more linguistic line of reasoning, most native speakers of any given language do not know the International Phonetic Alphabet, and cannot draw syntactic tree diagrams to show sentence structures; but they do produce sounds and sentences, and linguists are responsible for analysing these using the best tools available. If we are truly interested in investigating the nature of language, then we must note that 'whatever else languages may be, they are objects whose primary mode of existence is in time' (Lass 1987: 156–7). In other words, one property of language (or at least of all the languages studied so far) is that it changes, and linguists and linguistic theories should therefore be able to accommodate that fact, and ideally to say interesting things about the nature and causes of such change. It follows that, although historical investigation may be subsequent to synchronic analysis, since it involves the comparison of successive synchronic states, an adequate linguistic theory must involve a diachronic dimension, and synchrony and diachrony are intertwined. To come back to an earlier analogy, if we do not accept, and reflect in our theories, that 'tall oaks from little acorns grow', how much can we really claim to know about trees?

1.4   The organisation of this book

It follows from the discussion above that the aim of this book is to consider theories of language change as part of general linguistics: we will not simply catalogue changes, but use these to reflect on the nature of language, which, among other things, is inherently mutable. The changes we shall be considering affect all areas of the grammar: the sound system, or phonology; word-structure, or morphology; sentence-structure, or syntax; and meaning, or semantics. The changes will also be from a wide range of languages, although the bias towards Indo-European in historical linguistic research, and in my own background, will necessarily be reflected to some extent. In examining these changes, we shall also consider and evaluate a number of theories which have been formulated to account for them, and will return periodically to three related problems of linguistic change: the question of actuation, or how changes start; the transmission, implementation, or spread of change; and the more general issue of how and indeed whether linguistic changes can be explained.

The book is also divided into two halves, although the topics of the two sections are interrelated. Each of Chapters 2 to 7 focusses on changes in one particular area of the grammar: the phonetics and phonology in Chapters 2 and 3; the morphology in Chapter 4; the syntax in Chapters 5 and 6; and the semantics and lexicon, or vocabulary, in Chapter 7. The selection of changes reviewed in each of these chapters is by no means intended as exhaustive; rather, changes are included if they are of particular relevance in the history of the discipline, or of particular interest for a general account of change, or especially important for the relationship of synchrony and diachrony. Chapters 8 to 12 are more topic-oriented, and are not restricted to specific linguistic levels: thus, Chapter 8 deals with the effects of linguistic contact; Chapter 9 involves sociolinguistics and the study of linguistic variation; pidgin and creole languages are discussed in Chapter 10; language death in Chapter 11; and the question of linguistic evolution is the topic of the final Chapter 12. Each of the topics explored in Chapters 8 to 12 has been the focus of a good deal of recent work in historical linguistics, and all seem likely to be important for the development of the discipline.

Three questions of organisation should be considered a little further here. First, anyone with any knowledge of historical linguistics will notice that certain topics are absent from this book. In many cases, this is because I consider them to be more appropriate to a discussion of linguistic reconstruction than language change, although some areas, such as the consideration of written evidence and the problems of its interpretation, might plausibly be included in either field. I have also excluded extensive discussion of matters of prescriptivism, language academies, and other components of language planning, on the basis that 'language planning is *deliberate* language change' (Rubin and Jernudd 1971: xvi); we concentrate here primarily on unplanned, or involuntary changes. I apologise to any reader who finds his or her favourite topic omitted, but have been constrained in my selection by obvious considerations of space.

Secondly, each of Chapters 2 to 7 is restricted to a single area of the grammar purely as an aid to exposition; this does not reflect a view that the linguistic levels operate entirely in isolation and without reference to one another. In fact, this isolationist viewpoint will break down periodically throughout the first half of the book: for instance, in Chapter 3, interaction between the phonology and morphology is assumed, while Chapter 4, on morphological change, introduces the concepts of analogy, which re-appears in the syntax in Chapter 5, and of iconicity, which is of much more general relevance and plays a major part in Chapters 6 and 7. Similarly, Chapter 6 includes a discussion of grammaticalisation, a type of change involving not only the syntax, but also the phonology, morphology and semantics; and in Chapter 7, changes in both the semantics and the vocabulary are included, on the basis that it is not possible to talk about semantics in isolation from the words which express particular meanings. It might be argued that this framework of approaching changes as affecting or located in specific grammatical systems consequently breaks down too frequently to be useful. As noted above, it is adopted for purely presentational reasons; but having selected such a framework, one might then make it rigid, concentrating on changes which can be localised in particular areas of the grammar: however, I prefer to compartmentalise the grammar for reference purposes, while confessing that there are phenomena which cross compartmental boundaries, and not concealing from the reader the fact that interaction and sometimes confusion do occur. This approach reflects current practice in much synchronic linguistics, where individual grammatical areas are recognised, but interaction is also permitted.

The final organisational comment relates to the causes of linguistic change. Whatever our views on the explicability of changes, it seems clear at least that some have internal motivations, within the linguistic system itself, while others are motivated by external factors, and notably by contact between languages. I have chosen to examine the topic of language contact in Chapter 8, as an area of interest in its own right, although influences of one language on another will frequently be mentioned elsewhere. This partial isolation of the topic has the drawback of leaving the tension between internal and external causation implicit rather than explicit in most chapters: however, it is again more straightforward to deal with different motivations separately; we must simply ensure that we do not forget the degree of idealisation involved. With this caveat in mind, we now proceed to an exploration of sound change.

2   Three views of sound change

2.1   Introduction: types of sound change

In this chapter we shall investigate change in phonetics and phonology, primarily by outlining the approaches of three schools of linguists, in chronological order the Neogrammarians, Structuralists and early Generativists. This provides an opportunity to explore the development of sound change theory and introduce schools of linguistic thought which will be mentioned intermittently throughout the book. First, however, it may be useful to outline some of the types of sound change one might expect to encounter in any language.

Many sound changes affect single sounds, or vowel or consonant segments, and we shall concentrate on these below. However, some sound changes involve larger units, such as clusters of consonants, or diphthongs; and supra-segmentals such as rhythm, stress and intonation may also change. For instance, students of Germanic languages propose an early Germanic Accent Shift, which in general placed the main word stress on the first syllable of the stem; and English and German intonation patterns differ, although these languages are descended from a common source, so that we must assume changes in the intonational system of one or both daughters. It is certainly harder to study changes in suprasegmental features, since stress and intonation are rarely recorded in writing; but they do nonetheless occur.

Segmental sound changes can be conditioned, occurring in particular, specifiable environments, or unconditioned, applying to all occurrences of a particular sound. They may also be regular, or irregular and sporadic. One typically regular, conditioned type of sound change is assimilation, which involves one sound becoming more like another in its environment. Assimilation may be partial, in which case two sounds come to share certain features, or complete, producing two identical segments. Both possibilities are illustrated in (1a); in the West-Saxon dialect of Old English, the [v] of *efn* (or *efen*) [ev(ə)n] becomes nasal [m] before nasal [n], while the sequence [pt] becomes [tt] in Italian *sette*. Assimilations may be

14

anticipatory/regressive (with the affected sound coming first and the conditioning sound later), or progressive/perseverative, where the conditioning sound precedes the affected one (1b). Finally, the affected and conditioning sounds in distant assimilations are separated by other segments (see (1c)). Note that the arrowhead > indicates that one form becomes another, while the asterisk marks a reconstructed form.

(1)   Assimilation
  a.   partial: OE *efn* 'even' > West-Saxon *emn*
        complete: Latin *septem* 'seven' > Italian *sette*
  b.   anticipatory/regressive: *septem* > *sette*
        perseverative/progressive: Proto-Germanic *wulno > OE *wull* 'wool'
  c.   distant: *penkʷe > *kʷenkʷe > Latin *quinque* 'five'

Unlike assimilation, dissimilation tends to be sporadic and occurs only in isolated words, although it seems to happen more frequently with liquids, the cover-term for /r/ and /l/ sounds (2).

(2)   Dissimilation
        Latin   Old French   English loan
        peregrīnus > *pelerin*   *pilgrim*
        purpura   > *purpre*   *purpre* > *purpel* > *purple*

Segments may also be inserted, a process known as epenthesis, or lost. Epenthetic vowels often break up 'difficult' consonant clusters, while epenthetic consonants frequently arise due to mistiming (3). For instance, in the words *hamster* and *prince*, a nasal is followed immediately by a voiceless fricative, meaning that the vocal folds must be moved apart, the soft palate raised, and the complete oral closure relaxed simultaneously. However, the first two processes may precede the last, leading to an epenthetic voiceless stop.

(3)   Epenthesis
  a.   Latin *schola* 'school' > Old French *escole* (> French *école*)
  b.   *hamster* [hæmpstə(ɹ)], *prince* [prɪnts]

The terms for loss of segments depend on the unit being lost and the position it vanishes from: apocope is loss of a final vowel (4a), syncope affects medial vowels (4b), and haplology is the loss of a whole syllable from a sequence of similar syllables (4c).

(4)   Loss
  a.   apocope: Middle English [nɑːmə] > Modern English *name*
  b.   syncope: OE *munecas* > ModE *monks*
  c.   haplology: Old Latin *stipi-pendium > Latin *stipendium* 'tribute, soldiers' pay'
                     OE *Engla-lond* > ModE *England*

The types of loss shown in (4) tend to be sporadic, but loss may also be more regular. Regular cases involve the progress of a segment through a sequence of weakening changes, as shown in (5). The so-called sonority hierarchy, which runs from the (strongest) optimal consonants to the (weakest) optimal vowels, appears in (5a); weakening can be analysed as movement along this hierarchy in the direction of the arrow, generally through the stages in (5b).

(5)   a.   t   s   d   z   n   l   j   i   ii

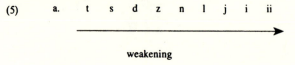

weakening

b. weakening: voicing > fricative / glide > vowel > zero

Finally, segments may be reordered, often by metathesis of adjacent segments, which is again sporadic and again tends to involve liquids (6). It is also possible to reorder segments in different syllables or words, producing Spoonerisms like *You have tasted the whole worm* (for *wasted the whole term*), but these are highly irregular.

(6)   Metathesis
         OE *ācsian* > *ask*
         OE *brid* > *bird*

The majority of the changes we have considered so far are conditioned, taking place in a restricted set of environments, and some seem to result from the actions of speakers, while others are arguably best explained with reference to hearers. For instance, epenthetic vowels may break up an articulatorily taxing sequence of consonants, while assimilation (see 2.2 below) is often explained in terms of ease of articulation, the theory that speakers prefer sequences of similar sounds, which are thought to be easier to pronounce than sequences of very different ones. Conversely, Ohala (1981, 1987) argues that listeners are responsible for dissimilation. Listeners learn by experience that speakers may distort certain clusters of sounds by assimilation, and work out corrective rules to help disentangle the intended pronunciation. However, invoking these corrective rules inappropriately leads to dissimilation.

For example (Ohala 1981: 188), Proto-Bantu *-bua 'dog' became Pre-Shona *bwa and Shona [bɣɑ], where the Pre-Shona labio-velar *w has become velar [ɣ] after a labial. By this dissimilatory change, a sequence of labial plus labial is replaced by labial plus velar. Ohala argues that listeners must have assumed that the preceding labial had distorted the next sound, and compensated by removing the labial component, leaving a plain velar, which they would then produce when acting as speakers. In other words, listeners are suspicious of sequences of similar sounds, and tend to alter one to undo the supposed assimilation; but sometimes their suspicion is misplaced and by trying to undo a non-existent assimilation they cause dissimilation instead.

Ohala's claims extend to distant dissimilation. For example, Grassmann's Law in Sanskrit de-aspirates the first of two aspirated sounds in a word. Ohala argues that aspiration spread from the two aspirated sounds to intermediate segments, but listeners reinterpreted this spread as emanating from a single, final aspirate, de-aspirating the rest of the word.

Ohala's work predicts that, in dissimilation, the first of two similar sounds will generally be the one affected, because assimilation is predominantly anticipatory; and that in cases of distant assimilation, the features affected will be those (like retroflexion, aspiration, and place of articulation features) which tend to spread over adjacent segments by assimilation. Both predictions seem broadly to be borne out.

I have emphasised this account of dissimilation to provide a counterbalance to the fact that 'in theories on the origin of sound change the speaker has usually been assigned the leading role: the speaker is claimed to have modified his pronunciation in order to reduce the energy expended in speaking, to have made his speech more distinct in order to make it more intelligible, etc.' (Ohala 1981: 178). As we have seen, certain types of sound change may prove more amenable to explanation from the speaker's point of view than the hearer's, while the opposite is true of others. However, since we all act as both speakers and hearers in normal conversation, the interplay of production and perception should not be neglected in our attempts to explain language change. We shall return to this periodically below, notably in the account of abduction in Chapter 4.

As well as the conditioned changes discussed so far, there are also unconditioned changes, the best-known being sound shifts, large-scale changes sometimes involving large numbers of sounds. In the next two sections, we shall encounter two famous sound shifts: Grimm's Law, which provides us with a good example of Neogrammarian theory; and the English Great Vowel Shift, which usefully illustrates Structuralist ideas.

2.2   The Neogrammarians

There must ... exist a rule for the irregularities; the task is to find this rule   (Verner 1978: 36)

2.2.1   *Introduction*

The Neogrammarians (*Junggrammatiker* or 'young grammarians' in German) were a group of scholars including Paul, Brugmann and Osthoff working mostly on Indo-European languages in and around Leipzig in the last quarter of the nineteenth century. By this time, attempts had been made at reconstructing Proto-Indo-European (PIE), and some changes affecting IE languages or subfamilies had been described. A beginning had also been made in the recognition of regularities in change. For example, the First Germanic Consonant Shift, which changed reconstructed Proto-Indo-European voiceless stops into Germanic voiceless fricatives, PIE voiced stops into voiceless stops, and PIE voiced aspirated stops into plain voiced ones, was first described by Rasmus Rask in 1814 (although we now know this sound shift as Grimm's Law, after Jacob Grimm who effectively publicised it). Similarly, Bopp seems to have been the first to use the term *Lautgesetz* 'sound law', which later became a mainstay of the Neogrammarian approach, in the 1820s. In work of this kind, we see clear forerunners of Neogrammarian ideas.

However, most discussion of sound change to date had been unsystematic and atomistic, consisting of a mere cataloguing of changes, or the rather directionless pursuit of individual forms down the branches of the family tree. Only rudimentary explanations, involving the Biblical Tower of Babel story, or the alleged effect of climate, diet or race on language, had been offered – for instance, frication of stops might result from speakers moving into mountainous regions, where the thin air made it harder to catch one's breath and the exertion of running up and down mountains promoted heavy breathing (Meyer 1901). Similarly, Grimm connects Grimm's Law with 'the Germans' mighty progress and struggle for freedom which inaugurated the Middle Ages and was to lead to the transformation of Europe' (1848: 417). 'Does there not', he asks us, 'lie a certain courage and pride in the strengthening of voiced stop into voiceless stop and voiceless stop into fricative?' (1848: 437; translation from Sampson 1980: 30).

Other pre-Neogrammarian historical linguists equated linguistic change with decay: language was seen as an organism, which is born, matures, then grows old and dies; and heavily inflected languages like Latin were considered to be highly developed, whereas later stages of Romance, like French, with its reduced inflectional system, were regarded as degraded and debased (see Chapter 12). The Neogrammarians, however, began to see that languages were not decaying at all. It is true that some languages sometimes lose elements of their morphological systems, as many of the inflectional endings have been lost from English and French. But this does not mean that they lose the capacity to express categories like tense; they simply evolve alternative strategies, like the use of auxiliary verbs. Furthermore, morphology may be gained as well as lost; so for instance in French we now have the productive adverbial ending *-ment*, from Latin *mens, mentis* 'mind' - forms like Old French *devotement* 'devotedly' therefore started out as Latin *devota mente* 'with a devoted mind'. Modern stages of languages are in fact just as useful as tools of communication as earlier ones, and no more debased than their ancestors. Instead of seeing changes as slovenly habits destroying the rules set down in some apocryphal Golden Age, the Neogrammarians attempted to rigorously define, describe and explain them.

2.2.2   *The regularity hypothesis*

In the late nineteenth century, science was becoming a legitimate pursuit and rather an exciting one, with the emergence, for instance, of Darwin's theory of evolution. The world was increasingly regarded as an orderly and law-governed place, and the Neogrammarians tried to show that this regularity extended to language by formulating principles and methodological assumptions about language change, and by studying sound change scientifically.

The Neogrammarians believed that only historical linguistics could be truly scientific, an attitude unfamiliar to late twentieth century linguists brought up to regard synchronic linguistics as primary. The Neogrammarians' view of the primacy of diachrony arose from their two main concerns. First, they were interested in explaining the regular, common similarities that exist among related languages. This concern encouraged the development of reconstruction, as divergent modern forms were traced back to a single form in the proto-language. Neogrammarian methodology involved first finding cognate words sharing similar sounds and meanings, like German *zu, zehn* and English *to, ten*, or Modern English *house, mouse* and Old English *hus, mus*. Next, correspondences of sounds such as those between English initial [t] and German [ts], or Modern English [aʊ] and Old English [u:], were analysed. The differences between these sounds were then ascribed to the operation of sound change.

Secondly, the Neogrammarians were worried about synchronic irregularities in language. For instance, the vast majority of Modern English nouns form their plural by affixing *-s*, but *foot* is irregular in having the plural *feet* rather than **foots* (note that * marks reconstructions, while ** indicates ill-formed, non-occurring forms). Labelling *feet* as a synchronic irregularity indicates that it is inexplicable given our knowledge about the present-day language. However, the Neogrammarians argued that such forms can be accounted for neatly if we assume that they were once quite regular, but that sound change(s) then operated and caused the apparent irregularity:

(7)   pre-Old English   *fōt   *fōti
         i-Mutation   *fōt   *føti
         Old English   fōt   fēt

| Great Vowel Shift | [fuːt] | [fiːt] |
| Modern English | [fʊt] | [fiːt] |

The development of *foot – feet* from pre-Old English is shown in (7). At this very early stage, we postulate a suffix on the plural form; the suffix vowel, high front [i], triggered a sound change called i-Mutation, a distant assimilation fronting the preceding stem vowel. The suffix was lost by Old English; the stem vowel remained front but had also unrounded, giving us the basis for the Modern English forms, with a back vowel in the present tense form, a front vowel in the past, and no suffix on either. The Great Vowel Shift, which we shall meet again in the next section, raised both stem vowels, and [uː] later shortened to [ʊ] in *foot*. Regular Modern English plurals, which lacked the high front vowel suffix, have a different history.

The main tool the Neogrammarians used in their account of cross-linguistic similarities and synchronic irregularities is the regularity hypothesis, a strong claim which in its most extreme form asserts that sound change is regular and exceptionless. Sound change was also thought to simultaneously affect all words with the same context in the language in question, and all speakers in the same speech community. The Neogrammarians also claimed that sound changes were purely phonetically conditioned, and could not refer to non-phonetic factors, such as the morphology, syntax and semantics. Sound change was therefore seen as operating with 'blind necessity', without concern for the grammatical consequences of its actions: if a sound change deleted a suffix distinguishing past from present tense forms, this was unavoidable and at best could be resolved later by alterations elsewhere in the language. The further claim that sound change proceeds by tiny, unobservable increments is probably related to this, since it was thought that if speakers knew a sound change was in operation and might have undesirable consequences for the grammar, they would try to stop it.

Although speakers do not generally seem to stop sound changes in progress, there is a 'housekeeping device' in the grammar which sometimes steps in after a sound change has occurred: this is analogy (see Chapter 4). The Neogrammarians saw sound change and analogy as opposing but interdependent processes. Since sound change operates regardless of the consequences for grammar or meaning, phonological and grammatical structure can get out of line; analogy is the process which effects realignment. However, analogy is sporadic; it clears up after sound change, rectifying mismatches of sound and grammar, but it does not apply in *all* such cases. Thus, only one of the irregular Old English nouns shown in (8a), *foot – feet*, is still irregular in Modern English. The other, if it had followed the same course, would now be *book – beek* or *book – beech*, but is in fact *book – books* due to the operation of analogy (8b).

(8) a.　　OE *fōt – fēt*　　　*bōc – bēc*
　　　b.　　*stone – stones = book –* X
　　　　　　　　　　X = *books*

Analogy makes some irregular form conform to a regular pattern, here illustrated by *stones*, which takes the weak *-s* suffix. This interaction between sound change and analogy is encapsulated in Sturtevant's Paradox: sound change is regular but creates irregularity, whereas analogy is irregular but creates regularity.

Finally, the Neogrammarians used the term sound change only for regular changes like assimilation and weakening. Changes like metathesis, haplology and dissimilation tend to violate the regularity hypothesis, since they are sporadic, applying in some words but not others with the same context, and are also observable: an interchange of two sounds can hardly happen gradually and imperceptibly.

2.2.3　*The motivation for sound change*

It is often said that the Neogrammarians saw all regular sound change as mechanical and physiologically motivated: for instance, they frequently invoked explanations like ease of articulation, explaining the assimilation from Latin *septem* to Italian *sette* by the assertion that a sequence of [t] plus [t] is easier to pronounce than a sequence [p] plus [t], with articulatory movements between the segments. However, the Neogrammarians also made use of some rudimentary psychology.

The Neogrammarian who speculates most on psychological causes of change is Hermann Paul (1978). His ideas make crucial reference to variation in a speech community, a notion clearly ahead of his time (see Chapter 9). Paul assumes that we produce sounds using muscles and motor nerves, and that this produces a motory sensation. The sensation is physical, but after the muscle activity dies away, a residual mental sound picture allows us to repeat the same sound again by matching the motory sensation with the sound picture. Normal speech involves a fair amount of deviation from the norm – as Paul says, 'even the most practised marksman misses his mark sometimes' (1978: 8) – but these deviations are generally too minute to hear, and will in any case proceed in both directions from the norm, ultimately cancelling one another out.

Occasionally, perhaps for reasons of convenience or ease of articulation, an imbalance will develop. If this happens for one speaker, it will be noticed and stopped, since Paul assumes communication will be impaired if some speakers are out of step with the rest of the speech community. But sometimes there will be a consensus, with all speakers producing a minute shift away from the target. If this imbalance outweighs deviations to the other side, the target itself will gradually shift, altering both the motory sensation and the sound picture (9).

(9)

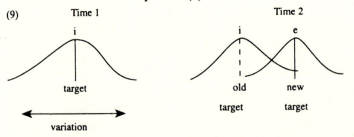

Unfortunately, Paul fails to explain why random deviations should ever become cumulative and directional. In addition, this mechanism is not intended to cover sporadic changes like metathesis and dissimilation; instead, Paul suggests that these are akin to speech errors and arise due to repeated mispronunciations which proliferate and ultimately become the norm. Thus, OE *ācsian* was presumably mispronounced as *āscian* so frequently between OE and ME that children learning the language heard the 'error' more frequently and reinterpreted it as the target – hence the modern form *ask*.

2.2.4   *Grimm's Law and the regularity hypothesis*

The most influential contribution of the Neogrammarians is arguably not any single explanation of sound change, but rather the regularity hypothesis itself. This has frequently been criticised on the grounds that absolute regularity is a myth, but the critics betray a failure to read the small print, since the Neogrammarians did not claim any such thing. In fact, the Neogrammarian notion of regularity is quite restricted. First, it excludes sporadic changes. Secondly, it is restricted to a particular speech community at a particular time; the Neogrammarians did not claim that the same sound in the same context in different languages or communities would always undergo the same change. Even with these exclusions, however, problems did arise.

The Neogrammarians seem to have seen their regularity hypothesis as an equivalent of one of the physical laws like the law of gravity, and therefore as an immutable consequence of the way the world is. Pursuing the same analogy briefly, imagine Sir Isaac Newton throwing an apple into the air and catching it, in the interests of testing his theory, until on one occasion the apple fails to come down. Sir Isaac looks around for a reason, sees that the apple is stuck in a tree, or has been carried off by a passing seagull, and the exception is explained. It is this kind of theorising which marks the greatest achievement of the Neogrammarians. Not every sound change they formulated turned out to be exceptionless. Instead, they tackled apparent exceptions in two ways: they assumed that the change had been inadequately formulated, and altered it; or they proposed an additional change. Thus, by minutely examining the data, they accounted for the counter-examples.

Let us now look at an extended example of this reasoning involving the First Germanic Consonant Shift, which appears in an informal and slightly simplified version in (10). The change is an unconditioned sound shift, affecting *all* occurrences of these sounds, not only those in specific contexts.

(10)   Grimm's Law
   a.   voiceless stop > voiceless fricative
        PIE *p t k > Gmc. /f θ x/
   b.   voiced stop > voiceless stop
        PIE *b d g > Gmc. /p t k/
   c.   voiced aspirated stop > voiced stop
        PIE *bh, dh, gh > Gmc. /b d g/

There are two main sets of exceptions to Grimm's Law as it stands in (10). First, as shown in (11), there is a set of items in which voiceless stops do not shift to fricatives.

(11)   Latin   Gothic   Old English
          cap*t*us   ha*f*ts   hæ*f*t   'prisoner'
          pis*c*is   fis*k*s   fis*c*   'fish'
          s*p*ūo   s*p*eiwan   s*p*īwan   'spit'

The words themselves are not exceptional, since the initial /p/ of *piscis*, for instance, has quite regularly become a fricative. On careful examination, however, it becomes clear that Grimm's Law simply has not been formulated carefully enough, and is missing the generalisation that voiceless stops *never* become fricatives when they follow another stop or a fricative. We do not, in fact, have exceptions, but rather a subregularity; (10a) can therefore be reformulated as in (12), reworking a basically sound idea to iron out the residual problems.

(12)   voiceless stop > voiceless fricative
                                    UNLESS directly following a stop or fricative

The second problem is rather more complex: although Grimm's Law predicts that PIE voiceless stops should become Germanic voiceless fricatives, they sometimes appear as Germanic voiced stops or voiced fricatives. PIE *bhrātēr- 'brother' becomes Gothic brōþar, with medial *t > /θ/, but PIE *pətēr- 'father' becomes Gothic fadar with a medial voiced /d/. The context causing this aberrant change is extremely hard to find, making the voicing development look truly irregular. However, Karl

Verner noted a connection with the position of the accent in PIE: voicing only occurred if the PIE voiceless stop occurred between voiced segments, *and* the previous syllable was unaccented; otherwise, the regular Grimm's Law change to voiceless fricatives took place.

One reaction to these discoveries might be to alter Grimm's Law further. Verner, however, considered this the wrong course to take, since the voicing he noted affected also the single fricative, *s, which existed in PIE before the operation of Grimm's Law. He therefore formulated an additional change, Verner's Law (13).

(13)   Verner's Law
          voiceless stops between vowels, when the preceding vowel is unaccented > voiced
          stops or fricatives

We can also work out the relative chronology of Grimm's and Verner's Law: Verner's Law must have operated after Grimm's Law historically, since it voiced the new fricatives /f θ x/ created by Grimm's Law as well as the pre-existing *s.

The Neogrammarian regularity hypothesis may therefore be generally upheld, although the sound changes first suggested might have to be supplemented or reformulated. This notion of regularity allowed the Neogrammarians to pioneer the explanation of apparent exceptions by rigorous examination of the data. The intention was not to deny the existence of exceptions, but to account for them: 'There must ... exist a rule for the irregularities; the task is to find this rule' (Verner 1978: 36).

2.3   The Structuralists

> Every modification must be treated as a function of the system of which
> it is a part   (Jakobson 1978:103)

2.3.1   *Saussure and the basis of Structuralism*

The tenets of Structuralism were first laid down by the Swiss linguist Ferdinand de Saussure in the early twentieth century, and subsequently borrowed into other fields, including literary criticism. Saussure was trained in Neogrammarian circles in Leipzig, but he taught mainly in Paris and later in Geneva where, between 1907 and 1913, he gave three courses of lectures on general linguistics. This was a new departure, given the Neogrammarian, historicist domination of contemporary linguistics, and given that Saussure's own published work was philological. After Saussure's death, two of his students, working from the notes of those attending the lectures, constructed the book which we know as the *Course in General Linguistics*, and which outlines Structuralist linguistic thought.

A number of different schools of Structuralist linguists developed during the first half of the twentieth century (Lepschy 1970), notably the Prague School, including Trubetzkoy and Jakobson, and the American Descriptivists, like Bloomfield and Hockett; but these share an adherence to Saussure's basic ideas. An account of Structuralist views of language change is therefore best prefaced by an introduction to Saussure's general theory of language.

Saussure's thought is often presented in the form of a series of dichotomies. First, he distinguished *langue* from *parole*. Parole is the individual, executive side of language, and the actual language, spoken or written, which results; while langue is the abstract system of units and rules underlying the surface variation. Saussure assumes that the linguist should be concerned primarily with langue. Secondly, Saussure distinguished synchronic from diachronic linguistics; but whereas the Neogrammarians had held that only historical linguistics was truly scientific, Saussure believed synchronic study to be primary, on the grounds that we can only understand language by considering how a particular linguistic system functions at a particular time; diachronic work involves comparing pre-established synchronic systems for two or more stages of a language. Saussure's third dichotomy involves syntagmatic as opposed to associative relations between units. Syntagmatic relations hold between sequentially ordered units, like the three segments in *cat* [kæt], or the words in the sentence *Anna is a teacher*. Associative relationships involve any relationships which speakers may perceive among words which are *not* sequentially arranged. For instance, speakers of French may associate all words ending in *-ment*, while an English speaker might associate the word *wine* with *glass* and *bottle*. In modern linguistics, one class of associative relations is of particular importance: these are now known as paradigmatic relations, and involve a choice between alternative elements at a single structural point. So, [bæt], [pæt], [mæt], [sæt] as opposed to [kæt] involve a substitution of the initial consonant; all these initial consonants are therefore paradigmatically related, in that they can all optionally fill the same structural slot. The same holds of the alternative agent nouns if *teacher* in *Anna is a teacher* is replaced by *carpenter / lawyer / doctor / taxi driver*.

The theory of syntagmatic and paradigmatic relations presupposes that, on each linguistic level, units will contrast or be opposed to one another, but will also combine in linear order to make up higher-order units. We might then expect that language could be analysed on the syntagmatic and paradigmatic dimensions both synchronically and diachronically. The Neogrammarians were particularly concerned with syntagmatic relations; for instance, they interpreted cases of assimilation as one sound influencing another, adjacent sound. However, as we shall see, the Structuralists were more interested in paradigmatic relationships.

Perhaps the central element of Saussure's theory is the idea of the linguistic sign. The sign has two parts, as shown in (14) – the signifier, or form, and the signified, or concept. The sign itself, the union of these two parts, is essentially arbitrary; there is no necessary connection between the word *glass* and the object it denotes, and either may change over time.

(14)

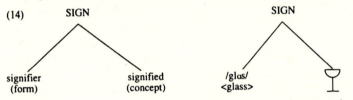

Saussure claims that signs are meaningful only when seen in their place in the system of a certain language at a certain time. Only the system is important, as we can see using the example of colours (Culler 1976). The spectrum is divided differently in different languages; non-native speakers of English, for instance, must therefore be taught the English colour terms. However, they will not learn what *blue* means by being put in a room with one hundred blue objects and told that this is the meaning of *blue*, since they will then be unable to generalise and to classify novel objects as blue or not-blue. This is because *blue* has no meaning in isolation; it is what is not-green, not-purple, not-black, not-white and so on, and such distinctions can only be grasped by considering all the colours together. The crucial thing is not the individual terms, but the way they contrast and interact within the system.

The units of language are likewise contrastive and relational, and can only be understood by considering their place within the language system. This assumption leads to a viewpoint rather different from that of the Neogrammarians, who were still essentially atomistic in their approach, considering individual units and changes. For the Structuralists, a language is crucially, in Meillet's terms, 'un système où tout se tient' – a system with a place for everything, and everything in its place. This must be borne in mind now, as we turn to the Structuralist view of sound change.

2.3.2   *Phonemic change: split and merger*

For the Structuralists, the central units of the sound system were phonemes. Like most other Structuralist terms, the phoneme is based on contrast: sounds are phonemic if they make a meaning difference between words. In English, /p/ and /b/ do contrast, as in *pat* versus *bat*, while the two /l/ sounds, clear [l] in *light* and dark [ɫ] in *hall*, do not. Native speakers are generally more aware of the first difference than the second, and the sounds which contrast, like /p/ and /b/, are phonemes, while the others, like [l] and [ɫ], which appear in predictable contexts and are variants of a single phoneme (in this case /l/) are called allophones. Each language has its own phonemic system; as (15) shows, Scots Gaelic does have a contrast between clear /l/ and dark /ɫ/.

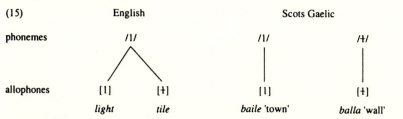

(15)   English   Scots Gaelic

phonemes   /l/   /l/   /ɫ/

allophones   [l]   [ɫ]   [l]   [ɫ]

              light   *tile*   *baile* 'town'   *balla* 'wall'

The Structuralist typology of phonemic change (Hoenigswald 1960) crucially involves split and merger: split involves one phoneme becoming more than one, while in merger, two or more phonemes collapse into one (see (16)).

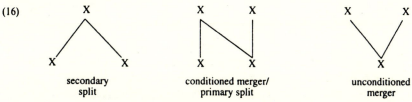

(16)   X   X   X   X   X

         X   X   X   X   X

        secondary   conditioned merger/   unconditioned
          split   primary split   merger

Unconditioned merger happens when the realisations of two phonemes fall together in all contexts, and is irreversible; a phoneme resulting from merger behaves exactly like a phoneme with a single source. In Sanskrit, for instance, PIE *a and *e merge to give /a/ in all environments; [e] becomes [a], and /e/ is lost. There is also conditioned merger, which is associated with primary split. Here, one phoneme develops a new allophone in a certain environment; this matches the realisation of some other phoneme, with which it merges, splitting from the phoneme to which it originally belonged. For instance, in Latin /s/ > [r] between vowels; this [r] sounded, we can assume, like [r] from the phoneme /r/, and was reinterpreted as a realisation of /r/ rather than of /s/ (some occurrences of [s] between vowels in later Latin, as in *ambrosia*, are the result of a subsequent change of /t/ > [s]; other cases appear in loanwords, for instance). Conditioned merger with primary split, unlike unconditioned merger, does not involve the loss of a phoneme; the phoneme system remains unchanged, but the distribution of its members alters. Secondary split, on the other hand, introduces a new phoneme into the system: here, a phoneme again develops a new allophone, but this does not correspond to an allophone of any other phoneme. The sound will remain allophonic unless the conditioning context which caused the original change is lost, in which case it becomes phonemic by primary split. An example is given in (17).

(17)   Pre-OE: i–Mutation /u/ > [y] / -- /i j/
        *trumian > *trymian 'strengthen'
        *trymian > OE *trymman*

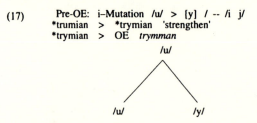

The pre-Old English sound change of i-Mutation fronted vowels when followed by high front /i/ or /j/. Later, however, the high front sounds conditioning the change were lost, making it impossible to predict where [y] might occur rather than [u]; earlier /u/ then split to /u/ versus /y/ in Old English.

2.3.3   *Structure and function*

The Structuralists, then, were interested in change as it affected the phoneme system, and studied such change by comparing successive systems. However, they also attempted to explain sound change.

As we saw in 2.2 above, the Neogrammarians concentrated on conditioned sound changes like assimilation, where one segment affects another to which it is related syntagmatically. Their explanations of ease of articulation or convenience might hold for these changes, but were unsuitable for unconditioned sound changes, or sound shifts, like Grimm's Law: the Neogrammarians formulated laws to say *what* happened, but were unable to say *why* the sounds should have followed their rather circular course. Why, for instance, would it be 'easier' to substitute voiceless fricatives for voiceless stops, and voiceless stops for voiced ones, than to maintain the status quo?

The Structuralists attempted to explain sound shifts by invoking the structure of systems and the function of language; and we shall look first at structure.

One important aspect of structure is symmetry; gaps in sound systems seem to be disfavoured. For instance, the pre-eighteenth century English fricative system appears in (18); there are three voiced – voiceless pairs, but two voiceless fricatives without voiced partners.

(18)   f θ s ʃ h
        v ð z

A new voiced partner, /ʒ/, has now evolved for /ʃ/. /ʒ/ arose from the combination of [z] + [j] in words like *treasure*, *pleasure*, and was also borrowed from French in loans like *beige*, *azure*, *rouge*. /h/, however, is not gaining a voiced equivalent, but may be disappearing from the language. Many English accents now have /h/-dropping, making *ham* and *am*, or *hit* and *it* homophonous; a corroborative story tells of an address dictated by a Cockney in which Harwich Harbour is heard and written as Arijaba. The social pressure maintaining /h/ may not hold out forever, so that the English fricative system may be gap-free relatively soon.

The idea of symmetry may also explain some unconditioned sound shifts, like Grimm's Law or the Middle English Great Vowel Shift, in which sounds (this time long vowels) again seem to move round in a circle. A rather simplified version of the Great Vowel Shift appears in (19).

(19)   The Great Vowel Shift

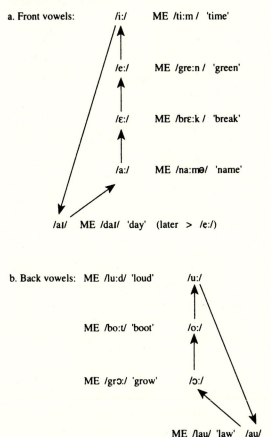

a. Front vowels: /iː/   ME /tiːm/ 'time'

                       /eː/   ME /greːn/ 'green'

                       /ɛː/   ME /brɛːk/ 'break'

                       /aː/   ME /naːmə/ 'name'

/aɪ/   ME /daɪ/ 'day'   (later > /eː/)

b. Back vowels: ME /luːd/ 'loud'   /uː/

         ME /boːt/ 'boot'   /oː/

         ME /grɔː/ 'grow'   /ɔː/

                       ME /lau/ 'law'   /au/

It is possible to see this shift as a drag chain, which involves one phoneme shifting, and leaving a space into which others will be pulled. In the case of the Great Vowel Shift, this analysis assumes that the high vowels diphthongised for some reason, and lower vowels were progressively raised to fill the abhorrent gaps: the diphthongising high vowels drag the rest of the long vowel system along behind them.

However, an alternative view might invoke function rather than structure. Martinet (1952, 1955), for instance, notes that the primary function of language is communication, and that change must not be allowed to jeopardise communication needs.

One change which might seriously disrupt communication is phoneme merger. If two phonemes fall together, an inevitable consequence is homophony; words with different meanings will begin to sound the same, and this might cause communicative difficulties if widespread. Martinet here refers to the notion of functional load, or the number of minimal pairs which exists for two phonemes. The opposition between /t/ and /d/, for instance, distinguishes a large number of pairs of words in English (including *tip – dip, at – add, hat – had, tear – deer, try – dry, writer – rider*), while the contrast between /n/ and /ŋ/ does relatively little work. The first opposition therefore has a high, and the second a low functional load, and pairs of phonemes with low functional load are more likely to merge, since this would cause less communicative damage. This conclusion, however, depends crucially on the structure of the language concerned; so, in English, although the contrast of /θ/ and /ð/ has a very low functional load, /θ/ and /ð/ are relatively unlikely to merge since they are distinguished by only one feature, voicing, which does a good deal of work elsewhere in the consonant system; nothing would therefore be gained in terms of economy if the /θ/ – /ð/ contrast were lost.

This notion of economy is also functionally relevant; sound systems tend toward economy as well as symmetry. Systems are most economical when they derive the maximal number of contrasts from the minimal number of features. Furthermore, systems with a wide margin of safety between sounds seem to be preferred, since well-defined distinctions can be more readily perceived. This might explain the frequent occurrence of triangular vowel systems like those in (20), where vowels are maximally distinct acoustically and articulatorily.

(20)   i   u   i   u
                              e   o
            a   a

Martinet's attempts to explain sound change in terms of maximum differentiation of phonemes, margin of safety, the best use of phonetic space, and the avoidance of wholesale mergers, might provide a second possible explanation for the Great Vowel Shift. Instead of a drag chain, we might propose a push chain, where one phoneme shifts and encroaches on the territory of some adjacent phoneme; this moves in its turn, again setting off a chain reaction. In the present case, we assume that one of the lower vowels was gradually raised; to avoid a merger, the next highest vowel shifted in the same direction, and the process was repeated until the original system of oppositions was restored, albeit with different vowels in different sets of lexical items.

It is certainly unwise to see the notions of structure and function as mutually exclusive, and indeed the preferable account of the Great Vowel Shift may involve both drag and push mechanisms, as data from Scottish English and other northern varieties suggest. The Middle English ancestors of these northern dialects did not have quite the same system as the southern dialects where the Great Vowel Shift began. Instead, they had the system in (21).

(21)   i: u:
         e: ø:
         ɛ: ɔ:
         a:
      aI   au

The main difference is that /oː/ had fronted to /øː/ in the north. In these northern areas, /uː/ also failed to participate in the Great Vowel Shift, so that modern Scots dialects still have /hus/, /mus/ rather than diphthongised /haus/, /maus/. /uː/ may have failed to diphthongise in these varieties because there was no /oː/ to push it, suggesting that this 'top' part of the Great Vowel Shift was a push chain. However, the other vowels did shift, indicating that the vowel to start the whole process may have been /ɔː/ (and similarly front /ɛː/), which moved up towards /oː/ where such a vowel existed, and dragged the other vowels along behind.

Structuralist notions of structure and function with respect to particular linguistic systems can therefore help us understand sound shifts as well as the smaller-scale conditioned changes discussed by the Neogrammarians. In addition, while the Neogrammarians considered each sound change as an independent process, operating blindly and without concern for the consequences, the Structuralists believed that one change might disturb the equilibrium of a system, provoking further changes until equilibrium was restored. Structuralist theory also permits a partial integration of synchrony and diachrony, since changes are seen as a function of the synchronic system in which they occur, and any laws governing the structure of synchronic systems will also determine and constrain change. These notions of the interaction and interdependence of synchronic principles and diachronic developments are crucial to much modern historical linguistics.

Although we have concentrated in this section on language-internal motivations for change, the Structuralists were very much aware that external considerations could also influence the onset and direction of linguistic changes. For example, Martinet notes that gaps in a system may remain empty for lengthy periods, and may be filled at a specific time due to external factors such as language contact. Similarly, Meillet accepts that some similarities between related languages appear only after divergence from the common ancestor, so that resemblances among languages may reflect parallel development rather than genetic relationship alone. Finally, Jakobson (in Keiler 1972) is at pains to point out that borrowing and linguistic convergence may have profound effects on language structure. We shall return to matters of language contact in Chapters 7–11, but should be aware that the Structuralists invoked external as well as internal causation in their search for explanations of change.

There are, however, two problems for Structuralist accounts of sound change. First, it is unclear how change is ever to happen, if every element in the system is dependent on every other element; and second, if units have no meaning in isolation, but only gain their significance from their place in the system of a certain language at a certain time, how can we compare different languages or different stages of the same language? Presumably comparison presupposes complete structural equivalence, which is extremely unlikely to exist; to pursue our analogy of colours, *blue* in English cannot, in strict Structuralist terms, be compared with the word for 'blue' in Russian or Welsh, since these cover slightly different areas of the spectrum, and are opposed to different sets of terms.

2.4   The Generativists
What really changes is not sounds, but grammars   (Postal 1968: 270)

2.4.1   *Generative Grammar*

In the last two sections, we have focussed on schools of linguistic thought which essentially constitute closed chapters in the history of the discipline. Diachronic (and synchronic) linguists have learned, and still can learn much from the approaches of the Neogrammarians and Structuralists; and indeed, the Generativists themselves might be described as Structuralist in their concentration on linguistic systems. However, there are now very few linguists working entirely within the Neogrammarian or Structuralist paradigms.

The Generative school, however, has not so far been superseded by a new, dominant paradigm, so that numerous linguists would still describe themselves as Generativists. In the last quarter-century, Generative syntax and phonology have both fragmented into a number of related but distinct synchronic and diachronic models. Since not all of these are yet fully developed, an up-to-date survey would necessarily be incomplete and also very complex theoretically. Consequently, this section will focus on early Generative work in the so-called Standard Model, as practised primarily in the 1960s. This has the advantage of allowing a relatively finished picture to be drawn, since Generativists today only very rarely adhere to the Standard Model. The picture might be seen as a rather old-fashioned one, but only if it is taken as an attempt to portray the current state of Generative linguistics, rather than a study of the beginnings of Generative theory included to maintain the historical perspective of this chapter. More recent aspects of Generative theory will be explored briefly in Chapter 3 (for phonological change) and Chapter 5 (for historical syntax).

Generative Grammar, with Noam Chomsky as its leading figure, came to prominence from the late 1950s with works on synchronic syntax (Chomsky 1957, 1965); the Generative approach spread to phonology (Halle 1959, Chomsky and Halle 1968), and later to sound change (King 1969a). One of its primary innovations was the realisation that the class of well-formed or grammatical sentences in any language is potentially infinite; consider the English sentence *I know Sarah and Clive and Aidan and Kathy...*, which obviously could be extended *ad infinitum*. Native speakers are also constantly producing novel sentences which they have not previously uttered. If I say *Alexandra fed forty-two lettuces to the llama*, I can feel reasonably confident that I have not uttered this sentence before; indeed, this may be the first time anyone has produced it. Even so, other native speakers of the same language can readily understand such newly-minted sentences, provided that they are grammatical.

Sentences in a human language will be grammatical if they follow particular patterns; they are not simply random collections of words thrown together in random order. Furthermore, the repeated patterns found in a given language will tend to be rather few, and this insight lies behind the Generative analysis of language and language acquisition. Many earlier studies had assumed that children acquire their native language by listening, memorising and repeating; however, this would mean that children could not move beyond the repertoire of sentences they had already heard, whereas in fact they often produce novel utterances. The Generative approach to this problem crucially involved regarding language as a rule-governed phenomenon: in acquiring a language, children would have to learn a small set of rules, and a larger but still finite set of words, and could then from these finite resources produce or generate a potentially infinitely large set of grammatical sentences.

Acquisition of even these rules or patterns, however, is not strictly a learning task, given Chomsky's further assumption that all human languages are analysable using the same sorts of rules and grammars. If the same types of structures are common to all languages, Chomsky reasons, then why should they not be already present in the mind at birth? A genetically inherited outline of language universals is consequently assumed to be innate. Children learn their own language by listening to linguistic data and filling language-specific details into this largely pre-set plan. This interaction between the innate Universal Grammar and heard, language-specific data allows the child to build a personal, internalised mental grammar. This internal grammar, which Chomsky calls competence, allows native speakers to understand and produce sentences, and represents their tacit or subconscious knowledge of their native language. The Generative linguist's task is then to build an explicit rule system which does the same job as this internal grammar. The Generativists were consequently concerned with the notion of a linguistic system, but while the Structuralists considered actual linguistic data, the Generativists concentrated on the underlying system of rules; whereas the Structuralists said 'phonemes change', the Generativists said 'rules change'. Indeed, actual language data, which Chomsky calls performance, was of strictly limited interest to the early Generativists, precisely because slips of the tongue, tiredness, lack of concentration and numerous other such factors ensure that many actual utterances do not entirely follow the rules which generate the idealised forms of competence. Chomsky hypothesises that children can abstract away from the limited and imperfect data they receive, in constructing their grammar. However, the primacy of competence is clear from the simplifying assumption that 'Linguistic theory is concerned primarily with an ideal speaker-listener, in a completely homogeneous speech-community, who knows its language perfectly and is unaffected by such grammatically irrelevant conditions as memory limitations, distractions, shifts of attention and interest, and errors ... in applying his knowledge of the language in actual performance' (Chomsky 1965: 3). It is easy to see that issues of variation were not addressed in early Generative theory.

Two short illustrative examples might be useful at this point. A Generative syntactician would assume that a native English speaker would regard the sentences in (22) as related.

(22)   *Alexandra fed the llama.*
        Did Alexandra feed the llama?
        Alexandra did not feed the llama.
        The llama was fed by Alexandra.
        Was the llama fed by Alexandra?
        The llama was not fed by Alexandra.

Early Generative syntax assumed that these sentences share essentially the same, rather abstract deep structure form, which might look something like ALEXANDRA FEED LLAMA, although each would also have markers to specify whether it would end up as a statement, negative or question on the surface. Transformational rules then turned the deep structures into the different surface structures; for instance, the rule for making questions said roughly 'add an appropriate form of the verb *do* at the beginning of the sentence'.

Similarly, in Generative phonology the goal was to assign to each morpheme, each meaningful part of a word, a single unique shape called the underlying form. The surface forms which actually appear in different contexts were then derived from this by rule. For instance, we might assume that native speakers of English know a unit meaning 'negative', with the underlying form /ɪn/. When this prefix is added to different adjectives, the nasal assimilates partly or completely to the first consonant of the adjective stem, as shown in (23). This variation is secondary and rather superficial; what really matters is that all these ostensibly different prefixes can be related, and the variations derived by rule.

(23)   /ɪn/ = negative prefix
       ɪ[n] *temperate*
       ɪ[m] *plausible*
       ɪ[ŋ] *coherent*
       ɪ[r] *relevant*
       ɪ[l] *literate*

Such alternations of sounds are very common; another example from English is *electri*[k] – *electri*[s]*ity* – *electri*[ʃ]*ian*, where the stem morpheme would again have a single underlying form, say /ɛlɛktrɪk/. Generative phonological reference to the morpheme, a non-phonological unit, also illustrates the Generative idea that phonology interacts with other components of the grammar, such as the morphology or syntax, so that sound change may be non-phonetically conditioned.

The Generative linguist, then, aims to write a grammar mirroring the native speaker's competence. However, the number of grammars which could generate the same set of sentences is potentially infinite, and it is unclear which we should prefer. The primary early Generative criterion was simplicity: we should assume that native speakers are creatures whose minds work on a principle of least effort. Their internalised grammars must therefore operate with minimal apparatus and fuss, generating all the necessary data with the minimum complexity; that is, they must be maximally simple. This requirement is a version of Occam's Razor, which states that <u>entia non sunt multiplicanda praeter necessitatem</u>, 'entities are not to be multiplied beyond necessity' – or, less formally, don't ask for more units than you need. If the linguist's formal grammar is to match the internal one, it must also be maximally simple, and in early Generative terms, simplicity was measured by counting the number of rules and units in the grammar, with lower numbers preferred (this, of course, is itself a slightly simplified outline).

2.4.2   *The Generative theory of sound change*
2.4.2.1   Introduction

In Generative theory, then, all sound change was seen as change in the grammar. Change between two related languages or varieties was established by constructing and comparing systems of rules and underlying forms for each stage or language. Logically, phonological change could only occur in the form, order or inventory of rules, or in the underlying representations.

The early Generative belief in evaluation procedures based on measurements of simplicity also led to the belief that all change must be simplificatory, translating more complex to simpler and more economical grammars. The Generativists therefore denied the functional motivation advocated by the Structuralists. For instance, King (1967) measured the functional load of various oppositions of sounds (that is, roughly, the number of pairs of words distinguished by the difference between these sounds). He used data from a number of Germanic languages, concentrating on sounds which are known to have subsequently undergone sound change, and his results contradict in part the predictions of the functional load hypothesis. For instance, /y/ has been lost by merger in Icelandic. There are two other Icelandic vowel phonemes close to /y/ in terms of their component features, with which /y/ might have merged; one is /u/, and the other /i/. The opposition /y/-/i/ had a functional load more than four times higher than that of /y/-/u/, but /y/ nevertheless merged with /i/.

In the next two subsections, we shall consider the mechanisms of phonological change proposed by the Generativists: first, the different types of rule change; then, restructuring of the underlying forms.

2.4.2.2   Rule change

2.4.2.2.1   *Rule addition*

Rule addition, which is also simply called innovation, was the most basic type of change recognised by the Generativists, and also the only sort of change which could affect the grammar of adult speakers; all the other changes to be discussed here take place between generations, as children acquiring language internalise a slightly different grammar from their parents'. In rule addition, the speaker adds a new rule to the end of his phonological rule system; this constitutes a response to the introduction of a sound change, and the change and the resulting phonological rule will generally be identical. Rule addition only changes the synchronic rule system, not the underlying forms of morphemes; any change at the underlying level will only take place later, if at all.

An example of an added rule is given in (24).

(24)
$$
\begin{bmatrix}
+ \text{ obstruent} \\
- \text{ continuant} \\
+ \text{ voice}
\end{bmatrix}
\longrightarrow [- \text{voice}]
$$

This rule, although formulated using Generative phonological notation, has identical results to the second part of Grimm's Law, in (10b) above, and states that voiced stops (or voiced, obstruent non-continuants) become voiceless; their value for voicing changes. A Generative statement of the diachronic sound change would differ from the synchronic phonological rule only in the conventional use of an arrow ($\longrightarrow$) in the latter, and a shaftless arrowhead ($>$) in the former.

The consensus view in later Generative work was that such rules would only be added at the end of the phonological rule system. Earlier, a process called rule insertion (King 1969a: 43) had allowed new rules to be added anywhere in the grammar. This was rejected because a rule introduced early in the inventory might operate cumulatively with later phonological rules to produce an output rather remote from the previous pronunciation, potentially impairing communication between generations. However, a rule added at the end of the rule component would alter pronunciations only according to its own effect, allowing communication with speakers as yet lacking the change.

2.4.2.2.2 'Rule loss

As well as appearing in a grammar, rules were said to disappear. King's (1969a: 46ff) example of rule loss involves final devoicing in Yiddish.

Yiddish ultimately derives from Middle High German, which underwent a sound change (and therefore added a rule) devoicing final stops and fricatives. This produced the alternations shown in (25b), which were not present in Old High German (25a) when the change had not yet operated. Most Modern German dialects retain this final devoicing rule, but Yiddish does not; as (25c) shows, voiced obstruents may appear finally in Yiddish.

(25) a. Old High German
        gab 'he gave' – *gabum* 'we gave'
        tag 'day' – *tage* 'days'

b.   Middle High German
   gap – gaben
   tac – tage
c.   Standard Yiddish
   tog 'day' – *teg* 'days'
   noz 'nose' – *nezer* 'noses'

We can hypothesise that final devoicing *did* apply in Yiddish, since isolated words like *avek* 'away' and *gelt* 'money' have voiceless final stops in Modern Yiddish, but had voiced ones in Old High German. Some Yiddish dialects also maintain final devoicing. In Generative terms, then, Yiddish did have a devoicing rule, but has lost it. Such loss probably should not be interpreted as the instantaneous disappearance of a rule, but rather as a gradual reduction in its scope; the process applies to fewer and fewer forms and ultimately fades out of the system.

2.4.2.2.3 *Rule reordering*

Two successive stages of a language, or two different dialects, sometimes seem to have the same two phonological rules applying in different orders. For instance, after German final devoicing was introduced, around AD 1000, another change lengthened vowels before voiced obstruents; so, in the fifteenth and sixteenth centuries, words like *lob* 'praise' and *veg* 'path' surfaced with short vowels in the nominative forms and long ones in the genitive (26a). This distribution is best accounted for if we assume that final devoicing preceded vowel lengthening, and that the synchronic order of rule application matched the chronological order of introduction of the sound changes. In Modern German, however, both nominatives and genitives have long vowels, suggesting that the rules have come to apply in the opposite order.

(26)   a.   underlier: lob   lobəs   veg   vegə

             final devoicing: lop   ——   vek   ——

             V lengthening: ——   lo:bəs   ——   ve:gə

       b.   underlier: lob   lobəs   veg   vegə

             V lengthening: lo:b   lo:bəs   ve:g   ve:gə

             final devoicing: lo:p   ——   ve:k   ——

One possible reason for such a rule reordering is suggested by Kiparsky (1978), who invokes the notion of rule simplification. Generative rules are regarded as simpler if they apply maximally and can be stated economically: an obvious case of simplification is shown in (27), where the simplified version has fewer features and applies potentially to more segments. The symbol # indicates a word boundary.

(27) a. $\begin{bmatrix} + \text{ obstruent} \\ + \text{ continuant} \end{bmatrix}$ $\longrightarrow$ [– voice] / ——— #

b. [+ obstruent] $\longrightarrow$ [– voice] / ——— #

Kiparsky argues that rule reordering also depends on the notion of maximal application, the requirement that each rule should do as much work as possible. In Kiparsky's terms, two rules may be ordered in feeding order, or in bleeding order. In feeding order, the first rule provides contexts for the next, as shown in (28a). But in bleeding order, the first rule robs the second of segments to which it could otherwise have applied, as in (28b).

(28) a.   Feeding order:

1. v $\longrightarrow$ f

2. f $\longrightarrow$ ϕ

b.   Bleeding order:

1. v $\longrightarrow$ f

2. v $\longrightarrow$ w

In (28a), rule 1 provides cases of /f/ for rule 2 to delete, but in (28b), rule 1 shifts all instances of /v/ to /f/, leaving no /v/s for rule 2 to apply to. Kiparsky argues that, to allow maximal application and thus increased simplicity, rules will tend to be reordered either into feeding order, or out of bleeding order. In the German final devoicing case, we see reordering out of bleeding order.

2.4.2.2.4 *Rule inversion*

The final type of rule change is rule inversion (Vennemann 1972), which involves the reinterpretation of original surface forms as underlying forms. One example involves the treatment of /r/ in certain accents of English, including Southern British English Received Pronunciation (RP). The operation of a number of eighteenth century sound changes in the ancestor of this variety meant that /r/ appeared after a restricted set of vowels, namely /ɔ:/, /ɑ:/, /ə/ and /ɜ:/, which we can regard as a long schwa (/ə/). Some examples are shown in (29).

(29)   /ɔ:/   *oar, floor, for, lore, shore* ...
          /ɑ:/   *star, bazaar, far* ...
          /ɪə/   *beer, fear, near, here* ...
          /ɛə/   *care, there, air, square* ...
          /ʊə/-/ɔ:/   *assure, pure, lure, poor* ...
          /ɜ:/   *stir, fir, fur, word, err, heard* ...

/aɪə/	choir, fire...
/aʊə/	flower, tower ...
/ə/	letter, father, sugar, figure ...

Subsequently, a process of /r/-deletion operated in a number of English accents, whereby /r/ was lost before consonants and pauses, as shown in (30). The resulting distribution of [r] is characteristic of so-called non-rhotic accents: rhotic varieties maintain [r] wherever it appears in the spelling.

(30)   /r/–Deletion: /r/ ———→ ⌀ ⊢——— $\left\{ \begin{matrix} \text{##} \\ C \end{matrix} \right\}$

       [r] retained initially: *red, robe, rate...*
       [r] retained intervocalically: *very, hurry, soaring...*
       [r] lost: *beard, heart, car...*

This conditioned loss of /r/ led to alternations of [r] and zero, with [r] appearing only in forms of a word with a following vowel: this pattern, shown in (31), is still very common among RP speakers, and is referred to as the use of linking [r].

(31)   Alternations of [r] – Ø:
        soar[Ø] – soa[r]ing – soa[r] in the sky
        fear[Ø] – fear[Ø]ful – fea[r]ing – fea[r] of flying
        for[Ø] – fo[r] Anna
        star[Ø] – sta[r]y; sugar[Ø] – suga[r]y
        letter[Ø] – put the lette[r] in here
        Peter[Ø] – Pete[r] isn't my favourite person

However, instead of learning that words like *soar* have underlying /r/, which is then deleted before consonants and pauses, some speakers seem to have undergone a rule inversion. These speakers analyse *soar* as having *no* final /r/ at the underlying level (after all, *soar* in isolation is never pronounced with [r] in their accent) and *insert* [r] instead after the vowels /ɔ: ɑ: ə/ when another vowel follows. This [r]-Insertion rule is given in (32).

(32)   [r]-Insertion:
        Ø ———→ [r] / /ɔ: ɑ: ə/ --- V

If *soar* is just /sɔ:/ underlyingly for speakers with [r]-Insertion, they should be unable to distinguish it from *saw*, which is also /sɔ:/; that is, they should apply [r]-Insertion to forms which had final /r/ historically *and* to forms with the same final vowel which did not. In fact, this prediction is borne out, since a growing number of people are producing so-called intrusive [r] – instances of [r], regularly inserted by [r]-Insertion, but in words which had no historical [r]. Some cases are given in (33).

(33)   *saw*[Ø] – *saw*[r]*ing*; *withdraw*[Ø]- *withdraw*[r]*al*
         banana[Ø] – *banana*[r]*y*; *magenta*[Ø] – *magenta*[r]*ish*
         Kafka[Ø] – *Kafka*[r]*esque*; *Shaw*[Ø] – *Shaw*[r]*ism*
         law[Ø] – *law*[r] *and order*
         comma[Ø] – *put the comma*[r] *in there*
         idea[Ø] – *the idea*[r] *is*
         Anna[Ø] – *Anna*[r] *isn't my favourite person*

Speakers who use intrusive [r] may also insert it when they are using foreign words or acronyms, or even speaking (or singing, in the case of the Latin) a foreign language (34).

(34)   Foreign words:
         the social milieu [miːljɜːr] *of Alexander Pope*
         the junta [xʊntər] *in Chile*

         Acronyms:
         as far as BUPA[r] *is concerned*

         Foreign languages:
         French: *j'étais déjà*[r] *ici*
         German: *ich habe*[r] *einen Hund*
         Latin: *hosanna*[r] *in excelsis,*
                  dona[r] *eis requiem*
         (Data partly from Wells 1982)

Furthermore, when vowels which would not otherwise trigger [r]-Insertion are reduced to schwa, [r] is regularly inserted, as shown in (35).

(35)   *tomato*[ər] *and cucumber production*
         the window[ər] *isn't clean*
         eyeshadow[ər] *and make-up*

         Cockney: *I'll tell you how* [jəræː]
                  to it [tərɪʔ]

         Norwich: *run over by a* [bərə] *bus*
                  out to[ər] *eat, quarter to*[ər] *eight*
         (data from Wells 1982, Trudgill 1974)

The data given in (33)-(35) above can only be accounted for if we assume that some speakers have undergone a rule inversion, so that, instead of analysing *soar* as /sɔːr/ and deleting /r/ in certain contexts, they internalise it as /sɔː/ and insert [r] in the opposite set of environments. For speakers who produce linking but not intrusive [r], we can either assume that the inversion has not taken place, or that they succeed in inserting [r] in *soaring* but not *sawing* by referring to the spelling.

2.4.2.3 Restructuring

As we have already seen, all rule changes apart from rule addition were ascribed to the child in early Generative theory: the child was seen as creative, constructing a grammar which is flexible for a time, then becomes fixed. Children were also said to be responsible for the second major type of phonological change, restructuring of the underlying representations.

King (1969a) provides an extended example of restructuring involving English /hw/ versus /w/. At an earlier stage of English (36a), adult speakers had contrasting /hw/ in *whales, which* and /w/ in *Wales, witch*, and this situation still persists in certain Modern English dialects, such as Scottish English. However, /hw/ gradually merged with /w/ in varieties like Southern British English, leading to the addition of a rule as in (36b). Adults, who can only add rules, would retain /hw/ in the underlying forms of *whales, which*, but cease to produce it.

The next generation of children have the target of constructing a maximally simple grammar of their variety of English. Since they will never hear [hw] from their parents, there is no motivation for them to postulate contrastive /hw/ and /w/, plus a merger rule; instead, they will hypothesise underlying /w/ in all previous /w/ and /hw/ words, as in (36c). This restructuring produces a revised, simpler grammar, without the rule merging /hw/ with /w/, but with the effects of that rule transferred into the underlying representations.

(36) a.   Adults: /hw/ [hw]   /w/ [w]
                        whales   *Wales*
                        which   *witch*
      b.   New rule: /hw/ ⟶ [w]
           Underlier: /hwɪtʃ/ *which*
           Surface: [wɪtʃ]
      c.   Children: /w/ [w]
                        which
                        witch
                        Wales
                        whales

2.4.2.4   Summary

A schematic representation of the Generative theory of sound change is given in (37).

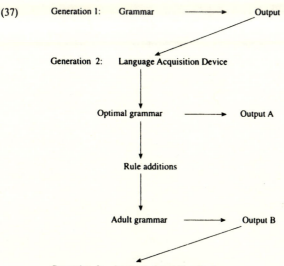

(37) Generation 1: Grammar ⟶ Output

Generation 2: Language Acquisition Device

Optimal grammar ⟶ Output A

Rule additions

Adult grammar ⟶ Output B

Generation 3: Language Acquisition Device

This Generativist model of change raises a number of difficulties. First, early Generative theorists tended not to consider the effects of change on the system of sounds in a language (the phoneme system in Structuralist terms). They consequently omitted from consideration Structuralist explanations of change, which centred on the structure and function of the system. Instead, the Generativists wrote formal phonological rules which reflect completed changes; but these are only restatements of the effects of the change, and are essentially non-explanatory.

Secondly, the notion of simplification, although it might be a candidate for explanation in the case of some changes, cannot be the cure-all the Generativists claimed it to be. Not all changes can be construed as simplificatory; it is hard, for instance, to see what a sound shift like Grimm's Law or the Great Vowel Shift might simplify, and Neogrammarian changes of the irregularity-creating variety certainly introduce complexity into the grammar. Even more basically, how can the addition of a new rule ever be considered a simplification? Furthermore, we have no entirely clear idea of what constitutes simplification. which is a relative rather than an absolute term. In other words, a particular change might be simplificatory under certain circumstances, but induce complexity in others. Finally, the characterisation of all change as simplificatory presumes a view of change as constantly creating ever simpler grammars. Languages, on this view, must have been getting gradually simpler ever since language began, a claim for which there is no evidence at all. Models promoting a single explanation in this way can all too easily be hijacked to promote a view of some languages as simpler or better than others, and of change as directed, cumulative and purposive, a view which we shall consider and reject in Chapter 12.

Even more serious problems are raised by Generative assumptions on the relationship of sound changes and synchronic phonological rules. If each change corresponds to one added rule, and instances of rule loss and reordering are infrequent, then the historical phonology of a language will be almost directly mirrored in the order of its phonological rules. The mechanism intended to deal with this was restructuring, but this was only sporadically invoked in the literature, allowing Chomsky and Halle (1968: 49) to claim that ' ... underlying representations are fairly resistant to historical change, which tends, by and large, to involve late phonetic rules. If this is true, then the same system of representation for underlying forms will be found over long stretches of space and time.' Such attitudes make for an extremely static model, and leave little scope for the divergence of dialects and languages to occur. Nonetheless, Generative theory has inspired a considerable amount of more recent work in historical linguistics, some of which we shall pursue in Chapters 3, 4 and 5.

2.5   The question of explanation

The three schools surveyed above have one common characteristic: they are all more successful at describing *what* happened than *why* it happened, although they all claim, with varying degrees of conviction, that they are explaining language change. Explanation can focus on one of two areas: the actuation problem, or the issue of why a change might start; or the transmission problem, the question of how a change, once initiated, spreads. The Neogrammarians attempted to tackle the actuation problem, suggesting physical causes such as ease of articulation, and psychological analogues, notably the notion of progressive directional displacement of pronunciation from an internalised target or sound picture. However, there is no explanation of why initially random displacements should become directional, nor any solution to the problem that assimilation, for instance, may operate in a given context in one language but fail in an identical environment in another. As for transmission, the Neogrammarians assumed only that change is lexically abrupt but phonetically gradual, and operates simultaneously for all members of a speech community; some problems for this hypothesis have already been raised in 2.2, and will be pursued in Chapter 3 below. The Structuralists did not really take issue with transmission, and failed to account adequately for actuation; although their notions of structure and function may explain the shape of a sound shift like the Great Vowel Shift once it has begun, there is no explanation for the movement of the first vowel. Finally, the

Generativists formulated changes, but this is descriptive rather than explanatory. Early Generative theory, with its emphasis on simplification, provided no adequate general account of actuation *or* transmission.

These inadequacies may be characteristic of the theories of change we have examined so far, or may be symptomatic of the inexplicable nature of linguistic change. Lass (1980) contends that language change simply is not amenable to explanation, if explanations are defined in deductive – nomological terms as strictly causal, universally valid covering laws which predict both <u>that</u> something will happen and <u>how</u>. Such an explanation has the structure '"X because it couldn't have been otherwise (because Y)"' (Aitchison 1981: 172); for instance, if someone's head is cut off, we can predict absolutely that he will die, since the heart cannot beat if it is disconnected from the brain, and a functioning heart is necessary for life. Such explanations, according to Lass, are unattainable in linguistics. For instance, the ease of articulation 'explanation' does not count since the same context may not always trigger the same change; similarly, functional 'explanations' are faulty because they are not universally valid.

It is certainly true that we cannot hope to explain linguistic change if we define explanation as rigidly as Lass does. However, seeking explanations of this type may be inappropriate in linguistics, which is not strictly comparable to the 'hard' physical sciences, but has a good deal more in common with biology. In the biological sciences, single absolute causes are rarely if ever to be found; sometimes, however, a cluster of interacting factors causing some phenomenon may be identified, although these are typically non-predictive and particularistic. Even in physics or chemistry, strongly predictive explanations may be a target rather than an achieved reality. Thus, Ohala (1987) argues that a physicist asked to predict the trajectory of a ball hit with a bat can only do so if she knows the angle at which bat strikes ball, the force of the blow, the speed and direction of the wind (and perhaps, if we now introduce chaos theory, even the whereabouts of all the butterflies in the world). In linguistics, we also have to specify contextual factors in this way, and consequently explanations in both fields can be probabilistic or statistical at best.

Arguably then, while seeking grand, unified explanations for language change, we should not reject intermediate, partial explanations specific to particular phenomena. For the moment, we may have to accept a lower-key definition of explanation at a less elevated but more commonsense level: explanation might then constitute 'relief from puzzlement about some phenomenon' (Bach 1974, quoted Greenberg 1979: 279). Our grounds for assessing explanations are not currently so well-developed as we might ultimately wish them to be, and we may sometimes fall back on insight and intuition; and the definition of explanation as providing relief from puzzlement with respect to a particular phenomenon does not reach the epistemological high ground occupied by Lass's deductive-nomological model. But in a discipline where the three theories of change we have explored so far frequently cannot even offer relief from puzzlement, we might profitably regard this less elevated type of explanation as a useful intermediate goal, and perhaps even as an ultimate one. As Lass says (1980: 146–7), ' ... even second-best is not the same as universal darkness, and there may well be areas in which second-best is best, because first-best is simply not possible in principle'.

In the chapters to follow, we shall consider further, generally particularistic and non-predictive, explanations of changes in all components of the grammar, while still striving to find general causes and motivations for change. In the next chapter, we shall look at two more recent bodies of work on sound change. The first, lexical diffusion theory, attacks the Neogrammarian solution to the transition problem. The second section focusses on the extension of Lexical Phonology, originally a synchronic phonological model, to the diachronic domain, and attempts to show that, despite the shortcomings of Standard Generative Phonology, its successors may cast light on sound change and on the relationship of synchrony and diachrony.

3 Sound change 2: the implementation problem

3.1 Introduction

In the last chapter, we considered the attempts of three successive schools of linguists, the Neogrammarians, Structuralists and early Generativists, to describe and explain sound change. We saw that all these theories are inadequate for much the same reason: although they may produce very elegant and ingenious descriptions, and although they all propose explanations for change, none comes very close to being truly explanatory. This is because none successfully tackles either the problem of actuation (why sound change begins) or the issue of implementation or transmission (how the change spreads): of course, these issues do overlap, since transmission can be interpreted as actuation for previously unaffected speakers. We shall return to the actuation issue in Chapter 9, when we consider the relationship between change and variation, and the transmission of a change through a speech community.

In this chapter, our main concern in Section 2 is the implementation of change in the grammar of the individual native speaker; this leads naturally to a discussion of the relationship between synchrony and diachrony, and specifically between synchronic phonological rules and diachronic sound changes, in Section 3.

3.2 Lexical diffusion

3.2.1 *The issue of transmission*

The issue of transmission involves the spread of a change, through the speech output and internalised grammar of the native speaker, and through the speech community as a whole. As we have seen, the Neogrammarians, with their methodological assumption of the imperceptibility of sound change, believed implementation to be beyond the scope of investigation. In the Neogrammarian view, sound change was lexically abrupt but phonetically gradual, proceeding by minute and inaudible increments and operating simultaneously in all eligible lexical items and for all speakers in the speech community. Moreover, the Neogrammarians believed that sound change was regular, and that 'it is the mechanical, blind, imperceptible, and inexorable nature of phonetic law that accounts for its absolute regularity' (Chen 1977: 198).

Neither the Structuralists nor the Generativists make such strong methodological claims for the inaccessibility of transmission, but neither school made its investigation a priority. The Structuralists, operating on their maxim that 'phonemes change', established successive phoneme systems and compared them. For instance, in Sanskrit there was a phoneme /k/, which underwent an assimilatory change palatalising it before the front vowels [e] and [i] (the latter may at the time have been a vocalic form of /j/). This change gave Sanskrit a phoneme /k/ with two allophones, and this situation, at time T_1, is shown in (1).

(1)   Sanskrit – T_1

$$/k/ \; > \; [t\int] \; / \; \underline{\qquad} \quad \begin{bmatrix} + \text{ syllabic} \\ + \text{ front} \end{bmatrix}$$

However, at a later time T_2, a further change had operated to merge /e/ with the back vowel /a/. After this merger, the contexts in which [k] and [t∫] appeared could not be distinguished, since the two sounds contrasted before /a/. Earlier /k/ therefore split, so that the phoneme system at T_2 includes /k/ and /t∫/ (2).

(2)   Sanskrit – T_2
       /e/ > [a] (> /a/)

       /k/ – /t∫/

The early Generative school would have dealt with the same change in a rather different way, assuming the addition of a new rule at T_2. At T_1, as shown in (3a), speakers have a rule assimilating /k/ to high front vowels, but at T_2 (see (3b)), they add a second, later rule changing all occurrences of /e/ into [a]. This account is in keeping with the Generative maxim that 'rules change'.

(3)a. T_1: Rule (i)   /k/ $\longrightarrow$ [t∫]/ --- [i e]
   b. T_2: Rule (i)   /k/ $\longrightarrow$ [t∫]/ --- [i e]
                Rule (ii)   /e/ $\longrightarrow$ [a]

Both these accounts establish a system, either of phonemes or rules, for each stage of the language, then compare these systems. However, neither tells us how the change proceeds; they compare T_1 with T_2 and describe the differences, but give us no insight at all into the interval between these times.

A sound change could be implemented in any one of four logically possible ways (see (4)).

(4) a.   phonetically gradual and lexically abrupt
    b.   phonetically gradual and lexically gradual
    c.   phonetically abrupt and lexically abrupt
    d.   phonetically abrupt and lexically gradual

Option a. of (4) corresponds to the Neogrammarian hypothesis that sound change operates by imperceptible phonetic increments, but simultaneously in all lexical items with the appropriate context. However, there are several good reasons for objecting to the Neogrammarian view of sound change, or at least arguments against considering it appropriate for all changes.

First, and most generally, sociolinguistic studies have now convincingly shown that sound changes in progress *can* be observed, by carrying out 'apparent-time' studies of speakers of different classes and ages within a speech community (see Chapter 9). Second, the notion that sound change is always phonetically gradual is unsuitable for a number of types of sound change (Wang 1969). Thus, for sound changes like some cases of metathesis, where two linearly related elements change places as in *ācsian* > *ask*, it is hardly possible even to imagine intermediate steps. Other sound changes may involve parameters like voicing or nasalisation: languages do not seem to exploit different degrees of these features, perhaps largely because our control of the appropriate articulatory processes is not very fine; sounds therefore tend to be either voiced or voiceless, and either nasal or oral, so that the notion of a continuum is again not particularly useful here. Finally, segments are fairly frequently inserted or deleted, and these seem to be absolute processes: languages do not appear to deal in half-vowels or quarter-consonants.

The phonetically gradual implementation of sound change might, then, be limited to certain types of change, perhaps including some assimilatory and weakening processes. We might then start to envisage some other changes as phonetically abrupt, each operating in a single, perceptible leap. This does not rule out the existence of variation in the speech community; all the assumption of phonetic abruptness entails is that, in a given word on a particular occasion of utterance, we have either phoneme X or phoneme Y, not something in between. However, one speaker may still undergo a change before another, so that variations in pronunciation between phonemes X and Y may still exist for some time in the speech community before the change spreads to all speakers.

This discussion removes from consideration options a. and b. of (4), for at least some changes. We must now choose between (4c) and (4d); that is, we must decide whether sound change is lexically abrupt or lexically gradual. The work of Wang (1969, 1977) and his associates (Chen and Wang 1975, Chen and Hsieh 1971, Chen 1977) argues for option (4d): in the view of these so-called lexical diffusionists, sound change is phonetically abrupt, and lexically gradual.

3.2.2   *Sound change as lexically gradual*

The main assumption of lexical diffusion theory is that not all eligible words are affected by a sound change at the same time. Instead, a change will originate in a small subset of morphemes. If we assume for the moment an abstract change of some phoneme X to some other phoneme Y, certain morphemes will undergo the change directly, but in others, pronunciation will fluctuate for a time, for individuals and/or for the community. This period of variation is characterised by the existence of doublets, morphemes with two possible pronunciations. Since all languages are constantly changing, we can assume that doublets will exist at any period of any language: for instance, Wang (1969) reports that in Chinese dialects many morphemes have alternative literary and colloquial pronunciations, while in present-day English we have *hat* with or without the initial [h], *car* with or without the final [r], and [sju:t] versus [su:t] 'suit', where the [j] glide seems to be disappearing.

Gradually, the sound change in progress will be confirmed in these morphemes. The change will also spread to other speakers, who may extend the new pronunciation into other morphemes with the same context. A change beginning in a small set of items may thus diffuse through the lexicon until it has, at least potentially, affected all morphemes with the appropriate environment.

Wang (1969) was not the first to propose the process of lexical diffusion, although he was the first to give it this name. Sturtevant (1917: 82) also held that:

… many sound changes are irregular when they first appear and gradually become more and more regular. The reason is that each person who substitutes the new sound for the old in his own pronunciation tends to carry it into new words. The two processes of spread from word to word and spread from speaker to speaker progress side by side until the new sound has extended to all the words of the language which contained the old sound in the same surroundings.

Similarly, Alf Sommerfelt, discussing a survey of Welsh dialects from the 1920s and specifically the loss of the uvular fricative /χ/ before /w/, notes that: 'at a given moment, /ware/ reaches a Welsh village and replaces /χware/, without it being necessary that, at the same time, /wanen/ should supplant /χwanen/ or /wa:ir/ 'sister' replace /χwa:ir/' (Sommerfelt 1962: 75, quoted Chen 1977: 215; my translation). Sommerfelt's evidence is especially valuable because he is clearly discussing a sound change still in progress. His data allow us to visualise a situation for Welsh at this period as illustrated in (5).

(5)	Time	t_1	t_2	t_3	t_4	t_5
	'to play'	χware	ware	ware	ware	ware
	'flea'	χwanen	χwanen	(χ)wanen	wanen	wanen
	'sister'	χwa:ir	χwa:ir	χwa:ir	χwa:ir	wa:ir

At time t_1, for the speaker concerned, the change deleting /χ/ has not yet begun. Stages t_2, t_3 and t_4 show its progress through the lexicon, and at t_5 it is completed. The same stylised table may be used to show diffusion through the speech community (see (6)).

(6)	Speaker	A	B	C	D	E
	'to play'	χware	ware	ware	ware	ware
	'flea'	χwanen	χwanen	(χ)wanen	wanen	wanen
	'sister'	χwa:ir	χwa:ir	χwa:ir	χwa:ir	wa:ir

As (6) shows, at a single given point in time, the change has not begun for speaker A, and has been completed for speaker E. In between are speakers B, C and D; for B, the diffusion has just started, and C has partial diffusion with idiolectal variation in one item, while for speaker D the diffusion is almost complete.

The theory of lexical diffusion is attractive to dialectologists as well as linguists, since it gives some theoretical status to the variation which emerges from dialect surveys, especially in transition areas between dialects. For instance, Sommerfelt's Welsh survey shows that Northern dialects have /χw/ consistently, and Southern dialects have lost /χ/ entirely, while the intermediate Central Welsh dialects show variation between /χw/ and /w/. Such variation indicates a double diffusion; not only some morphemes, but some dialects show change sooner than others. This areal diffusion is not restricted to related dialects, but may also apply to shared developments in related languages. Krishnamurti (1978), for example, traces the history of a series of changes which he collectively calls apical displacement in the South-Central subfamily of Dravidian. He reports that this set of changes has affected around 75 per cent of the Kui lexicon, 65 per cent of the vocabulary of Kuvi, Pengo and Maṇḍa, but only

20 per cent in Gondi and Konda, and ascribes this variation to a gradual diffusion from morpheme to morpheme within each language, and also from language to language. These changes, to judge from written evidence from Telugu, have been going on for at least 2,000 years, and are still in progress in some South-Central Dravidian languages.

We shall return to the connection of diffusion theory with dialectology and sociolinguistics in Chapter 9. Here, our next question concerns the rate of lexical diffusion. The simplest assumption would be that change diffuses through the lexicon steadily, at a uniform rate, affecting the same proportion of words in each unit of time. In fact, we have a way of testing this hypothesis, since a fairly large number of sound changes in progress have now been observed and discussed in the literature. If diffusion does proceed at a uniform rate, we should be able to observe changes at any stage of their development; our corpus of changes in progress should include some which have affected 20 per cent of the eligible vocabulary, and others which have covered 40 per cent, 60 per cent, 80 per cent and 100 per cent. However, changes are only very rarely found at or around the 50 per cent mark; they are almost always at one of the extremes, having affected around 20 per cent or 80 per cent of relevant lexical items.

These observations refute the proposal that changes diffuse at a constant rate. Instead, diffusion can be represented using the S-curve model shown in (7).

(7)   % of lexicon
       affected

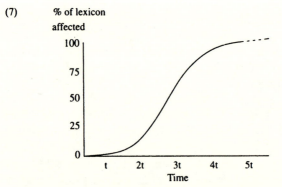

This S-curve graph, which can be interpreted as showing the progress of a change for a single speaker or for the whole speech community, represents the hypothesis that changes begin slowly, perhaps in a very small number of morphemes, and gradually build up speed. There is a rapid increase in the rate of diffusion from around 20 per cent, and the middle 60 per cent of vocabulary is covered relatively quickly; then, for the last 20 per cent or so of its range, the change slows down again. The S-curve model is also known as the snowball model, since snowballs under construction follow the same slow-quick-quick-slow pattern of movement: a snowball initially has to be pushed down a hill, then takes off under its own momentum, and gradually slows down and stops at the bottom. If this model does accurately reflect the pattern of lexical diffusion, we would predict that most changes would be observed during the slow periods below 20 per cent and above 80 per cent, and as we have seen, this prediction is supported by reports on sound change in progress.

3.2.3   *Residual forms*

So far, we have been assuming that a diffusing change will continue to completion, that is until it has covered 100 per cent of morphemes with the appropriate environment. This assumption helps us accommodate the Neogrammarian idea of lexically abrupt sound change, since if a diffusing change runs its full course, it will look to all intents and purposes as though it had affected all the relevant vocabulary at once: no traces are left of its intermediate stages. However, lexical diffusion theory is particularly enlightening in cases of apparent irregularity, when exceptional, unaffected forms remain. These 'can be regarded as residual forms of a sound change which has not yet completed its course, has come to a premature end, or has been thwarted by a competing sound change overlapping with it along the time dimension' (Chen 1977: 244).

If sound change is taken to be lexically gradual, its course is neither inevitable nor inexorable, even after it has begun. The Neogrammarians, however, saw change as lexically abrupt or instantaneously implemented, and did not have recourse to explanations for exceptions which rely on graduality. Instead, the Neogrammarians invoked two factors, those of analogy and dialect borrowing. Analogy, at least within the paradigm, cannot be the only explanation for residual forms, since many examples of diffusion are drawn from Chinese; and Chinese, as an isolating language, has no inflectional morphology and hence no paradigms. Lexical diffusionists object also to the invocation of dialect borrowing, which the Neogrammarians do tend to use as a last resort, all-embracing explanatory strategy: Chen (1977: 205) complains that 'the abandon and insouciance with which certain otherwise careful and meticulous scholars make use of dialect borrowing threatens to turn [it] into a waste-basket category into which all sorts of unexplained irregularities are thrown together'. The main argument against dialect borrowing is that it is unfalsifiable – even if it is demonstrable that such borrowing could not have taken place at time X, it is impossible to prove that it did not happen before or after time X (or, as Wang (1969: 21) puts it, 'we cannot prove that the platypus does not lay eggs with photographs showing a platypus *not* laying eggs'.) This lack of any potential counter-evidence makes dialect borrowing an undesirably weak explanation.

Four alternative explanations for exceptional residual forms are offered within lexical diffusion theory. These are detailed below.

1 The existence of residual forms may simply indicate that a diffusing change is not yet completed; its further progress may ultimately make these apparent exceptions regular.

2 A diffusing sound change may run out of momentum before affecting the last few eligible lexical items; this potential tailing off is signalled by the dotted line at the upper extreme of the S-curve in (7). For instance, the Middle English change of Trisyllabic Shortening shortened long vowels three or more syllables from the end of the word, giving [dɪvi:n] – [dɪvɪnɪti] (earlier [dɪvi:nɪti]) for Modern English *divine – divinity*, and [sɛre:n] – [sɛrɛnɪti] (earlier [sɛre:nɪti]) for *serene – serenity*; *divine*, *serene*, with long vowels, subsequently underwent the Great Vowel Shift to give the present-day forms. However, Trisyllabic Shortening failed to apply in *obesity* (earlier [obe:sɪti]), which retains a long vowel and has undergone the Great Vowel Shift like its base form *obese*. Since Trisyllabic Shortening stopped operating centuries ago, there is now no possibility that *obesity* will be made regular by the sound change.

3 Some sound changes begin, but then reverse themselves. So, in Stockholm Swedish (see Chen and Wang 1975) there is an optional deletion of final [d] in words like *ved* 'wood', *hund* 'dog' and *blad* 'leaf'. This deletion used to be possible in many more nouns, and also in other grammatical categories. It seems that a sound change deleting final [d] began in a subset of nouns, then started to diffuse through the lexicon. However, final <d> does appear in the spelling, and, due perhaps to the dramatic increase in literacy in Sweden this century, there has been a resurgence of final [d]; in diffusionist terms, a final-[d] epenthesis rule has developed, and is now spreading through the lexicon in turn. Similarly, in the Paris area, [r] changed to [z], but this was also reversed, leaving only a single trace in the form of the word *chaise*, 'chair'. The lexical diffusion model gains strong support from such cases, which cannot adequately be described as a wholesale shift in one direction followed by an equally sudden reversal, but seem rather to show a gradual ebb and flow.

4 Finally, lexical diffusion is particularly useful in cases where a sound has developed in different directions in a single phonetic environment. If changes were implemented instantaneously, we would expect them to operate successively, like the rules in a Generative phonology. However, changes diffusing over a relatively long period of time are likely to intersect with other diffusing changes, and the longer the period of diffusion, the more likely and the more frequent such intersection will be. Intersection in

time covers the three relations of coincidence, incorporation and overlap, shown in (8).

(8) a.   Coincidence
          — — — — — — — — —   Change A
          — — — — — — — — —   Change B

     b.   Incorporation
          — — — — — — — — —   Change A
          — — — — — —   Change B

     c.   Overlap
          — — — — — —   — — — — — — —   Change A
          — — — — — —   or   — — — — — —   Change B

Two changes coincide if their periods of operation are precisely the same, as in (8a). In (8b), change A incorporates change B, since the period of diffusion for change A entirely includes that of change B. Overlap is a more loosely defined relationship; the periods of diffusion for two overlapping changes (as in (8c)) must be partially coincident.

In the majority of cases, the intersection of two sound changes will make no difference to the progress of either, since each will affect a different set of input sounds in a different context. However, in some cases, the intersecting changes may potentially apply to the same inputs, leading to competition, defined by Wang (1969: 18) as a situation where 'there are morphemes whose phonetic histories would differ according to the sequence in which the rules are applied'. These notions of intersection and competition may account for the apparently irregular outcomes of some sound changes.

One example of competing changes, from Peking Chinese (Chen and Hsieh 1971) is illustrated in (9).

(9)a.   Middle Chinese   Peking dialect
         b'ai   p'ai   'signboard'
         b'ai   pa   'to cease'
         tş'ai   tş'ai   'hairpin'
         tş'ai   tş'a   'to cross'

     b.   Middle Chinese
      i.   Offglide dropping: [ai] > [a]
      ii. Low vowel fronting: [ai] > [æi] (> [ai])

As (9a) shows, Middle Chinese [ai] has developed in two distinct and unpredictable ways, to become Modern Peking dialect [ai] or [a] in identical phonetic contexts. The diffusionist solution appears in (9b); we postulate two intersecting sound changes for Middle Chinese, both competing to apply to the same [ai] vowels. It is entirely fortuitous which change reached which morpheme first, and this competition produced the ostensibly puzzling Modern Peking distribution of [a] and [ai].

A number of explanations are available, then, for apparent exceptions; but these rely on the assumption that at least some sound changes are lexically gradual. There are undoubtedly questions still to be answered by the diffusionists – for instance, we do not know what factors determine which lexical items will be affected first by a change, and it is unclear what determines the momentum of a diffusing change. On the whole, however, lexical diffusion theory should be seen as a promising development in historical linguistics, which makes an important contribution to our understanding of the transmission problem.

3.3   Lexical Phonology and sound change

3.3.1   *Introduction*

This section follows from the last in that it again concentrates on the transmission problem, but it also has three aims of its own. First, we shall see that both the Neogrammarian and the lexical diffusionist views of sound change are correct, since there are two types of sound change. Secondly, it will be established that different dialects of the same language may undergo quite different developments, as a preliminary to the discussion of dialectology and historical linguistics in Chapter 9: I shall illustrate this here by introducing Scots dialects and Scottish Standard English. Finally, the account of Standard Generative Phonology and its theory of sound change in Chapter 2.4 above may have left the impression that current phonological theories, developed to deal with synchronic data, can contribute little or nothing to historical linguistics. I hope to show that a successor of Standard Generative Phonology, Lexical Phonology, can in fact cast light both on the relationship of synchrony and diachrony, and on problems within the theory of sound change, and that this has advantages for both historical linguistics and phonological theory.

3.3.2   *The 'Neogrammarian controversy'*

As we saw in Section 2 above, the Neogrammarians held that regular sound change (excluding, as usual, sporadic changes like metathesis) was phonetically gradual and lexically abrupt. Neither of these characteristics, however, can be universally upheld. For instance, some changes (like epenthesis, or changes involving dimensions like voicing or nasalisation) cannot appropriately be seen as phonetically gradual since they do not lend themselves to a formulation with intermediate steps. On the other hand, some convincing examples have been reported of sound changes (like the loss of the voiceless uvular fricative before /w/ in Welsh) which do not seem to be lexically abrupt, but rather diffuse gradually across the lexicon from morpheme to morpheme. We have, then, two entirely opposed characterisations of sound change: in the Neogrammarian view, it is phonetically gradual and lexically abrupt, whereas in the opinion of the lexical diffusionists, it is phonetically abrupt and lexically gradual.

Much of the work on lexical diffusion was done in the late 1960s and early 1970s, producing a situation of stalemate partially relieved only by the publication of William Labov's 1981 paper 'Resolving the Neogrammarian controversy'. Labov is one of the pioneers of sociolinguistics, who established, as we shall see in Chapter 9, that much of the variation to be found among the speakers in a speech community can be interpreted as ongoing sound change. He was therefore one of the first linguists to refute in practice the Neogrammarian contention that sound change is unobserv-able, by reporting on a large number of changes in progress, especially in New York City.

Labov's attempt to resolve the question of whether sound change has Neogrammarian or diffusing properties involved taking a sample of changes in progress and assessing which model characterised these best. His reasoning was that previous analyses rested on changes which were long since completed, and which could not be absolutely proved to have operated in one way or the other, while changes currently under way could more readily be investigated. However, Labov's data did not fall unambiguously into one category or the other. Instead, he found that the Neogrammarian system accounted beautifully for some changes (in-volving, for instance, fronting, backing or rounding of vowels), while the diffusing model worked equally well for others (including lengthening and shortening changes).

Initially, then, it seemed that Labov's attempts to solve the Neogram-marian controversy had failed, producing only an apparent *impasse* where we are 'faced with the massive opposition of two bodies of evidence: both are right, but both cannot be right' (Labov 1981: 269). Labov, however, suggests an alternative solution. It is clearly impossible to claim either that all sound change is phonetically abrupt and lexically gradual, or that it is phonetically gradual and lexically abrupt. Labov therefore accepts that there are two distinct types of sound change: one behaves as predicted by Neogrammarian theory, while the other is implemented by diffusion. Labov then attempts to distinguish the two types as precisely as possible, and the result is the classification in (10).

(10)		Lexical diffusion	'Neogrammarian' change
Discrete		yes	no
Phonetic conditioning		rough	fine
Lexical exceptions		yes	no
Grammatical conditioning		yes	no
Social affect		no	yes
Predictable		no	yes
Learnable		no	yes
Categorised		yes	no
Dictionary entries		2	1
Lexical diffusion		yes	no

As (10) shows, diffusing changes are discrete; in other words, they produce a binary output, such as voiced as opposed to voiceless, or long as opposed to short sounds. Neogrammarian changes, being phonetically gradual, can produce variation between these poles, making segments longer or shorter, rather than categorically long or short. Neogrammarian changes are very sensitive to the phonetic facts, but are never affected by grammatical ones, whereas diffusing changes may be grammatically conditioned, but are typically only roughly phonetically conditioned. Diffusing changes may have lexical exceptions; as we have seen, these may result from a change tailing off before affecting 100 per cent of the eligible vocabulary. However, Neogrammarian changes tend to apply across the board, without exceptions.

Neogrammarian changes are also socially relevant, occur in predictable environments, and can be learned by speakers who may move into the dialect area where the change is operating, while the opposite is true of diffusing changes. Lexically diffusing changes, on the other hand, can be categorised – that is, speakers can generally distinguish the input to such changes from the output, whereas Neogrammarian changes are characteristically unobservable. This relates to the fact that diffusing changes typically involve a contrast between two elements; they therefore involve two phonemes, or two dictionary entries. Neogrammarian changes operate at a lower, non-contrastive level. Finally, and rather obviously, (10) shows that lexically diffusing changes operate by lexical diffusion!

The properties in (10) ought to allow us to classify any sound change as either Neogrammarian or diffusing. However, I would like to suggest that these two types of sound change are not simply polar opposites, but that Neogrammarian changes may become diffusing changes over time. I shall illustrate this claim in the next section, using the example of the Scottish Vowel Length Rule.

3.3.3   *Scots, Scottish Standard English, and the Scottish Vowel Length Rule*

Today, Scots dialects are spoken over most of Scotland, except in the very far North and the Western Isles, where Gaelic has generally given way directly to English, and Scots has never been spoken. Scots dialect speakers are likely to have non-standard features in all areas of the grammar, and some examples of distinctively Scots vocabulary, syntax and phonology are given in (11), (12) and (13) respectively.

(11)   *beagie, tumshie, neap* 'turnip'
         (regional variants)
         puddock 'frog'
         wabbit 'tired'

(12)   *I didnae see naebody.*
         To get that job, you have to can type.
         I might could go to that party.

(13)   [hem] 'home'   [snɔ:] 'snow'
         [mus] 'mouse'   [fa:] 'who' (Aberdeenshire)

It is a common misapprehension to assume that Scots is the way it is because of influence from Gaelic, a Celtic language introduced from Ireland in the fifth century AD, which itself displaced Pictish. There are in fact remarkably few Gaelic borrowings in Scots, only a few lexical items such as *galore* from Gaelic *gu leoir* (which means 'enough' in Gaelic but 'more than enough' in Scots and English). The source of the peculiarities of Scots is actually primarily a dialect division in Old English; Scots is descended from Old Northumbrian, rather than the West Saxon, Mercian and Kentish dialects which are the ancestors of Southern English English. Scots was introduced into southern Scotland when the Anglo-Saxons conquered Lothian in the seventh century, and has been driving Gaelic into the hills ever since.

Scots has not, however, benefited consistently from the problems of Gaelic, but has itself been progressively disenfranchised by English. There are two main reasons for the success of English in Scotland. First, the Unions of the Crowns (1603) and of the Parliaments (1707) of Scotland and England, and the concomitant movement of the Scottish court and parliament to London, led to a drive towards anglicisation, since Scots wishing to gain influence had to go south, and therefore to speak English. Second, after the Reformation, an English Bible was introduced as there was no available Scots translation. And if God appeared to speak English, we can hardly blame the Scots for trying to do the same.

From the eighteenth century on, upwardly mobile middle-class Scots consequently attempted to learn English, usually with the aid of books which promised to weed out unwelcome Scotticisms. These, however, tended to concentrate on features of morphology, syntax and vocabulary, which could easily be set down in writing, while largely ignoring phonetics and phonology. The resulting amalgamation of Standard English grammar and vocabulary with some Scots phonology seems to have been found acceptable, with even Dr Johnson's companion Boswell (himself a Scot and part of the anglicising movement) claiming that 'a small intermixture of provincial peculiarities may, perhaps, have a pleasing effect' (Kay 1988: 84).

These developments produced Scottish Standard English (SSE), an accent which differs from Southern British English Received Pronunciation (RP) only in its phonology, and which today exists alongside Scots dialects. Like RP, SSE is a social rather than a regional accent; the accent of Standard English as it is spoken in Scotland.

There are few differences in consonant phonology between SSE and RP, although Scots and SSE retain [hw] in *whales*, *which* as opposed to [w] in *Wales*, *witch*, and are rhotic, meaning that [r] is always pronounced wherever <r> appears in the spelling (see (14)).

(14)   <u>RP – non-rhotic</u>   <u>Scots/SSE – rhotic</u>
          car [kɑː]   *ca*[r]
          car keys [kɑːkiːz]   *ca*[r] *keys*
          car engine [kɑːrɛndʒɪn]   *ca*[r] *engine*

More interesting discrepancies between RP and SSE involve the vowels, as illustrated in (15).

(15)   RP   SSE
          beat   iː   i
          bit   ɪ   ɪ
          bait   eɪ   e
          bet   ɛ   ɛ
          balm   ɑː   ⎱
          bat   æ   ⎰ a
          bought   ɔː   ⎱
          bomb   ɒ   ⎰ ɔ
          food   uː   ⎱
          foot   ʊ   ⎰ u
          boat   oʊ   o
          but   ʌ   ʌ
          bite   aɪ   aɪ
          bout   aʊ   au
          boy   ɔɪ   ɔɪ
          Before /r/:
          bird   ⎱   ɪr
          word   ⎰ ɜː   ʌr
          heard   ɛr

beer	ɪə	ir
bear	ɛə	er
car	ɑː	ar
poor	ɔː	ur

A number of differences between RP and SSE can be extracted from (15). For instance, SSE sometimes has monophthongs, like [e], [o], where RP has diphthongs, such as [eɪ], [oʊ]; RP has some additional vowels, including [ɜː] and the centring diphthongs [ɪə], [ɛə] where SSE has vowel + [r]; and SSE lacks three contrasts which RP has, between the vowels in *bat* and *balm*, *bomb* and *bought*, and *foot* and *food*. However, the main difference between RP and Scots/SSE involves vowel length.

In RP, there are six long-short pairs of vowels, as shown in (16).

(16)   /iː/ – /ɪ/
         /eɪ/ – /ɛ/
         /ɑː/ – /æ/
         /uː/ – /ʊ/
         /ɔː/ – /ɒ/
         /oʊ/ – /ʌ/

The left-hand member of each pair is always long, and the right-hand one is always short. In Scots/SSE, however, the members of these pairs are either distinguished only by quality (as for /i/ – /ɪ/, /e/ – /ɛ/, /o/ – /ʌ/), or the pair is replaced by a single vowel (/a/ for /ɑː/ – /æ/, /ɔ/ for /ɔː/ – /ɒ/, and /u/ for /uː/ – /ʊ/). Vowel length is not contrastive in Scots/SSE; in other words, no vowel is consistently long, but almost all become long in certain phonetic environments, and the controlling process is the Scottish Vowel Length Rule (17).

(17)a.

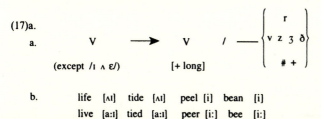

a.   V   ⟶   V   / ──{ r / v z ʒ ð / # + }

    (except /ɪ ʌ ɛ/)   [+ long]

b.   life [ʌɪ]   tide [ʌɪ]   peel [i]   bean [i]
          live [aːɪ] tied [aːɪ] peer [iː] bee [iː]

An outline of the Scottish Vowel Length Rule (SVLR) is given in (17a), and some examples of its effects in (17b) (see also McMahon 1991). SVLR operates in present-day Scots dialects and SSE, and makes all vowels (except /ɪ ʌ ɛ/, which are always short) long before /r/ or voiced fricatives, and before a word (#) or morpheme (+) boundary – that is, at the end of a word or before a suffix. In general, SVLR *only* lengthens vowels, but the diphthong /aɪ/ also undergoes a quality change, giving short [ʌɪ] in *life, lice, tide* but long [aːɪ] in *live, lies, tied*.

Our concern here is not with the formulation of the modern SVLR, but rather with its history. It may be an isolated process, characteristic only of Scottish varieties; or it may be related to some other change in the history of English.

It seems, in fact, that SVLR is linked with another vowel lengthening process, which affects most present-day English dialects (apart from some in the north of England) and which has even been claimed to be universal. This process involves what is known by phoneticians as the 'voicing effect' - the fact that vowels become progressively longer according to the hierarchy of following consonants in (18).

(18)

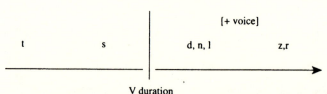

		d	z
t	s	n	r
		l	
voiceless	voiceless	voiced stops,	voiced
stops	fricatives	nasals, /l/	fricatives, /r/

vowel duration

In other words, vowels become longer when they precede voiced sounds. In fact, vowels are longest of all before pauses, but (18) shows only consonantal environments. In accents like RP and General American (the most widespread variety of English in the USA, excluding the Deep South and New England), there is a measurable jump in vowel length before voiced consonants, or in contexts to the right of the vertical line in (19).

(19)   RP / General American

		[+ voice]	
t	s	d, n, l	z,r

V duration

The change which caused this 'voicing effect' lengthening in RP and General American (and which is still operative as a phonological rule in many varieties of present-day English) has all the characteristics of a Neogrammarian sound change. For instance, the results are not discrete; vowels do not become categorically long or short, but both long and short vowels become longer depending on the environment. The process is clearly phonetically conditioned, but has no grammatical conditioning, and it applies across the board, with no lexical exceptions. Furthermore, the 'voicing effect' change is not categorised, in that its operation is not perceived by speakers; and there is no evidence of lexical diffusion.

We return now to the historical SVLR; there are a number of different formulations of this change, and an alternative to the one proposed here is given in Lass (1974). We have already established that, in most varieties of English, all vowels lengthened according to the hierarchy in (18). In Scottish varieties, probably in the late sixteenth century, all vowels but /ɪ ʌ ɛ/ underwent extra lengthening before voiced fricatives and /r/, which are in any case the contexts most conducive to lengthening and which I have labelled voiced continuants in (20).

(20)   SSE/Scots

This extra lengthening was probably audible to speakers, who might then have stopped thinking of vowels as long or short, and started to classify them all as short, with the majority lengthening before /r/ and voiced fricatives.

In Scots / SSE, the extreme environments of the voicing effect hierarchy were therefore isolated from the voicing effect process, and became a new, separate change, SVLR. Although SVLR has developed from the voicing effect, however, it does not behave like a Neogrammarian change. On the contrary, it shows the properties of a lexically diffusing sound change. For instance, SVLR does have discrete results, since it produces long vowels while unaffected vowels, and all vowels outside SVLR long contexts, are short. It is partly phonetically conditioned, but also grammatically conditioned, operating word-finally and before inflections so that vowels are long in *tie*, *tied* and *ties*, but short in *tide*, where no boundary follows the vowel. We have already observed that vowels are universally longest before pauses. I assume that pre-pausal lengthening was extended to word-final position as in *tie*, even when no pause followed, and that this lengthening was then extended to other forms sharing the same stem, including *ties* and *tied*; this extension probably involved analogy, which we shall consider in more detail in the next chapter. SVLR is also cate-gorisable, since speakers tend to be able to distinguish long vowels, to which SVLR has applied, from short ones. Furthermore, SVLR is beginning to show lexical diffusion. At the moment, this is only true of one vowel, the diphthong /aɪ/, which as already noted has the short realisation [ʌɪ] and the long one [aːɪ]. The long realisation is obviously expected in the usual SVLR long contexts, before /r/ and voiced fricatives, word-finally and before suffixes. However, long [aːɪ] is beginning to diffuse, so that forms like *pylon, spider, viper*, which by SVLR should have short vowels, now frequently have long ones. This phenomenon is still sporadic and speaker-specific, but is clearly lexical diffusion. Finally, this incipient diffusion is providing lexical exceptions for SVLR, in the form of words like *spider* to which it ought not to apply but does, supplying a further property of diffusing change.

The voicing effect change, then, is certainly a Neogrammarian sound change, while SVLR is equally clearly a diffusing change. If we are to accept both that there are two types of sound change, and that SVLR and the voicing effect lengthening are connected as demonstrated above, our only option is to assume that changes may initially have Neogrammarian properties, but may subsequently begin to diffuse. This is the course which SVLR has followed, albeit only in some varieties of English. Neogrammarian changes, then, may become diffusing changes over time.

3.3.4   *Lexical Phonology and sound change*

In the last chapter, we saw that the theory of sound change promoted within Standard Generative Phonology was inadequate in various respects. One notable inadequacy is the failure of the standard model to suggest a valid pathway whereby sound changes may be integrated into the synchronic grammar; it is not enough simply to say that sound changes and phonological rules are identical. In addition, Labov's two types of sound change have no analogues in Standard Generative Phonology, which recognises only one type of phonological rule.

This failure of Standard Generative Phonology has encouraged the attitude of certain historical linguists that modern linguistic theories, conceived to deal with synchronic data, have no diachronic dimension, and that synchronic and diachronic linguistics are necessarily isolated from one another. Given that languages change, adequate linguistic theories ought to incorporate an analysis of this fact. We should therefore prefer linguistic theories which have a contribution to make to historical linguistics.

Although Standard Generative Phonology cannot incorporate Labov's two types of sound change, we shall see that Lexical Phonology, one of its successors, can. If this is so, it is advantageous for historical linguistics, since a closer connection between synchrony and diachrony will be demonstrable, and for Lexical Phonology, since it will have been shown to be exempt from one of the major failings of its predecessor, the Standard Generative model.

Lexical Phonology is a Generative model, and therefore involves the assignment of a single underlying form to each morpheme, and the subsequent operation of phonological rules on these forms to produce surface phonetic representations. However, Lexical Phonology (LP) is innovative in two main respects. It is less abstract than Standard Generative Phonology, since underlying and surface representations are generally very similar, while in the standard model underlying forms often bore little resemblance to the eventual phonetic forms. Fewer and less powerful rules are therefore required in LP. However, the main innovation of LP is in the organisation of the phonological component of the grammar, which is seen as integrative, with phonological and morphological rules interacting.

The main motivation for LP, which began developing in the early 1980s, is the kind of data in (21), where the addition of certain suffixes seems to correlate with a movement of the stress on the stem, while other suffixes do not affect stress placement.

(21)a.   átom   b. édit
         atómic   éditor

The solution offered within LP is to split the phonology up into ordered levels, or strata, with a certain inventory of phonological and morphological rules applying on each level. The result, for the limited data in (21), is given in (22). In *atom*, the Stress Rules apply on Level 1, followed by an affixation rule. Level 1 is a cyclic level, where rules can apply more than once to successively larger constituents. The addition of *-ic* therefore allows the Stress Rules to operate again; and because the rules are applying to a different form, they assign the stress to a different syllable. However, for *edit*, the Stress Rules apply, but no affix is added; instead, the form passes to Level 2 where the rule attaching *-or* is located. This process operates, but the stress pattern cannot then be altered, since the Stress Rules apply only on Level 1, and once a form has left this level, it cannot go back.

(22)a.   Level 1: átom   Stress Rules
                   átomic   −*ic* affixation
                   atómic   Stress Rules

   b.   Level 1: édit   Stress Rules

                        ↓

         Level 2: éditor   −*or* affixation

The basic structure of a Lexical Phonology, for English, appears in (23).

(23)

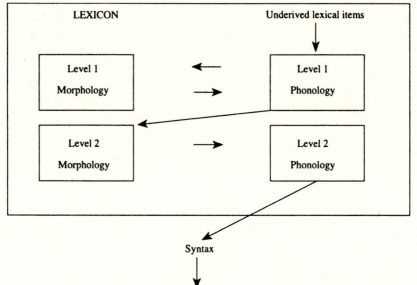

Postlexical Phonology

As this outline shows, lexical items are passed through phonological and morphological rules on Levels 1 and 2 (see Kaisse and Shaw 1985 for more details), then emerge from the lexicon into the syntax. Here, individual words are joined together into sentences, which pass finally into the postlexical phonology. Not all phonological rules apply in the lexicon; some operate in this postlexical component instead (or as well). Typically, lexical rules are those which have some link with the morphology, like the Stress Rules; have lexical exceptions; and apply only within words. Postlexical rules, on the other hand, may apply across words, like the rule deleting /r/ in English varieties with linking but not intrusive [r] (see Chapter 2), which applies whenever a consonant follows, whether this is in the same word (*dark* [dɑːk]) or in the next (*car park* [kɑːpɑːk]). Postlexical rules also lack exceptions and are not subject to morphological conditioning. A set of properties summarising the differences between lexical and postlexical rules is given in (24).

(24) *Lexical*   *Postlexical*
      Discrete, binary output   Gradient output
      May be morphologically conditioned   Purely phonologically conditioned
      May have lexical exceptions   Apply across the board
      Input and output distinguishable by   Speakers unaware
        speakers

| Operate on and introduce only contrastive units | May introduce novel segments and features |
| Apply within words | Apply across words |

It is at this point that we return to sound change. If the characteristics of lexical and postlexical rules in (24) are compared to those of diffusing and Neogrammarian changes in (10) (repeated as (25) for convenience), a high degree of overlap becomes apparent; lexical rules and lexically diffusing changes, and postlexical rules and Neogrammarian changes, have markedly similar sets of properties.

(25)

	Lexical diffusion	'Neogrammarian' change
Discrete	yes	no
Phonetic conditioning	rough	fine
Lexical exceptions	yes	no
Grammatical conditioning	yes	no
Social affect	no	yes
Predictable	no	yes
Learnable	no	yes
Categorised	yes	no
Dictionary entries	2	1
Lexical diffusion	yes	no

Some of these properties show direct matches. For instance, both lexical rules and diffusing changes tend to be discrete, producing binary outputs; may be morphologically as well as phonetically conditioned; are categorised, or have observable outputs; and may have lexical exceptions. Postlexical rules and Neogrammarian changes, on the other hand, have gradient outputs and are not observed by speakers; apply across the board without exceptions; and are sensitive only to phonetic information. One or two further comparisons can be made: for example, the requirement that lexical rules may operate only on contrastive features can be linked with the fact that diffusing changes involve two dictionary entries (and hence two distinctive units); and lexical diffusion may also produce lexical exceptions, since one sort of exception involves application of a rule outside its original conditioning context, and this may be due to the diffusion of a change, as in the over-application of SVLR in items like *spider*, *pylon*.

We can conclude, then, that lexically diffusing changes correlate with, and therefore enter the synchronic grammar as, lexical phonological rules, while Neogrammarian changes, once implemented, become postlexical rules. However, just as Neogrammarian changes may ultimately begin to diffuse, so postlexical processes must be allowed to become lexical. Again, this transition may be illustrated using SVLR. The voicing effect change must initially have been a postlexical rule; in English today it still produces a gradient output, is unobservable, has no exceptions and is sensitive only to the phonetic context. SVLR, on the other hand, has a number of lexical characteristics. For instance, as we have already established, it has begun to diffuse, and has thereby acquired lexical exceptions like *spider*, *viper*, *pylon*, which lack a lengthening context but undergo SVLR all the same. SVLR also has a binary rather than a scalar output, producing long as opposed to short vowels, and many Scots speakers can distinguish these categories. Finally, we saw above that SVLR spread, probably by analogy, from pre-pausal to word-final to pre-suffixal position (that is, from utterance-final *tie* to all cases of *tie* and thence to *ties* and *tied*). Due to this analogical extension, synchronic SVLR is sensitive to morphological information, another indication of lexical application.

We have established, then, that Labov's two types of sound change have direct analogues in the two types of phonological rules of Lexical Phonology. The establishment of connections between Neogrammarian changes and postlexical rules, and diffusing changes and lexical rules, and the discovery that the former may develop into the latter, is advantageous for historical linguistics in that it provides a partial answer to the question of implementation. It is also helpful to linguists attempting to formulate theories which embrace both synchrony and diachrony, since this analysis suggests a way of incorporating change into the synchronic grammar, and indicates that initially synchronically based theories like LP may have a diachronic dimension. Finally, Lexical Phonology gains in two respects. Its two types of rules provide parallels for sound change which were unavailable in Standard Generative Phonology; and the gradual penetration of initially Neogrammarian changes deeper into the grammar provides a mechanism for dialect and language differentiation conspicuously absent from earlier phonological theory.

Lexical diffusion theory, then, provides a partial answer to the transmission question. We shall return to the issue of implementation, in the speech community rather than the individual grammar, and to the so far entirely unsolved problem of actuation, in Chapter 9. First, however, we must extend our investigation of language change beyond sound change into the domains of morphology, syntax, semantics and vocabulary.

4 Morphological change

4.1 Introduction

We move now from the study of change in the phonetics and phonology to change in other areas of the grammar, and specifically to change in the morphology, or the structure of words. Morphology, of course, is not isolated from other components of the grammar, and integrates both synchronically and diachronically with the phonology and syntax. For instance, most Modern English nouns make their plurals by adding -s, whereas a few, like *foot*, instead change the stem vowel in the plural. Historically, the *foot* – *feet* alternation was part of the phonology, not the morphology: in earlier *fōt – *fōti, the final vowel showed plural number, but the sound change of i-mutation subsequently fronted /o:/ whenever /i/ appeared in the next syllable, giving *fōt – *fø̄ti. The vowel in the plural form unrounded in OE to give *fēt*, and the suffix dropped, leaving *fōt – fēt*, which ultimately became *foot - feet*. This loss of the final -*i* meant that the changed stem vowel was no longer predictable on the basis of phonological context, becoming instead a morphological fact about a particular word. Syntactic features may also become morphological: for example, auxiliary verbs may in time cease to be independent units and instead attach themselves to the main verb as person, number or tense affixes. This process of morphologisation of syntactic elements, known as grammaticalisation, will be discussed much more fully in Chapter 6.

Morphological facts cannot therefore be divorced entirely from syntactic or phonological, or indeed semantic concerns, as we shall see periodically below. However, our main concern in this chapter will be change in the morphology itself. 'Unfortunately,' as Anderson (1992: 365) notes, 'theories of such changes are not well developed, and real results or established principles are hard to find. Explicit theories of morphological structure within the context of a full formal grammar are still comparatively new, and the literature devoted to change in such systems is quite limited.' The obvious solution is to concentrate on the one immensely well-documented area of internal morphological change, namely analogy, which was much discussed in earlier, traditional historical linguistics; and this will indeed take up most of the current chapter. However, we should not ignore newer and ongoing work, and a final section will therefore introduce the theory of Natural Morphology (Dressler 1985, Wurzel 1989).

4.2   Analogy

4.2.1   *The anatomy of analogy*

Analogy is a term which we have encountered already in this book, so that readers will already have a rudimentary idea of what analogy is and how it operates. For example, the Neogrammarians saw sound change and analogy as interacting but opposing forces, a view summed up clearly in Sturtevant's Paradox, which says that sound change is regular but produces irregularity, while analogy is irregular but produces regularity. Analogy is therefore seen as a kind of housekeeping device, which resignedly picks up at least some of the mess made by the more impetuous sound change as it hurtles blindly through the grammar.

One major difference between sound change and analogy is that the former tends to involve only phonetic factors – in fact, both the Neogrammarians and the Structuralists made this a primary condition on sound change, which could never be sensitive to morphological, syntactic, or semantic information. Analogy, however, is primarily concerned with the link between sound and meaning, which combine to express particular morphemes or meaningful units. The task of analogy is then to maintain this link by keeping sound structure, grammatical structure and semantic structure in line, especially when sound change might have made their relationship opaque.

There is one similarity between sound change and analogy: both can be divided into more and less regular subtypes. Regular sound changes might include assimilation and weakening, while some irregular, sporadic subtypes are haplology, metathesis and dissimilation. In this section, we shall consider a similar typology for analogy, noting the subtypes which are generally recognised and assessing their regularity. It is worth bearing in mind, however, that there are few, if any, cases of absolutely regular analogy.

4.2.1.1 Systematic analogy

The two most systematic, regular subtypes of analogy are analogical extension and analogical levelling.

4.2.1.1.1 *Analogical extension*

The main characteristic of analogical extension is the generalisation of a morpheme or relation which already exists in the language into new situations or forms. One of the most famous examples of such generalisation involves the <-s> plural of Modern English.

In present-day English, by far the most widespread and regular method of marking the plural on nouns is the addition of an <-s> suffix, pronounced [-əz] or [-ɪz] after the sibilants /s z ʃ ʒ tʃ dʒ/ (*horses, bushes, churches*), [-s] after other voiceless consonants (*cats, drops, oafs*) and [-z] after other voiced sounds (*dogs, loaves, loans, hills, pennies*). Old English, however, had a far wider variety of ways of forming the plural, with no one strategy dominating. In fact, OE had no method of signalling plural number alone – instead, inflections indicated a combination of gender, case and number information. Furthermore, adjectives, pronouns and the definite article also varied for gender, case and number. The OE system of inflectional morphology was therefore much more complex than that of modern English, and more closely resembled the Latin system, where there are also different declensional classes for nouns (and conjugational classes for verbs), each characterised by different sets of suffixes and modifications to the stem. Three illustrative OE noun paradigms are given in (1).

(1)a. Weak feminine noun: *sunne* 'sun'

	sg.	pl.
Nominative	*sunne*	*sunnan*
Accusative	*sunnan*	*sunnan*
Genitive	*sunnan*	*sunnena*
Dative	*sunnan*	*sunnum*

b. Strong masculine noun: *stān* 'stone'

	sg.	pl.
Nominative	*stān*	*stānas*
Accusative	*stān*	*stānas*
Genitive	*stānes*	*stāna*
Dative	*stāne*	*stānum*

c. Strong neuter noun: *scip* 'ship'

	sg.	pl.
Nominative	*scip*	*scipu*
Accusative	*scip*	*scipu*
Genitive	*scipes*	*scipa*
Dative	*scipe*	*scipum*

Between Old and Middle English, this complex system of inflections began to break down. In fact, this erosion was already under way by OE: for instance, OE rarely differentiates the nominative and accusative cases, as shown in (1), although in Gothic, an older relative, separate inflections are attested for all case and number forms (see (2)).

(2)   Gothic *dags* 'day'

	sg.	pl.
Nominative	*dags*	*dagos*
Accusative	*dag*	*dagans*
Genitive	*dagis*	*dage*
Dative	*daga*	*dagum*

Final nasals, which seem cross-linguistically to be rather unstable and difficult to perceive, were lost first; and the vowels in final unstressed syllables then became confused, ending up in Middle English mostly as schwa [ə]. Ultimately even these schwas, which no longer adequately differentiated grammatical categories, also dropped.

However, some nouns like *stān* in (1b) did not only include inflections consisting of vowel or vowel plus nasal in their paradigm; they also added suffixes with /s/, as in the genitive singular *stānes* or the nominative and accusative plural *stānas*. This /s/ proved more stable, and the paradigm of such nouns in ME became [stɑ:nəs] (later [stɑ:nz], even later [sto:nz] / [stoʊnz]) in the possessive and the plural, but [stɑ:n], with the earlier inflections lost, everywhere else. This /s/ was then reinterpreted as a marker of the plural and the possessive.

So far, analogy has played no part in these developments; we have witnessed only a reinterpretation of the /s/ inflection in the paradigms of certain nouns. Analogical extension next stepped in, gradually generalising the new /s/ plural marker to many nouns, like *scip* and *sunne*, which had never used /s/ to mark the plural in any case (although, as (1c) shows, *scip* had had /s/ in the genitive singular). Such nouns had lost the inflections which signalled their plurals in Old English, and the distinctive /s/, which was historically appropriate only to the *stān* class, was introduced to replace these. It is now characteristic of all regular English nouns.

This type of analogy is often called proportional analogy, because the mechanism of extension seems to involve the construction of a proportion like the one in (3). Proportions generally encode a relationship among four terms, giving the phenomenon its other common name of four-part analogy.

(3)   *stān* : *stānes* = *sunne* : X
          X = *sunnes*

The overgeneralisation of surface forms characteristic of analogical extension is particularly noticeable in child language; children frequently produce analogically regularised forms like *foot – foots* or *bring – brang – brung*. If corrected, children may respond by producing their proportional model; that is, a child told that the past tense of *bring* is actually *brought* may object that *sing* has the pattern *sing – sang – sung*, so that the analogous patterns *bring – brang – brung* and *swing – swang – swung* must also be correct.

Although many English nouns have adopted the <-s> plural, analogy is rarely as regular and exceptionless as some sound changes can be. Nouns have been filtering out of the irregular class and into the regular one from Old English to the present day: for instance, *book* was irregular *bōc – bēc* in OE and would have ended up with the plural *beek* or *beech* if it had not been analogically regularised to *books*; while *shoe* had the plural *shoon* well into Middle English. Irregular plurals still remain in Standard English; these include *foot – feet*, *ox – oxen* and *sheep – sheep*, which show no tendency towards regularisation (except in child language). Such a residue of irregular forms is characteristic even of the more regular subtypes of analogy. It has been suggested that residual words are often the most frequently occurring, which will be heard and learned earliest by the child and which are furthermore most susceptible to correction if the child does produce a regularised form like **foots. Some objections can be raised; for instance, *ox* is not a particularly common noun in modern English – although it probably occurred rather frequently in Middle English. *Ox* might have been expected to regularise as it became less common, but this decrease in frequency probably overlapped with the rise of literacy, which tends to slow down analogical change. In general, the connection of resistance to analogy with frequency seems to hold.

4.2.1.1.2 *Analogical levelling*

If analogical extension involves patterns, then the second systematic type of analogy, levelling, involves paradigms. In languages which organise their inflectional morphology in terms of regular additions of affixes or modifications to the stem, a paradigm is a set of inflectional forms with the same stem morpheme, like those shown in (1). Paradigms seem to have some degree of psychological reality for native speakers, and are often the units used in teaching foreign learners; and they also form the domain for certain changes. Levelling also exhibits the clearest connection of analogy with sound change: sound change will tend to apply to certain forms in a paradigm, but not to others, and it therefore sets up alternations, or allomorphy, resulting in the existence of different phonological forms for the same morpheme. In the paradigm of the morpheme *foot*, for instance, there are two forms, *foot* and *feet*, in which the vowels /ʊ/ and /i/ alternate. Levelling 'levels out' such diversity in the paradigm.

An example of levelling is given in (4) (and is further discussed in Hock 1986, Chapter 9).

(4)		OE	ModE	
	present	cēo[z]an	choose	[z]
	past sg.	cēa[s]	chose	[z]
	past pl.	cu[r]on	chose	[z]
	past participle	(ge-)co[r]en	chosen	[z]
		OHG	ModG	
	present	kiu[s]an	küren	[r]
	past sg.	ko[s]	kor	[r]
	past pl.	ku[r]un	koren	[r]
	past participle	(gi-)ko[r]an	gekoren	[r]

Both Old English and Old High German (OHG) have alternations, variously involving [s], [z] and [r], within the paradigm of the verb 'to choose'. The alternation of [s] and [z] in OE results from Verner's Law, and [r] appears due to another Germanic sound change, called rhotacism, which turned [z] into [r] in certain contexts. The operation of these regular sound changes, and the resultant allomorphy, makes the semantic relationship between the forms of the verb in OE and OHG, and the fact that they belong to a single paradigm, rather opaque. In Modern English and German, analogical levelling has removed this opacity: one alternant has been selected ([z] in English and [r] in German) and extended throughout the paradigm, levelling out the earlier variation. Analogical levelling can be thought of as implementing an association of one form with one meaning; this requirement of iconicity will be explored further in 4.2.3.3 below.

Levelling has sometimes been interpreted as reversing a sound change; in fact, there is never a complete reversal, only a subsequent analogical change in certain sectors of a paradigm which may restore an earlier phonological form. For instance, English *sword* had the [w] pronounced at an earlier stage of the language; [w] was then lost between [s] and a back vowel, in *sword* and other words with the appropriate context like *swore*. In *swore*, however, the [w] has been restored by analogical levelling, since it was retained in the related *swear*. Analogy therefore interferes with the output of sound change, but does not reverse it completely.

4.2.1.2 Sporadic analogy

We shall now look briefly at some less systematic subtypes of analogy, namely contamination, back-formation, and folk etymology.

The effects of contamination can be seen in English *father*, which cannot be regularly derived from PIE *pǝtēr-. Grimm's and Verner's Laws should have changed the medial *t to *ð in Germanic; medial *ð then regularly developed to [d] in OE, to give expected **[fadǝ(r)]. However, the expected voiced stop is not found in modern English; instead, we find a fricative. It seems that this [ð] is included by analogy with *brother*, which has the medial voiced fricative derived quite regularly and has 'contaminated', or influenced *father*. Contamination most frequently affects forms from related semantic fields, such as kinship terms; some further examples are the reformation of Armenian *ustr* 'son' after *dustr* 'daughter', or the replacement of **synove*, the expected plural of Russian 'son', with *synov'ja*, by analogy with *brat'ja* 'brothers' (Anttila 1977).

Contamination is also fairly common in words which occur in lists, such as the days of the week, months of the year, and especially numerals. For instance, English *four* should have initial [k] (compare Latin *quattuor*, Scots Gaelic *ceithir* or Sanskrit *catvāras*), but has been contaminated by the adjacent numeral *five*. Similarly, Russian *dev'at'* should have initial [n], like *nine* or Latin *novem*, but has been contaminated by *des'at'* 'ten'. The sporadic nature of contamination is clearly illustrated by the fact that such changes have happened only in certain numerals and in certain languages – so the [t] of English *ten* has not spread to *nine*.

Finally, there are occasional cases of bidirectional contamination. For instance, Old French *citeain* and *deinzein*, both meaning 'inhabitant', became Anglo-Norman *citizein* and *denizein*, clearly showing mutual influence.

A second sporadic type of analogy is back formation, seen operating in (5).

(5)   *scare* : *scary*
       smell : *smelly*
       X   : *lazy*   X = *laze*

English speakers know that adjectives can be formed from many verbs by adding -*y* to the verb stem; so, when they encounter *lazy*, they assume that it is derived from a verb *to laze*, although historically there was no such verb. In back formation, a new form is coined by analogy with other pairs of words which are related by a productive morphological process; the new form is the result of reversing this process.

Some instances of back formation also indicate the relationship of analogy with reinterpretation. When French *cerise* 'cherry' was borrowed into Middle English, the final [z] was reinterpreted as a plural marker. Consequently, a new singular form was produced by removing this [z], by back formation according to the proportion in (6).

(6)   *pears*   : *pear*
       cherries : X
       X   = *cherry*

Our final type of irregular analogy is folk etymology. Here, a word which seems opaque to the native speaker, often because it has a foreign origin, is reinterpreted or has its morphological boundaries shifted so that its semantic and morphological structures coincide, making it transparent. Some well-known English examples are the dialect form *sparrowgrass* for *asparagus*, and the name of a particular area of London, the *Elephant and Castle*, which derived ultimately from *Infanta of Castile*. Similarly, Latin *margarīta* 'pearl' is borrowed into OE as *meregrota*, where *mere* means 'sea' and *grota* means 'grain'; this is a motivated compound, in that each element means something, and the meanings of the parts contribute to the meaning of the whole. Finally, Anttila (1972) observes that Finnish *jaloviina*, literally 'noble liquor', bears a chance resemblance to English *yellow wine*, which is therefore what British tourists call it.

4.2.2   *Constraints on analogy*
4.2.2.1   Introduction

So far, we have established that there are various subtypes of analogy, some more regular and others more sporadic, and have introduced an elementary classification. However, we have given no indication of what limits exist on analogical processes. Furthermore, there has been no evidence that we can assess either when analogy will occur, or what pathways it can follow when it does operate. That is, the account of analogy given above is entirely non-predictive.

The sporadic nature of analogy almost certainly means that we shall never be able to formulate a strongly predictive theory of analogical change; even the most regular types of analogy do not lend themselves to prediction, since they never seem to be obligatory, but represent only one possible reaction to a particular situation. However, some attempts have been made to propose constraints on analogy, or to discern some tendencies indicating the directions in which analogical processes typically proceed. Such attempts may help us to understand, and perhaps formalise, analogical change.

Two main sets of generalisations about analogy have been produced, by the Polish linguists Kuryłowicz and Mańczak. Neither claims to be able to predict when analogical change will happen, but both attempt to specify what such a change may do, if activated. Kuryłowicz (1949: 37) actually has an analogy for this: he says that we cannot tell exactly when it is going to rain, but have a fair idea of where the rain will go when it does, since there are pipes, drains and gutters which the water is likely to flow down. Similarly, we cannot know with any certainty whether analogy will be triggered by a particular set of circumstances or not, but there are certain characteristics it will tend to exhibit once it starts to work.

Kuryłowicz and Mańczak have rather different approaches to their work on analogy. Kuryłowicz bases his generalisations on the intuitions about change which he built up over a number of years of research into analogy, and states his ideas as laws. Mańczak is rather more circumspect, stating his generalisations as tendencies; he also works more empirically, basing these tendencies on a statistical survey of analogical processes constructed from historical grammars and etymological dictionaries of various European languages.

Kuryłowicz proposes six laws, and Mańczak nine tendencies. I shall discuss these selectively below, and some will not be mentioned at all; those wishing to pursue the topic may consult Kuryłowicz (1949), Mańczak (1958, 1980) and the surveys in Hock (1986, Chapter 10) and Vincent (1974).

4.2.2.2 Kuryłowicz's laws

According to Kuryłowicz's first law, bipartite markers of particular grammatical categories tend to replace unitary ones; more generally, complex markers replace simple ones. For instance, in German there is a class of nouns, including *Gast – Gäste* 'guest', which mark the plural using both a suffix and umlaut on the stem vowel; and this bipartite marking has now been generalised to other nouns which historically only had the affix, such as *Baum – Bäume* 'tree' for earlier plural *Baume*. Hock (1986) suggests that we should accept the spirit rather than the letter of the first law, and rephrase it to say that more overt marking is preferred. This would include cases like the German one, as well as instances of *any* marker replacing a zero marker, such as the generalisation of the /s/ plural in English to nouns which had lost their plural suffixes.

Kuryłowicz's second law says that any analogical development should proceed from a basic or simple form to a derived form. This works relatively well in most cases of proportional analogy; for instance, *stone* in English represents a simple form and the plural *stones* a derived one, and this pattern has been generalised by analogical extension to other nouns like *sun*, producing the new derived form *suns*.

However, certain problems do arise with the second law. First, it seems to rule out back formation which, as we have seen, produces a new basic form, like *laze*, from a derived form, such as *lazy*. It is also notoriously difficult to define basic and derived. For instance, in contamination, it is unclear why the form affected should be less basic than its model; why should *dev'at'* 'nine' be less basic than *des'at'* 'ten' in Russian, or *five* more basic than *four* in English? Finally, in the case of levelling, it is impossible to say that one alternant within a paradigm is more basic than another. The paradigms of the verb 'to choose' in Old English and Old High German are given in (4) above; the equivalent forms in modern English and German show that English has generalised the [z] alternant, while German has selected [r]. If Kuryłowicz's second law is accepted verbatim, we must also accept that the [z] forms were more basic in English, but the [r] forms in German.

Kuryłowicz's fourth law initially seems less problematic. The argument here is that, when one form is split into two by analogy, the new, analogically derived and regular form will take on the basic meaning or function, while the older, irregular form will remain in a subordinate role. The standard example here is English *brother*, which has the archaic plural *brethren*, but has moved from the strong to the weak noun class over time, and has consequently acquired the new, analogically derived plural *brothers*, with the regular [z] plural suffix. *Brothers* is now the form used in semantically unmarked contexts, while *brethren* is restricted to rather specialised semantic areas, such as religious usage. Similarly, *stretch*, *work* and *melt* had past participles *straight*, *wrought* and *molten* earlier in English; these have been replaced by the regular, analogical forms *stretched*, *worked* and *melted* in past participle uses, but have remained as adjectives and in some compounds like *wrought iron*, *molten lava*.

The fourth law has been challenged by Kiparsky (1974). Kiparsky presents a number of counterexamples, all of which show regularisation of a form in some special function, but the retention of irregularities in the primary function. For instance, the plural of *mouse* is *mice*, but that of *mickey mouse* 'a notoriously easy course' is *mickey mouses*; the plural of *sabertooth* (*tiger*) is *sabertooths*, not ****saberteeth*; and the verb *weave* has the strong past tense *wove* when referring to cloth, but analogically derived *weaved* when used to describe the movement of a vehicle through traffic. Hock (1986) defends the fourth law by claiming that, in these cases, the semantic change involved preceded the morphological reformation, but this argument is at best impossible to prove, and Kiparsky's counter-examples must at least cast doubt on the universal validity of the fourth law.

Finally for our purposes, Kuryłowicz's fifth law asserts that, if the speakers of a language have a choice between keeping a contrast of rather marginal significance, and abandoning it in favour of reinstating a more basic distinction, then they will abandon the marginal contrast and reestablish the basic one. Again, this can be illustrated using the example of the generalisation of the English <-s> plural. In Old English, there had been no way of signalling plural number alone: case and number could only be marked together. It seems that, cross-linguistically, marking number is more important than marking case, and so when the markers of different morphological categories fell together in late OE, speakers seem to have selected a form, the /s/ suffix, which could mark plurality, even if this meant sacrificing the ability to mark case.

4.2.2.3 Mańczak's tendencies

I shall discuss these generalisations selectively, paying particular attention to whether Mańczak's tendencies agree with, conflict with or supplement Kuryłowicz's laws.

Mańczak's first and third tendencies are linked, proposing respectively that longer words, and longer inflectional forms are more usually remade on the basis of shorter ones than the reverse. These are connected with Kuryłowicz's laws in two ways. First, they are two aspects of the second law, which holds that analogy proceeds from basic to derived forms, since it might be argued that shorter forms are more basic than longer ones. Secondly, the idea that longer forms are preferred, which is implicit in Mańczak's tendencies, accords well with our extended version of Kuryłowicz's first law, which expressed a preference for more overt marking. Mańczak (1958) reports that he tested his first hypothesis on etymological dictionaries of French, German and Czech, and found that 91 per cent, 99 per cent and 89 per cent of reformations respectively did proceed in the predicted direction. The third tendency was checked using Romance and Germanic data: 85 per cent and 83 per cent of developments respectively support Mańczak's hypothesis.

According to Mańczak's second tendency, alternation within paradigms is more often abolished than introduced; in other words, a paradigm with a single stem form will be preferred to one with a number of alternating variants. The second tendency seems to be an attempt to deal with levelling, the major analogical mechanism disposing of alternation in the paradigm. This is, then, a real contribution, since Kuryłowicz did not succeed in dealing with levelling (more accurately, it can be argued that the third law is intended to cover levelling, but its interpretation is rather fraught, and I do not propose to discuss it here). However, even the second tendency, which seems to be on the right lines, clearly *is* a tendency rather than an absolute constraint, since there are cases of alternants being extended; this is the case for the German composite affix-plus-umlaut plural marker, which has been generalised from nouns like *Gast* to historically non-umlauting nouns like *Baum*. Mańczak claims that 93 per cent of his data show loss of alternation, but on this occasion these are drawn only from a single Polish dictionary.

Mańczak's fourth and fifth tendencies hold that zero endings are more usually replaced by full endings, and monosyllabic endings by polysyllabic ones, than *vice versa*. Again, this extends and makes more explicit the preference for overt marking implicit in Kuryłowicz's first law. Finally, Mańczak's sixth and seventh tendencies classify the indicative mood and present tense (to which can be added third person and singular number) as basic, and state that other moods and tenses (and persons and numbers) will characteristically be reworked on the basis of these unmarked categories. Again, this tendency follows Kuryłowicz's second law, which claims that analogy proceeds from basic forms, although Mańczak gives more information on what is actually basic. Although these tendencies seem intuitively promising, and are again supported by between 58 per cent and 100 per cent of cases in the various etymological dictionaries and grammars Mańczak consulted, they would have to be tested on a sizeable and consistent corpus of data from various language families before being validated; indeed, Mańczak (1980) argues strongly for statistical testing of his tendencies and Kuryłowicz's laws to settle the various controversies between them, but such testing has not so far been carried out.

4.2.2.4 Summary

As we have seen, Mańczak's tendencies are by no means a mere restatement of Kuryłowicz's laws. A more detailed discussion of both sets of generalisations would certainly reveal cases where they make opposing predictions, but constraints of space mean that we can neither explore these discrepancies nor attempt to resolve them here. Instead, I shall end on a positive note, by stating three superordinate generalisations (after Vincent 1974) which include most of the important aspects of the laws and tendencies, and give us at least some idea of the courses analogical changes may take.

First, some categories are more basic than others – these might include indicative mood and present tense, and perhaps shorter as opposed to longer forms. These will tend to be used as the model for analogy, which will remake other forms on the basis of these unmarked ones.

Secondly, there is a tendency to form clear exponents of grammatical categories, which should be as strong as possible. Longer, more overt, and complex markers are consequently favoured.

Thirdly, redundancy, or multiple expression of the same information, will tend to be eliminated, as will alternation or allomorphy within a paradigm.

4.2.3   *Analogy and the form and construction of grammars*
4.2.3.1   Introduction

The previous section reported attempts to constrain analogy and to specify general characteristics of analogical change. However, we are still left with a rather loose definition at best. Recent work on analogy has sought to cast light on the phenomenon by studying its interaction with other aspects of the grammar, and we shall investigate three such attempts in this section. First, we shall briefly consider the Generative view that analogy is a formal principle of grammar; we then turn to more fruitful connections of analogy with *non*-formal principles, beginning with an exploration of iconicity, and ending with the relationship of analogy and language acquisition.

4.2.3.2   Generative grammar and analogy

Since Generative historical linguistics aims at formality and explicitness, its practitioners might be expected to be ill-disposed to the vagueness of analogy. King especially criticised the Neogrammarian reliance on analogy as a default solution to any conceivable problem with sound change, claiming that analogy had become a 'terminological receptacle devoid of explanatory power' (1969a: 235). King, and Kiparsky (1974, 1978), identify two particular problems with earlier work on analogy. First, they claim that proportion based accounts of analogy assume that all analogical change is gradual and sporadic, whereas in fact levelling and extension may be relatively regular. Second, there are no clear conditions on the forms related by proportions: should they share more than two phonemes, or rhyme, or what? Without such conditions, we cannot rule out preposterous proportions, like Kiparsky's example in (7); but it is not clear whether conditions can be specified, or whether the constraints on proportions are perhaps semantic rather than formal.

(7)   *ear*:*hear* = *eye*:X
             X = *heye*

The solution the Generativists proposed was to move away from the idea of proportions, and construct instead a formal, rule-based theory of analogy as simplification of phonological rules. Specifically, Kiparsky argues that children acquiring a language will learn the simplest possible grammar. This may differ from their parents' grammars by being simpler in the form or ordering of rules; and such inter-generational developments are said to correspond to analogical changes in the following ways.

Kiparsky (1978) and King (1969a) associate analogical extension with simplification of the structural description of a rule, and analogical levelling with simplification of its structural change. In the schematic rule in (8), A and C constitute the structural description, showing the input and environment for the rule respectively, and B is the structural change, indicating the work the rule actually does.

(8)   A ⟶ B / — C

     A, / — C = structural description

                    (or structural analysis)

     B   = structural change

There are no convincing examples of simplification in the structural change of a rule corresponding to analogical levelling. However, an example of simplification of the structural description, discussed by Kiparsky (1978), is given in (9).

(9)   OE:

$$\begin{bmatrix} + \text{ syllabic} \\ - \text{ cons} \end{bmatrix} \longrightarrow [-\text{long}] \; / \; — \, CC \left\{ \begin{array}{c} C \\ \ldots V \ldots V \ldots \end{array} \right\}$$

      ME:

$$\begin{bmatrix} + \text{ syllabic} \\ - \text{ cons} \end{bmatrix} \longrightarrow [-\text{long}] \; / \; — \, C \left\{ \begin{array}{c} C \\ \ldots V \ldots V \ldots \end{array} \right\}$$

As (9) shows, vowels in Old English shortened either before three consonants, or before two consonants and two following syllables. This process shortened only a few words such as *bræmblas* (< *bræmblas) 'brambles / blackberries', *enlefan* (< *ænlefan) 'eleven' and *samcucu* (< *sām-) 'half-alive'. In Middle English, a similar but much more productive change shortened vowels before two consonants, or one consonant plus two syllables, creating alternations like *keep – kept*, *meet – met*, *holy – holiday*, *divine – divinity*. It is clear that some sort of extension has taken place here, but its classification as an *analogical* extension is dubious in the extreme. The OE and ME rules may look formally similar, but have rather different effects; and indeed, it is unlikely that the few shortened forms of OE could have created a pattern suitable for analogical extension. This development is arguably better analysed as a phonetically motivated generalisation of a phonological rule with no input from analogy at all.

Kiparsky (1978) also proposed a link of analogical change with rule reordering. As we saw in Chapter 2, certain rule orders are assessed in Generative phonology as simpler than others. Rules may feed one another, in that the earlier rule may provide inputs for the later one, or the earlier one may bleed a later one by depriving it of potential inputs. Kiparsky contends that it is simpler for all rules to apply maximally; consequently, he argues that rules will be reordered historically to maximise feeding order and minimise bleeding order. Furthermore, Kiparsky hypothesises that reordering into feeding order leads to analogical extension, while reordering out of bleeding order creates levelling.

Unfortunately for Kiparsky's case, there are no good, clear and relatively uncontentious examples to illustrate the proposed parallel of reordering into feeding order with extension. However, reordering out of bleeding order does seem to be linked with analogical levelling. For instance, in certain Low German dialects (Kiparsky 1978), a rule turning postvocalic voiced stops into fricatives was added after the now familiar process of final devoicing, as shown in (10).

(10)		tag	tagə
	Devoicing:	tak	----
	Stop to fricative:	---	taɣə

This situation creates alternation within the paradigm involving both voicing and the stop-fricative distinction. Kiparsky argues that rule reordering has now taken place in a number of these dialects, producing the revised derivation in (11).

(11)		tag	tagə
	Stop to fricative:	taɣ	taɣə
	Devoicing:	tax	----

The surface alternation is now one of voicing alone. It is true that this development leads to only partial levelling, since the output is still [tax] – [taɣə] rather than **[taɣ] – [taɣə] or [tax] – **[taxə], but levelling it certainly is. Moreover, the levelling process can be ascribed to a rule reordering out of bleeding order, since in (10) Devoicing bleeds Stop to fricative of one input, while in (11) both rules apply maximally.

Although some cases of analogical levelling and extension can be analysed as resulting from rule simplification or rule reordering, the discussion above should indicate that the Generative view of analogy is not always well supported by the facts. Furthermore, analogy may complicate, rather than simplify the grammar, rendering untenable the Generative equation of analogy with simplification. For instance, *brother* has acquired the new, regular, analogical plural *brothers*. It might be argued that this does constitute simplification, as part of a general tendency towards the regularisation of plural formation in English, and indeed it might have been acceptable as simplificatory had *brothers* emerged as the only plural of *brother*. In some cases, the extension of plural < -s > has certainly contributed to the simplicity of the grammar, since nouns which were formerly marked for other pluralisation strategies have lost these lexical markings, and certain minority pluralisation rules have disappeared from the grammar. *Brother*, however, has retained its archaic plural *brethren* alongside the new, regular *brothers*; the operation of analogy has therefore increased the complexity of the grammar. It is true that *brother* no longer has to be marked as an exception to the regular plural rule, but it must still be marked as having the irregular plural *brethren*; and moreover, since the two plurals are not in free variation, a stylistic rule governing their usage will be required.

Finally, it should be noted that the Generativists do not even attempt to extend their equation of analogy with simplification to cases of sporadic analogy, such as contamination or back formation, and it is unclear how they would have dealt with these. For instance, in Middle English the form *femelle* was restructured to *female* by analogy with the semantically related *male*. This is clearly a case of contamination, producing phonetic similarity between two semantically linked words. However, in a Generative account, all that could be said is that *femelle* has been restructured. Since surface forms have no theoretical status in Generative phonology, the reason for this restructuring (the influence of *male*) remains entirely opaque.

It seems, then, that although attempts to constrain analogy and to formulate generalisations about its operation (such as those by Mańczak and Kuryłowicz) are useful and increase our understanding of analogical change, the Generative attempt to formalise analogy entirely, and to locate it in the grammar as simplificatory rule change, is ultimately obscurantist. Analogy is not concerned with competence, or the structure of the native speaker's internalised grammar, alone; it is also intimately involved with the shape of surface forms, and with the movement towards formal similarity of semantically related items. As Vincent (1974) suggests, analogy may not be part of competence or performance, but rather a bridge between them. We therefore move now to proposed connections of analogy with *non*-formal aspects of the form and construction of grammars.

4.2.3.3   Analogy and iconicity

4.2.3.3.1   *Introduction*

Saussure's characterisation of language as composed of a system of arbitrary signs, which are symbolic and conventional with no necessary link between the signifier (the linguistic unit) and the signified (the concept or object in the world), suggests a minimal link between language and non-linguistic reality. However, there is also an opposing principle, that of iconicity, which seems to favour related surface elements which are similar in form as well as in meaning, and which more generally binds language to the non-linguistic world: we have already seen iconicity at work in analogical levelling, which reduces or eliminates alternation within the paradigm. In this section, we shall first isolate some subtypes of iconicity, and give some linguistic examples of these, then consider a case study relating iconicity to analogical change.

4.2.3.3.2 *Iconicity in language*

The notion of the icon has been best developed by the philosopher Peirce, and can be generally defined as 'a non-arbitrary intentional sign – that is, a designation which bears an intrinsic resemblance to the thing it designates' (Wescott 1971: 416). Peirce in fact divides iconicity into two types, distinguishing iconic images from iconic diagrams.

Iconic images are signs which directly resemble their referents in some respect; this may be visual, as in the case of statues or paintings, or may not. Iconic images are less important than iconic diagrams for linguistic purposes, but some examples can still be found. For instance, Wescott (1971: 418) reports that 25 per cent of the signs in the Dictionary of American Sign Language of 1965 are classified as pantomimic or imitative. Furthermore, in written language many apparently non-motivated signs, like those in modern alphabets, derive ultimately from iconic, pictorial images. Thus, Latin A is from Semitic *'alif* 'ox', represented in the Sinaitic script as ▽, an ox's head complete with horns; while B, from Semitic *beth* 'house' was Cretan hieroglyphic △ (Wescott 1971). There are fewer iconic images in speech, the best example being onomatopoeia. Onomatopoeic words mimic some vocal aspect of their referent, but do not do so entirely non-language specifically; so, British cockerels say *cock-a-doodle-doo*, German ones *kikeriki* and French ones *cocorico*. This classification of onomatopoeic forms as iconic images may, however, solve a problem with analogy and regular sound change, which characteristically do not affect onomatopoeias. For example, in Middle English, chicks said [pi:p] – the verb *pipen* – with a long high front [i:] vowel. This vowel went through the Great Vowel Shift to [ai], so that *pipe* (N.) is now [paip] rather than [pi:p]. However, the formerly homophonous [pi:p] (V.), describing the noise made by chicks, has remained [pi:p] rather than developing to [paip]; and Modern English chicks still say *peep*. We might then hypothesise that onomatopoeias are not affected by sound change or analogy because they are already maximally iconic.

Iconic diagrams are more relevant for our purposes, and there are numerous linguistic examples. An iconic diagram is defined by Haiman

(1980:515) as 'a systematic arrangement of signs, none of which necessarily resembles its referent, but whose relationship to each other mirrors the relationships of their referents'. Haiman in turn divides linguistic dia-grammatic iconicity into two types, which he calls isomorphism and motivation.

Isomorphism probably represents the unmarked, or default meaning of iconicity, referring to a one-to-one, biunique association of form and meaning, or signifier and signified. When the numerous markers of plurality in OE were more or less reduced to -s, so that plural number is now usually signalled by -s and -s means plural, or when *bōc – bēc* underwent levelling to the invariant stem *book*, we see a movement towards isomorphism. As we have seen, isomorphism may be interrupted by regular sound change, and restored by subsequent analogy; isomorphism is also violated by homonymy (as in *sole* and *soul*), synonymy and syntactic ambiguity. Haiman (1980) attempts to identify factors which may overrule the universal tendency towards isomorphism in particular circumstances, but this is beyond the scope of our discussion.

Iconic motivation is a rather more loosely defined concept, embracing widely differing cases where some linguistic form, or set of forms, in some sense mirrors non-linguistic reality. Examples are to be found in syntax, morphology and phonology.

Perhaps the clearest case of iconic motivation in syntax involves the correspondence of linear order of constituents with the temporal order of events. For instance, in the Latin *vēnī, vīdī, vīcī*, 'I came, I saw, I conquered', the actions described took place in the stated order; that is, the conquering followed the seeing, and so on. Similarly, the much greater frequency of languages with word-orders SOV, SVO or VSO, in which the Subject precedes the Object, than those with the minority orders OSV, OVS or VOS, in which the Object precedes the Subject, might be ascribed to the greater relevance or perceptual salience of the Subject in real-world situations; in linguistic representations of these situations, the Subject therefore comes first.

In morphology, greater markedness of categories seems to correlate with greater length of form: Haiman (1980), for instance, quotes Jakobson, who asserts that some languages have no explicit marker for singular number (note English *cat*, *table* with a bare stem) but that all languages have at least some markers of the plural. One might also note that, in many languages, the forms of the positive, comparative and superlative in adjectives are literally *long*, *longer* and *longest* – or in Latin, *longus, longior* and *longissimus*. Finally, Haiman (1980) claims that grammatical opera-tions may be iconically motivated; for example, reduplication, the repetition of some element of the base form, frequently marks plurality, as in Daga and Dakota; repetition, as in Cree and Yokuts; or intensification, as in Chamorro and Turkish. As illustrated in (12), reduplication signals all three semantic categories in Tagalog. In all these cases, semantic repetition is signalled by morphological repetition.

(12)   Tagalog:
   a.   Reduplication of first syllable of adjective root = plurality in adjectives
         (*ma*)*yaman* 'rich' (sg.), (*ma*)*ya-yaman* 'rich' (pl.)
   b.   Reduplication of first syllable of verbal root = repetition in verbs
         l(*um*)*akad* 'walk (now, once)',
         (*mag*)*la-lakad* 'walk (repeatedly)'
   c.   Reduplication of entire verbal root = intensification of verbs
         (*ma*)*basag* 'get broken',
         (*magka*)*basagbasag* 'get thoroughly smashed'
                     (after Haiman 1980)

Examples of iconic motivation in phonology are perhaps hardest to find, although Wescott (1971: 420–21) does suggest a connection of high front vowels with diminutives, and low back vowels with augmentatives. For instance, English *wee*, *teeny* and *little* have high front stem vowels, while *vast*, *huge* and *large* have back ones (and *big* is a much-quoted problem). Spanish has [i] or [e] in all its diminutive vowel suffixes, including *-illo*, *-in*, *-ito*, *-ico*, *-ete*, *-ejo*, and [ɑ], [o] or [u] in all the augmentatives, such as *-al*, *-azo*, *-ote*, *-udo*. In non-Indo-European languages, the same connection seems to hold, for instance in Tungus *xexe* 'woman' versus *xaxa* 'man', Mandarin *ching* 'light' versus *chung* 'heavy', and Proto-Polynesian **i'i* 'small' versus *oho 'large'. Some rather more fanciful instances of phonological motivation have also been suggested, and these can be harder to accept. I simply quote the following from Wescott (1971: 422): 'Dentality, since it involves articulation with the teeth, iconically connotes steady projection. In many of the world's languages, the names of various projections from the earth or the body contain dental obstruents. Among these are : Proto-Indo-European *ed 'bite' and *dent- 'tooth'; Efik *-ot* 'head' and *eto-* 'tree'; and Mixtec *tu-* 'tail', *thuk'* 'horn', *t'e* 'woods', and *duti-* 'mountain''.

4.2.3.3.3   *A case-study*

We have now considered the various subtypes of iconicity, and their possible manifestations in language. I shall conclude this section by outlining a case-study (Robertson 1983) which explicitly relates analogical change to iconicity.

Robertson claims that the number of possible forms in any grammatical subsystem must be 2^m, where m is the number of values in the system. For instance, the English verb phrase has four values: the modals, such as *will*; the perfective *have ... -ed*; the progressive *be ... -ing*; and the passive *be ... -ed*. This gives $2^m = 2^4 = 16$ possible spaces in the system; all 16 occur and are listed in (13).

(13)   *close*
       will close
       has closed
       is closing
       is closed
       will have closed
       will be closing
       will be closed
       has been closing
       has been closed
       is being closed
       will have been closing
       will have been closed
       will be being closed
       has been being closed
       will have been being closed

However, not all grammatical systems have all logically possible spaces filled. Instead, they may have gaps, or syncretism – that is, more than one meaning may be represented by a single form. For instance, in the English pronoun system, the singular forms show gender as well as number, as shown by *he, she, it*. However, the plural does not have the three possible corresponding forms, only *they* (see (14)).

(14)

	singular	plural
masculine	*he*	*they*
feminine	*she*	*they*
neuter	*it*	*they*

Robertson proposes that systems characterised by a good deal of iconicity tend to have all possible spaces filled, whereas those with a high degree of symbolism also have more syncretism. Furthermore, when a system expands to include a new category which was previously logically possible but not realised (that is, when a new grammatical category is created), this must be preceded by an analogical change from symbol to icon elsewhere in the system. Regularisation by analogical levelling must therefore precede realisation of a new grammatical category.

The example of such a development suggested by Robertson involves a complex of changes occurring between Common Mayan and modern Yucatecan – specifically, the San Quintín dialect of Lacandón. Mayan has two cases, the ergative (which marks the subjects of transitive verbs and the possessors of nouns) and the absolutive (which marks the subjects of

intransitive verbs and the objects of transitives), and two numbers, singular
and plural. An early development in this case / number system seems to
have affected the third person forms, as illustrated in (15), where Stage 1 is
Common Mayan and Stage 2 is modern San Quintín.

(15)

	Absolutive 3rd sg.	Absolutive 3rd pl.
Stage 1:	Ø	*ob'
Stage 2:	Ø	ob'

	Ergative 3rd sg.	Ergative 3rd pl.
Stage 1:	*ru > u	*ki
Stage 2:	u	u ... ob'

At Stage 1, the ergative third person plural form was symbolic *ki;
however, Robertson argues that this is semantically a combination of the
absolutive third plural, and the ergative third singular, and indeed at Stage
2 morphological reanalysis has established iconicity by introducing the
new, motivated form *u ... ob'*, which combines the absolutive third plural
and ergative third singular markers.

A similar development in the ergative second person plural, which is
symbolic at Stage 1 but at Stage 2 has been morphologically reformed and
contains the ergative second singular and part of the absolutive second
plural marker, is shown in (16).

(16)

	Absolutive 2nd sg.	Absolutive 2nd pl.
Stage 1:	*at	*eʃ
Stage 2:	etʃ	etʃeʃ

	Ergative 2nd sg.	Ergative 2nd pl.
Stage 1:	*a	*e
Stage 2:	a	a ... eʃ

The changes in the second and third persons are clearly analogical, and
involve both levelling and an increase in iconic isomorphism. However,
these developments show only regularisation in the paradigm; for a case of
realisation, and the introduction of a new grammatical category into the
system, we must turn to the first person.

Changes in the first person in the San Quintín dialect build on the
previous, regularising developments in the second and third persons, and
furthermore introduce new categories. Whereas in Common Mayan there
was only one first person plural 'we' form, in San Quintín there are three;
an exclusive form ('we' = 'me and them, not you'), an inclusive dual ('we'
= 'me and you singular') and an inclusive plural ('we' = 'me and you
plural'). The forms are shown in (17).

(17)   Stage 1 – Common Mayan:
        Absolutive 1st sg.   *in
        Ergative 1st sg.   *nu

Absolutive 1st pl.	*o'ŋ
Ergative 1st pl.	*qa

Stage 2 – San Quintín:

Absolutive 1st sg.	en
Ergative 1st sg.	in
Absolutive 1st pl. exclusive	enob'
Ergative 1st pl. exclusive	in ... ob'
Absolutive 1st pl. inclusive dual	o'n
Ergative 1st pl. inclusive dual	ik
Absolutive 1st pl. inclusive plural	'oneʃ
Ergative 1st pl. inclusive plural	ik ... eʃ

A comparison of (17) with the third and second person forms in (15) and (16) also shows that these new grammatical categories of inclusive and exclusive 'we' have predominantly analogically derived, regular and iconically motivated forms. For instance, although the first person inclusive dual forms, *o'n* and *ik*, simply reflect symbolic Common Mayan *o'ŋ* and *qa*, the exclusive 'we' form is composed of the non-second plural marker *ob'* plus the first singular marker *in* or *en*, reflecting literally its meaning of 'me and them'. Similarly, the first person inclusive plural is composed of the reflexes of Common Mayan first plural *o'ŋ* or *qa*, plus the second plural *eʃ*, again mirroring the meaning 'me and you (plural)'.

4.2.3.4 Analogy and abduction

4.2.3.4.1 *Introduction*

In the last section, we explored the relationship of analogy to iconicity, essentially a constraint on surface structures. However, analogy seems also to be relevant to the psychological domain, with connections to acquisition as well as various conceptual constraints and principles. Although the Generative attempt to locate analogy in the grammar has been shown to be ill-founded, analogy *does* have an influence on the form of grammars, through its links with perception and acquisition. We shall now explore three proposed areas where perceptual or conceptual factors overlap with analogy; the first two will be considered only briefly, but we shall dwell on the third, abduction, for a little longer.

4.2.3.4.2 *Humboldt's Universal*

Vennemann (1978) contends that human language would be conceptually ideal if it were entirely iconically isomorphic, with one form always corresponding to one meaning. However, this conceptual ideal may conflict with what is phonetically ideal; sound change may then operate, violating isomorphism and creating allomorphy. From this tension arises the conflict between sound change and analogy summarised by Sturtevant's Paradox – that is, the claim that sound change is regular but creates irregularity, while analogy is irregular but creates regularity. Vennemann further proposes that isomorphism is maintained as far as possible, and re-established after its interruption by sound change, by an 'innate principle of linguistic change' (Vennemann 1978: 259) which he calls Humboldt's Universal. This principle is essentially a statement of the superiority of iconic isomorphism, and says that 'Suppletion is undesirable, uniformity of linguistic symbolization is desirable: both roots and grammatical markers should be unique and constant' (Vennemann 1978: 259).

The operation of Humboldt's Universal is particularly clear in child language acquisition, and is responsible for such analogically regularised forms as *go – goed, mouse – mouses*, and *keep – keeped*. It is also consistent with cases of analogical change which do not constitute grammar simplification. For instance, certain shifts of gender and declension class in Latin, including the attraction of third declension neuter nouns with nominatives in *-us* like *tempus, corpus* into the second declension, and the reinterpretation of second declension neuter tree names such as *pīnus, prūnus* as masculine, cannot be analysed as simplificatory, since the third declension remains open and there are still second declension neuters. However, these shifts are certainly in line with analogical developments implementing Humboldt's Universal; the ambiguous surface sequence *-us* is gradually being restricted to the single meaning 'second declension masculine'.

4.2.3.4.3   *Morphological perceptual strategies*

The operation of analogy has also been linked with the influence of perceptual strategies. These strategies help the hearer to decode sentences, and this task is facilitated if the markers of grammatical categories are relatively long, maximally clear, and maximally uniform. As we have already seen, analogical change frequently increases the overtness and uniformity of markers. However, these requirements of an efficient perceptual system may conflict with conditions such as ease of articulation which facilitate speech production; and here we have another interpretation of the tension between sound change and analogy (Vincent 1974).

Bever and Langendoen (1971) offer an example of the role of such perceptual strategies in linguistic change. Their argument is essentially that the loss of inflections in Old and Middle English created certain ambiguous, perceptually difficult constructions, notably in relative clauses; these perceptual problems were resolved by the loss of the ambiguous constructions.

For instance, it becomes gradually obligatory for a relative marker (*who, which, that ...*) to appear on a non-initial noun which is the subject of a relative clause; so, in modern English, (18a) is acceptable but (18b), with the relativiser omitted, is not.

(18)a.   Clive saw a cat which had no tail.
   b.   **Clive saw a cat had no tail.

In Old English, constructions like (18b) would have been acceptable, since the noun phrase corresponding to *a cat* would have been inflectionally marked as an object. However, as inflections disappeared, such constructions, like the Middle English ones in (19) below, seem to have become perceptually difficult. Bever and Langendoen ascribe this difficulty to the development of a perceptual strategy specifying that a sequence of Noun Verb should be interpreted as Subject Verb unless otherwise indicated. This strategy reflects the greater reliance on word order made necessary by the loss of inflections, but could easily lead to initial misinterpretations of sentences like that in (19).

(19)   He sente after a cherl was in the toun.
          'he sent after a man (who) was in the town'
              (Chaucer, *Canterbury Tales*)
          – is this: He sente after [a cherl was in the toun]?
                  (after Bever and Langendoen 1971: Appendix 2, Stages 2–3, (3))

In response to these potentially incorrect perceptual segmentations, constructions lacking a relative clause marker have gradually died out. Again, it is possible to relate this development to analogy if we assume that relativisers were inserted in constructions like the one in (19) by analogy with other sentences where a relative marker did appear.

4.2.3.4.4 *Abduction*

There is a long-standing tradition of relating analogy to language acquisition. Bloomfield (and earlier Paul, for instance) saw analogy as the major mechanism of language learning, although this view is no longer dominant; Kiparsky attempted to explain analogical change as the residue of imperfect learning; and Vennemann sees Humboldt's Universal as partially controlling language acquisition. I shall now introduce a further step in the same direction, Henning Andersen's (1973) account of abductive language acquisition, and show that this can also be related to analogy. In this section, we shall also consider cases of analogy outside the morphology. Andersen illustrates his concept of abduction using a phonological change in particular dialects of Czech. In Old Czech, until the thirteenth century, plain dental and labial consonants were opposed to palatalised ones. However, between 1300 and the late fifteenth century, this opposition was lost, first in dentals and subsequently in labials. Palatalised dentals merged with plain ones; and palatalised labials either merged with the plain set, or became sequences of plain labial plus /j/, except in a set of dialects which Andersen calls the Teták dialects, where palatalised labials became dentals before /i e r/. This situation persisted until the nineteenth century, when contact with neighbouring speakers of non-Teták dialects increased. The Teták use of dentals where all other Czech dialects have labials quickly became stigmatised, and the Teták speakers were ridiculed by their neighbours. Ultimately, dental pronunciations became associated with low social class, and were replaced by labials. By the late nineteenth century, dental reflexes of Old Czech palatalised labials persisted only in a few frequently occurring lexical items, such as /koutit/ (Standard Czech *koupiti* 'buy'), /di:lej/ (Standard Czech *bílý* 'white') and /nesto/ (Standard *mesto* 'town'), and even then only for older speakers.

These developments, Andersen argues, can be divided into an evolutive change, characteristic of the Teták dialects and motivated by their internal structure, and a later adaptive change removing the dentals, motivated externally by contact with non-Teták speakers. In what follows, I shall concentrate on the evolutive change, returning finally to the adaptive loss of the dentals.

Andersen argues that the change of palatalised labials to dentals in the Teták dialects results from phonetic ambiguity and reclassification. The frequency continuum, as shown in (20), can be segmented in a number of ways; and if mergers take place in the system, reinterpretations may occur. In this case, heightened low tonality may be perceived as an exponent of low tonality and assigned to the /p/ phoneme, as happened in most Czech dialects, or, as in the Teták dialects, it may be reanalysed as a realisation of high tonality and assigned to /t/.

(20)a.   Most Czech dialects:

	Stage 1	Stage 2	Stage 3
Heightened high tonality	t^j		
High tonality	t	t	t
Heightened low tonality	p^j	p^j	
Low tonality	p	p	p

   b.   Teták dialects:

	Stage 1	Stage 2	Stage 3
Heightened high tonality	t^j		
High tonality	t	t	t
Heightened low tonality	p^j	p^j	
Low tonality	p	p	p

Andersen's aim is to account for the acquisition of this change, and also to explain how the results of such a perceptual recategorisation could be accepted in the speech community. To do so, 'what is needed is a model of phonological change which recognises, on the one hand, that the verbal output of any speaker is determined by the grammar he has internalized, and on the other, that any speaker's internalized grammar is determined by the verbal output from which it has been inferred' (Andersen 1973: 767). A schematic representation of such a model is given in (21); and the process by which a grammar is inferred from verbal output in the environment is what Andersen calls abduction.

(21)   <u>Speaker 1</u>   <u>Speaker 2</u>

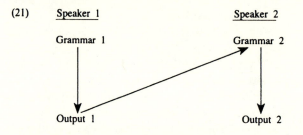

In fact, Andersen proposes that grammar construction, testing and use involve the three logical strategies of deduction, induction and abduction. Of these, deduction is probably the most familiar: given a law, such as 'all men are mortal', and a case, such as 'Socrates is a man', one deduces the result, 'Socrates is mortal'. In induction, cases and results are used to establish a law; so, if Socrates is a man and mortal and so are Aristotle and Plato, we may induce that all men are mortal. In both cases, nothing is asserted that is not in the premises, and if the premises are true, then the conclusion must also be true. Abduction, however, operates rather differently: given a particular result, such that Socrates is dead, and a law, that all men are mortal, one abduces that Socrates may have been a man, inferring from a law and a result that something may have been the case. Abduction is unreliable, since it is relatively easy to invoke the wrong law, so that the truth of the conclusion need not follow from the truth of the premises; thus, if Socrates is dead and I invoke the law that all fruit flies are mortal, I abduce that Socrates may have been a fruit fly. However, abduction is also immensely important, since it is the only one of the three types of logical inference which can introduce and create novel ideas.

In terms of grammar construction, the child hears language in her environment, construes it as a result and guesses at the structure of the grammar which produces it, with the help of whatever linguistic laws we assume to be innate; this is abduction. The grammar built by the child can then be tested in two ways. She may hear novel structures, and check whether her grammar can produce them; this is induction. If the grammar fails, further abductive innovations are required. Additionally, the child may attempt to produce utterances, testing the output of her grammar on other speakers; this is deduction. If her listeners misunderstand or correct her, she must again revise her grammar.

Let us now apply these notions to the Teták changes. Adults in the speech community produce palatalised labials, [pʲ]; children perceive heightened low tonality, analyse this as a manifestation of high tonality, and abduce that the correct underlying form is a dental; they then produce dental [t] in all words where their parents have palatalised labials. Thus, an innovation is introduced into the grammar by an abduction, in which the children have invoked the wrong law ('heightened low tonality = high tonality' rather than 'heightened low tonality = low tonality'). Andersen assumes that parents would tolerate this production of dentals in very young children, but that these children would be corrected as they grew older, and encouraged to produce palatalised labials. Some children would then, by deduction, revise their grammars and replace underlying dentals in particular words with palatalised labials. Most, however, would not implement such a radical revision, but would simply introduce an adaptive rule leaving the underlying dentals untouched but creating palatalised labials on the surface to please their parents ('in words X, Y and Z, change [t d n] to [pʲ bʲ mʲ]').

Andersen further assumes that these speakers, with underlying dentals but surface labials, would be more sympathetic to subsequent generations of children who produced dentals. Gradually, the adaptive rule would then die away, being first used only to speak to very old people, then ultimately lost completely.

The opposite process probably led to the loss of the distinctive Teták dentals in the late nineteenth century. Teták speakers, seeking to avoid ridicule from speakers of other dialects, would implement an adaptive rule replacing dentals with labials in certain words. Gradually, only labials would be used, and children would then abduce underlying labials rather than dentals, leading to the loss of the Teták features.

It remains to link this process of abduction with analogy. Lightfoot (1979a) presents a syntactic case from Middle English which illustrates just such a connection.

In Old English, the verb *līcian* (which has become modern English *like*) meant 'to give pleasure to' rather than 'to derive pleasure from': Lightfoot's (1979a: 352) example is the sentence *þam cynge līcodon peran* 'pears are pleasing to the king'. There are two clues to the Object Verb Subject (OVS) interpretation of this construction, since *þam cynge* is case-marked as the object, and the *-on* ending on the verb shows agreement with the plural subject, *peran*. As inflections were lost in late OE and ME, sentences like (22a) resulted. This is ambiguous and could be interpreted as

OVS or SVO. However, sentences like (22b) and (22c) must still be interpreted as OVS.

(22)a.	The king liked pears.	OVS? SVO?
b.	The king like pears.	OVS
c.	Him liked pears.	OVS

In present-day English, however, we have the constructions in (23); the SVO analysis has clearly been favoured and generalised.

(23)a.	The king liked pears.	SVO
b.	The king likes pears.	SVO
c.	He liked pears.	SVO

Lightfoot explains this change with reference to both abduction and analogy. He notes that, as inflections became less reliable and ultimately disappeared, English speakers were forced to rely on word order in decoding sentences (recall here the discussion of perceptual strategies in 4.2.3.4.3 above), and evolved the strategy that a sentence-initial sequence of Noun Phrase plus Verb should be interpreted as Subject plus Verb. Furthermore, the relatively free word order of Old English became constrained, producing an unmarked order, SVO, and various marked minority orders signalled by syntactic or prosodic means; one example is Object Topicalisation, with the fronted Object intonationally marked as in *That book I can't stand*. These factors conspired to create a predominance of SVO constructions; by analogy with these, children abduced the structure SVO for sentences like *The king liked pears*. This interpretation was then generalised to (22b) and (22c), creating the revised structures in (23b) and (23c) and leading to a semantic change in the verb *like*, which now means 'to derive pleasure from'. Abductive innovations, then, may be motivated by analogy.

We have seen, then, that analogy is a strong force in linguistic change, but one which eludes formalisation. However, this failure to entirely predict or explain analogy should not force us to abandon the concept. Instead, we should follow Kuryłowicz and Mańczak in attempting to constrain the phenomenon, and also explore its connections both with surface-structure conditions like iconicity, and higher-order principles, including Humboldt's Universal and abduction. Lightfoot sums up these points admirably. He contends that 'analogy is a principle governing the construction of grammars, influencing the form of grammars, but in no sense directly represented in those grammars' (1979a: 371); thus, although the shift from OVS to SVO is an analogical process for the Middle English child, no analogical rule appears in the grammar of parent or child. However, we should not be discouraged by the elusiveness of analogy.

'The fact that many re-analyses can be interpreted as analogical extensions does not make analogy a principle of change or anything more than a pre-theoretical concept. On the other hand, the fact that the *form* of re-analyses cannot be predicted beyond imposing very general bounds on possible surface structure extensions, does not belittle the role of analogy in governing language acquisition and therefore historical change' (Lightfoot 1979a: 373).

Despite this encouraging note, there is a residual problem. Although we have ascribed various changes, such as the reanalysis of OVS to SVO in Middle English, to the machinations of analogy, we have not yet determined why such a change became necessary, or why such a revising abduction should occur, beyond the vague invocation of ambiguity. We shall pursue this matter further in the next chapter, when we consider one of the earliest attempts to explain syntactic change, Lightfoot's Transparency Principle. First, however, let us turn to the developing theory of Natural Morphology, to illustrate a different approach to morphological change.

4.3   Natural Morphology

4.3.1   *Introduction*

The term 'natural' has had a rather chequered history in linguistics: it has been multiply defined, and often avoided on the grounds that it cannot be sensibly defined at all. In the early 1970s, the theory of Natural Phonology (Stampe 1972) was developed as an attempt to define and formalise phonological naturalness. Stampe based his idea of naturalness on markedness, and claimed that marked features are those which strain the human language capacity most. Unmarked features and processes are genetically determined; however, marked features, which conflict with these, may arise in languages through processes of change. Children therefore face two tasks in acquiring a language: they must suppress the innate, natural phonological processes in certain language-specific contexts, and learn morphophonological rules which are the synchronic residue of sound changes in their language.

It is now generally agreed that Natural Phonology failed, largely because naturalness was still not adequately defined, and perhaps also because the laws proposed were too specific. However, from the late 1970s, there have been attempts to transfer the ideas of Natural Phonology into morphology. The main proponents of Natural Morphology are Dressler (1985), Wurzel (1989) and Mayerthaler; Bauer (1988; Chapter 12) also provides an introduction. Natural Morphology is important for us because it not only seeks to explain morphological change, but also to account for synchronic aspects of morphology in terms of the history of the language concerned, thus illustrating the interdependence of synchrony and diachrony which is one theme of this book.

4.3.2   *Defining naturalness*

In Natural Morphology (NM), naturalness is again defined in terms of markedness; unmarked forms and constructions are said to be preferred by speakers. There is a checklist for assessing markedness: unmarked or natural features occur frequently cross-linguistically; appear often and in numerous contexts in languages where they occur; are relatively resistant to change but often result from changes; occur in pidgins and are introduced early in creoles; and are acquired early by children, but unaffected or lost late in aphasia. Furthermore, borrowings and neologisms in a language will typically follow the unmarked pattern; and it is rarely affected by speech errors, although marked forms are commonly assimilated to the unmarked pattern in error.

By assessing which categories and types of expression of these categories adhere most closely to these desiderata, NM can establish which are most natural. The prediction that morphological change moves towards naturalness can then be assessed, and general principles underlying naturalness may be identified. For instance, Wurzel (1989) claims that certain categories are semantically unmarked, including Subject (as opposed to Object), animate (versus inanimate), and first person, present tense, indicative mood and singular number. More importantly for us, Wurzel discusses the relative naturalness of different ways of symbolising or expressing semantic categories morphologically, and claims that the optimal symbolisation will obey the three principles of constructional iconicity, uniformity and transparency. These are all aspects of what we called iconicity in 4.2.3.3 above. Constructional iconicity, which corresponds to Haiman's (1980) iconic motivation, is maintained if what is semantically 'more' is reflected in 'more' form; for instance, plural is semantically 'more' than singular, and cross-linguistically it is extremely common for nouns to have no marker of singular, but some marker of plurality. Uniformity is the 'one function, one form' condition; transparency is closely related to this, favouring derived forms or processes in a paradigm to have only a single meaning. These are both aspects of Haiman's (1980) isomorphism. To exemplify these principles, let us return to the Gothic paradigm of *dags* 'day' from (2) above, repeated as (24).

(24)   Gothic *dags* 'day'

	sg.	pl.
	sg.	pl.
Nominative	*dags*	*dagos*
Accusative	*dag*	*dagans*
Genitive	*dagis*	*dage*
Dative	*daga*	*dagum*

This paradigm is partly constructionally iconic, in that the semantically marked plural is longer than the singular by one syllable in the nominative and accusative cases, and by one segment in the dative – the genitive is problematic in having a slightly longer singular form. Transparency is also adhered to, since each suffix signals a single combination of case and number information: the addition of *-os* can only mean 'nominative plural', for instance. However, this paradigm is not uniform: each form does indeed have one function, but the same function is not always expressed by the same form. That is, we cannot isolate one element of the suffix and say that it always corresponds to the meaning 'plural' or 'genitive'. Thus, there is a *-s* in the nominative and accusative plurals, but it does not appear in the other plurals, and *does* appear in the nominative and genitive singular. If we were to imagine a version of Gothic made uniform as well as transparent and constructionally iconic, its paradigm for 'day' might look like the invented one in (25) – although of course, to measure morphological naturalness in Gothic or any other language as a whole, we would also have to know whether all noun paradigms are structured in this way.

(25)   Uniform Gothic *dago* 'day'

	sg.	pl.
Nominative	*dago*	*dagos*
Accusative	*dagan*	*dagans*
Genitive	*dage*	*dages*
Dative	*dagum*	*dagums*

4.3.3   *Naturalness, frequency and change*

NM aims to explain why certain morphological phenomena never occur in languages: these might be in conflict with all the principles of constructional iconicity, uniformity and transparency. As we shall see in the next sections, natural morphologists also try to explain the occurrence of unnatural phenomena, and to make predictions about the solutions to conflicts among the various criteria for naturalness. However, NM also seeks to predict and explain the direction of morphological change; and the principal claim is that this will gradually make morphological structures more natural by increasing conformity with the three principles defined above. Natural processes and structures are therefore also expected to occur more frequently.

Dressler (1985) assesses the constructional iconicity of a number of morphological strategies. We have already seen that, because plural is semantically marked as compared with singular, constructional iconicity will be greatest if the singular of a noun has no marker or a shorter marker. Thus, *dog – dogs* in English is maximally constructionally iconic, while *sheep – sheep* is noniconic. A strategy whereby the singular was formally more marked than the plural would then be countericonic, 'because less form contradicts more meaning' (Dressler 1985: 328); such strategies would therefore be unnatural, and would be predicted in NM to be very rare. Dressler reports that there are no such countericonic strategies, not only for number but for any morphological categories, in Standard German, English, the standard Romance languages, Georgian, Tzotzil, Diegueño, Kalispel, Pengo or Palau. There may be one case in Russian and Polish, and there is one case of subtractive place naming in the Australian language Yidiɲ. The Hessian dialect of German has some subtractive plurals like *hond* 'dog', *hon* 'dogs' (compare standard German *Hund – Hunde*). There is also one case in Hungarian, where diminutives are productively formed by shortening, so that *Erzsébet* 'Elizabeth' has the shortened form *Erzsi* 'Lizzy, Betty', and *zongora* 'piano' corresponds to *zongi* 'little piano'. However, even though meaning is being added and form subtracted here, it may be significant that the added meaning is diminutive, so that the shorter form may indeed be more appropriate, and indeed iconic in a conflicting way.

NM would predict that subtractive morphological processes should be rare and more often lost than gained in morphological change, and Dressler's survey seems to bear this out. This is also the case for suppletion. Weak suppletion is the unpredictable alternation of segments as in *child – children*, while strong suppletion is stem alternation of the *am, is, are, was, were, be* variety; and NM predicts that the stronger types in particular should be very rare and should tend to vanish over time. Again, Dressler (1985) provides data to support these predictions. This time, he concentrates on one language, giving a complete list of Italian suppletions in approximately two pages. For instance, there are three cases of weak plural suppletion, *uomo – uomini* 'man', *bue – buoi* 'bull' and *dio – dei* 'god'; some comparatives have strong suppletion, including *cattivo* 'bad', *peggiore* 'worse', *pessimo* 'worst'; there is some strong suppletion in the personal pronouns; and the verbs *have, must, can, will* and *be* (see (26)) are highly suppletive.

(26)   Italian – the verb 'be'

1	sg	*sono*	future	*sarò*
2		*sei*	imperfect	*ero*
3		*è*	preterite	*fui*

1 pl	*siamo*	participle	*stato*
2	*siete*		
3	*sono*		

A few main verbs like 'know' and 'make/do' also have weak suppletion, and some numerals like *uno* 'one' – *primo* 'first' have suppletion between the cardinal and ordinal forms; and finally, some adjectives derived from country and city names are suppletive.

The brevity of the list certainly supports Dressler's claim that suppletion is rare. Dressler (1985: 333) also argues that 'suppletions are subject to analogical levelling in language acquisition and language change'. Since suppletive formations are opaque, analogical levelling will increase naturalness by increasing transparency. Thus, many suppletive forms in Latin have regularised in Italian. As for those which remain, Dressler contends that suppletive forms are most resistant to analogical levelling when they are most frequent and learned earliest. So, Latin *hominēs* 'men, people', which has given weakly suppletive Italian *uomo – uomini*, was probably the commonest noun in the group with singular *-ō* and plural *-inēs* (the competition was *virgō* 'virgin', *origō* 'origin', *hirundō* 'swallow', *cardō* 'door hinge', and a few de-adjectival abstract nouns with the suffix *-tūdō* 'ness'). Similarly, the affected Italian comparatives are among the most frequent, while the low numerals and verbs like 'have' and 'be' are among the commonest word forms in any language, and are therefore likeliest to remain suppletive. Finally, as Dressler (1985: 333) notes, 'analogical influence is easier within large classes where many regular forms can exert a higher analogical pressure on exceptions than within small classes. Clearly articles, pronouns, auxiliary and modal verbs ... and number names all form small classes.'

4.3.4   *Conflicts of naturalness*

The last section has begun to suggest that, although natural phenomena are preferred, unnatural ones may also be maintained in a language under certain circumstances. The next question is how these unnatural forms and processes arise.

We have seen already that naturalness cannot be defined in terms of a single criterion. The problem is that the various criteria may not always point in the same direction, and may therefore conflict. For instance, phonological naturalness involves optimal articulation (for the speaker) or perception (for the hearer), whereas morphological naturalness is charac-terised by optimal symbolisation of grammatical categories. Thus, natural sound changes may shorten words, and cause morphological difficulties. So, the Proto-Germanic nominative plural of the noun 'drop' was *drupan-ir, which was progressively reduced to *drupan in Proto-Norse, then *drupa* in Old Swedish. This was easier to pronounce, but morphologically unnatural in that in Old Swedish *drupa* was not only the nominative plural form, but also the genitive, dative and accusative singular and the genitive and accusative plural! This situation clearly runs counter to both uniformity and transparency, and consequently in later Swedish, the nominative plural *drupa* became *drupar*, a form peculiar to the nominative plural. However, postvocalic /r/ seems phonologically unstable, and so in casual speech and certain dialects of Swedish, *drupar* has again reduced to *drupa*. Phonological naturalness may therefore lead to some change, which causes morphological difficulties and provokes a response in the shape of a change restoring morphological naturalness; but this in turn may create unnatural phonology, and lead to further change, a cycle we have already discussed in relation to Humboldt's Universal (4.2.3.4.2 above). As Wurzel (1989: 21) puts it, 'the conflicts of naturalness cause a continuous mutual influencing of the individual components of the language system. Thus, they represent a continuously driving force toward language change.' As we shall see in Chapter 6, this sort of spiral development, involving different components of the grammar, is also characteristic of grammaticalisation.

Conflicts among the various principles of morphological naturalness may also develop. For instance, transparency is highly natural, and as Bauer (1988) suggests, so are relatively short words, with the optimal length being perhaps three syllables, plus or minus two. In agglutinating languages, like Turkish or Swahili, transparency is very generally maintained, with a distinctive affix being added for each grammatical category expressed; however, words may then become rather long. Conversely, inflecting languages like Latin and Welsh typically have shorter words, but at the cost of some opacity. One of the main tasks of NM must now be the formulation of predictions or at least the observation of tendencies as to what happens in such situations of conflict between universal parameters of naturalness.

Conflicts may also arise between system-independent or universal measures of naturalness, like the principles of constructional iconicity, uniformity and transparency, and system-dependent or language-specific criteria. These may also lead to change, and are discussed at length in Wurzel (1989).

System-dependent naturalness can be measured in two ways. First, certain inflectional classes in any language will be more normal than others, in that they have more members and are more stable and productive. For instance, in modern German, the weak class of verbs is more normal than any strong class: borrowings and neologisms are weak;

nonsense verbs are conjugated as weak by most speakers; first and second language learners master weak before strong inflection; aphasic patients suffer greater and faster impairment of strong inflection; and errors typically make strong verbs weak rather than the reverse. Furthermore, many strong verbs have become weak historically, including *bellen* 'bark' and *mahlen* 'grind'. Others, like *gleiten* 'glide' and *triefen* 'drip' are now becoming weak. However, no verbs are now moving from the weak to the strong class (Wurzel 1989).

In this case, universal naturalness and language-specific norms seem to go together, since the German weak verbs express tense and person by suffixation, while strong verbs also use the less natural technique of stem modification: compare weak *ich tanze* 'I dance' - *ich tanzte* 'I danced' with strong *ich komme* 'I come' - *ich kam* 'I came'. However, this is not always true. For instance, Old Swedish had masculine *u*-stem and *i*-stem nouns, with identical paradigms except for the *-u* and *-i* endings in the accusative plural. These both involve affixation and are therefore equally natural from a universal point of view; yet the *u*-stems have now been lost and the *i*-stems correspondingly generalised. Wurzel (1989) argues that, in such situations, frequency is the controlling factor, with smaller classes tending to give way to larger ones; and indeed, the Old Swedish *i*-stems were more numerous than the *u*-stems. Larger classes therefore become progressively more dominant in a language; however, the effects of sound change and grammaticalisation will tend to collapse existing classes or create new ones so that systems will never reach absolute stability with only a single inflectional class.

The second measure of language-specific naturalness involves what Wurzel (1989) calls system-defining structural properties, which again define normal morphological behaviour for a particular language and can be ascertained by answering the questions in (27).

(27)   Parameters of the inflectional system
   a.   Which categories are there (e.g. for nouns, number, case) and which features (e.g. singular, plural; nominative, accusative, genitive)?
   b.   Is there stem or base-form inflection (i.e. does the basic form, usually nominative singular for nouns, have a suffix or marker, or is it unmarked)?
   c.   Are features from different categories (e.g. genitive and plural) marked separately as in agglutinating languages, or in bundles as in inflecting ones?
   d.   How much formal distinctiveness is there, and how much syncretism or multiple use of markers?
   e.   What types of marker occur (e.g. prefixes, suffixes, stem modification)?
   f.   Are there inflectional classes, and if so, how many?

Children learn the answers to these questions gradually, as they master the morphological structure of their language. So, a child acquiring

Swahili will learn that many prefixes are used as markers, and that there is distinctive, separate marking for each category, since Swahili is an agglutinating language. A child learning Welsh will perceive that suffixes are often used, and that different categories are generally marked in bundles, following the pattern of an inflecting language. Children therefore use their growing experience of the language to learn the unmarked or typical system-defining structural properties. These are neither innate nor universal, but again NM claims they direct language change: generalisation of unmarked options is frequently found both in child language and in diachronic morphology.

In German (Wurzel 1989), base-form inflection is clearly the system-defining structural property for nouns: the norm is represented by forms like *der Tag – die Tage* 'day', *die Uhr – die Uhren* 'clock', and *das Kind – die Kinder* 'child'. Stem inflection, where the nominative singular has a suffix, is extremely rare and occurs only in a few non-native words like *die Firm-a – die Firm-en* 'firm, business', *der Glob-us – die Glob-en* 'globe', and *das Kont-o – die Kont-en* 'account'. Pressure seems to have developed to assimilate this marginal, stem inflecting class to the norm, so that many of the stem-inflecting nouns now have base inflecting variants, as in (28), created by reinterpreting the singular suffix as part of the base. These variants are still characteristic of informal speech and non-standard dialects, but NM would certainly predict that they should gain ground.

(28) | *die Firma* | *die Firmas* | 'business' |
      | *die Aroma* | *die Aromas* | 'aroma' |
      | *die Tuba* | *die Tubas* | '*tuba*' |
      | *das Konto* | *die Kontos* | '*account*'|
      | *der Globus* | *die Globusse* | 'globe' |
      | *der Radius* | *die Radiusse* | 'radius' |

It should again be noted that this change is triggered for language-specific, not universal reasons: base-form inflection is no more natural than stem inflection in global terms, but happens to represent the system-defining structural property of modern German. Although in this case, the choice between the two strategies is neutral with respect to system-independent naturalness, this is not always so, and conflicts may again arise. For instance, according to the universal principle of constructional iconicity, suffixation is more natural than stem modification. Consequently, in modern German where both techniques are available for pluralisation, we might expect a movement of nouns from the umlaut to the affixing class. This is indeed happening for neuters, so that *das Boot* 'boat', which had the umlaut plural *die Böte*, has now acquired the new plural *die Boote*. However, masculine nouns are changing in exactly the opposite way, and are developing new umlaut plurals, as shown in (29).

(29)   *der Hund – die Hunde > die Hünde*   'dog'
         der Strand – die Strande > die Strände   'beach'
         der Zwang – die Zwange > die Zwänge   'compulsion'

Wurzel (1989) again explains this apparently unpredictable change in terms of frequency: since most masculines now have umlaut in the plural, the exceptions are gradually coming to conform, although this conflicts with system-independent naturalness. 'That is, where universal and language specific naturalness criteria conflict, the language specific ones seem to take precedence' (Bauer 1988: 193). This seems to be exactly what we would expect, if NM has indeed adopted the idea from Natural Phonology that children acquire language by suspending universals in language-specific contexts. Furthermore, this coheres with Bickerton's (1981, 1984) Bioprogram Hypothesis, which we shall meet in Chapter 10; this holds that instructions from the innately specified bioprogram only surface during language acquisition if a child hears no conflicting data. Nonetheless, the question of which universal or language-specific criteria for naturalness prevail, and under what conditions, must be an area of future investigation for NM.

Finally, system-defining structural principles, being neither innate nor universal, are also subject to change: thus, Old High German had stem inflection predominating; in Middle High German, base-form inflection came to dominate and all stem inflection was lost; while in modern German, stem inflection has been reintroduced in some loan words but is, as we have seen, now disappearing again. However, Wurzel claims that 'morphology itself is conservative. It will maintain the already existing system defining structural properties but will not itself produce any new ones' (1989: 104). Again, changes in these properties result from change in other components of the grammar. For instance, sound change may erase a marker and leave two categories formally identical, or one category unexpressed: thus, in Old English, case and number were marked together on nouns, while intervening sound changes have made case irrelevant to nouns in Modern English. Alternatively, new categories may develop through grammaticalisation, as an independent word becomes an affix. In Hungarian, the noun *bele* 'the interior', in constructions like *ház belén* 'in the interior of the house', has now coalesced with *ház* as a suffix, giving *házban* 'in the house' and producing a new case category. This development is also due to sound change, this time to changes in the accent system (Wurzel 1989: 98). Over time, NM predicts that the morphology will change to increase coherence with the new system-defining structural properties.

Dressler (1985) argues that NM establishes general laws which languages must follow. However, as we have seen, the universal aspect of NM is tempered by a language-specific component, and the interaction of the two mean that irregularities and unnatural phenomena can and do arise, and may even, in certain circumstances, be maintained and extended. Consequently, NM identifies tendencies rather than absolute universals, and its principles 'express "only" universal TENDENCIES and not completely universal PROPERTIES of natural language necessarily occurring in every language' (Wurzel 1989: 189). This should not be seen as an admission of defeat: although much remains to be done, Natural Morphology represents a step forward in its acceptance of interaction between the universal and the language-specific, between morphology and other components of the grammar, and between synchronic morphology and morphological change. In Chapter 6, we shall explore in more detail the question of whether absolutely general, universal laws could ever be applicable to linguistic change. First, however, we must explore change in the syntax.

5   Syntactic change 1: the Transparency Principle

5.1   Introduction

> Diachronic syntax lay, like the Sleeping Beauty, in a deathlike coma for
> the first half of this century. In the late sixties and seventies there was a
> flurry of activity as increasingly large numbers of linguists realised the
> importance of the subject, and attempted to hack their way through the
> thorns encircling the Sleeping Beauty's castle and into the central issues
> of the topic ... [David Lightfoot's] is the first book which has attempted
> both to provide a fully-fledged theory of syntactic change, and to clarify
> the relationship between a theory of change and a theory of grammar. As
> such, [his] work is of great significance, since he may be viewed as the
> Prince who woke the Sleeping Beauty from her long sleep. Nevertheless,
> although he has woken her, he is not necessarily the answer to all her
> prayers. As with many pioneers, his work is perhaps more important for
> the questions it raises than for the solutions it provides.
>
> (Aitchison 1980: 137)

This rather long and romanticised quotation is from a review of Lightfoot's
book *Principles of Diachronic Syntax* (1979a), and outlines the direction
we shall take in this chapter. We shall begin by considering earlier work on
syntactic change, but will focus on Lightfoot's contribution. One of his
case studies, and his general theory, will be outlined in 5.3, while 5.4
reviews some reactions and criticisms provoked by his ideas, and 5.5
introduces aspects of his more recent work (Lightfoot 1988, 1991).

5.2   Earlier work on syntactic change

5.2.1   *Pre-generative work*

In a sense this section title is a misnomer, since there was remarkably little
work on historical syntax before the 1960s. While the Neogrammarians
contributed much basic work on sound change and analogy, they did not
leave a similar legacy for syntactic change, since their methodology does
not generalise well to syntax. The cornerstone of the Neogrammarian
study of sound change was the establishment of phonological correspon-

dences between languages or stages of a language, but while a word or sound from an earlier stage may correspond to a later word or sound, it is unclear how an individual Old English sentence can correspond to a Middle English one. Certainly such correspondence is unthinkable without any notion of a formal grammar. The Neogrammarians did make some attempts at reconstructing earlier surface syntactic patterns, specifically for Proto-Indo-European, but these were unsuccessful on two counts. First, reconstructive methodology had not been perfected, and the results tended to resemble Sanskrit more closely than the patterns we now ascribe to PIE. Secondly, although some comparisons were made between reconstructed and attested stages, these were purely descriptive; differences were noted and classified, but there were very few attempts to explain or motivate changes.

These initial investigations were barely supplemented by the Structuralists: it was not until after the establishment of Generative syntax in the 1960s that substantial research on syntactic change was carried out.

5.2.2   *Generative syntax*

The advent of Generative theory put the main focus of linguistics squarely on synchronic syntax, and it was perhaps inevitable that this interest would spread to the study of syntactic change (following in the footsteps of Generative Phonology, which had, as noted in Chapter 2, made itself diachronic almost as an afterthought). In early Generative syntax, all syntactic change was analysed as simplificatory grammar change. Instead of comparing sets of surface sentences, as the Neogrammarians had done, the Generativists compared successive grammars which they constructed for, say, Old High, Middle High and Modern German, and attempted to show that any surface changes were due to changes in the syntactic rules. These could be added or lost, their form or order could alter, and children could construct a different, simpler grammar from their parents'; the mechanisms of change were therefore identical to those assumed in historical Generative Phonology.

Before considering two examples of early Generative work on syntactic change, I shall briefly outline the theory of grammar which these analyses assume, the early Chomskyan model expounded in *Aspects of the Theory of Syntax* (1965).

5.2.2.1 The *Aspects* model

Chomsky's central assumption is that we do not learn language by listening, memorising and repeating; the linguistic stimulus we receive is too incomplete and degenerate. He hypothesises that children succeed in acquiring a native language so quickly and from such inadequate data because we each have a genetically encoded Universal Grammar (UG), a set of consistent, universal principles of language which forms part of an innate language faculty. Linguistic data are passed through UG and the two interact to build a grammar. The child's grammar is part of his competence, or tacit knowledge of his language, and it is generative, since it produces or predicts all and only the grammatical sentences of the language. It also allows for the child's creativity in producing and understanding sentences he has never heard, since a finite number of patterns with different lexical items can produce a potentially infinite set of structures. The grammar which the linguist writes is intended to mirror the child's, and is therefore also essentially generative.

Within the grammar are various components – phonological, syntactic and semantic. We shall concentrate here on the syntactic component, which itself has two subcomponents, a base and a set of transformational rules. The base consists of a lexicon and a set of Phrase Structure Rules (PSRs). In the lexicon, each word is listed along with some information; we can look up its word class, features like animacy for nouns, and instructions for nouns and verbs which have irregular plurals or past tenses. Verbs will also have a specification of what constituents must or can follow them; thus, BITE may have a following Object Noun Phrase while WALK does not. The PSRs then specify the configurations in which strings of lexical items may appear. In each PSR, the possible components of the category on the left of the arrow are spelled out on the right. The arrow means that the left-hand expression consists of, or technically, rewrites as, the units on the right: so PP ⟶ P NP would translate as 'a Prepositional Phrase consists of a Preposition plus a Noun Phrase'. Categories in brackets are optional. Examples of lexical entries and PSRs for a fragment of English are given in (1) and (2) respectively.

(1)   Lexicon:
         CAT   (N, [+ animate])
         DOG   (N, [+ animate])
         BITE   (V, irregular past *bit*, (+ NP))
         WALK   (V)
         BLACK   (Adj.)
         THE   (Art.)

(2)   Phrase Structure Rules:
         S   ⟶ NP VP
         NP ⟶ Art. (Adj.) N
         VP ⟶ V (NP)

Combining the two components of the base would allow us to generate infinite well-formed structures. Of course, the material in (1) and (2) is too restricted for this, but with a few minor additions can produce at least the examples in (3).

(3)   Dog[+ plural] walk.
        The cat bite[+ past] the black dog.
        The dog walk[- past].
        The dog bite[- past] the black cat.
        The black cat walk[- past].
        Cat[+ plural] bite[- past] dog[+ plural] ....

Strings such as those in (3), which are specified by the base component, are referred to as the deep structures, and must be put through a set of later rules, called the transformations, to create surface structures. These are less abstract, and will eventually, after phonological and semantic information has been supplied, become the actual spoken or written utterances. Transformational rules will spell out the past and present tense, and plural markers in (3). These structures would surface as declarative and positive, but could also be marked as negatives, questions or passives, which are all derived by transformation from similar deep structures to capture the generalisation that speakers will regard paradigms of sentences like the one in (4) as related. Possible deep structures eligible for such transformations are given in (5a), with simplified versions of the transformations used for questions, negatives and passives, and the resulting surface structures, in (5b).

(4)   *Cats bite dogs.*
        Do cats bite dogs?
        Cats do not bite dogs.
        Dogs are bitten by cats.
        Are dogs bitten by cats?
        Dogs are not bitten by cats.

(5)a.   Dog [+ plural] walk Q
        Dog [+ plural] walk NEG
        Cat [+ plural] bite [- past] dog [+ plural] PASSIVE

   b.   Questions:
        NP VP $\longrightarrow$ DO NP VP
        Dogs walk $\longrightarrow$ Do dogs walk?

        Negatives:

        NP VP $\longrightarrow$ NP $\begin{Bmatrix} \text{Aux.} \\ \text{Modal} \\ \text{DO} \end{Bmatrix}$ NOT VP
        Dogs walk $\longrightarrow$ Dogs do not walk

        Passives:

        NP_1 V NP_2 $\longrightarrow$ NP_2 BE PPartV BY NP_1
        Cats bite dogs $\longrightarrow$ Dogs are bitten by cats

In general, early historical work considered the tranformational component to be the major locus of change. We shall now consider two analyses of this type.

5.2.2.2 Klima's analysis (1964)

Klima's claim is that the order of application of transformational rules may change between generations, and his evidence involves the distribution of *who* and *whom* in English. Klima identifies two varieties of Modern English; Variety 1, shown in (6a), is more archaic than Variety 2, in (6b), a more recent and spreading development.

(6)a.   Variety 1:
    i.   *Who saw John?*
    ii.   *Whom did John see?*
    iii. *Whom did John give it to?*
    iv.   *To whom did John give it?*

  b.   Variety 2:
    i.   *Who saw John?*
    ii.   *Who did John see?*
    iii. *Who did John give it to?*
    iv.   *To whom did John give it?*

Klima accounts for the facts of Variety 1 by invoking two transformations. The first is Pronoun Case-Marking, formulated in (7), which governs the alternation of *who* and *whom*, and *he* and *him*.

(7)   Pronoun Case-Marking:

X	$\left\{ \begin{array}{c} V \\ \text{Prep.} \end{array} \right\}$ Pro.		Y	$\longrightarrow$		[+ oblique]	
1	2	3	4		1	2	3	4
John	saw	he		$\longrightarrow$	John	saw	him
John	saw	who		$\longrightarrow$	John	saw	whom

Rule (7) says that pronouns, like *he* and *who*, will become oblique *him* and *whom* when they are preceded by a verb or preposition. This works for (6aiv), where *who* is preceded by a preposition, *to*, and will consequently become oblique, and for (6ai), where the pronoun is not preceded by a preposition or a verb and does not become oblique. However, in (6aii) and (6aiii) *whom* surfaces, and this is not predicted by (7) since this pronoun does not follow a preposition or verb, at least on the surface.

Klima's solution is to posit a second transformation, Wh-Movement, which operates after Case-Marking. He assumes that the object pronouns originate in deep structure at position 3, as shown in (8). Case-Marking first applies, while *who* still follows a verb or preposition in (8 b-d); the results are shown in (9). Objective *wh-* pronouns are then fronted by a rule (10), which moves *whom* or, optionally, a prepositional phrase containing *whom*.

(8)   Deep structures:
  a.   Who saw John
  b.   John saw who
  c.   John gave it to who
  d.   John gave it to who

(9)   Case-Marking:
  a.   Who saw John
  b.   John saw whom
  c.   John gave it to whom
  d.   John gave it to whom

(10)   Wh-Movement:
  (i)   X   V   Y Prep. Wh-
        1   2   3 4   5 $\longrightarrow$ 5   1   2   3 4
        John saw   whom $\longrightarrow$ whom John   saw
        John gave it to   whom $\longrightarrow$ whom John   gave it to

  (ii) X   V   Y Prep. Wh-
        1   2   3 4   5 $\longrightarrow$ 4 5   1   2   3
        John gave it to   whom $\longrightarrow$ to whom John gave it

Finally, two transformations introducing auxiliary DO and inverting the Subject and DO are applied to produce the surface structures in (11).

(11)a.   *Who saw John?*
    b.   *Whom did John see?*
    c.   *Whom did John give it to?*
    d.   *To whom did John give it?*

For Variety 1, then, Pronoun Case-Marking necessarily precedes Wh-Movement. However, the same derivation is inappropriate for Variety 2, where *whom* only surfaces in sentence (d). This is also the only case where the *wh-* pronoun follows a verb or preposition on the surface. Klima accounts for this variety by positing the same deep structures and transformations, but assuming that the two transformational rules have changed their order of application so that Wh-Movement operates before Pronoun Case-Marking. The derivation for these sentences in Variety 2 is given in (12).

(12)   Deep structure:
        a. Who saw John
        b. John saw who
        c. John gave it to who
        d. John gave it to who

        Wh-Movement:
        a. Who saw John
        b. Who John saw
        c. Who John gave it to
        d. To who John gave it

Pronoun Case-Marking:
a. Who saw John
b. Who John saw
c. Who John gave it to
d. To whom John gave it

Other transformations:
a. *Who saw John?*
b. *Who did John see?*
c. *Who did John give it to?*
d. *To whom did John give it?*

As (12) shows, it is only when Wh-Movement optionally shifts *to* as well as *who* in sentence (d) that the appropriate context for Pronoun Case-Marking is maintained, accounting for the narrower distribution of *whom* in Variety 2. The change in surface structure between Variety 1 and Variety 2 therefore results from a change in the order of application of two transformational rules.

5.2.2.3 Traugott (1972)

Traugott's study focusses on the history of the Auxiliary (Aux) constituent in English, and her intention is to show that changes may occur in both the transformations and in the PSRs. Her technique is a very rigidly Saussurean one (see Chapter 2), in that she writes grammars of ninth century Old English (OE), fifteenth century Middle English (ME), sixteenth century Early Modern English, and Modern English (ModE), and then compares these. We shall concentrate here on the differences she proposes between OE and ModE.

Traugott proposes that the PSRs relating to Aux in ModE are as shown in (13).

(13)   Modern English:
          S   ⟶ NP VP
          VP ⟶ Aux Main V
          Aux ⟶ T (M) (have-PP) (be-PresP)

In other words, the basic word order is SVO, each Verb Phrase contains the Auxiliary constituent as well as a main Verb, and Aux itself consists of a tense marker (which will attach to the first verb of the clause), then optionally a modal and/or the auxiliaries *have*, which takes a following past participle, and *be*, with a following present participle. These rules generate sentences like those in (14).

(14)   *I shall go.*
             Aux MV
          Anna's parrot has died.
                       Aux MV

Simon is going to the party.
　　Aux MV

In ModE, then, Aux is the first element of the Verb Phrase. In OE, however, Aux appears last in the clause, as shown in (15), except in main clauses (16) where the first auxiliary appears before the main verb.

(15)　　*þā　Darius geseah þæt hē oferwunnen bēon wolde.*
　　　　then D.　　saw　that he conquered　be　would
　　　　　　　　　　　　　　　　　　　　MV　　[　Aux]
　　　　　　　　(Orosius 128.5)

　　　　&　him æfterfylgende wæs
　　　　and him following　　was
　　　　　　　　　　MV　　Aux
　　　　　　(Orosius 236.29)

(16)　　*þa Scipio hæfde gefaren*
　　　　when S.　had　gone
　　　　　　　　　Aux　MV
　　　　　　(Orosius 196.12)

Nū ic wille ēac þæs māran Alexandres gemunende bēon
now I will also the great A.　　considering be
　　Aux　　　　　　　　　　　　　MV　　　Aux
　　　　　(Orosius 110.10)
　　　　　　(after Traugott 1972)

Traugott accounts for these differences by proposing that OE and ModE do not have the same PSRs; in OE, Aux is generated before rather than after the main Verb, as shown in (17).

(17)　　Old English:
　　　　S ──→ NP VP
　　　　VP ──→ MV Aux

These rules allow the sentences in (15) to be generated, but an additional transformation, shifting the first auxiliary in front of the main Verb, is also required to account for the constructions in (16).

　　Finally, Traugott argues that OE manifests more restrictions on the contents of Aux than ModE, since the sequences in (18), which are permitted now, were outlawed in OE. She consequently writes some rather complex rules governing possible combinations of units within Aux.

(18)　　OE: **M Have-PP　　　　ModE: *I might have seen it*
　　　　OE: **Have-PP Be-PresP　ModE: *I might have been dancing*

　　Although Traugott concentrates on cataloguing such changes in her paper, she aspires to a higher goal: the construction of a 'diachronic grammar' for English. Such a grammar would 'provide rules accounting for diachronic relatedness between grammatical systems, such that the different systems may be regarded as modifications or extensions of a given system' (Traugott 1972: 212). Grammars of different stages would thus be related both to one another and to some central 'grammar of English'.

A number of problems arise in connection with Traugott's ideas and methods; some of these apply also to Klima's work. First, both show an inadequacy we have encountered already in our discussion of historical Generative Phonology in Chapter 2: it is certainly possible to account for language change in terms of rule change, but only at a descriptive rather than an explanatory level. In calling a linguistic change a rule change, we merely restate it; there is no investigation of motivation. There is also a lack of constraint and restrictiveness, and possible changes cannot readily be distinguished from impossible ones, since rules can be written ad hoc. Changes consequently appear to be accidental. Under these circumstances, it is hard to argue for one analysis over another; why should the accounts given by Traugott and Klima be the right ones, and how, in any case, will we ever recognise the right analysis when we find it? As Lightfoot (1979a: Chapter 1.3) sees it, this confusion results from the lack of an adequately formulated theory of change, and the failure to integrate work on change with a sufficiently restrictive theory of grammar.

Lightfoot also argues against Traugott's use of arguments ex silentio – from silence. Traugott assumes that certain constructions were ungrammatical in OE since no examples are found in the corpus, and consequently formulates complex rules to stop such sentences from surfacing. However, ModE does have such sentences, and Lightfoot (1979a: 30) argues that there is no known language with the properties Traugott assumes for OE, so that OE itself is rather unlikely to have had these characteristics. A preferable hypothesis might be that these constructions were extant but rare in OE, and have not survived in the texts we have.

Traugott also tends to assume that, if a particular constituent or process is a property of ModE, it must have an OE and ME equivalent. For instance, she assumes a category of Modal for OE because modals exist in the present-day language; as we shall see in the next section, Lightfoot regards this category as a relatively recent innovation. Lightfoot argues that assumptions about one stage of a language should not be allowed to colour our view of others; instead, 'particular grammars... must be written independently and then be compared only after the formulation' (Lightfoot 1979a: 34).

Finally, there have been strong objections to Traugott's notion of diachronic grammars, 'which were intended to encompass facts about various stages of a language and the transitions among those stages' (Lightfoot 1979a: 307). There are two main problems with this idea. First, diachronic grammars will necessarily contain a large number of rather complex rules, 'but since the statement that, for instance, this or that re-ordering took place at some stage, provides no insight into the *cause* of the change, formulating such rules appears to be a useless exercise' (Fischer and van der Leek 1981: 306). Furthermore, diachronic grammars propose links among grammars of different synchronic stages; however, such links cannot in reality exist, since 'grammars are by definition discontinuous entities' (Fischer and van der Leek 1981: 306). In other words, each speaker in each generation acquires a grammar which is self-contained and potentially different from her parents'; adult speakers do not pass on a grammar to their language-learning children. Writing rules to link such grammars formally is therefore, as Lightfoot (1979a: 307) puts it, 'a wild goose chase'.

5.3   Lightfoot's (1979a) theory of syntactic change

During the 1970s, it was felt that Generative syntactic theory was permitting too much abstractness. Deep structures were growing increasingly distant from surface forms, and the transformations, which join the two levels, were correspondingly becoming complex, unwieldy and unconstrained, and perhaps unlearnable. To combat this abstractness, the scope and operation of the transformational component was severely curtailed and the deep and surface structures consequently brought much closer together. Relatively few transformational rules remained in this so-called Extended Standard Theory (Radford 1981) – and indeed, subsequent developments have followed the same route, so that an even more recent Generative theory, Government and Binding (Chomsky 1981a, 1986) retains only a single transformation, Move-α. Of course, these few rules must also be tightly constrained if the deep and surface structures are to remain close.

Lightfoot (1979a) is set within the Extended Standard Theory, a more restricted syntactic theory than the earlier and more permissive *Aspects* model. The comparative lack of transformations within this model means that syntactic change could no longer be described solely or predominantly in terms of changes in these rules. Lightfoot's response to these innovations is a new approach to syntactic change, which we might see in broad terms as a catastrophe theory of historical syntax. Before expanding on this brief definition, however, we should consider Lightfoot's best-known example, his 'paradigm case' (Lightfoot 1979a: 81), which involves the English modals.

The ModE modals, and their OE predecessors the premodals, are listed in (19). The premodals are given in the first person singular present form, since not all the infinitives are attested.

(19)
	can	may	will	shall	must
OE	*ic can*	*ic mæg*	*ic wille*	*ic sceal*	*ic mōt*

The essence of Lightfoot's argument is that the premodals in OE shared the characteristic syntactic and morphological properties of verbs, so that OE had a single grammatical category of Verb which included the modals. However, in ModE modals behave in ways which set them apart from verbs, and Lightfoot therefore proposes that English has undergone a category change and innovated a new category of Modal. This clearly does not involve a rule change, but a category change in the base; although this will, of course, have repercussions for the rules.

Lightfoot notes that, between OE and around 1500, four developments progressively isolated the premodals from other verbs; these Predisposing Changes are listed in (20).

(20)   Predisposing Changes:
   a. all other preterite-present verbs become obsolete
   b. modals alone take a following bare infinitive – **I will to look
   c. 'past tense' forms of modals no longer signal past time reference – *I might go next week*
   d. modals cannot take a nominal object – ***I can a bicycle.*

In OE, the premodals were by no means the only preterite-present verbs – that is, verbs using historically past-tense forms as their present tenses, and thus lacking the characteristic third person singular present tense inflection (*-s*, in ModE). Instead, there was a fairly large class of such verbs in OE, including *dugan* 'to be of value', *munan* 'to think', *witan* 'to know', but all non-premodal members became obsolete or moved into the weak class during ME, leaving the premodals isolated. Secondly, all OE verbs took a following infinitive ending *-an*, but most also had a so-called inflected infinitive; thus, *singan* 'to sing' stood beside *to singenne*. As the *-an* inflection dropped during late OE, the *to* infinitive took over. However, the premodals are not attested with following *to* forms in OE, perhaps because the inflected infinitive had the meaning 'for the purpose of', 'in order to', which was not compatible with the senses of the premodals; ***ic wille to singenne* would mean 'I want in order to sing'. Consequently, the modals alone now occur with a following bare infinitive, a further isolating factor. Finally, the examples in (21) show that the premodals could have both nominal objects and past time reference in OE; the subsequent loss of these properties has increased the isolation of the premodals from other verbs.

(21)   *seþe sculde him undred denera*
        'he who owed him a hundred denarii'
        (*Rushworth Gospels*, Matthew xviii 28, c.975)

heora non swaþeah nolde befrinian hwæt hēo þær wolde
'none of them, however, would ask what she wanted there'
(Aelfric, c.1000)

Lightfoot argues that, if the premodals are still verbs, they must be marked as exceptions to many of the generalisations applying to verbs. Instead, he proposes that a radical reanalysis took place in the sixteenth century, whereby these exceptional forms were reinterpreted as members of a new category, Modal. This category change took place deep in the base of the grammar and thus was not directly observable, but is reflected in a number of related surface changes which were manifested more or less simultaneously. These are outlined in (22).

(22)a.   modals lose infinitive forms – **to may*
    b.   modals become incompatible with *-ing*, losing gerund and possessive forms:
          John's maying go annoyed me
          I am musting see her
    c.   modals are no longer found in perfective constructions – **She has mayed go*
    d.   sequences of modals disappear (except dialectally; in Scots some combinations are still permitted, as in *I might could go*).

Modals therefore lose all nonfinite forms, and no more than one modal is permitted in a clause. Lightfoot contends that these changes are explained by the category change he posits, which was itself motivated by increased exceptionality in the analysis of modals as verbs. Before the category change, the relevant PSR would be that in (23a), but afterwards, this would have been replaced by those in (23b).

(23)a.   S $\longrightarrow$ NP VP
        (modal = V, so part of VP)
    b.   S $\longrightarrow$ NP Aux VP
        Aux $\longrightarrow$ Tense (Modal)
        (modal = separate category, not part of VP)

Since the properties in (22a-c) are characteristic of verbs, we would expect the modals to relinquish these if they ceased to be verbs. Furthermore, the rules in (23b) allow only one modal per clause. The observed surface changes therefore follow from the changes in the base.

Lightfoot finally suggests that this reanalysis may be responsible for the developments in (24).

(24)a.   Only modals (and the auxiliaries *be, have, do*) can invert with the subject in questions and take a following negative marker.
    b.   New verbs *be going to, have to,* and *be able to* are introduced.

In OE *all* verbs could invert and take a following negative, giving patterns like those in (25).

(25)   Old English:
        He can go   Can he go?   He cannot go
        He goes   Goes he?   He goes not

However, from the sixteenth century, these properties become characteristic of only auxiliaries and modals; if none is present, a form of *do* must
instead be introduced, as shown in (26).

(26)a.   Did he go?   **Went he?
    b.   He didn't go.   **He went not.
    c.   Can he go?   **Does he can go?
    d.   He can't go.   **He doesn't can go.

Lightfoot accounts for these changes by proposing that the transformational rules for question and negative formation in OE inverted or
placed the negative marker with the first verb in the VP. However, once
there are two constituents, Aux and VP, these rules have to be made
sensitive to one or the other or both, and the observable changes show that
they came to refer to Aux alone. From the sixteenth century, Subject-Verb
Inversion and Negative Placement therefore affected the first lexical item in
Aux; if Aux was empty but for Tense, a form of *do* was then inserted to
carry tense, invert and take the negative. Finally, the introduction of *be
able to*, *have to* and *be going to* would, on this account, follow from
expressive difficulties in the language resulting from the departure of the
modals from the class of verbs. The solution was to create new verbs with
the same semantic content as the modals *can*, *must* and *shall/will*, but
without their syntactic deficiencies.

We can now use this example to illustrate Lightfoot's theory of change
– although, as we shall see, he actually concentrates much more on the
theory of grammar, regarding the theory of change itself as peripheral,
impoverished and relatively unimportant. The Extended Standard Theory
incorporates the hypothesis that children have a genetically prepro-
grammed specification of the characteristics of a possible grammar, and
therefore of a possible language. This aspect of Universal Grammar will
then include an upper bound on possible changes, since no change will be
allowed to create an impossible grammar. No formal limit on change will
be required, provided that the theory of grammar is sufficiently restrictive.

One of Lightfoot's most important contributions is his suggestion that
part of the theory of grammar is a Transparency Principle, which Lightfoot
treats as an independent principle, although admitting that 'it may be
possible to regard the principle as a specific consequence of a general
evaluation measure' (Lightfoot 1979a: 137). The Transparency Principle
(TP) controls the amount of opacity, or exceptionality that can be
tolerated in a grammar. Broadly, 'the Transparency Principle requires
derivations to be minimally complex and initial, underlying structures to

be 'close' to their respective surface structures' (Lightfoot 1979a: 121); it is therefore a control on abstractness in the syntax and can be seen as part of the move to restrict the scope of the transformations and approximate deep and surface structures which characterises the Extended Standard Theory. The TP clearly tells us about the properties of possible grammars, and is therefore part of the theory of grammar. However, as we shall see, it is also deeply involved with syntactic change.

Lightfoot proposes that complexity, opacity or exceptionality may build up in a grammar across time, perhaps through such factors as foreign influence or speakers' attempts to be expressive. The Predisposing Changes of ME, which progressively isolated the premodals from other verbs, would fall into this category. Eventually, exceptionality increases to the point where it violates the TP by passing the permitted level of complexity, and at this stage the TP requires a catastrophic change or radical reanalysis in the grammar, making underlying forms conform more closely to surface structures, as the modals were reanalysed as belonging to a novel category. This deep change in the grammar will be manifested on the surface by the emergence of a whole series of simultaneous changes, like the sixteenth century changes affecting the modals. These changes, as we have seen, follow from the underlying category shift, but without that deeper change and the TP which necessitates it, they would look accidental and unrelated. Lightfoot's principle is that, if a whole series of changes seem to have occurred near-simultaneously, a suitably restrictive theory should offer a single, unifying explanation for them; and the explanation he offers is the notion of transparency. Conversely, the discovery of simultaneous changes is the main signal that the TP has been in action.

Lightfoot tells us that too much complexity will violate the TP, but does not formulate the principle explicitly or give a measure of the opacity required to trigger it. However,

one may set up as a goal for work in syntactic change the formulation of such a Transparency Principle, [and] the determination of the tolerance level for initial structure opacity. How much opacity can a language take before being driven to re-analyse its initial structures to bring them closer to their surface structures and eliminate the exceptionality? How much 'work' can the transformational component perform? To put it differently, how smart are language learners? What is the limit to the abstractions that they postulate? (Lightfoot 1979a: 129)

Lightfoot hopes that these questions may be answered by considering further cases of simultaneous surface changes traceable to an underlying reanalysis; the point at which reanalyses occur should identify for us the limit of the grammar by showing us where the TP steps in. This goal is in fact bipartite: we would then be able to formulate the TP, and since our knowledge of possible grammars would also be improved by our discovery of what would be *im*possible grammars, we would have supplemented the theory of grammar. Change helps us verify the theory of grammar, while the theory of grammar, including the TP, delimits and explains change.

However, although the TP should ultimately be able to predict <u>when</u> change will become necessary as a therapy to some extravagant level of opacity, Lightfoot is adamant that it will never predict what form this therapeutic change will take; his argument is that a large number of strategies are available to any language at any time, and we cannot hope to predict which will be selected. Moreover, the TP applies to solve purely local problems; as we saw earlier, the recategorisation of certain verbs as Modals in the sixteenth century reduced exceptionality in the grammar, but caused further complications which lead to a revision of the procedures for question and negative formation and the introduction of new verbs. The operation of the TP may not be the solution to all the grammar's problems; instead, it may be the starting point in a chain of changes.

It follows from what has been said so far that the only formal distinction between possible and impossible changes comes from the theory of grammar, and therefore that the better, or more restrictive that theory of grammar is, the more rigidly possible changes can be defined. The task of a theory of change is consequently greatly curtailed, and in fact Lightfoot sees the theory of change as composed only of the four statements in (27). Assuming an impoverished theory of change does not, however, devalue the study of diachronic syntax; rather, it takes the important step of integrating change with the rest of the model, making it responsible to the theory of grammar in the same way as synchronic facts.

(27)a.   communicability must be preserved between generations
   b.   grammars practise therapy rather than prophylaxis
   c.   less highly valued grammars are liable to reanalysis
   d.   certain therapeutic changes are more likely than others.

Property (27a) is fairly obvious, and is assumed in most work on sound and syntactic change. The statement in (27b) tells us that grammars and speakers are not prescient, and thus cannot stop changes which may cause complexity although they may clear up the complexity afterwards, a point reminiscent of the relationship of sound change and analogy (see Chapter 4 above). Property (27c) simply recapitulates that therapeutic changes will be required in low-valued grammars; we are not told which grammars are low-valued since this information will be supplied by the theory of grammar and specifically by the TP. Finally, (27d) is hypothetical, and again a goal for further research; Lightfoot's only contribution here is to say that changes are more likely if they conform to the TP, and obviously a more explicit characterisation must await a formulation of that principle.

The discussion so far may have given the misleading impression that the

TP provokes only category change, and to remedy this imbalance we shall conclude this section with a brief look at a quite different type of change, involving word order, which Lightfoot also ascribes to the operation of the Transparency Principle.

We have encountered this particular word order change before, in the discussion of analogy and abduction in 4.2.3.4.4. In fact, it seems quite natural that Lightfoot's theory should have links with these phenomena, since his TP is an attempt to formalise the intuitive feeling among theorists of change that when the patterns of a language become confused, they will in time be reorganised. The force generally thought to be responsible for such tidying-up is analogy; and one way of implementing analogical change is innovation by children using abductive reasoning (Andersen 1973).

In OE, sentences like (28) must be interpreted as Object – Verb – Subject, as is made clear by the case and number morphology.

(28)   *þam cynge līcodon peran.*
       O   V   S
      'pears (plural) were pleasing (plural) to the king (dative singular)'

However, as inflections were lost in late OE and ME, (28) turned into (29), with no overt signal of which noun is Subject and which Object, leaving an ambiguous structure which could be interpreted as OVS or SVO.

(29)   *The king liked pears.*

Lightfoot's hypothesis is that this ambiguity was unacceptable since it violated the TP, which therefore demanded some resolution of the problem, although it did not stipulate a particular strategy. A child learning ME would, however, have heard large quantities of surface SVO sentences, since the canonical, basic word order for English had become SVO rather then SOV by the late twelfth century, and might therefore have abduced that the order of sentences like (29) was likely to be SVO. Again, this deep reanalysis is signalled by various simultaneous surface changes: sentences like those in (30), which are clearly OVS, are replaced by the SVO constructions in (31); and the meaning of the verb *like* alters from 'give pleasure to' to 'receive pleasure from'.

(30)a.   Him liked pears.   OVS
   b.   The king like pears.   OVS

(31)a.   He liked pears.   SVO
   b.   The king likes pears.   SVO

Our only remaining mystery is why clearly marked OVS constructions like those in (30) did not combat the reanalysis. Lightfoot's current work is dedicated to answering this question (Lightfoot 1991), and we shall return to it in 5.5 below.

5.4 Reactions and criticisms

5.4.1 *Introduction*

Reviewers of Lightfoot's book, while offering various criticisms of his approach, are generally agreed that his work is important and marks a significant step forward in historical syntactic theory. Fischer and van der Leek (1981: 301) provide a typical comment in their contention that 'with this book Lightfoot ... has made a very important and lucid contribution to the study of diachronic syntax. Its importance lies first and foremost in the fact that he develops a (hitherto sadly lacking) sound methodology for the study of syntactic change.' However, praise of this kind tends to be tempered with blame in the reviews, and in this section we shall therefore concentrate on critiques of Lightfoot's work. These can be divided into two broad categories: first, problems of the interpretation of data; and second, difficulties concerning the Transparency Principle itself.

5.4.2 *Lightfoot's data*

Warner (1983) provides a careful analysis of the data invoked by Lightfoot in his 'paradigm case' of the English modals, showing that Lightfoot's division of the developments involved into three distinct series of changes (the Predisposing Changes, loss of nonfinite forms, and subsequent consequences) is over-simplificatory and conceals various difficulties.

First, Lightfoot includes in the set of Predisposing Changes, which distance the premodals from the verbs, the loss of direct objects of premodals. Warner (1983) points out that this change did not take place entirely before the sixteenth century, giving attestations of *can*, *may* and *will* with direct objects from the sixteenth and seventeenth centuries. This development cannot therefore be a predisposing change, but must be treated as a signal of the deep reanalysis of premodals as Modals, or even as a later consequence of this. Lightfoot (1991) has now accepted this. The question must then be whether the three remaining predisposing changes are sufficient jointly or severally to violate the limit of tolerable opacity in the grammar and thus activate the TP.

The next data problem relates to the possible analysis of the ModE modals as a subclass of verbs with certain exception features to signal their deviant behaviour. Lightfoot (1979a) rejects this analysis on the grounds that the sixteenth century changes comprising the loss of nonfinite forms occurred simultaneously, and that an explanation of this simultaneity, which cannot be provided by the mere addition of exception markers, is therefore required.

However, Fischer and van der Leek (1981) are concerned that Lightfoot's analyses 'are ... not always in accordance with existing data' because 'in his search for changes occurring simultaneously ... Lightfoot often overlooks the existence of data that occur too early for his convenience' (1981:301). A case in point is Warner's (1983) observation that the loss of nonfinite forms of all modals could not have occurred simultaneously, since *can* and *may* lost their nonfinite elements by the mid-sixteenth century, but *will* not until the early seventeenth century, while there is only patchy and unreliable evidence of nonfinite forms of *shall* and *must* from even OE and ME, suggesting that these must have been lost considerably earlier than the sixteenth century.

If this is so, then Lightfoot's objection to the analysis of the modals as verbs with defective paradigms collapses. It may be that this analysis is preferable in any case. For instance, modals and verbs behave much more similarly than any other pair of categories; they take NP subjects, and appear in much the same position in the sentence. M and V will therefore have to have certain common features, requiring repetition in the grammar. Indeed, Warner (1983) notes that Early ModE modals were even closer to verbs than present-day ones, since although they lacked the third person singular present -*s*/-*th* inflection, both modals and verbs retained the second person -*st* ending, as in *thou could(e)st, thou canst, thou sing(e)st*. Furthermore, treating modals as a subclass of verbs might solve the problem of intermediate cases like *ought, need* and *dare*, which behave in some respects like modals but otherwise like verbs, as shown in (32). Forms do not generally fall between two word classes in this way.

(32)   Ought I to go?   I oughtn't.
         Dare I do it?   You needn't tell me.
         He needs a book.   He ought to see her.
         **I am oughting to go.

Finally, modals would not be unique among verbs in having defective paradigms; there are other verbs which require exception features. For instance, *beware* has an infinitive, as in *I warned him to beware* and an imperative, found in *Beware the Ides of March!*, but arguably no finite forms; it is not even clear to me whether the past tense would be *he bewared, he bewore*, or perhaps even *he was ware*.

Again, Lightfoot (1991: 142) accepts Warner's correction, admitting that the loss of nonfinite premodals 'may not have been as cataclysmic as I claimed'. However, he does not accept the analysis of modals as defective verbs. For one thing, there is probably a difference between a form like *beware*, which simply lacks certain verbal properties, and the modals, a small class distinct in both morphological shape and behaviour. As we shall see in 5.5, Lightfoot's most recent work includes other arguments against this analysis, as well as incorporating a more gradualist view of syntactic change.

Finally, Lightfoot (1979a) argues that several tidying-up changes took place after the reanalysis of modals as a separate category; these involve question and negative formation, and the coining of the new verbs *be going to*, *have to* and *be able to*. Warner again provides counter-evidence to these claims. First, he notes that new question and negative constructions with *do* co-existed with the older type until the late seventeenth century, a full century after the supposed reanalysis, so that the new constructions are scarcely an immediate consequence of this change. Finally, Warner notes that *be able to* and *have to* are both listed in the *Middle English Dictionary* for the fourteenth century with the appropriate senses, while *have to* also has an ME attestation in the poem *Pearl*. *Be going to* is not recorded in ME, but a number of equivalents, such as *be to* and *be upon point to*, are. It follows that the emergence of these verbs could not be a direct consequence of the movement of *can*, *must* and *will/shall* out of the verb class.

Consequently, although the modals have undergone various changes through the history of English, these are not so neatly ordered as Lightfoot (1979a) suggests. We shall return to Lightfoot's (1991) reanalysis of this 'paradigm case' in 5.5 below.

5.4.3   *The Transparency Principle*

In this section, we shall concentrate on criticisms of Lightfoot's unformulated Transparency Principle, which is intended to control the amount of opacity or exceptionality in the grammar, and which steps in to demand reanalysis if a grammar exceeds the permitted amount. One of the most vocal opponents of the TP is Romaine (1981), who sets out to demonstrate that the principle does not work; we shall review her arguments first, before moving to two broader criticisms of the TP noted by Warner (1983).

5.4.3.1 Romaine's critique

Romaine begins by noting that, in order to accept the TP, one must also accept the Extended Standard Theory, of which it forms part (although she produces no evidence against this theory to show why this is objectionable). This point may be partially valid, although it might be argued that since the TP is intended to combat abstractness, and since any syntactic theory is likely to need some mechanism to serve this purpose, a modified version of TP might be a desirable constituent of all syntactic theories. A more substantive point is Romaine's assertion (1981:284) that 'in order to 'explain' syntactic change to the fullest extent, we would have to predict both the change and its mechanism', something Lightfoot explicitly says the TP cannot do. Lightfoot (1981b) is dismissive of Romaine's point, arguing that prediction is not a necessary element of explanation (see also Chapter 2 above). He contends that Romaine's goal of

a theory of change which ... is fully predictable ... is not necessary in order to obtain explanations; after all, biology, in dealing with evolutionary concerns, is not a predictive science (like history), but this does not deprive evolution theory of explanatory force. If I understand her correctly, then I think that she is too ambitious. Her theory will need to be able to predict at least which stylistic innovations speakers will make and when, and what and when they will borrow from a neighbouring language ... perhaps she will achieve such a theory in future work; meanwhile I am not holding my breath (Lightfoot 1981b: 363).

Romaine proceeds to argue that the TP does not work, and that there are two methods of falsifying the principle. The first is to demonstrate differential failure, whereby change occurs which is not predicted by TP or where the TP does not operate as predicted; and the second involves proving that syntactic change is not radical reanalysis, but is instead gradual.

The first of these arguments is not particularly convincing. Lightfoot does not claim that all change is predictable by the TP; indeed, he notes explicitly that some changes which cumulatively breach the limit of tolerable opacity may be motivated by factors like foreign influence or attempts to produce expressive language; such changes may trigger TP but are not caused by it. Romaine's claim of differential failure is no more successful. She suggests that the reanalysis of OVS constructions to SVO in English should be mirrored in other languages under similar circumstances. However, Romanian is SVO, but has OVS structures with verbs like *a placea* 'to please', as shown in (33).

(33)   *îmi   place cartea aceasta*
        me-DAT pleases book this
        'I like this book'
                (after Bennett 1979: 852)

The same mismatch of deep SVO and surface OVS structures presumably exists in Romanian and existed in ME, but reanalysis has taken place only in the latter; hence Romaine's claim of differential failure.

However, the TP is not necessarily disproved. First, Lightfoot (1981b) notes that we do not know that English and Romanian speakers analyse these structures identically. This is perhaps not a strong point, since we equally do not know that the two languages do *not* have an identical analysis; but in any case, a much clearer counter-argument appears in

Bennett (1979), who notes that Romanian, unlike English at the appropriate stage, has a case system (of course, this point is stronger for nouns than for pronouns, which are still case-marked in English). Case-marking means that Romanian shows no surface ambiguity between SVO and OVS structures, and Bennett (1979: 853) concludes that 'deep-surface "distance" can be tolerated provided that there are clues to enable speakers to assign the "correct" structure to a sentence'.

Further evidence along the same lines comes from language acquisition. For instance, Jakobson (1963: 269) reports that small Russian children tend to analyse NP-V-NP constructions as SVO even when these are case marked as OVS, while English children interpret passives like *Anna was hit by Jane* as semantically equivalent to *Anna hit Jane* (Bennett 1979: 855). Bennett quotes a developmental universal formulated by Slobin which covers both analyses, claiming that 'sentences deviating from standard word order will be interpreted at early stages of development as if they were examples of standard word order'. This leads to Bennett's conclusion that

... when children begin to analyse an SVO language, they first interpret NP-V-NP strings as SVO and active. Only later do they begin to pay attention to nominal or verbal morphology, and at this stage their initial misinterpretation may be revised. But only if there is clear evidence that their initial analysis was incorrect (as with the Russian OVS construction and the English passive) will there be a revision. In the case of *the king liked pears*, there is nothing to show that the SVO hypothesis is wrong, hence the perpetuation of it (1979: 855).

This clearly relates to Bever and Langendoen's (1971) notion of perceptual strategies discussed in 4.2.3.4.3 above.

We do not, then, have any disproval of the TP due to differential failure. Our only remaining mystery, again, is why OVS does not persist in clearly marked ME constructions like *him liked pears*; we return to this in 5.5.

Romaine's second allegation may be more damaging, at least when supplemented with evidence from Aitchison (1980). Romaine argues that some syntactic changes show gradual diffusion, like diffusing sound changes; she claims that this fact is inconsistent with Lightfoot's view of syntactic change as radical reanalysis, and that the TP cannot therefore be upheld. However, this is not necessarily so: the catastrophic/instantaneous and gradual analyses are incompatible only for any *one* change. We have already established (in Chapter 3 above) that there are two types of sound change, gradual and non-gradual; it is unclear why two parallel types should not also be included in diachronic syntactic theory.

Romaine herself does not show that any of the changes examined by Lightfoot are gradual; however, Warner (1983) claims, as we have seen, that the loss of nonfinite forms in the modals in all likelihood spread from *must, shall* to the others, raising a further question-mark over the 'paradigm case'. Aitchison (1980) takes this further. She points out initially that, in sound change, one often finds a series of diffusing changes which, seen in retrospect, look like a single change; such a configuration is analysable using the S-curve model discussed in Chapter 3. Aitchison generalises this analysis to syntactic change, and specifically to the modals, arguing again that Lightfoot's claims for simultaneity do not hold water, so that it is impossible to distinguish a set of predisposing changes, a following set of simultaneous changes in the sixteenth century involving the loss of nonfinite forms, and a further simultaneous set of seventeenth-century consequences. Instead, she identifies three overlapping stages: Stage 1 is a slow movement of the premodals away from the central class of verbs between OE and the fifteenth century; Stage 2 is a faster section of the same process through the sixteenth century; and Stage 3 is a final, slower stage extending into the seventeenth century. This slow-quick-slow development is clearly reminiscent of the S-curve motion of gradual sound changes.

This may not be the end of Lightfoot's hypothesis that some syntactic changes are instantaneous. He attempts to retaliate (Lightfoot 1981b) by arguing that his notion of simultaneity refers solely to the time of change in the grammar, not the subsequent spread across the community, a distinction Aitchison's S-curve account may blur. Furthermore, to be conclusive it would have to be demonstrated that all the changes reviewed by Lightfoot were gradual. It must also be noted that it is extremely hard, if not impossible, to demonstrate the simultaneity of changes from the philological record, since written data do not necessarily reflect perfectly the situation in speech. For instance, changes which are simultaneous in speech may not be reflected in the writing system at the same time; while changes which take place gradually in the spoken language may arrive in writing as the result of a fairly abrupt change in orthographic practice. In any case, as we shall see in 5.5, Lightfoot has more recently slackened his requirement of simultaneity and incorporated graduality into his model of syntactic change.

5.4.3.2   Broader criticisms

Warner (1983) and Aitchison (1980) both note two further and broader difficulties with the TP. First, they are concerned that the TP is absolute rather than relative; indeed, Aitchison (1980: 143) argues that Lightfoot 'is perhaps unique in thinking that opacity can be quantified and a tolerance level specified'. Her main evidence is her contention that some languages seem to tolerate higher levels of opacity than others; for instance, Ancient Greek is more tolerant than Latin, as can be seen from the greater number of optional stylistic devices in Latin. This begs the question of whether

Greek and Latin have the same number of opaque constructions in the first place, but nonetheless raises an awkward objection to Lightfoot's characterisation of the TP as a constant element of Universal Grammar.

An even stronger objection to the TP, although one with a potential solution, is that it is too broad and wide-ranging. As Aitchison points out (1980: 143–4), 'it seems to be a catch-all, *post-hoc* explanation designed to cover different types of change. [Lightfoot] rightly criticises linguists of the 1960s for believing that all change was inexorable simplification. He himself is falling into a similar trap in calling to his aid an all-powerful, but ill-defined Transparency Principle... Unless he can tighten up and sub-divide his Transparency Principle in some way, he is simply replacing one over-simplistic explanation with another.'

Lightfoot in fact accepts this criticism to some extent, agreeing that the TP 'covers different kinds of complexity and... it is unlikely that one principle, when properly formulated, will cover them all' (1981b: 360). Again, however, he holds out hope that further research will 'provide more precise ideas about what the Transparency Principle was groping towards' (Lightfoot 1981b: 360). This has been the topic of his more recent work, which I shall survey in the next section.

5.5   Lightfoot and the principles and parameters model

Lightfoot (1981a, 1988, 1991) claims significant advances in the recasting of the Transparency Principle. The Extended Standard Theory, within which the original TP was couched, is now rather out of date; and Lightfoot is now working with its successor, the Government and Binding or principles and parameters model. The transformational component has been even further reduced in this model, and it is argued that the grammar is divided into a set of interacting modules. Each module has its own principles, which are part of the child's genetic inheritance, and other principles operate throughout the grammar. Furthermore, the child is equipped with various innate parameters, which are set with reference to incoming language data to show whether, for example, the object precedes or follows the verb in the language being learned, in much the same way as we set switches on a computer printer to specify whether we are going to use A3 or A4 paper.

Chomsky and others (see Hornstein and Lightfoot 1981) have now attempted to formulate some of these innate principles, and it seems that reference to these may supersede an independent Transparency Principle while maintaining the same effect. For instance, if we return to the English OVS > SVO reanalysis, we find the derivation in (34) for OE, on the usual assumption that deep structure word order in OE was SOV.

(34)   Deep structure:

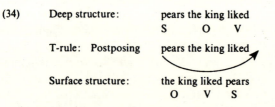

T-rule: Postposing

Surface structure:

However, from the late twelfth century ME had innovated canonical SVO order at deep structure, so that the derivation in (35) would be required to produce the same output, with two transformations swapping the Noun Phrases around.

(35)   Deep structure:

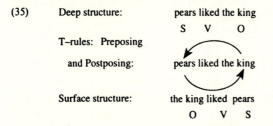

T–rules: Preposing

and Postposing:

Surface structure:

Lightfoot's early (1979a) account managed to link the subsequent word order reinterpretation with the change in meaning of the verb *like*, and 'noted that a derivation involving a permutation of subject and object seemed to be opaque in some undefined sense' (Lightfoot 1988: 309), but was not entirely successful in explaining this opacity. Instead, the derivation is rather pretheoretically ruled out by the TP, which bulldozes excessive opacity, regardless of its source, out of the grammar.

However, with the introduction of more specific principles and constraints, more specific accounts may be forthcoming. One of the principles proposed in the revised model is the Trace Erasure Principle, which states that a Noun Phrase, when moved by a transformational rule, leaves behind a trace to indicate its original location, as shown in (36).

(36) OE: pears$_i$ the king$_j$ liked
    T-rule: $_i$ the king$_j$ liked pears$_i$

The theory specifies that a gap may be filled, and the trace occupying it erased, by certain specially designated elements such as *there* or *it*, but not by any random NP. It follows that an analysis swapping the NPs in *pears liked the king* to produce *the king liked pears* is prohibited in this model since it would involve two Noun Phrases moving, both leaving traces, and each illegally moving into a space already occupied by a trace. This tells us both why the derivation produces opacity, and why a reanalysis is required. In this case, the particular change selected is to retain the order *the king liked pears* but interpret it analogically as SVO; the underlying order then changes to match, and there is a concomitant alteration in the semantics of *like*. Lightfoot (1988) even proposes that the Trace Erasure Principle can be subsumed under a more general Projection Principle, although we need not pursue this here. Either way, the account remains substantially the same: an excess of opacity or exceptionality arises in the grammar, and a reanalysis is required because some principle is contravened. The only difference from Lightfoot (1979a) is that different changes may violate different principles, rather than the TP alone.

One note of caution must be sounded, however: it is essential for us to establish that this theory of grammar is truly restrictive; otherwise, there might be a temptation to introduce a new principle to solve each new problem, producing an unwieldy grammar full of *ad hoc* principles. We must assess which is worse: to propose one principle like the TP which has to cover so many eventualities it becomes impossible to formalise, or to allow an indefinitely large, unconstrainable set of principles. Proposing individual conditions like the Trace Erasure Principle, then subsequently seeking to derive them from a smaller number of more far-reaching constraints such as the Projection Principle, could be either the way forward or an uneasy compromise.

These specific misgivings are not applicable to the most recent reworking of these ideas (Lightfoot 1991). Here again, Lightfoot discusses the interconnections of linguistic change, language acquisition and formal grammar: this time, however, the spotlight is on acquisition. Lightfoot points out that generative grammar has seen first language learning in terms of parameter setting, or '... fixing option points defined in Universal Grammar' (1991: ix) for around a decade; but very little has been said about how these parameters are actually set, or what data might be available to the child. Lightfoot sets out to define the range of this data, the child's triggering experience, largely with reference to language change.

Lightfoot (1991) argues that existing studies of parameter setting seem to assume that children have access during acquisition to negative data – that is, they work out what is *un*grammatical. It is hard to see how children might attain this sort of knowledge: of course, children do hear ungrammatical and degenerate data, but these seem not to affect the child's own production, while parents do not habitually produce ill-formed sentences and explain their ill-formedness. Access to rather uncommon data, or to very complex sentence types, is also often assumed: for instance, Wexler and Culicover (1980) claimed that children acquire language on the basis of simple, main clauses like *Anna left*, and also embedded clauses, or structures of degree-1 complexity like *I thought* [*that Anna had left*], and degree-2 structures containing two embedded clauses such as *I thought* [*that you said* [*that Anna had left*]].

Lightfoot (1991), on the other hand, suggests that only common, robust and simple structures are involved in acquisition. Children do not use the same data linguists would in writing a grammar, so that ' … the triggering experience … does not include information about ungrammatical sentences, comparative data from other languages, exotic and subtle judgments about quantifier scope, and much more that occurs in a typical issue of *Linguistic Inquiry*' (1991: 13). Consequently, not every linguistic experience can act as a trigger: and more precisely, Lightfoot claims that essentially, only main clauses matter in setting parameters. That is, children are degree-0 learners; they have access only to main clauses and to certain well-defined units at the beginning of embedded clauses (which we need not specify here) in setting parameters.

This is clearly a very restrictive hypothesis, which requires verification, and Lightfoot suggests that language change represents a useful testing ground. That is, ' … the nature of some linguistic changes suggests that children are degree-0 learners. Under certain conditions they are insensitive to complex data that should have inhibited the new parameter settings actually adopted' (Lightfoot 1991: 40). One of the syntactic phenomena Lightfoot discusses is word order in Dutch, German and Old English, which all have predominantly VO main clauses and OV subordinate clauses: however, in Modern English VO is universal, whereas no change has taken place in the other languages. First, Lightfoot demonstrates that children could collect enough clues from frequently occurring, robust main clauses to set their parameters appropriately in Dutch and German, producing embedded OV order. In OE, some similar triggers were available in main clauses, but these were much less clear and consistent than in Dutch and German. In fact, OV order in *main* clauses declines steadily throughout OE, while VO increases; clues to OV order therefore become fewer and fewer, and OV ultimately becomes unlearnable, leading to a new parameter setting. Consequently, a gradual change in the frequency of a certain construction eventually causes a parameter to be reset, producing VO in embedded as well as main clauses, just as increasing opacity in the grammar triggered the Transparency Principle in Lightfoot's earlier work: now, however, the opacity referred to is essentially acquisitional. And again, as with the TP, an underlying change deep in the grammar (here, the parameter resetting) causes a catastrophic, sudden change on the surface: in this case, although OV order had formed an average 66 per cent of embedded clauses until 1122, it declined extremely sharply to 11 per cent in the period 1122–1140. Of course, this rapid decline in embedded OV order can only follow from a parameter resetting if children are degree-0 learners; if they were not, but set parameters according to data from subordinate clauses, they would have had plenty of robust OV structures right up to the twelfth century, which would presumably have inhibited the parametric change from happening at all.

Interestingly, this sort of analysis is also illuminating for formal grammar, since a survey of the surface changes which follow a parametric change will tell us what structures are connected in the grammar. Here, main and subordinate clause order are shown to be linked since a change in the parameter setting for one affects the other. Sometimes, these connections are rather obvious, but in other cases they may not previously have been suspected: just as the French rivers Loue and Doubs were only found to be linked in 1901 when an accidental spillage at the Pernod factory on the Doubs temporarily turned the Loue into a gigantic free apéritif.

This claim of degree-0 learnability, although crucially underpinning Lightfoot's recent work, is not of direct relevance to the two changes we have focussed on in this chapter, namely the alleged recategorisation of the modals and the loss of OVS order in *the king liked pears*, which is of degree-0 complexity. Lightfoot here introduces the argument that even degree-0 structures may not always act as part of the triggering experience, in a particular set of circumstances: morphological change may lead to the resetting of a parameter, which may in turn mean that certain constructions (such as *Him liked pears*) become unanalysable for children with the new parametric value. These constructions then become obsolescent, as a by-product of the parametric change.

Let us turn first to the decline of impersonal OVS constructions like those in (37).

(37)   *ac gode ne līcode na heora gelēaflēast. ...*
        dat.   nom.
                  (Aelfric *Homilies* xx 71)
        'but their faithlessness did not please God'

        þæm cynge līcodon peran
            dat.sg. pl.   nom.pl.
        'pears pleased the king'

        him ofhrēow ðæs mannes
        dat.   gen.
        'he pitied the man'

In OE, about 40 verbs can appear, as in (37), with two NPs, neither of which is a nominative subject. However, some of these verbs (like *ofhrēowan*) vanished by late Middle English; others developed an expletive *it* subject as in (38); and still others had one NP reanalysed as the subject and made nominative, as happened with *līcian > like*.

(38)   OE   *snīwð*
        ModE   *it is snowing*

OE	*rīnde*
ModE	*it rained*

Lightfoot's explanation of these changes relies heavily on theory-internal arguments, which I can only summarise superficially here. One of the modules in Government and Binding theory involves case. Anyone familiar with Latin, German or OE will be used to the idea that certain verbs or prepositions make nouns appear in a particular case: thus, OE *ofhrēowan* always makes its left-hand noun dative and its right-hand one genitive; Latin *in* followed by an accusative noun means 'into', while *in* plus ablative means 'in'; and German *auf* means 'on' with a dative noun and 'onto' with a following accusative. In these languages, case is generally overt; that is, the case of a noun is signalled by a suffix. However, Government and Binding claims that, even in languages like Modern English where no overt signals of case appear, abstract case is still assigned to nouns. Without having either overt or abstract case, no NP can ever surface in any language: a caseless noun would violate the so-called 'case filter', and cause the construction to be rejected as ungrammatical.

Case can be assigned in two ways. First, certain verbs and prepositions can mark their argument NPs for particular cases at deep structure. If a noun is not case marked at that level, it will have to acquire structural case at surface structure: since structural case is assigned only to nouns in certain structural positions, the NP will have to occupy a certain slot in the construction before it is eligible to receive case.

Lightfoot assumes OE lexical entries like those in (39) for verbs like *līcian* and *ofhrēowan*. Each will have two argument NPs, an experiencer and a theme: *līcian* assigns inherent dative case to its experiencer and no case to the theme, which will acquire structural nominative case later; while *ofhrēowan* assigns dative to the experiencer and genitive to the theme.

(39)   *līcian*:   experiencer-dative; theme
        ofhrēowan: experiencer-dative; theme-genitive

However, Lightfoot (1991) argues that the assignment of lexical case at deep structure depends on the appearance of overt morphological case-marking on the surface in the language concerned. In early OE, case is morphologically marked and thus the lexical entries in (39) are appropriate. But as the morphological case system broke down later in OE, children would not learn overt case marking, and would consequently not have the ability to assign inherent case at deep structure, leaving a lexical entry like (40) for *līcian* in their innovatory grammar.

(40)   *līcian*:   experiencer; theme

Previously, the construction O (dative) VS (nominative) had been permissible because the dative case was assigned at deep structure. However, after the loss of morphological dative case, this is no longer possible and both NPs must be assigned structural case. Crucially, two NPs in the configuration NP V NP can only be assigned structural case in one way: the first must be nominative, and therefore the subject, and the second will be oblique, and the object. The reinterpretation of *The king liked pears* from OVS to SVO, and the concomitant change in the meaning of *like*, follow. Children would still hear structures like *Him liked pears* for some time, from adults with the older grammar, but these would not form part of the triggering experience since they could not be analysed by a child with the new parameter setting. The obsolescence of these structures therefore follows from the parametric resetting, which in turn is a by-product of inflectional loss.

This analysis has certain advantages over Lightfoot's earlier account. First, earlier work explained the OVS > SVO change in terms of ambiguity: if a child heard *The king liked pears*, she would parse this automatically as SVO, by analogy with the very frequent SVO constructions which do *not* have an alternative OVS reading. However, Lightfoot (1991) admits that, in the texts, most of the supposedly ambiguous structures are in fact disambiguated by a pronoun, and are therefore of the *Him liked pears*, not the *The king liked pears* variety. Secondly, this new analysis takes account of the existence of variation in the community. Lightfoot's earlier work relied, as we have seen, on assumptions of simultaneous change. Here, however, he attempts to incorporate the considerable OE and ME variation in impersonal constructions into his account, by hypothesising a situation where each member of the speech community would have one of two grammars, the archaic one with inherent case assignable at deep structure, or the innovating one with structural case alone. The link of inherent case with morphological case, and the gradual loss of the latter, allows Lightfoot to explain the gradual shift of the population from the old grammar to the new one, and the gradual obsolescence of OVS structures. Unusually for a syntactic theory, Lightfoot's (1991) account therefore incorporates matters of variation and gradual change. Finally, this account requires no special principles: neither the TP nor the Trace Erasure Principle is relevant.

Let us now turn, finally, to the matter of the modals. Although Lightfoot (1991) has made certain alterations to his earlier account, due largely to Warner's (1983) emendations, the crux of the argument remains the same, albeit stated in newer terminology. Essentially, the OE premodals, which were ordinary verbs, were gradually distanced from other verbs by a number of predisposing changes; these again are morphological, since they cumulatively make the premodals the only verbs lacking a following *to* infinitive and the third person singular present tense -*s*. This small, morphologically definable class is then input to a syntactic change, whereby the class membership of the premodals is altered and they cease to be verbs, as signalled by their loss of nonfinite forms and inability to take direct objects. Children would again hear degree-0 structures like *I am canning do it* and *I have could do it*, but would no longer be able to analyse these since *can* would not, for them, be a verb. Such constructions would therefore not be part of the child's triggering experience and would not influence his production; and again, their gradual obsolescence follows from the child's altered grammar. Similarly, old negative and question structures, with negation or inversion of any verb, also obsolesce as new generations involve only modals and auxiliaries in these constructions. Furthermore, Lightfoot's hypothesis that children are degree-0 learners provides another argument against the alternative idea that modals are still verbs which have simply acquired an increasing number of exception features during the history of English. These exception features would, in Lightfoot's terms, be unlearnable, since they rely on negative data or a knowledge of what is ungrammatical, which Lightfoot assumes to be unattainable for the child. Such accretions of exception features could therefore provide a description of what changes have occurred, but cannot be linked with language acquisition and are therefore not explanatory.

Lightfoot (1991) finally integrates his various case-studies into a general outline of syntactic change. He suggests that languages, like biological populations, are continually in flux. Linguistic constructions may increase in frequency, or forms may be borrowed, producing novel structures; however, these are necessarily random and unpredictable, giving language the character of a chaotic system. Now and again, however, such random changes, along perhaps with gradual morphological change, may cumulatively alter the input data to the extent that children acquiring the language will set some parameter differently from the previous generation. The new parameter setting will be manifested in the language by a number of surface changes which take place very rapidly (if not quite simultaneously) and will characteristically follow the S-curve pattern, not a more gradual straight-line graph. Obsolescence of potentially robust, degree-0 constructions will gradually follow as the innovating grammar becomes the norm in the community; and a chain of further changes may also be initiated. New parameter settings therefore correspond to relatively short periods of rapid change in a language, interrupting the normal stasis of the grammar, like the notion of 'punctuated equilibrium' in evolution.

These hypotheses are attractive for a number of reasons. They incorporate the idea of gradual, diffusing change rather than clashing with it as the original Transparency Principle may have done. They also stress the importance of variation, as we shall in Chapter 9, and links of diachronic linguistics with evolutionary biology, to which we return in Chapter 12. The price, as Lightfoot (1991) cheerfully admits, is a good deal of theory-internal argument, and reliance on Universal Grammar and Government and Binding syntax. This may lead, again, to a problem. We have seen that the TP is undefinable, and that the derivation of its effects from conditions like Trace Erasure may lead to an unwelcome proliferation of principles. Here, our concern must be for the reliance we are forced to put on UG. For instance, when Lightfoot (1991) argues that some property x is unlearnable by children, perhaps because it relies on negative data, he is not necessarily saying that property x is unavailable in grammars; it could instead be genetically given as part of UG. An argument that x is unlearnable and must therefore be impossible is one thing, but one which says x is unlearnable and must therefore be innate might be quite another. We do not know the limits of UG, but must surely be conscious of making them too permissive, so that effectively nothing is ruled out.

If we are to follow Lightfoot in making analyses of syntactic change responsible to a theory of grammar, we have to be sure that our theory of grammar is responsible, too.

6 Word order change and grammaticalisation: language change and general laws

6.1 Introduction

In the last chapter, we explored the insights into syntactic change which might be gained by operating within the confines of a formal model of grammar. Here, we shall consider syntactic change as part of an investigation into whether there are general laws which languages must obey, and whether such laws might somehow compel language-internal changes to proceed in a particular direction.

The observation of directionality in syntactic (and other) change is not new, and has been discussed under various labels in the literature. One of the most famous is probably Sapir's (1921: 150) suggestion that 'Language moves down time in a current of its own making. It has a drift.' Sapir argues that, although individual variation is random, drift in a language is directional, and operates by the unconscious selection of variants which change the language in a particular, cumulative way. Each individual change will therefore be part of a series, being prefigured by earlier developments which it continues, and providing an input for subsequent changes. Sapir isolates three particular morphosyntactic drifts in English, which might well be expected to recur cross-linguistically: these are the levelling of case distinctions; the fixing of word order; and the tendency towards invariable words.

There seem to be two ways of making sense of the rather mystical concept of drift. The first is to assume an evolutionary framework – and indeed Malkiel, in a detailed survey of Sapir's notion of drift and its various interpretations, defines drift as 'a single, isolated, undisturbed evolutionary strain or streak' (1981: 566). Evolutionary theory in biology also makes use of the idea of unintentionally cumulative developments, notably in the metaphor of the blind watchmaker, who slots pieces into a pattern which he cannot perceive as a whole. In a similar vein, Aitchison (1987, 1989a) sees linguistic evolution as the invention of solutions to problems: since we are all human, and speak human languages, the problems and solutions are apt to be common ones, but any solution selected may reduce the options speakers have at the next stage, thus creating apparent chains of changes. We return to linguistic evolution in Chapters 10, and especially 12, below.

Drift might alternatively be explained within a framework more specific to language than evolutionary theory, by invoking laws which languages must obey, or which govern the direction of change. Thus Lakoff, identifying a drift from synthetic to analytic in Indo-European, attributes it to 'a metacondition on the way the grammar of a language as a whole can change' (1972: 178). However, we saw in the last chapter that conditions on change arguably follow from conditions on grammars; it is unclear how Lakoff's metacondition could operate in this way, since certain Indo-European languages are still relatively highly inflecting, and there are certainly languages outside this family which disobey her law.

In this chapter, we shall explore two drifts which have been observed cross-linguistically. First, in 6.2, we consider so-called consistency in word order, whereby the heads of phrases are predicted to have modifiers either to the left or the right across all the constructions of a language; then, in 6.3, we turn to grammaticalisation, in which independent lexical items move from the syntax into the morphology. In both cases, we shall investigate attempts to derive changes from general laws, but will find that functional rather than formal explanations, and a careful invocation of natural tendencies rather than the postulation of rigid laws, are more illuminating.

6.2   Typology and consistency in word order

6.2.1   *The typological approach*

Languages may be classified genetically, according to their relationship with others descended ultimately from the same proto-language; areally, according to the geographical region in which they are spoken; and typologically, according to their own inherent characteristics. We shall concentrate here on the contribution of typology, and the associated search for linguistic universals, to the study of word order change, and must consequently begin by defining the terms typology, word order and universals as they will be used below.

When linguists consider the typology of a language, they are interested in its properties, and the possibility of classifying it in relation to other languages with potentially different properties. Typological theory covers all areas of the grammar: the phonology, morphology, syntax, semantics and vocabulary. Phonological typology might involve assessing the number and type of vowel or consonant sounds in a given language, or its preferred syllable structure; while morphological typology distinguishes isolating languages like Vietnamese (with invariable words) from agglutinating languages like Turkish (where morphs are glued together in an invariable order and each realises one morpheme) and inflecting ones like Latin (where it is almost impossible to segment words unambiguously into morphs and even harder to say which morph expresses which morpheme(s)). However, the best-developed area of typology probably involves the syntax, and specifically word order.

Word order typology revolves around 'various permutations of the magical letters S, V and O' (Watkins 1976: 305); however, the Subject, Verb and Object of a sentence may consist of considerably more than one word, as shown in (1).

(1)a.   *Simon saw David.*
         S   V   O

  b.   [*The tall young man in the rather fetching*
        spotted bow tie] [*caught a quick glimpse of*]
        S   V
        [*the trainee librarian who was gazing out of*
        O
        the window of the Number 47 bus]

'Word order' is therefore only convenient shorthand, and our concern is with the order of constituents in the sentence. Of all the constituents we are likely to encounter, S, O and V are the most central, since these provide the building-blocks of basic clausal order.

Basic order is generally taken to appear in unmarked constructions; this would normally exclude negatives and questions, and cases where one constituent has been focussed by fronting, as in English *Alexandra I really cannot stand*, which is OSV. Ideally, basic clausal order should also be the most frequently occurring word order in a language. Sometimes these criteria produce a fairly unambiguous result, so that English is SVO, Turkish SOV, Scots Gaelic VSO, Malagasy VOS and Hixkaryana (an Amazonian language) OVS. However, sometimes it is rather harder to isolate a single, basic, unmarked word order. For instance, in some Australian languages like Warlbiri and Dyirbal, all possible permutations of S, V and O produce grammatical sentences, and there seems to be no particular preference for one over another, so that selecting a basic order would be arbitrary (Dixon 1980, cited by Comrie 1981). Furthermore, some languages exhibit a word order split; German, for instance, has SVO order in main clauses and SOV in subordinate clauses, as (2) shows.

(2)a.   *Das Mädchen kennt meine Tante.*
         'the girl knows my aunt'
         S   V   O

b.   *Ich glaube, dass das Mädchen meine Tante kennt.*
       'I believe that the girl my aunt knows'
                  S   O   V

It is not even clear that categories like 'subject' can be defined in the same way for all languages. Even preliminary typological classification can therefore be controversial.

Work on typology has been linked with the search for language universals since Greenberg's (1963a) pioneering investigations in the 1960s. Greenberg searched for surface properties which would, in the strongest case, be common to all human languages, or which all possible human languages must have, by comparing data from a wide-ranging sample of languages. Greenberg's initial paper (Greenberg 1963a) on universals was based on a preliminary survey of 30 languages, but data gathering and processing is now much more efficient, with computer-based samples covering up to 600 languages.

Working with his initial, restricted database, Greenberg noted a number of universals. Not all of these are absolute and exceptionless; few universals are, although one good candidate appears as (3a). The majority of Greenberg's universals are implicational, like (3b) and (3c), predicting that if a language has one property, it will have another. Implicational universals 'state a dependency between two logically independent parameters' (Croft 1990: 47), making a connection that might not automatically be suspected.

(3)a.   All languages have vowels.
   b.   If a language has front rounded vowels, then it also has front unrounded vowels.
   c.   If a language has nasal vowels, then it also has oral vowels.

Even implicational universals can be too strong for Greenberg, who is extremely cautious (his article begins 'the tentative nature of the conclusions set forth here should be evident to the reader'). Consequently, Greenberg frequently proposes implicational universal *tendencies*, predicting that if a language has property A, it will probably also have property B. A Greenbergian universal is therefore not necessarily 'universal' in its strongest sense.

Greenberg's universals are predominantly syntactic, and are based on the order of S, V and O, and of elements within the Noun Phrase and Verb Phrase, including the order of determiners, adjectives and relative clauses with respect to nouns, auxiliaries relative to main verbs, and nouns relative to adpositions (the cover term for prepositions, which precede nouns, and postpositions, which follow them). Greenberg's major discovery was the existence of strong correlations among these logically independent word order properties. Certain properties therefore tend to cluster together in languages; some examples (from Greenberg 1963a) are given in (4).

(4)   Universal 2: In languages with prepositions, the genitive almost always follows the governing noun, while in languages with postpositions it almost always precedes.

Universal 3: Languages with dominant VSO order are always prepositional.

Universal 4: With overwhelmingly greater than chance frequency, languages with normal SOV order are postpositional.

Other syntacticians, notably W. Lehmann (1973b) and Vennemann (1974, 1975) have subsequently modified Greenberg's initial, basic correlations. We shall now assess their claim that these implicational universals are relevant to syntactic change.

6.2.2   *Implicational universals and syntactic change*

If we reduce Greenberg's correlations to just four basic parameters, these being basic order within the clause, the choice of preposition or postposition, and the order of noun and genitive and noun and adjective, twenty-four logically possible language types arise from their combination; but only four (see (5)) are found in significant numbers of languages.

(5)a.	VSO	Prep.	NG	NA
b.	SVO	Prep.	NG	NA
c.	SOV	Post.	GN	AN
d.	SOV	Post.	GN	NA

These four types could arguably be reduced even further. (5c) and (5d) are identical but for variation in the order of the adjective and noun; we might ignore this and collapse the two as the single OV type in (6b). (5a) and (5b) also fall together given the further assumption that the position of S relative to V is unimportant; the crucial point is the order of V and O. (5a) and (5b) together then give the VO type in (6a). There is some support for this move: Greenberg's initial survey contained no VOS languages, since none had then been discovered, but Malagasy and Gilbertese are now known to be VOS, and are also prepositional, NG and NA.

(6)a.	VO	Prep.	NG	NA
b.	OV	Post.	GN	AN

Work linking syntactic typology to word order change began from this distillation of Greenberg's word order correlations. Regarding the correlations as random or coincidental is incompatible with the tendency in modern linguistics to seek for universals; we therefore require some factor to unify these properties. Furthermore, the synchronic clusters of properties may also have a diachronic aspect: as Croft (1990: 203) puts it, 'if linguistic types fall into universal cross-linguistic patterns, then it is worth investigating if the cross-linguistic patterns also govern changes in linguistic type'.

Lehmann and Vennemann argue that the two linguistic types in (6) are indeed involved in change, and that the correlations shown there are not coincidental, but rather follow from the operation of a particular linguistic principle. Lehmann calls this 'a structural principle of language' or 'the principle of modifier placement' (1973b: 48); Vennemann (1974) christens it 'the principle of natural serialisation'. Since the last title is probably the most common in the literature, I shall use it here.

In any construction, it is possible to isolate a head, the central, governing element, and subsidiary modifiers. The head often exerts some linguistic influence on its modifiers: for instance, prepositions in Latin and German may require following nouns to take the accusative or dative case, while Italian determiners and adjectives agree with their head noun in gender and number; prepositions and nouns are therefore the heads of their phrases. Modifiers tend to be omissible while heads are not, as shown in (7), and heads give their name to the phrases in which they appear, so that *to the castle* is a Prepositional Phrase and *a red bus*, a Noun Phrase.

(7)a.   *She lives opposite the church.*
         She lives opposite.
         ***She lives the church.*

  b.   *Large drinks drown sorrows.*
         Drinks drown sorrows.
         ***Large drown sorrows.*

Vennemann notes that the clusters of properties in (6) follow from the assumption that *all* modifiers, or operators, in a language will appear consistently on one side of their heads, or operands; VO languages have head-modifier order, while OV languages are modifier-head. The principle of natural serialisation, which states that 'operators either all follow or all precede their operands, in the natural case' (Vennemann 1974: 347), will hold ideally for all languages and for all constructions in each language, and underlies Greenberg's word order universals.

Lehmann and Vennemann take the order of V and O to be the central parameter, which determines the serialisation of the language as operand-operator for VO, and operator-operand for OV languages. Languages which adhere strictly to one of the two types, with all their word order properties in harmony (that is, all operator-operand or all operand-operator) are termed consistent languages; consistency is said to be natural and preferred. Languages may become inconsistent, due to a shift in the order of V relative to O; a period of inconsistency will then follow as all other word order parameters move into line with the new basic clausal order. Gradually harmony will be restored, although the language will have changed from one consistent type to the other. We therefore have the hypothetical scenario in (8) for a change from VO to OV.

(8)a.   VO, Prep., NG, NA
         – consistent language, operand-operator
   b.   VO > OV
         OV, Prep., NG, NA
         – violates natural serialisation
   c.   Prep. > Post. other parameters gradually
         NG   > GN shift into line with the
         NA   > AN altered clause order.
   d.   OV, Post., GN, AN
         – consistent language, operator-operand

Matthews (1981: 9) suggests that Lehmann and Vennemann

think of a language in transition as like a drunk moving unsteadily between two lamp-posts. Latin, for example, had somehow lost its grip on the OV lamp-post and, in acquiring prepositions, had taken one step towards the other side of the road. Later, over the centuries, it took others ... In this way, the typological laws explain particular historical changes, or series of changes. It is because the lamp-posts are there that the drunks are seen to lurch ... in one direction or the other.

Vennemann clearly assigns a directly causal role to natural serialisation; the appearance of any discrepancy which violates it will trigger a chain of word order changes, reestablishing the ideal state of harmony. Inconsistent languages are in a temporary state of flux, in transition between harmonic types.

There is one clear, major flaw in this argument. If natural serialisation is indeed a causal principle, then it is relatively clear why the other word order parameters realign once V and O have reversed their order; but we have no motivation for the initial violation of consistency. However, Vennemann does offer an explanation, at least for changes from SOV to SVO.

Vennemann notes that many languages topicalise constituents, for emphasis, by moving them to sentence-initial position. If the Object is fronted in this way in an SVO or VSO language, the resulting word order is clearly distinct from neutral order; but in SOV languages alone, neutral and topicalised order are both NP NP V, as shown in (9).

(9)   Neutral order   O fronted
   a.   SOV NP_s NP_o V NP_o NP_s V
                The girl the boy loves   The boy the girl loves

   b.   SVO NP_s V NP_o NP_o NP_s V
                The girl loves the boy   The boy the girl loves

   c.   VSO   V NP_s NP_o NP_o V NP_s
                Loves the girl the boy   The boy loves the girl

It follows that OV languages alone 'require some additional means of indicating whether a certain structure (NP NP V) is a basic S-O-V structure or a secondary O-S-V structure' (Vennemann 1974: 365). The 'additional means' identified by Vennemann is consistent morphological case marking of the subject and object constituents, which resolves any ambiguity. Classical Latin, assumed to have a predominantly SOV order, is able to function because it possesses such a case system, as shown in (10).

(10)   Latin – SOV
        Neutral: *puella puerum amat*
                     S   O   V
                   'the girl the boy (+ accusative) loves'

        O-fronted: *puerum puella amat*
                     O   S   V
                   'the boy (+ accusative) the girl loves'

The case morphology of Latin and also Old English, both SOV languages, has however decayed across time, and the modern Romance languages such as French, as well as Modern English, have innovated SVO order. Vennemann explicitly links the SOV > SVO change to the loss of consistent morphological case-marking, claiming that, if sound change destroys case markers in an OV language, and no new morphological signals develop, the language will become VO with a more rigidly fixed word order.

However, Vennemann does not argue that SOV languages acquire SVO order immediately; instead, he proposes an intermediate strategy of TVX – a topic, the verb, then any other material. This is still problematic in the absence of morphological markers, as the topic could be either S or O. Consequently, since topics are most frequently identical with subjects, we have a further reinterpretation of TVX as SVX, or SVO. Subjects are now initial in the unmarked word order; if we wish to topicalise an object, it must be placed initially, but before S rather than instead of S, as shown in (11).

(11) Modern English – SVO
        Neutral: *I can't stand Alexandra*
                     S   V   O
        O fronted: *Alexandra I can't stand.*
                     O   S   V

It is true that some languages undergoing a change of this sort, like German, retain XV order in subordinate clauses; however, Vennemann sees this as evidence for his proposal rather than against it, since topicalisation in subordinate clauses is perhaps less likely.

Once the basic, central parameter of OV has changed to VO in this way, the principle of natural serialisation will be activated, levelling out the discrepancy which has been created by causing all other word order parameters to shift into line, and re-creating consistency. Vennemann therefore sees Greenberg's correlations as diachronic implicational universals.

Vennemann and Lehmann suggest a number of other reasons for the OV > VO change; these include borrowing, and the grammaticalisation of afterthought patterns, so that sentences like *I the dog saw – Rover* would ultimately become *I saw Rover* and *I saw the dog*. However, we do not know why such afterthoughts might be grammaticalised, although of course we do know why they occur sentence-finally. Very little attention has been paid to the opposite change of VO > OV, although Vennemann speculates that it might occur if a language developed consistent morphological markers for S and O. The only strategy which has been worked out at all consistently is therefore Vennemann's SOV > TVX > SVO pathway. We shall consider criticisms of this strategy, and of the whole typological approach to historical syntax, in the next section.

6.2.3   *Criticisms of the typological approach.*
6.2.3.1 Vennemann's SOV > TVX > SVO strategy.

Vennemann's claims that SOV becomes SVO via a stage of topicalisation, that this is due to morphological decay, and that it forms the necessary first step in an overall realignment of word order parameters, are all open to criticism. For instance, if there is so much typological pressure on a language to stay consistent, why should SOV languages not fix their word order as SOV and develop an alternative topicalisation process rather than violating natural serialisation? Moreover, although the TVX > SVO change is quite transparent, the motivation for the earlier SOV > TVX stage is not clear, since it solves no problems. The link with the loss of morphological marking of S and O also cannot be consistently maintained; for example, some languages like Ijo maintain fixed SOV word order but lack case morphology, while Proto-Niger-Congo, the ancestor of Ijo, was also arguably SOV without case-marking – which does not explain the fact that many Niger-Congo languages *have* changed to SVO (Hyman 1975, cited in Comrie 1981). Conversely, VO order has evolved in some languages which retain nominative and accusative case markers, such as Lithuanian, which preserves perhaps the most archaic case system of any Indo-European language (Comrie 1981). Finally, the order of V relative to O cannot universally be the initial step in a change of word order patterns, since Latin changed its Noun Phrase properties to Noun Genitive and Noun Adjective and acquired Prepositions before basic clausal order shifted from OV to VO. We shall return to the transition from Latin to the modern Romance languages in 6.2.4 below.

6.2.3.2 More general criticisms

There are two main criticisms of theories like Vennemann's and Lehmann's. First, the claim that natural serialisation is explanatory and causal is questioned; the typological data and the notion of consistency are then seen as factors to be explained rather than being truly explanatory themselves. Secondly, Lehmann and Vennemann are accused of weakening Greenberg's cautiously formulated implicational universals by producing composite statements, while at the same time seeing these universals as expressing natural states towards which languages should progress: as Watkins (1976: 306) says, ' ... in Lehmann's work broods a theory which elevates some of Greenberg's interesting quasi-universals to the dubious status of an intellectual straitjacket, into which the facts of various Indo-European languages must be fitted, willy-nilly, rightly or wrongly'. These themes will recur throughout the discussion below.

Hawkins (1979) sees Lehmann and Vennemann as formulating 'trigger-chain theories', where an initial change activates a principle which in turn motivates a subsequent set of changes. He argues that 'trigger-chain theories are internally inconsistent. They assume that language universals can be both weak and strong constraints on language evolution' (Hawkins 1979: 641). Thus, the universals must exert a sufficiently weak hold on linguistic development to allow the initial violation to occur; but they must also be strong enough to require a complete word order reanalysis once a single parameter *has* shifted. Lightfoot (1979b: 389) challenges specifically this last attribute of natural serialisation, arguing that 'it is certainly oversimplified to posit a simple syntactic drag-chain, set off in the parent language and relentlessly followed by the daughters'. For instance, Lehmann and Vennemann crucially claim that the Indo-European languages manifest a gradual drift from SOV to SVO. As Lightfoot points out, however, their case rests on the reconstruction of PIE as an SOV language; and they make no mention of the pitfalls inherent in syntactic reconstruction. In fact, PIE may not have been consistently SOV, or had any single, basic word order; non-OV orders are attested with at least equal frequency in early Indo-European daughter languages. Problems of interpretation arise here, since the daughter languages studied in most depth may depend on the word order a linguist wishes to reconstruct; consequently, those preferring to see PIE as SOV tend to focus on Sanskrit and Hittite, rather than early Greek.

We have, as Lightfoot points out, very few attested cases of complete typological shifts; those which are cited, such as the PIE – Latin – French change from SOV to SVO, rely partly on reconstructed evidence, take millennia to operate, and often even then are left incomplete – French, for instance, is almost consistently SVO but maintains the modifier-head order Determiner Noun, as in *la maison, des enfants*, in the Noun Phrase. Lightfoot notes that the concept of lag has been introduced for cases where one property may develop long after another, but as we have seen, French is in no apparent hurry to tidy up its Noun Phrase, while Persian has had OV clause order but all the other characteristic properties of a VO language for thousands of years. It seems that invoking lag is unhelpful, only showing explanations based on consistency to be particularistic rather than universal: as Smith puts it (1981: 49),

if a language acquires a characteristic that brings it into typological line, this is supposed to be due to the pressure of typological consistency; if, on the other hand, changes occur which are not susceptible to this explanation, they are due to social forces ... pragmatic factors ... and above all to borrowing. When all these variables are excluded there is always the ultimate escape-hatch that language X has not undergone this change yet.

One might argue that an initial change in one word order parameter sets a target of regaining harmony which the language must reach, irrespective of the length of time this may take. However, this implies that the change, once it has begun, is inevitable and has a predetermined end-point, a conclusion redolent of teleology, the notion that linguistic development is preordained and directional and that languages in some sense 'know' where they are going. We shall return to this unwelcome philosophical corollary in Chapter 12; for the moment, it should be noted that the inevitability of change, for instance from SOV to SVO in Indo-European, simply cannot be upheld, unless we maintain that Hindi, which remains OV, is an exceptionally slow starter, while the Celtic languages, which are VSO, got lost on the way to SVO but will make it in the end.

Lightfoot (1979b) argues that there are no independent diachronic principles of change such as natural serialisation, and accuses Lehmann and Vennemann of proposing a mystical approach; after all, if children build their grammars independently and have no access to their parents' grammars, what could the domain of such diachronic principles be?

Languages are learned, and grammars constructed, by the individuals of each generation. They do not have racial memories, so as to know in some sense that their language has gradually developed from, say, an SOV type and towards SVO, or that it must continue along that path. After all, if there were a prescribed hierarchy of changes to be performed, how could a child, confronted with a language exactly halfway along this hierarchy, know whether the language was changing from type X to type Y, or vice versa? (Lightfoot 1979b: 389)

Instead, explanations for changes must follow from the structure of the grammar, or from external factors such as language contact.

Smith (1981) provides a further critique of the typological approach.

Smith considers that 'properties of normality, unmarkedness, etc., do not distinguish consistent from inconsistent languages and the notion is either vacuous, being merely a label for arbitrarily segregated (groups of) languages; or points up a statistical property which is itself in need of explanation' (Smith 1981: 40), and supports this view by considering and rejecting four predictions which should be borne out if pressure towards consistency is a valid explanation for syntactic change.

a   *Consistent languages should be statistically preponderant*

Smith believes that we know too little about too many of the world's languages to produce a decent definition of consistency. If we accept Lehmann's and Vennemann's definitions, we are still faced with a problem, since consistent languages do not seem to form a strong majority. In fact, Lehmann himself admits in later work that 'it would be remarkable if any language were completely consistent' (1978: x), and that 'few languages are even approximately consistent' (1978: 400). To return to Matthews' analogy of the drunks and the lamp-posts, it follows that 'we cannot actually point to any language which is leaning gratefully, even for the odd century or two, against either of our typological lamp-posts. Some are very close to one of them, but not quite there. Others can be seen to stagger purposefully in one direction. Others ... are just swaying about somewhere in the middle' (Matthews 1981: 10). The existence of disharmonies cannot disprove the claim that harmonic languages are natural or preferred; but we will then have to regard the majority of attested languages as being in transition. This is scarcely convincing, particularly since inconsistent languages take so long to remedy the situation, if indeed they ever do so at all.

b   *Consistent languages should be easier to learn*

As Smith (1981: 43) notes, 'there is no reliable evidence that any language is, overall, harder for children to learn than any other'. One might acquire evidence on this hypothesis by considering bilingual children who are learning both consistent and inconsistent languages, or by studying the speed with which children acquire inconsistent and consistent constructions in a single language. However, no such experiments have been carried out.

However, Smith's view on this prediction seems to have altered somewhat in more recent work, following developments in Chomskyan syntactic theory, which now hypothesises principles and parameters as part of our innate language faculty. That is, Universal Grammar 'consists of a highly structured and restrictive system of principles with certain open parameters, to be fixed by experience. As these parameters are fixed, a grammar is determined' (Chomsky 1981: 38; see also Chapter 5 above). To take for the moment parameters relating to word order, there is a major division between languages with some basic word order and those, like Warlbiri and Dyirbal, where every order of words gives a well-formed sentence. As Chomsky notes, one could set such a parameter on the basis of rather little data. In languages without free word order, another parameter would be set according to the basic word order, and this might itself set further parameters: for instance, if all VSO languages have prepositions, a child learning Welsh and consequently setting the basic word order parameter at VSO might also automatically have the adpositional parameter set for prepositions.

Smith (1989: 69) suggests that the principles and parameters model 'is capable of making implicational or correlational statements over grammars not just over data' - earlier typological work concentrated on data and not on grammars or rule systems. Smith proposes that there may be a head-first / head-last parameter, which would be set according to whether the majority of constructions in the language being acquired were operand-operator or operator-operand. In consistent languages, children would have to learn only one phrase-type; setting the parameter would generalise this to all constructions, so that a considerable amount of acquisition would be 'free'. A child learning a non-consistent language would be obliged to learn the exceptional constructions individually.

This hypothesis again shows the benefits which may follow from combining a restrictive formal model with a functional approach. Smith's (1989) predictions might profitably be tested using child language data: for instance, he argues that the setting of a parameter should create certain specific errors in children's speech. There is still, however, the problem of why consistent languages are so few, if their advantages in acquisition are so great.

c   *Consistent languages should be more stable*

Lehmann's and Vennemann's theories would predict that consistent languages should generally maintain their harmonic characteristics, while any which have become inconsistent should move back towards consistency. Unfortunately, this suggests that more languages should now be consistent, and all languages more consistent, than in the past; and this evidently is not the case. Smith denies that shifts from one type to another are explicable in terms of a drift towards consistency, or are even particularly meaningful: notably, since languages must be either VO or

OV, 'clearly a change from one must be towards the other, but this is no more revealing than the old claim that languages undergo "cyclic" changes from analytic to synthetic and back again' (Smith 1981: 49).

d   *Consistent languages should be easier to process*

A benefit which might theoretically follow from consistency, or motivate a movement towards consistency, is ease of processing or understanding. Again, there is little or no relevant data, and again Smith (1981: 50) is dismissive: 'that some language should be overall more difficult to process than another seems *a priori* implausible and barely testable'. However, certain *structures* may be harder to process than others, partly due to inconsistency. Smith still sees consistency as something to be explained, not as an explanation; but ease of processing may supply part of the motivation for harmony. That is, 'it is ... mistaken to view consistency as providing an explanation for perceptual ease or difficulty. Rather, what consistency there is, is itself explained in part by the effects of perception' (Smith 1981: 51). We shall pursue this point in the next section, as we review some attempts to salvage the connection of typological consistency and syntactic change.

6.2.4   *Amendments to the typological view*
6.2.4.1 Introduction

In the light of these criticisms, we should perhaps abandon consistency and, indeed, any link of typologically established universals with syntactic change. Not all critics of Lehmann and Vennemann would see this as the right way forward; Harris (1984b: 183), for instance, argues that 'while some of the more extreme claims made in favour of the utility of a typological approach to historical syntax cannot be upheld, it is nevertheless the case that any theory which ignores the insights gained by such an approach is substantially reduced by so doing'. In this section, we shall examine some emendations of the typological view, which include consistency as a factor implicated in syntactic change without regarding it as explanatory or causal. First, we shall consider John Hawkins' work; and secondly, we shall pursue the connection of perceptual factors and ease of processing with linguistic typology and syntactic change.

6.2.4.2 Hawkins' contribution

As we have already seen, Hawkins (1979, 1980, 1983) has two main objections to Lehmann's and Vennemann's 'trigger-chain theories'. If Greenberg's universals really are universals, then they should not be readily contravened; yet Vennemann must assume that the synchronic implicational universals are violated by an initial change to activate natural serialisation, which will then (eventually) restore consistency. Furthermore, Hawkins is concerned that ' ... the reformulation of Greenberg's universals by Lehmann and Vennemann introduces an intolerable number of exceptions, misses more patterns, and misrepresents the careful balance between non-statistical and statistical statements in Greenberg's work' (1979: 622). In an attempt to remove these difficulties, Hawkins reformulates Greenberg's implicational universals in a more constrained way; abandons and replaces the principle of natural serialisation; and attempts to account for the rise of disharmony.

Hawkins claims that languages will never violate synchronic universals; this is akin to Lightfoot's idea that no change will ever create an impossible grammar. However, to uphold this claim, he must make Greenberg's implicational universals exceptionless. He does this in general by adding conditions and making the statements more complex. For instance, the implication SOV > GN (in SOV languages, the genitive precedes the noun) is not exceptionless, since there are some SOV languages with NG order; however, Hawkins increases the scope of the implication, noting that in SOV languages with the adjective before the noun, the genitive also always precedes the noun (SOV $\supset$ (AN $\supset$ GN)). The resulting statement may be less sweeping, but does have the virtue of being exceptionless, allowing Hawkins to predict that no language violating this (or any other) universal will arise. Moreover, if these universals are exceptionless rather than statistical tendencies, they might plausibly be inherited by children as part of Universal Grammar, meaning that no independent, extra-grammatical diachronic principles need be proposed, while again connecting a theory of change with a theory of grammar.

Hawkins also does not see consistency as inviolable, and does not assume that a language must serialise all operators on one side of their operands. Instead, he introduces the principle of Cross-Category Harmony (CCH), which asserts that 'there is a quantifiable preference, across languages, for the ratio of preposed to postposed operators within one operand category to generalise to the other operand categories' (Hawkins 1979: 644–5). Moreover, 'CCH predicts that the more similar the balance in operator preposing and postposing across the different operand categories, the greater the number of languages – and the more dissimilar, the fewer the languages' (Hawkins 1979: 646). In other words, no head need consistently take its modifiers to left or right, but there will be a certain proportion of head-modifier to modifier-head constructions for any given head, and that proportion will tend to spread to other heads. The more heads in a language follow this pattern, the more common and popular the language type will be. The major prediction, then, is that more languages and more constructions within languages will follow Cross-Category Harmony than the converse; and this seems to be borne out statistically.

Cross-Category Harmony also predicts that, if one head-modifier order alters significantly, others will follow. Hawkins proposes two external explanations for this initial change. First, he introduces a Mobility Principle, which predicts that certain specifiable modifiers will shift away from the characteristic serialisation pattern of a language before others. Secondly, he formulates the Heaviness Serialisation Principle, which states that light or short modifiers, like determiners in a Noun Phrase, will typically appear on the left of their phrase, while heavy modifiers like relative clauses will tend to be on the right.

Some of the criticisms of Lehmann's and Vennemann's work in 6.2.3 also apply to Hawkins' - and there are some new ones. For instance, Smith (1981: 42) is concerned about Hawkins' complex universals, arguing that ' ... multi-valued implicational statements can be devised *ad hoc* to cater for ... new complexities, but the strong impression remains that no counter-examples to any of these universals would be a very great surprise: in brief, anything seems to be possible'. Just as worryingly, Hawkins' principles of heaviness and mobility are neither sufficiently detailed nor convincingly explanatory. Which modifiers are mobile and why? When does a modifier become heavy, and why should it then develop a preference for final position? We may have at least a partial answer to the last question; and to find it, we must return to perceptual factors.

6.2.4.3 Perceptual factors and syntactic change

Work on perceptual factors might help our investigation of historical syntax and typology by explaining why consistency might be violated, and perhaps also why a certain degree of consistency might be preferred. Let us start with some evidence that matters of perception can indeed contribute to syntactic change.

Bever and Langendoen (1971, 1972) argue that both adults and children use certain perceptual strategies in interpreting sentences; for instance, English speakers and learners will preferentially analyse a sequence of NP V NP as SVO. However, although adults seem to switch these strategies off when faced with certain constructions, children cannot; thus, as we saw in the last chapter, young children learning English tend to interpret passives like *The dog was bitten by the cat* as equivalent to *The dog bit the cat*, while adults have learned that passives contravene the usual 'Subject/ agent first' rule. Bever and Langendoen further argue that these perceptual strategies may be responsible for certain changes, and their example involves English relative clauses.

In Modern English, the sentences in (12a) and (12b) are grammatical, while those in (12c) and (12d) are not. The question is how this pattern of acceptability arose.

(12)a.   *The girl who needs to see the doctor is sitting outside.*
   b.   *The receptionist comforted the girl who needed to see the doctor.*
   c.   ***The girl needs to see the doctor is sitting outside.*
   d.   ***The receptionist comforted the girl needed to see the doctor.*

Throughout the history of English, sentences like (13) have been ill-formed; however, (14), where *ancient* refers to the object, was acceptable until about 1700.

(13)   ***The boy read the book was clever.*

(14)   *The boy read the book was ancient.*

After 1700, a relative pronoun became obligatory in sentences like (14), although some related constructions, as in (15), are still acceptable for some speakers. It may be that the constructions in (15) do not really involve relative clauses in close dependency on the noun; they are therefore permissible in a way that, for instance, ***There are people like parsnips*, where *People who like parsnips* clearly is a relative clause, would not be.

(15)a.   *There are lots of vulgar people live in Grosvenor Square.* (Wilde)
   b.   *It was haste killed the yellow snake.* (Kipling)
         (from Bever and Langendoen 1971: 442)

According to Bever and Langendoen, this change in relative clause formation follows from a perceptual strategy specifying that a Noun Phrase should be interpreted as the beginning of a sentence, and a Verb Phrase as the end. Sentences in which a verb introduces a relative clause must therefore carry some special marker to warn listeners against implementing this strategy. In (13), the sequence *the book was clever*, being NP VP, would always have been misinterpreted as an independent (and semantically anomalous) sentence without some relative marker earlier in the string, accounting for the unacceptability of (13) at all periods of English. However, sentences like (14) would be unproblematic in Old English, since case-marking and less rigid word order would make the perceptual strategy less crucial. Only as case morphology disappeared and word order became more fixed did the NP VP = S strategy become both reliable and necessary. From this period, sentences like (14) would be misanalysed, creating ambiguity and perceptual complexity, as shown in (16).

(16)a.   *The boy read [the book was ancient]*
                    NP   VP   = main clause
   b.   *He sente after [a cherl was in the town]*
                    NP   VP = main clause
         'he sent after a man (who) was in the town'
                                      (Chaucer)

Since the application of the perceptual strategy in (16) would enable many false segmentations of NP VP as main clauses, causing potential misunderstandings, these constructions died gradually out of the language; the change is gradual since we can assume that the ambiguity created did not significantly endanger communication. The perceptual strategy is, however, maintained, presumably due to its usefulness in many other types of constructions.

Let us return to the relationship of perceptual strategies with consistency. We have already noted Smith's (1981) objection that there is no evidence that consistent languages are easier to process overall than inconsistent ones. However, Kuno (1974) produces evidence that certain constructions may be more perceptually problematic than others, and that these may show a correlation with discrepant serialisation. For instance, natural serialisation predicts that SOV languages will have relative clauses preceding their head noun, while in VSO languages relative clauses will be postnominal. Kuno links this fact to the perceptual difficulties created by centre-embedding.

Centre-embedding makes two clauses or phrases into one by inserting one into the middle of the other. As shown in (17), this creates sentences which are so difficult for native speakers to analyse that they are generally judged to be ill-formed.

(17)a.   ** *The cheese [the rat [the cat chased] ate] was rotten.*
   b.   ** *That [that [the world is round] is obvious] is dubious.*

If these structures are made right-embedded, then they are perfectly intelligible (see (18)), showing that centre-embedding is clearly the source of the difficulty.

(18)   *The cat chased the rat [that ate the cheese [that was rotten]].*

Whereas English characteristically has postnominal relative clauses, Japanese, an SOV language, has prenominal relative clauses and therefore left-embedding, as shown in (19). However, while left-embedded structures like (19) are easily interpretable, centre-embedded sentences like (20) are extremely difficult for Japanese speakers to process.

(19)   *Neko go oikaketa nezumi ga tabeta cheese wa kusatte ita*
        cat   chased rat   ate   rotten was
          'the cat chased the rat that ate the cheese that was rotten'

(20)   *John ga [Mary ga [Jane ga aisite iru] syoonen ni*
                                   loving is   boy to
        kaita] tegami o yonda
        wrote letter   read
        'John read the letter that Mary wrote to the boy that Jane was in love with'

Kuno conjectures that centre-embedding demands too much of our short-term memory; presumably we function best linguistically if we can analyse and understand a sentence section by section, instead of having to listen to the entire construction and interpret it as a whole. Centre-embedding is certainly a relatively unpopular strategy cross-linguistically, and languages tend to evolve procedures to avoid or minimise it. Kuno (1974) shows that postnominal relative clauses in SOV languages, and prenominal relatives in VSO languages, guarantee frequent centre-embedding, which arises much more rarely when SOV languages have prenominal, and VSO languages postnominal relative clauses. He therefore hypothesises that these language types predominantly show the latter type of relative clause/noun order (which happens to fit their expected serialisation patterns and therefore contributes to consistency) to reduce the risk of perceptual ambiguity arising from centre-embedding.

For much the same reason, VSO languages tend to have prepositions and SOV languages, postpositions. As shown in (21), the opposite, non-harmonic order would produce difficult centre-embedded structures with clusters of adpositions initially or finally.

(21)   VSO a. Prepositions
                    colour [of flowers [in vase [on table]]]
              b. Postpositions
                    colour [flowers [vase [table on] in] of]

        SOV a. Prepositions
                    [of [in [on table] vase] flowers] colour
              b. Postpositions
                    [[[table on] vase in] flowers of] colour

Vincent (1976: 55) sees Kuno's hypothesis that 'the universals uncovered by Greenberg are due to limitations on the human perceptual mechanisms' as a solution to two now familiar difficulties with consistency. First, since Greenberg's correlations are not absolute, but statistical or probabilistic, they allow mixed types; and it is unclear why these should *necessarily* be under pressure to change. Second, the notion of change determined by a drive towards consistency assumes goal-directed change and is therefore teleological. Vincent argues (1976: 55) that invoking perception solves both these problems:

perceptual factors are of necessity 'fuzzy', since the degree to which they obtrude on the successful performance of any act of linguistic communication varies with the amount of context non-linguistically recoverable, or more generally with the amount of redundancy. Hence any constraints on languages deriving from limitations on the perceptual system would only make themselves felt gradually over a period of time, thereby allowing for the existence of intermediate stages and mixed types. Furthermore, problems of the processing of speech impinge directly on the speaker's conscious linguistic ability, where reference to goal-directed explanations is inherently admissible.

Moreover, Vincent (1976) reports a further case of apparent avoidance of centre-embedding, this time from Latin.

Although Classical Latin shows very considerable freedom of word order, the basic order is SOV. However, while Verb Phrases are modifier-head, as expected in a harmonic OV language, Noun Phrases are head-modifier, so that relative clauses, adjectives and genitives are typically postnominal. Classical Latin also has prepositions, whereas consistent OV languages like Japanese have postpositions.

Vincent accepts that Proto-Indo-European was SOV, at least at some stage. Since the modern Romance languages are fairly consistently SVO, the split of NP and VP properties in Classical Latin may indicate a large-scale change in progress: Latin is in transition from SOV to SVO. Some corroborating evidence is available within Latin; for instance, the early Latin modifier-head order of standard-(marker)-adjective in comparatives, as in *tē maior* 'you bigger', gradually gives way to the head-modifier construction adjective-marker-standard *maior quam tū* 'bigger than you': the latter pattern is characteristic of VO languages.

Vincent does not address the question of how SOV began initially to shift, but notes that once it does, the SOV basic order with postnominal relative clauses will produce numerous, perceptually problematic centre-embedded structures. We would thus predict the occurrence of the Latin constructions in (22); all are centre-embedded, and show the typical build-up of verbs sentence-finally.

(22)   *Puerum quem Maria amabat advenit.*
        boy who Mary loved arrived

        Puerum quem Maria amabat Claudia laudavit.
        boy who Mary loved Claudia praised

        Claudia puerum quem Maria amabat laudavit.
        Claudia boy who Mary loved praised

        Puella puerum qui libros quos voluit
        girl boy who books that he-wanted
        repperit laudavit.
        he-found praised
        (From Vincent 1976: 56)

However, Latin seems to have had two strategies to prevent such structures from surfacing. Vincent calls the first Extraposition from Noun

Phrase, a process shifting relative clauses to sentence-final position, as shown in (23).

(23)   *Mulierem quae pisces vendit aspicio.*
        woman who fish sells I–see

Extraposition

Mulierem aspicio quae pisces vendit.

The second strategy is Heavy NP Shift, which this time moves an entire Noun Phrase to the end of the sentence; as shown in (24), this produces SVO order. This movement of long or complex phrases is in accordance with Hawkins' Heaviness Serialisation Principle, which holds that heavy modifiers may follow the head even though lighter ones precede it.

(24)   *Natura homini addidit [rationem qua regerentur appetitus]*
        'nature to-man has added reason by-which may-be-governed appetites'

Extraposition seems to have been the preferred process for avoiding centre-embedding until the start of the Christian era, by which time the morphological system of Latin was breaking down. Since Extraposition maintained SOV order, it required case-marking to minimise ambiguity, and the reduction in morphological marking consequently led to a decline in Extraposition. Heavy NP Shift was then employed to a far greater extent, producing SVO constructions; these were gradually generalised, leaving SVO as the majority word order type. This allows for the change from OV to VO; in fact, as Comrie (1981: 207) observes, 'most SOV languages, even those that are often classified as rigidly verb-final (e.g. Turkish, Japanese), do in fact allow some leakage of noun phrases to the right of the verb, so all that would be required would be an increase in this possibility'. In Latin, this increase is motivated by the decline of inflectional morphology; and the subsequent change of other Verb Phrase parameters to head-modifier order may have followed because of the perceptual advantages of consistency.

Our introduction of perceptual factors has effectively returned us to Vennemann's (1974) original claims concerning syntactic change. His central hypotheses are that ambiguity, or opacity, arises in SOV languages which lose case morphology; that this ambiguity requires resolution, which takes the form of reanalysis to SVO basic order; and that this central change introduces disharmony and violates the principle of natural serialisation, which sets in motion a subsequent series of changes bringing all other word-order parameters into line with the new basic clausal order.

We have seen that certain changes may increase consistency because discrepant serialisation often favours the occurrence of perceptually problematic constructions, such as centre-embedded sentences. However, no syntactic change of this kind seems to be necessary; inconsistent languages are likely to become more consistent only if problems of ambiguity arise – and even then, the reintroduction of harmony is one of many possible routes speakers might take in resolving difficulties of interpretation.

It is not at present clear why so many resolutions of perceptual difficulties involve a movement towards consistency; but one tentative suggestion might help us to unify our findings on perceptual problems with Hawkins' ideas on Cross-Category Harmony. It may be that the main problem with accounts such as those of Lehmann and Vennemann is the specific nature of laws like natural serialisation. The factor favouring consistency might instead be an extremely general one, namely the phenomenon of iconicity.

Iconicity was defined generally in Chapter 4 as a non-arbitrary link between some aspect of language and some aspect of the world. Haiman (1985: 1) notes that compelling functional explanations could be, but have not generally been, based on iconicity. Such explanations would show

that linguistic forms are frequently the way they are because, like diagrams, they resemble the conceptual structures they are used to convey; or, that linguistic structures resemble each other because the different conceptual domains they represent are thought of in the same way. These ideas are not new; they are simply somewhat unfashionable at the moment. They will probably continue to be unfashionable until and unless linguistics gets over its envy of physics.

Iconicity may initially seem an unlikely explanation for consistency, since there is little overt reflection of the world in either order of head and modifiers. However, this imitation of properties of the referent or the situation described is only characteristic of isomorphism (the one-form-one-meaning condition) and motivation, the two subtypes of iconicity discussed in 4.3.3. There is another, language-*internal* subtype of iconicity, which we might call automorphism (Haiman 1985: 4), and which holds that linguistic elements which are alike semantically should also resemble one another formally or morphologically. That is, automorphism deals with correspondences or shared behaviour between two or more units in a linguistic system.

Automorphic iconicity is relevant to word order in that, presumably, verbs are to objects as prepositions are to noun phrases or nouns to adjectives: in other words, the semantic relationship of all heads to their modifiers is the same. This conceptual relationship would be reflected in formal similarity if the order of heads and modifiers was the same across the constructions of a language – in other words, if Cross-Category Harmony was maintained.

Iconicity represents a general tendency in language, but is by no means a law forcing change in a particular direction. Counericonic structures may therefore arise; but at the same time, it seems natural that, given a choice of a number of alternative strategies to resolve a perceptual problem, speakers might select one conforming with such a broad, conceptually-based tendency. Where languages fall into types, this should consequently not be seen as a cause, but as an effect of iconicity.

In other words, consistency is not a perfect state towards which all languages eternally struggle, driven by the irresistible force of a principle like natural serialisation; instead, it is a tendency observable in languages, which itself requires explanation. Part of this explanation may involve iconicity and perceptual mechanisms; but even these do not make consistency fully explicable. Instead, we may have to see consistency as similar to analogy (with which iconicity shows clear links, both being concerned with parallels of form and meaning), in 'providing a preferred pathway for change once that change has been independently motivated' (Harris 1984b: 188): and again like analogy, iconicity is too unconstrained a concept to be either predictable or predictive.

6.3   Grammaticalisation

6.3.1   *Introduction*

Meillet (1912: 131), in the first discussion of the phenomenon, defines grammaticalisation as 'le passage d'un mot autonome au rôle d'élément grammatical' ('the shift of an independent word to the status of a grammatical element'): words from major lexical categories, such as nouns, verbs and adjectives, become minor, grammatical categories such as prepositions, adverbs and auxiliaries, which in turn may be further grammaticalised into affixes. Full words, with their own lexical content, thus become form words, which simply mark a particular construction; and this categorial change tends to be accompanied by a reduction in phonological form and a 'bleaching' of meaning. Thus, grammaticalisation is not only a syntactic change, but a global change affecting also the morphology, phonology and semantics. As preliminary examples, we might include the Old English nouns *hād* 'state, quality' and *līc* 'body', which have become the Modern English suffixes *-hood* and *-ly*; German *Viertel* 'quarter' and *Drittel* 'third', which contain reduced forms of the noun *Teil* 'part'; and the development of Spanish verbal suffixes from originally autonomous verbs shown in (25). The forms on the left are Spanish reflexes of Latin *habēre*, which has grammaticalised to give the suffixes on the right.

(25)   Spanish
          tu hás 'you have' – *tu comprar-ás* 'you will buy'
          ellos hán 'they have' – *ellos comprar-án* 'they will buy'

If grammaticalisation is not purely syntactic, why should it be included here? So far, attempts have been made in this book to consider changes involving a single area of the grammar in each chapter. However, although this approach of presenting each component of the grammar as diachronically self-contained may be helpful for expository purposes, readers should not be over-protected from the fact that changes may affect more than one level of a language, or that a change on one level may motivate further developments elsewhere. Indeed, such cases have already been presented: we have seen that analogy may operate on syntactic as well as morphological structures, and that sound change may affect the morphology by removing or altering morphological markers. In the last section, it was also established that such morphological loss may be a contributing factor in the fixing of word order, indicating that chains of changes may build up across linguistic components, and over time.

Grammaticalisation is the cross-componential change *par excellence*, involving as it does developments in the phonology, morphology, syntax and semantics, but is discussed here for three reasons. First, grammaticalisation was discovered through typological surveys, providing a clear link with the work reported above. Secondly, grammaticalisation represents a directional change – or more accurately, a directional syndrome of related changes – and can consequently be dealt with under the heading of drift. Finally, we shall see below that grammaticalisation is also connected with iconicity.

Before exploring these theoretical issues further, however, we shall exemplify grammaticalisation in more detail by exploring the most famous and most commonly quoted case of grammaticalisation, which involves the French negative.

6.3.2   *The French negative*

Classical Latin (Harris 1978) had two negative particles, the sentential qualifier *non*, and *haud*, which negated single constituents as in the phrase *haud male* 'not badly'. *Haud* gradually disappeared, perhaps disfavoured since all other Latin negative markers had initial [n] like *non*, while *haud* clearly did not (see (26)).

(26)   *numquam*   'never'
        nihil   'nothing'
        nullus   'nothing'
        nemo   'no-one'

Latin passed the remaining *non* negative on to its Romance daughters. The majority retain a single negative marker, like Italian *no(n)*, Spanish *no* and Portuguese *não*, but in Old French two distinct negatives, *non* and *ne*, developed.

Initially, *non* appeared in stressed, and *ne* in unstressed positions. In Modern French, however, the distinction has become a grammatical one, so that *non* is now used disjunctively, everywhere except when the negative is directly conjoined to the verb phrase, while *ne* is used conjunctively, adjacent to the verb (27).

(27)   *ne*
        elle ne dort pas   'she is not sleeping'
        pour ne pas exagérer   'not to exaggerate'
        ne le faisant pas   'not doing it'

        non
        non-fumeur   'non-smoker'
        vous venez ou non?   'are you coming or not?'

In early French, *ne* began to be reinforced by the particles *mie*, *point*, *goute* and *pas*, which had been independent nouns; their meanings and some examples are given in (28).

(28)a.   *pas* < Latin *passus* 'a step'
          blet n'i poet pas creistre
          'wheat cannot grow there'
              (Chanson de Roland)
          Je ne vais pas
          'I am not going'

   b.   *point* < Latin *punctum* 'place, spot'
          Belin ne crienst point sa menace
          'B. did not fear his threat'
            (Roman de Brut, Wace, 1155)
          Je n'ai point de café
          'I have no coffee'

   c.   *goute* < Latin *gutta* 'drop'
          Je n'ai goute d'argent
          'I have no money'
              (Foulet: *Petite Syntaxe de l'Ancien Français*, Paris 1968)
          Je n'y vois goutte
          'I don't see anything'
              (modern colloquial)

d.　*mie* < Latin *mīca* 'crumb'
　　Altrement ne m'amerat il mie
　　'Otherwise he will not love me'
　　(Chanson de Roland)

These particles may initially have carried an emphatic, reinforcing meaning, like English *I don't give a damn, I don't care a bit/a fig/one iota*. Such negative reinforcers are a popular emphatic strategy in language; in Latin, for instance, 'nouns designating such concepts as feathers, straws and pips frequently reinforce nouns in representations of popular speech' (Harris 1978: 25). The French 'negative auxiliaries' later lost their emphatic meaning and marked the end of the scope of negation, before becoming semantically negative themselves (Posner 1985: 171). However, in French one of these reinforcers, *pas*, has triumphed over its rivals to become a fixed and necessary component of the negative construction. We shall therefore concentrate here on the history of *pas*.

Price (1984) asserts that, as well as being an emphatic form, *pas* would initially have been used to reinforce verbs of motion, where its meaning of 'step' would have been particularly appropriate. However, by its earliest written attestations in the early twelfth century, *pas* could be used with any verb (see (29)).

(29)　*Je ne vais un pas*　'I'm not going a step'
　　　↓
　　Je ne vais pas　'I'm <u>not</u> going (a step)'
　　Blet n'i poet pas creistre　'Wheat cannot grow there'
　　　↓　　　　　　　　　　(Chanson de Roland)
　　Je ne peux pas le faire　'I can't do it'

By the earliest texts, *pas* often does not seem particularly emphatic, and is simply a negative particle, having lost its original nominal meaning and changed category from noun to adverb. Until the mid fifteenth century, it shared this role with *point*, *mie* and *gout(t)e*. However, *pas* was the preferred particle in the centre and west of France and in Paris, and as literary French became equated with the Parisian variety, *pas* became correspondingly popular. It first ousted *mie*, which was geographically restricted to the north and east, and although *point* and *gout(t)e* are still used occasionally, the latter in colloquial contexts only, *pas* is now the only negative particle in common use in the majority of spoken and written French; it has been compulsory in negative constructions since at least the seventeenth century.

The use of *pas* has now entered another phase, since in modern colloquial French it is not only a necessary marker of negativity but often the sole marker; *ne* is being progressively dropped. Sentences like *Je suis pas allée*, 'I didn't go', *J'ai pas dit ça* 'I didn't say that' are becoming increasingly acceptable. Ashby (1981) collected data from 37 speakers from Tours, and found that all deleted at least some instances of *ne*, although the precise amount varied considerably, from categorical deletion to 94 per cent retention, depending on a number of sociolinguistic and linguistic factors. The former included the speaker's age, gender and class, while the latter included matters of style (*ne* was produced more often in formal speech); of phonology (*ne* was more likely to be retained postpausally, or intervocalically if one vowel was nasal); and of clause type (*ne* appeared more often in subordinate than in main clauses).

Pas has therefore become so well established in the negative construction that it has acquired a negative value. In the same way, *personne*, *rien*, *jamais*, *plus* and *aucun*, which, as shown in (30), initially had positive meanings, have acquired a negative sense through continual use in negative constructions and a consequent association with negativity.

(30)   *personne* < Latin *persōna* 'person'
        Qui est là? – Personne
        'Who is there? – No-one.'

        rien < Latin *rēm* 'thing'
        Que dis-tu? – Rien
        'What did you say? – Nothing.'

        jamais < Latin *iam* 'now, already' + *magis* 'more'
        Tu l'as vu? – Jamais
        'Have you seen it? – Never.'

        plus < Latin *plūs* 'more'
        Plus de questions!
        'No more questions.'

        aucun < Latin *alicunus* < *aliquis* 'someone' + *ūnus* 'one'
        Est-ce que vous savez l'addresse? – Aucune idée
        'Do you know the address? – No idea.'

Meillet (1912) suggests that the motivation for grammaticalisation is the speaker's desire for expressiveness. Words which are used frequently lose their expressive force, and require reinforcement; originally autonomous words are then drafted in for emphasis, but become, with repetition, expected elements of the construction. Further cycles of phonological and semantic attrition followed by further reinforcement set in, leading to a spiral development. For instance, in French negation, the initial desire for reinforcement results from the fact that the Proto-Indo-European negative particle *ne, and its direct descendants like Sanskrit *na*, Gothic *ni* and Slavic *ne*, were short, unstressed and relatively inexpressive words. In Old Latin, a new emphatic negative *noenum* arose from the combination of *ne* 'not' with *ūnum* 'one'; this then became the normal, unemphatic form and reduced to *non*, which gives rise to French *non* and *ne*. *Ne*, another short, unstressed particle, required further reinforcement, supplied by the use of *mie*, *pas*, *point* or *goutte*. The increasingly dominant *pas* in turn is bleached of its nominal meaning 'step' in negative contexts and is integrated into the negative construction; and in modern French emphatic negatives must now be marked in novel ways, perhaps using *pas du tout* 'not at all' or *absolument pas* 'absolutely not'. As Meillet summarises (1912:140), 'Les langues suivent ainsi une sorte de développement en spirale: elles ajoutent des mots accessoires pour obtenir une expression intense; ces mots s'affaiblissent, se dégradent et tombent au niveau de simples outils grammaticaux; on ajoute de nouveaux mots ou des mots différents en vue de l'expression; l'affaiblissement recommence, et ainsi sans fin.' ('Thus, languages follow a sort of spiral development: they add extra words to intensify expression; these words weaken, decay and fall to the level of simple grammatical tools; one adds new or different words on account of expressiveness; the weakening begins again, and so on endlessly.')

A similar example, again illustrating the interplay of semantic, syntactic, phonological and morphological change in grammaticalisation, involves the rise of auxiliary verbs in Tok Pisin (Aitchison 1989b). Tok Pisin is one of the official languages of Papua New Guinea, initially a pidgin language based on English and various indigenous languages, and now undergoing creolisation (see Chapter 10). Pidgins characteristically have little or no morphology, and creoles often acquire markers of tense, mood, and aspect in the form of new auxiliaries. In fact, Givón (1979) asserts that a small group of verbs very consistently become auxiliaries and perhaps subsequently affixes marking particular grammatical categories, and some typical pathways are shown in (31).

(31)   want > FUTURE
         go   > FUTURE
         finish > PERFECTIVE > PAST
         have > PERFECTIVE > PAST
         be   > PROGRESSIVE – HABITUAL > FUTURE
         know > can > HABITUAL-POSSIBLE-PERMISSIBLE
         done > PERFECTIVE > PAST
                (after Givón 1979: 222)

Aitchison (1989b) gives several examples of Tok Pisin verbs which undergo these developments. For instance, Tok Pisin *save* 'to know' has developed into a habituality particle, *sa*. This change has several stages, illustrated by the examples in (32).

(32)a.   *God i save olgeta samting.*
         'God knows everything'
    b.   *Colgate i save strongim tit bilong yu.*
         'Colgate knows how to/is accustomed to/can strengthen your teeth'

c. *Yu save smok?*
    'Do you smoke?'
d. *Mi sa kirap long moning long hapas siks.*
    'I usually get up about half-past six in the morning.'
e. *Mi bin sa go long skul.*
    'I used to go (habitually) to school.'

Initially, *save* is an independent verb, as in (32a), but gradually verb serialisation develops, as shown in (32b) where *save* occurs alongside another verb, *strongim*. At the same time, a bleaching of meaning begins, the sense shifting from 'know', through 'know how to', 'be able to', to 'be accustomed to'. Phonological reduction to *sa*, as in (32d) and (32e), accompanies this semantic change. *Sa* is then reanalysed as a preverbal particle marking habituality, and becomes fully integrated into the construction as signalled by its increasingly frequent and redundant use; in (32d) and (32e), for instance, context alone would indicate that habitual, repeated actions are under discussion, yet *sa* still appears. Finally, *sa* is used along with other preverbal particles, including *bin* (the past tense marker, from English *been*) in (32e).

6.3.3 *Lehmann's analysis*

We turn now to three attempts to establish the regular, recurring components of grammaticalisation, and to integrate these into more formal frameworks. In later sections, we shall discuss Traugott's analysis of grammaticalisation from the semantic-pragmatic point of view, and attempt to relate grammaticalisation to iconicity, but we shall first introduce C. Lehmann's (1985) account.

Lehmann argues that 'the more freedom with which a sign is used, the more autonomous it is. The grammaticalisation of a sign detracts from its autonomy' (1985: 306). The measures of autonomy are the weight, cohesion, and variability of the sign, and each has both a paradigmatic interpretation (which concerns selectional aspects of the sign) and a syntagmatic one (which concerns its combinatorial potential). The paradigmatic weight of a sign is its *integrity*, its phonological or semantic size, while its syntagmatic weight is its *scope*, the extent of the construction it is part of. Paradigmatic cohesion is *paradigmaticity*, the degree to which the sign is integrated into a paradigm, and syntagmatic cohesion is *bondedness*, the extent of dependence on or attachment to other signs. Finally, the *paradigmatic variability* of a sign is the possibility that it may be substituted or omitted; its *syntagmatic variability* is its potential for movement within the construction.

A sign becomes grammaticalised if it loses weight and variability and/or gains cohesion, and Lehmann coins the following terms (which are not always particularly felicitous ones) for such losses and gains in both the syntagmatic and paradigmatic sphere.

1   The loss of paradigmatic weight, or integrity, is <u>attrition</u>, 'the gradual loss of semantic and phonological substance' (Lehmann 1985: 307). For instance, Ancient Greek *thélo hína* 'I want that [something should happen]' has been reduced to Modern Greek *tha*, the subjunctive marker.

2   The shrinking of scope, or syntagmatic weight, is <u>condensation</u>, whereby a sign begins to combine with less and less complex constituents. Thus, *thélo hína* governed a subordinate clause, while *tha* controls only a finite verb.

3   A gain in paradigmatic cohesion, or paradigmaticity, is <u>paradigmaticisation</u>, and involves the integration of syntactic forms into morphological paradigms. For instance, modern French *avoir* and *être* are used in the expression of tenses and are therefore part of the paradigms of other verbs, while this was not the case, at least in early Latin, for their ancestors *habēre* and *esse/stāre*.

4   A gain in bondedness, the syntagmatic aspect of cohesion, is <u>coalescence</u>. Syntactic elements become morphological and may fuse with other constituents. So, French *de*, *à* fuse with the article to form *du*, *au*, although Latin *dē*, *ad* did not undergo such fusion; and the Latin periphrastic future *cantāre habet* (literally 'he/she has to sing') has become French suffixed *chantera*.

5   The loss of paradigmatic variability is <u>obligatorification</u>, whereby the choice of members of a paradigm becomes rule-governed. Lehmann notes that Latin *dē* was often substitutable by *ab* 'from' or *ex* 'out of', as in phrases like *cadere dē/ā/ex manibus* 'to drop from the hands', but French *de* is not replaceable by other elements in phrases like *le début de l'année* 'the beginning of the year'.

6   Finally, a loss of syntagmatic variability is <u>fixation</u> within a construction, such that 'the grammaticalised sign tends to occupy a fixed syntactic, then a morphological position and becomes a slot filler' (Lehmann 1985: 308). Again, Latin *dē* and *ad* could appear in a number of positions within complex noun phrases, but French *de*, *à* must precede these.

Lehmann's identification of the elements of linguistic change involved allow a measurement of relatively stronger or weaker grammaticalisation. He also attempts to explain such changes, and agrees with Meillet (1912) in ascribing them to linguistic creativity. Again, speakers are said to strive constantly for originality and expressiveness, but since they have only a limited range of linguistic possibilities to choose from, there tends to be a general movement in one direction; the result becomes commonplace, and so the development must begin again. This hypothesis is clearly related to Meillet's notion of spiral development, and may help account for the recurrence of particular grammaticalisations cross-linguistically – for instance, many languages derive definite articles from demonstratives meaning 'that', and indefinite articles from the form for the numeral 'one'. Grammaticalisation arises, then, because speakers 'do not want to express themselves the same way they did yesterday, and in particular not the same way as somebody else did yesterday. To this extent, language is comparable to fashion. The two are also comparable in another respect: given that, for reasons inherent in the nature of things, there is only a limited number of possibilities, after having run through a grammaticalisation scale, we are back to its start' (Lehmann 1985: 315). Furthermore, the invocation of the search for expressiveness is also said to explain the unidirectionality of grammaticalisation chains (Lehmann 1985: 315), since 'the converse movement...would presuppose a constant desire for understatement, a general predilection for litotes. Human speakers apparently are not like this.'

The spiral development characteristic of grammaticalisation may therefore have an explanation in the creative use of language; but this spiral also has a linguistic aspect, which Givón (1971, 1979) sees as part of the far larger cycle in (33).

(33)   Discourse $\longrightarrow$ Syntax $\longrightarrow$ Morphology $\longrightarrow$ Morphophonemics $\longrightarrow$ Zero

That is, forms which originally help build a coherent discourse become part of the syntax; grammaticalisation then embeds them in the morphology, and subsequent phonological attrition fuses them into morphophonemic markers, then finally deletes them altogether. Bleaching or reduction consequently takes place both cumulatively and within each component. Givón sums this up in the statement that 'today's morphology is yesterday's syntax' (1971: 413): a consideration of present-day morphology might therefore help us to reconstruct the syntax of earlier periods. But this is beyond the scope of our discussion.

6.3.4   Traugott's analysis

Traugott (1982) is another attempt to establish general characteristics of grammaticalisation, but unlike Lehmann (1985), Traugott focusses on the semantics and pragmatics. Her goal is to ascertain 'the actual types of semantic-pragmatic shifts that occur in the process of grammaticalisation' (Traugott 1982: 247) and to establish a typology of such changes.

Traugott assumes three functional-semantic components in language, namely the propositional, textual and expressive components. The propositional component contains the basic resources a language has for talking about some situation, including those relating to truth and falsehood. The textual component contains elements 'directly linked to the unfolding of the speech event itself' (Traugott 1982: 248) and those dedicated to keeping the discourse coherent: these would include connectives like *but* and *therefore*, and the mechanisms involved in anaphora and cataphora (reference back to something already mentioned, or forward to something about to be mentioned in the text). Finally, the expressive component includes linguistic elements which express personal attitudes to the topic or to other participants; these would include honorifics or turn-taking markers.

Traugott formulates various hypotheses based on semantic shifts within or between these components. I shall consider two of these, and the first, Hypothesis A, is reproduced in (34).

(34)   'Hypothesis A. If a meaning-shift in the process of grammaticalisation occurs within a component, it is more likely to involve "less personal to more personal" than the reverse.'
(Traugott 1982: 253)

Traugott assumes that meaning changes within a component will involve increasing concern with more personal aspects of the interaction, like the speaker's or hearer's feelings about the situation or relationships with her interlocutors. For example, Old English *ān* 'one' gives the modern indefinite article *a(n)*; while the numeral shows that the object referred to is singular, the article is more personal in that it alerts the hearer to expect reference to new material. Similarly, textual connectives such as *but* come from forms which refer to place or time, like Old English *būtan* 'on the outside'; these are still within the textual component, but do not reflect the speaker's attitudes so directly and are therefore less personal. The shift of second person plural forms like French *vous* to deferential second person singular pronouns also involves a shift from less to more personal; from expressing a distinction of number, they move to encode the social relationships of the participants.

However, not all shifts occur within components, and Traugott asserts that meaning shifts between components are also predominantly uni-directional (see (35)).

(35)   'Hypothesis B. If there occurs a meaning-shift which, in the process of grammaticalisation, entails shifts from one functional-semantic component to another, then such a shift is more likely to be from propositional through textual to expressive than in the reverse direction.'
(Traugott 1982: 256)

Traugott is careful to note that no shift is obligatory; forms may not move along the whole chain or through all the components. However,

Hypothesis B predicts that the direction from propositional to textual to expressive will be more common for elements which *do* move between components. Again, Traugott uses a number of predominantly English examples to support her case. For instance, the English definite article *the* is from the Old English demonstrative *se, sēo, þæt*, which signalled that the entity referred to was relatively distant from the speaker. The demonstrative and the article both have the textual function of anaphora, since *that dog* and *the dog* can both refer back to some entity previously mentioned; but *the* has now also acquired an expressive, participant-oriented meaning, so that in *Put the cat out*, the particular cat is established as common ground between speaker and hearer, while a novel beginning *The girl was getting tired* attempts to include the reader and draw him into the story by assuming linguistically that both author and reader know which girl is intended. A shift from propositional to expressive may also be found in the case of intensifiers like *awfully, terribly*, which were once content words related to *awful* and *terrible*, but now mean 'very'; *very* itself has followed the same route, and was in earlier English an adjective meaning 'true', as French *vrai* still does.

Traugott's classification is certainly partially successful in establishing, as Lehmann also does, shared features for disparate cases of grammaticalisation. Traugott's Hypotheses A and B could clearly be stronger (although more data and more rigorous testing would be required first), and it is true that the boundaries between the three functional-semantic components she distinguishes are rather vague, so that it can be hard to see why certain meaning-shifts are analysed as occurring within components but others as moving between them. However, this work is only part of an ongoing programme of research (see also Traugott 1989), in which Traugott attempts to find 'paths of change, or constraints on the directionality of semantic change' (Traugott 1989: 33). This more recent work also involves a number of higher-order tendencies, which partly overlap with Hypotheses A and B above. For instance, Traugott suggests that meanings referring to the external, described situation will frequently develop into meanings based in the speaker's internal perceptual or cognitive situation, just as Old English *fēlan* 'touch' later acquired the sense 'feel'. Meanings will also tend to become increasingly subjective, reflecting the speaker's attitudes and beliefs so that, for instance, English temporal *while* (*I read a book while she was on the telephone*) has developed a concessive sense with increased subjectivity (*While I don't mind her singing, the whistling really gets me down*). These tendencies are clearly relevant to grammaticalisation; for example, the development of verbs like *go* into future auxiliaries may involve an increase in subjectivity. However, their scope is wider and extends to semantic change in general. Traugott's work will therefore be discussed at greater length in the next chapter, on semantic and lexical change.

6.3.5   *Grammaticalisation and iconicity*

One further explanation for grammaticalisation arises from Bybee's observation (1985: 11) that 'elements that go together semantically tend to occur close together in the clause'. This takes us back to the notion of automorphic iconicity (see 6.2.4.3 above), which states broadly that units which are related in the semantic or conceptual domain should also ideally be related in the formal domain. This relatedness could take one of three forms. First, related elements might resemble one another physically; this is frequently the outcome of the operation of analogy (see Chapter 4). Secondly, the related units might behave in similar ways: for instance, we noted in 6.2 that according to Cross-Category Harmony, heads tend to occur relatively consistently first or last across a range of constructions in a given language, and attempted to account for this by hypothesising that, since heads bear the same relationship to modifiers irrespective of their specific construction, they might quite naturally be ordered similarly with respect to those modifiers across constructions. As Vincent (1980) notes, however, we cannot relate grammaticalisation to typological work directly at this point, since typological relations are taken to be both synchronic and diachronic, giving rise to the problem of consistency we encountered earlier, while grammaticalisation is a purely diachronic phenomenon; and 'chains of grammaticalization are unidirectional or unilateral' (1980: 58), in that lexical items can be grammaticalised but grammatical units cannot be lexicalised, while the strongest typological relations will be bilateral.

However, there is a third way in which semantically like elements can be related formally, which depends on position in the construction: the more closely related two units are, the closer together they are likely to be located; Matthews (1991) calls this 'syntagmatic iconicity', making explicit the link with the linear order of elements. Bybee (1985) investigated this hypothesis by considering verbal inflections, suggesting that those grammatical categories most relevant to the verb would be closest to the verb stem, and most likely to be fused with it. Bybee established the hierarchy of relevance to the verb as having aspect first, then (in descending order) tense, mood and person, and found in a survey of 50 genetically and areally unrelated languages that aspect was typically nearest the stem, and was the category which most often fused with or conditioned changes in the stem.

What we seem to have here is a sequence of two stages, approximation and fusion, the first showing the influence of iconicity and the second, of grammaticalisation. Iconicity will tend to ensure that the material closest to the verb (or any other element) will be most closely related semantically, even when the verb and the expressor of the grammatical category are independent units in the syntax. Any subsequent fusion will be due to grammaticalisation, which is likely to affect forms which are spatially close. Furthermore, forms are likely to coalesce only if they are semantically close, since the resultant single word will have to be understandable as a single, semantically coherent unit; and the formal proximity of semantically related forms therefore facilitates their coalescence. Fusion will be followed by semantic weakening as the grammaticalised form gradually loses its own identity and merges with the stem, and this has repercussions in the phonological and syntactic domains. The weakened form, attached to the stem, then becomes a bound, fixed characteristic of a particular construction.

Paradoxically, as the grammaticalising form weakens, becoming more integrated into the construction but losing more of its own identity, it becomes gradually less iconic, and develops into a symbol of its particular construction, at which point its independent, iconic origins are no longer perceived. It follows that a change motivated initially by iconicity in the syntax, and specifically by the spatial proximity of semantically related elements, eventually contributes to the rise of symbols. Grammaticalisation, in other words, is the gradual fusion of icons into symbols, and the weakening processes involved in grammaticalisation involve a shift from the iconic to the symbolic. It is this link with iconicity that leads to the essentially unidirectional but cyclic nature of grammaticalisation. This cyclicity arises from the fact that various fates may befall a grammaticalised element. It may be weakened to the point of loss, allowing the cycle to begin again. It may become attached indiscriminately to all units in a particular class, as is the case with the Classical Nahuatl nominal suffix -tl as in coyo-tl 'coyote', cihua-tl 'star' (Croft 1990: 229), which was earlier an article. Nahuatl is now back at the start of a well-known grammaticalisation cycle which involves the development of articles from anaphoric demonstratives. Finally, grammaticalised elements may lose their initial meaning but be recycled with a new one; Lass (1990) calls this process exaptation, and we shall explore it further in Chapter 12.

It seems, then, that both consistency and grammaticalisation involve some sort of drift, or natural tendency, which historical linguists have attempted to explain in various ways. One popular approach has been to posit some general law: this might be natural serialisation in the case of consistency, and semantic weakening in grammaticalisation. However, neither phenomenon is sufficiently predictable or constrained to be the reflection of an all-encompassing, rigidly general law; instead, what we find in both cases are tendencies, which may indicate the operation of deep principles of linguistic and conceptual organisation. One of these, which we have explored to some extent but do not fully understand yet, is iconicity.

Our consideration of grammaticalisation, however, leaves us with a quite different problem. In this chapter, and so far throughout this book, we have been presenting and analysing changes as almost uniformly internally motivated. This assumption is not uncontroversial. For instance, we have seen that one general route by which languages acquire definite articles involves the grammaticalisation of demonstratives like *that*. It might indeed be the case that each language showing this development has undergone it independently; but surely it is also possible that the pattern could have spread from one language to another, perhaps via bilingual speakers? In Chapter 8, this matter of external motivation will be discussed in more detail.

7   Semantic and lexical change

7.1   Introduction

One of the quickest and easiest ways of introducing a sceptical non-linguist to the fascination (if not the relevance) of historical linguistics is to mention some titbit of information like the fact that *silly* used to mean 'blessed'; that the word *blurb* was invented (by the American humourist Gelett Burgess) in 1907; or that *lobster* and *locust* were both borrowed into English from the same Latin word. All three nuggets of information relate to the lexicon, the repository of words and meanings in a particular language. Changes in meaning and in lexical inventory tend to have a higher profile among native speakers than other types of change, as witness letters to the British press denouncing 'Americanisms', and the attempts of the Académie Française to regulate the influx of English loans into French, to give just two examples. This does not necessarily mean that historical linguists have been particularly successful in accounting for such changes, as we shall see in 7.2, when we attempt to ascertain how semantic changes in the meaning of existing words might be classified and explained. The rest of this chapter deals with lexical creativity, or the formation of new words using a language's own resources, including productive morphological processes and compounding. In Chapter 8, we turn to lexical borrowing, or the introduction of new words from other languages, and to the general issues of external motivation for language change, and the broader consequences of language contact.

7.2   Semantic change

7.2.1   *Introduction*

It is often said that there is less resistance to change in the semantics than in other areas of the grammar (Ullmann 1957, 1962), so that meaning changes relatively quickly and easily. Most native speakers will thus be aware of semantic changes which have taken place within their lifetime: for instance, the English word *gay* meant 'bright, cheerful' before the 1960s, and now generally means 'homosexual', while ongoing changes in English might include the movement of the sense of *flaunt* towards that of *flout*, as in recent press allegations that businessmen have *flaunted* the laws on share dealing. This awareness of recent or ongoing change is particularly marked for semantics, and is evidenced by the fact that native speakers often comment (generally adversely) on meaning changes. For instance, *hierarchy* was first used in English for the medieval classification of angels into various ranks, including cherubim, seraphim, powers and dominions. In the seventeenth century, *hierarchy* was extended to the ranking of clergymen, and thereafter to any system of grading. Hughes (1988: 192) quotes a letter to the *Daily Telegraph* from 1976 which clearly harks back to the earlier meanings, complaining that 'in your issue of March 3 you refer to the "Soviet Communist Hierarchy". I eagerly await your publication of a photograph of Mr. Brezhnev wearing a cope and chasuble – or even wings.'

Our purpose in this section is to assess proposed generalisations or explanations in semantic change. Are there regular semantic changes, with recurring types; or must we accept that 'every word has its own history'? The latter view of meaning as fundamentally unformalisable has influenced the study of historical as well as synchronic semantics: thus, we find Ullmann (1957: 154) bewailing the fact that 'the existence of ... regularities is in most cases extremely hard to demonstrate, and their very possibility is still doubted by many scholars'. One of the main obstacles to the analysis of semantic change is the inextricable link of meaning with culture. This means that to understand a change in meaning we may also require a good grasp of the socio-cultural situation within a speech community, as shown by two semantic changes discussed by Anttila (1972). First, English *mint* and *money* come from the same root as Latin *monēre* 'to warn, admonish, advise', because money in ancient Rome was made in the precincts of the temple of Juno Monēta – Juno the Admonisher. The name has been transferred due to historical accident. Similarly, early Latin *prōclīvis* meant 'downhill', but later came to mean both 'easy' and 'difficult'; only the first change seems readily comprehensible. Anttila suggests that the 'difficult' interpretation arises because goods in Rome were transported in large, cumbersome ox-carts without adequate brakes, which would indeed have been rather difficult to drive downhill. In cases like these, apparently inexplicable meaning changes can be accounted for if we know about the cultural context of the speech community; but cultural context is an extremely specific factor which does not generalise to other changes.

However, not all linguists would agree that the nature of meaning militates against the identification of explanations for semantic change:

Jespersen (1946: 212) claims that 'there are universal laws of thought which are reflected in the laws of change of meaning ... even if the Science of Meaning ... has not yet made much advance towards discovering them'. In corroboration, Sperber ascribes our failure to discern laws of semantic change to a lack of data, or at least widespread investigation of data, arguing that 'The idea of building a system of classification of general validity on the basis of so inconsiderable a collection of facts strikes me as hardly more promising than an overall botanical scheme drawn up by someone who only has detailed knowledge about the poplar, the toadstool, and the daisy' (quoted Ullmann 1957: 199–200).

In the next section, we shall identify conditions conducive to semantic change. In 7.2.3, we turn to some suggested classifications of semantic change, and provide a critique of such classifications, which are not laws determining the direction of change, although they may be partially explanatory. We then proceed, in 7.2.4, to a discussion of some recent work by Traugott (1985, 1989), which suggests that certain types of semantic change may be regular and recurrent enough to be predictable.

7.2.2   *Conditions for semantic change*

There seem to be at least three identifiable aspects of language in general, and meaning in particular, which allow semantic change to occur. First, words are typically polysemic; each has various meanings or covers a whole range of shades of meaning. This flexibility is necessary since words are used in a wide variety of contexts by many different speakers, who may vary in the meaning they wish to convey, and is probably best illustrated by all-purpose, 'portmanteau' words like *get*, *do*, *thing*, *bad* and *nice*. Words can lose or gain meanings relatively easily, due to this elasticity; and they do not have to lose an earlier sense to gain a new one. Bloomfield (1935), following Hermann Paul, suggests that each word will naturally have one central meaning and various occasional, marginal meanings, and that semantic change occurs when speakers stop using the central meaning and reinterpret a marginal sense as the central one. This may happen because new, analogical forms encroach on the central meaning, as the spread of *slowness* ousted earlier *sloth*. *Sloth* was related to *slow* as *truth* still is to *true*, but is now retained in its previously peripheral meaning of 'laziness' (and in the name of an animal popularly thought to embody this characteristic). Alternatively, a loanword may take over the central meaning of a native form, which may then become obsolete or be retained with an altered, marginal sense, as shown in (1). It is notable that the native terms have also often lost status in the process; the new meaning is frequently less socially elevated than the old one.

(1)	stōl	'throne'	>	stool
	dēor	'animal'	>	deer
	wyrm	'dragon'	>	worm
	wamb	'stomach'	>	womb
	fugol	'bird'	>	fowl
	steorfan	'die'	>	starve
	spillan	'destroy'	>	spill

It can sometimes seem unlikely that a word should have simultaneously been usable with two meanings as disparate and unrelated as the old and new ones; however, this impression often results from the loss of an intermediate, linking meaning. For instance (Guilbert 1975), French *voler* can mean 'fly' or 'rob'; the now obsolete intermediate sense was from falconry, where *voler* was applied to a bird snatching prey while in flight.

Secondly, language is transmitted discontinuously: children do not receive a fully-formed grammar from their parents, but create one for themselves on the basis of incoming data (with, in the Chomskyan theory, some help from innate constructs). Children may therefore learn imperfectly, or make abductive inferences which alter the language. This may have permitted the change of Old English *(ge)bēd* 'prayer' to Modern English *bead* 'small wooden or other ball on a string'. If an adult using a rosary explains to a child that she is *counting her beads*, we have an ambiguous context: the adult intends to convey that she is saying her prayers, but the child sees only the accompanying concrete action involving the movement of the little spheres which make up the rosary. *Bead* consequently alters its sense.

Finally, semantic change is sanctioned by Saussure's doctrine of the arbitrariness of the linguistic sign. Recall that the sign is bipartite, made up of a signifier (an actual string of letters or sounds) and a signified (a concept). These two components are arbitrarily linked; there is no reason beyond convention why French *arbre* should refer to a tree and not a book or a seagull. Before the idea of arbitrariness became current, semantic change could not really be studied at all: for instance, one common view among the Ancient Greeks was that every word had its own true meaning – ἔτυμον, which gives us *etymology*, is the neuter form of the adjective *etymos* 'true'. Although words might be used with different meanings poetically, this was purely synchronic and no historical change of meaning was visualised. Arbitrariness now allows us to regard the signifier and the signified as essentially independent; either may therefore change with time. In the relatively rare case of onomatopoeia, where a motivated or non-arbitrary link exists between signified and signifier, there tends to be greater stability: onomatopoeiac forms tend to resist both sound change and semantic change. In the unmarked case, however, we have arbitrariness, allowing change to occur more freely. Non-linguists have not accepted the doctrine of arbitrariness quite so readily, and still tend to call upon etymological arguments in support of older, 'true' meanings; this is implicit in the letter on the use of *hierarchy* quoted above. Of course, appeals to etymology depend on how recent and catastrophic a meaning change is; surely not even the most etymologically-minded English speaker would now insist that *treacle* means 'an antidote to the bite of wild animals'.

7.2.3   *Classifications of semantic change*

Bréal (1964; original edition 1897), who coined the term *semantics*, approached meaning change by formulating purportedly universal laws, involving for instance restriction and expansion of meaning. This approach of setting up classes 'according to the logical relations that connect the successive meanings' (Bloomfield 1935: 426) was pursued, among others, by Jakobson, who suggested a classification based on metaphor and metonymy, and Meillet, who identified three categories of causes of meaning change. In 7.2.3.1 – 4, I shall outline the most commonly found of these classifications, before discussing their drawbacks in 7.2.3.5.

7.2.3.1   Extension and restriction

Semantic change may broaden or narrow the range of meanings conveyed by a word. Restriction (or specialisation, or narrowing) of meaning paradoxically also involves an increase in information conveyed, since a restricted form is applicable to fewer situations but tells us more about each one. Bréal (1964 = 1897: 30) argues that the introduction of a new word, by borrowing or neologism, may cause an older one to 'recoil' (see also (1) above). For instance, Modern English *starve* means 'to die of hunger' (or often 'to be extremely hungry'; and dialectally, 'to be very cold'), while its Old English ancestor *steorfan* meant more generally 'to die', as does the Modern German cognate *sterben*. Similarly, OE *mete* meant 'food', and appears as a translation of Latin *cibus* 'food'. In addition, *voyage* in earlier English meant 'a journey', as does French *voyage*, but is now restricted to journeys by sea; *hound* once meant 'dog', like German *Hund*, but now refers specifically to dogs of a particular breed used in fox-hunting; and Modern English *dole* 'payment to the unemployed' derives from Old English *dāl* 'part, portion'.

Conversely, extension (or generalisation, or broadening) increases the number of contexts in which a word can be used, although again, paradoxically, reducing the amount of information conveyed about each one. Examples are fewer than for restriction, but might include English *arrive*, from Vulgar Latin *<u>arripare</u> (*ad* 'to' + *rīpa* 'shore, bank') 'to come to shore'; or *broadcast*, which once referred solely to sowing seeds. Similarly, Latin *panarium* 'bread basket' becomes French *panier* 'basket'.

7.2.3.2   Pejoration and amelioration

The attitude of speakers and hearers to particular words may also change, as the value assigned to the referents of words alters. Pejoration, a downward move in evaluative attitude, is frequently due to social prejudice (and very often involves words for women or foreigners): for instance, *maîtresse*, Modern French 'mistress', once meant 'bride'. Similarly, *sely* 'blessed' has become *silly*, and French *crétin* moves from meaning 'Christian' to 'stupid', a shift which Anttila attributes to the good Christian habit of turning the other cheek when attacked. Hughes (1988) notes that shifts in societal attitudes may trigger pejoration; for instance, the contemporary distrust of élitism, which is now more often denounced as a vice than seen as a virtue, has robbed *élite* of prestige, while the French revolution and the subsequent rise of democracies have damaged *aristocracy*. One specific source of pejoration is euphemism (see 7.2.3.3): in avoiding some taboo word, speakers may use an alternative which in time acquires the meaning of the original and itself falls out of use. Thus, in English, *disinformation* has replaced *lying* in some political contexts, where it has recently been joined by *being economical with the truth*.

Amelioration, on the other hand, involves an improvement in assigned value: Old English *cniht* 'boy, attendant, servant' clearly has less exalted connotations than its descendant *knight*, and *sophisticated* now means 'worldly-wise, intellectually appealing, cultured' rather than 'artificial'. Sometimes amelioration involves weakening of an originally strongly negative meaning: so, *annoy* is from Late Latin *inodiāre* 'to make loathsome', in turn from the Latin phrase *mihī in odiō est* 'it is hateful to me'; and French *regretter* has lost the meaning 'to lament over the dead'. Likewise, *terribly* and *awfully* have weakened to become alternatives for *very*. Hughes (1988) associates this type of amelioration with the popular press, and labels it 'verbicide', citing *tragedy* which can now, in journalistic usage, be applied to an earthquake killing thousands or to a missed goal in football.

7.2.3.3   The causes of semantic change

The most commonly cited causal classification of semantic changes was formulated by Meillet, who proposed three causes, namely linguistic, historical and social; to these Ullmann (1962: Chapter 8) adds a fourth, psychological category.

Linguistic causes are language-internal, and have nothing to do with external, contextual factors like the material culture. Probably the best example of linguistically conditioned semantic change is grammaticalisation (see Chapter 6 above): recall the case of French *pas*, from Latin *passus* 'step', which remains a noun with this meaning in Modern French, but has also become an adverb marking the negative.

Historical causes involve a change in the material culture. Referents frequently change, usually due to technological innovation, but the name remains the same. Thus, Latin *carrus* 'four-wheeled vehicle, chariot' has given English *car* 'automobile', and Eskimo *umiaq* originally meant 'eighteen-foot sealskin boat', but now refers to any boat or ship.

Meillet's last category involves social causes; here, a word tends to acquire a new meaning due to its use by a particular social group, or a word used in a specific sense by some group comes into common currency with an extended meaning. For example, *lure*, now 'to attract', comes from falconry where it referred originally to the bundle of feathers with which a falconer attempted to attract his hawk. Conversely, English *bishop* and French *éveque* come from Greek *episkopos* 'overseer'; their religious sense results from use within the Christian community, while Latin *trahere* 'pull' became French *traire* 'milk' as part of its restriction to farming contexts. An interesting case concerns *autumn* and *harvest*. *Harvest* is the native Germanic word, cognate with German *Herbst* 'autumn'. However, after the Norman Conquest, the upper classes adopted a great many French words, including *autumn*. This borrowing promoted a semantic shift: *autumn* became the normal word for the season, while *harvest* was reserved for the agricultural labour the peasantry would have been performing at that time.

Hughes (1988) outlines the main social developments in English-speaking society over the last millennium and the resultant trends in meaning change. For instance, religious terminology has tended to secularise, as shown in (2), as the influence of the church has waned.

(2)   *cell* 'monk's living space' > scientific domain
       office 'church service' > commercial domain
       sanction 'imposition of penance' > political/legal domain
       Also: *hierarchy, passion, mercy, sanctuary, novice ...*

Hughes (1988: 172) also identifies a general 'monetarization of transactional terms'. Changes like Latin *pecūnia*, etymologically 'wealth in livestock', to 'money', and the parallel OE *feoh* 'cattle' > 'money' (note Modern English *fee*) occur fairly frequently cross-linguistically, and to these Hughes adds *rich* 'noble, powerful' > 'wealthy', and *finance*, which initially means 'end' (note Latin *fīnīre* 'to end', *fīnis* 'end'), then 'settlement of a debt', and by the mid-sixteenth century, 'borrowing money at interest'. The growing link of power with money is well illustrated by the history of *fortune*, which around 1300 means 'chance', shifts around 1400 to 'good luck', then by the sixteenth century to 'an amount of wealth'. In the earlier period, *fortune* controlled people; but by Elizabethan times, those with enough money were clearly seen as controlling it. Other terms, like *interest*, *duty*, and *business* have also acquired specialised financial senses alongside their more general meanings.

Finally, Hughes (1988) outlines the English political vocabulary, which developed as the commands of kings gave way to the discussion and persuasion of elected governments. This vocabulary is almost entirely borrowed from other domains; for instance, *canvass* originally meant 'to toss in a sheet of canvas', while *heckle* meant 'to dress flax'. The rapid growth of the semantic field of politics in the nineteenth century is illustrated by the fact that *Conservatism*, *Socialism* and *trade union* all appear in one year, 1835.

Ullmann suggests the addition of a fourth, psychological category of causation. This might cover cases of reinterpretation by children, as seen above in the history of *bead*. In addition, Ullmann hopes to capture Sperber's Freudian analysis of semantic change under this heading. Sperber asserts that, if we are deeply concerned with some topic, we are likely to refer to it frequently even when ostensibly discussing other matters; this hypothesis might account for the clusters of related metaphors which appear in languages. For instance, in sixteenth century France, when religion was a topic of overwhelming general interest, many religious metaphors (such as *vray comme la messe* 'as true as mass') were introduced, while in the nineteenth century we find an influx of railway metaphors. Unfortunately, this claim is non-reciprocal; the lack of a large stock of metaphors based on a given topic does not necessarily mean there is no interest in it.

Psychological factors also figure largely in taboo and euphemism. Often religious concepts, dangerous animals and acts or objects which are thought of as unpleasant or distasteful become taboo; their names cannot then be used, and euphemisms are substituted, causing a semantic change in the euphemistic expression. Weasels, wolves and bears are frequently tabooed in Indo-European languages. For instance, Sanskrit *ṛkṣah* and Latin *ursus* maintain the Indo-European root for 'bear', but English *bear* originally meant 'brown', as its Lithuanian cognate *béras* still does, and we have various other euphemistic forms like Lithuanian *lokys* 'licker', Russian *medv'ed* 'honey-eater' and Middle Welsh *melfochyn* 'honey-pig'. Frequently, the Devil cannot be referred to directly, hence the wealth of Scots euphemisms including *Auld Nick* and *Clootie*; and the same is true of God, who is often referred to by euphemisms meaning 'master', as in English *Lord* and French *Le Seigneur*.

Hughes (1988) observes that war and violence provide fertile ground for euphemism in English (as in other languages), with *liquidation* 'murder', *intervention* or *military operations* 'war', and the relabelling of the *Ministry of War* as the *Ministry of Defence* all satisfactorily distancing the listener or reader from what is really happening. A recent example is the coining of *collateral damage* for 'dead or injured civilians' during the 1990–91 Gulf War. Euphemisms also arise from political propaganda, and may form chains as each is displaced by a new, 'anaesthetic' form (Hughes 1988: 206): thus, the South African government has successively relabelled apartheid *separate development, plural democracy, vertical differentiation* and *multinationalism*. Similarly, *positive discrimination*, retaining too many echoes of ordinary, negative discrimination, is giving way to the supposedly more upbeat *affirmative action*.

As Hughes notes, euphemistic terms in English generally involve latinate vocabulary, partly because such words tend to have more prestigious connotations (see Chapter 8 below), and partly because their meaning will be less transparent to the casual observer. Latinisation also figures largely in the current trend, inspired by 'political correctness', of renaming occupations to enhance their status, so that *dustbin man* becomes *refuse collector*, while in American English (Hughes 1988: 229) *rat-catcher* might become *rodent operative* and *greengrocer, vegetable executive*. Handicaps and perceived disadvantages are also euphemised, giving a current spate of terms including *visually challenged* 'blind' and *financially challenged* 'poor'. Such formations quickly become ludicrous, as witness *vertically challenged* 'short' and the voguish replacement of *disabled* by *differently abled*.

7.2.3.4 Contiguity and similarity of meaning

According to Ullmann (1957, 1962), meaning changes may result from a similarity in the senses of two words, leading to metaphor; a contiguity of sense, giving metonymy; a similarity of form, producing folk etymology; or a contiguity of form, giving ellipsis.

We shall begin with metaphor, which involves similarity of meanings. An imagined link is established between two concepts, allowing the transfer of a label from one to the other: the human *foot* is the lowest part of the body, just as the *foot* of a hill is the lowest part of the hill. People may be *owlish, mulish* or *catty*, if their behaviour matches some (real or imagined) characteristic of the animal concerned. Metaphors often shift meanings from concrete to abstract; thus, *grasp* means 'to take hold of something' mentally as well as physically, while *to cast light on something* may mean 'to make something understandable' as well as 'to make something visible'. *Eliminate*, from Latin *elīmināre* 'to put out of the house', exhibits a similar metaphorical extension. The transfer of a word or phrase from specialised into general use may also entail metaphor; outside discussions of space travel, French *être sur orbite* 'to be in orbit' now means 'to be very successful' (Guilbert 1975).

Metonymy arises from contiguity of meanings, and involves a real rather than an imagined link between concepts. In the most common, part-for-whole type, one characteristic of an entity is directly referred to but the whole entity is understood: examples include *town and gown, redhead, first violin* which includes the player, and *Washington* for 'the American government', as in *Washington said that action would be taken if necessary*. Inventions are also called after their inventor, as in *wellington boots*, or *sandwich*, or items after their area of provenance, as with *jersey, champagne*, and *calico*, called after the port of Calicut (Kōḷikōḍu in Malayalam) on the coast of Malabar in India.

Folk etymology involves a change in meaning due to the similarity of two words, usually in sound. One word is mistakenly connected with another which sounds similar, and a transfer of meaning then occurs. For example, *country dance* gives rise to French *contredanse*, and German *sint-vluot*, the earlier name for the Biblical flood, has become *Sündflut*, literally 'sin-flood' (with *Sünde* 'sin'). A more recent example is the American replacement of *Alzheimer's Disease* with *Old Timers' Disease*.

Coates (1987) bewails the scant attention that historical linguists have paid to folk etymology; most cite only English dialectal *sparrowgrass* for *asparagus*, which 'barely survived the nineteenth century' (Coates 1987: 321). Coates sees folk etymology as analogical change (see Chapter 4 above), since semantic resemblance between the affected and affecting words is sometimes relevant, but formal resemblance is always essential. Thus, meaning resemblances are clearly at work in *Old Timers' Disease*, and in French *lavanche*, which becomes *avalanche*, incorporating *aval* 'downhill'. However, in the remaking of Amoy *koë-tsiap* as *catsup* (and then *ketchup*), the resemblance to *cat* is purely formal, and is not semantically relevant. Coates notes that such cases are explicable if we accept that words are stored in the mental lexicon according to sound as well as meaning, and can be looked up and retrieved phonetically as well as semantically.

Meaning similarity is naturally relevant in cases where synonyms are involved, such as Middle English *citiyen* ⟩ *citizen* by analogy with *denizen*, and with antonyms or complementary terms, including Latin *gravis* 'heavy' becoming *grevis* under the influence of *levis* 'light', and English *femelle* > *female* by analogy with *male*. These cases would commonly be labelled as contaminations, but Coates observes that the changes involved are of exactly the same sort as folk etymology, and suggests that 'willingness to ascribe a change to folk-etymology varies directly with the morphological complexity of the affected or resultant forms and maybe also the risibility of the product. Funny forms are the best folk-etymologies' (Coates 1987: 326).

Standard cases of folk etymology typically involve hyponymy: the affecting form designates a superordinate term, and the affected one comes to resemble the superordinate term formally and denote a subtype semantically. Thus, French *écrevisse* becomes English *crayfish*, which is seen as a sort of *fish*, and French *apentis* is reformed to English *penthouse*, a particular sort of *house*. Unfortunately, the semantic connections are not always so clear: for instance, OE *titmase* is reshaped as *titmouse* – but the creature concerned is a kind of bird, not a kind of mouse.

Finally, ellipsis results from the habitual contiguity of two forms; one ultimately drops, and the leftover form stands for the whole string. We therefore have *private* (*soldier*), (*with*)*drawing room*, *daily* (*paper*), *to win a gold* (*medal*), *navy* (*blue*), *a first* (*class degree*) and *taxi* (*meter cab*); and similarly, French *le périphérique* 'ring road' is shortened from *le boulevard périphérique*, and *une automobile* 'car' from *une voiture automobile* (Guilbert 1975).

7.2.3.5 Discussion

The elementary typology of semantic change given above is neither complete nor unproblematic. It is true that, as Bloomfield (1935: 427) notes, 'Collections of examples arranged in classes like these are useful in showing us what changes are likely to occur.' We can also go some way towards explaining particular changes, for instance in social or technological terms. However, it is not appropriate to see these classifications as universal, predictable laws, as Bréal (1964) and his followers did in formulating a Law of Restriction of Meaning, a Law of Metaphor and so on. As Lyons (1977: 620) observes, 'the laws of semantic change that were proposed did little more than reflect the prior classification of the data'.

There are other difficulties with our classifications. First, some of the classes included arguably do not involve semantic changes at all, as in some instances of folk etymology and ellipsis, which arise from relationships of form rather than meaning, although they may have semantic consequences.

Second, we must accept that our categories are not mutually exclusive, but overlap. For instance, the shift of Eskimo *umiaq* from 'eighteen-foot sealskin boat' to 'boat, ship' is an extension with historical causes. The development of *belfry* also illustrates such interaction: Middle High

German *bercfrit* 'watch-tower' (from *berc* 'protection', *frit* 'security') was borrowed into Old French as *berfroi* and thence into Middle English as *berfray*. However, Modern English *belfry* has acquired a connection with *bell*. This new meaning of 'bell-tower' arises through a combination of folk etymology and metonymy: in part because the meaningless *ber* sounds like *bell*, and in part because bells were often hung in watch-towers, and church towers containing bells were often used for defensive purposes. One useful direction of future research might involve assessing which causes, results and types of change typically go together, to identify any restrictions on possible combinations.

Finally, these categories are not exhaustive, but we must be cautious in revising or extending them. First, we should not simply add new categories *ad hoc*, every time we encounter data which does not slot easily into our current classification. Second, we must beware of vast, all-subsuming categories, so huge they become meaningless, like Waldron's (1967) category of shift, which contains essentially any semantic change which has no clear place in another category.

These difficulties of classification, which apply even more strongly to explanation, result largely from two general characteristics of meaning. First, it is intrinsically connected with social history. Semantic change is frequently socially conditioned, and crucially involves language use; thus, the meaning of a word alters because one sense is favoured and another disfavoured in a particular context. Lack of evidence makes historical work extremely difficult in such cases: we may know that a certain Old English word had a particular meaning because of its use in a translation, or the definition given in a glossary, but we cannot establish its full range of senses, or the connotational meanings it had at the relevant period. We can understand recent or ongoing changes much more easily; but of course it is not always easy or wise to extrapolate current situations back into the linguistic past.

Secondly, semantic change is highly unlikely to be as regular and predictable as, say, sound change, because the units involved and the constraints on them are entirely different. Sounds are basic, and there tend to be relatively few phonemes, generally of the order of forty–fifty, in a language. Words, however, are derived, and form a much larger and more open class; and as we have seen, meanings are not limited to one per word. Similarly, the sound sequences we produce are partially constrained by physiology, and this also constrains sound change; but it is not clear what limits there are on semantic change. Presumably, such constraints result from the structure of the brain or the memory, about which we know very little. Finally, the formulation of phonological theories has cast some light on sound change; our understanding of semantic change is unlikely to progress significantly in the absence of a comprehensive and generally accepted theory of synchronic semantics.

One way forward might involve the application of Structuralist principles to semantic systems, although since these will by their nature be more amorphous than phonological systems, the usefulness of such principles will be more limited. The acquisition of a new meaning by one word will affect others in the same semantic field, and also the word(s) which previously carried that meaning; thus, the specialisation of *meat* to mean 'edible animal flesh' affected *flesh*, which has now lost this meaning. There are also a few attested cases of wholesale semantic shifts, two of which I shall mention here. The first (Anttila 1972) involves Latin legal terminology and is illustrated in (3).

(3)

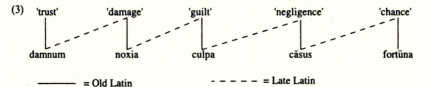

Between Old and Late Latin, the connections between form and meaning shift, in a regular chain reaction.

The second case is from the intellectual semantic field of German (Trier; discussed in Ullmann 1957). Around 1200, this semantic field included *kunst*, *list* and *wîsheit*: *kunst* referred to higher branches of knowledge and specifically courtly knowledge, and to social behaviour; *list* referred to lower, technical knowledge and skill; and *wîsheit* was a synthesis, involving the ideas of man's social, religious, courtly and intellectual aspects. However, by around 1300, the relevant terms were *wisheit*, referring to religious and mystical knowledge; *kunst*, which specifically concerned art, without its previous social connotations; and *wizzen*, the new general word for knowledge of any kind. It is not simply the case that *list* has been lost and *wizzen* introduced; the meaning of each element in the system and the relations between the elements have also changed.

These examples indicate that changes in the semantics, like those in the phonology, may involve sets of units. Consequently, such semantic chain-shifts might be subjected to analyses of the sort used in phonology, introducing Structuralist notions like systemic equilibrium and push- and drag-chains. In the next section, however, we turn to a different attempt to analyse more regular types of semantic change.

7.2.4   *Traugott* (1985, 1989)

We return here to Traugott's work on semantic and pragmatic change, which was discussed above in connection with grammaticalisation, but is not relevant to grammaticalisation alone. As we saw in Chapter 6, Traugott (1982) hypothesises that originally propositional meanings tend to develop into textual and then expressive senses. So, OE *þa hwīle þe* 'at the time that' refers to a particular temporal situation and is propositional; ME *while* develops a textual sense, since it links not only two events but also two clauses; and Modern English *while*, in *While I like to see her, she tires me out*, is expressive since it indicates the speaker's attitude.

Traugott (1989) sees this shift from propositional to textual to expressive meanings as part of a general process in semantic change which involves increasing subjectivisation, or description of the speaker's point of view. She considers this process regular enough to allow predictions to be made about 'paths of change, or constraints on the directionality of semantic change' (Traugott 1989: 33), and identifies three tendencies (see (4)): Tendency I characteristically feeds Tendency II, while either may feed Tendency III.

(4)   Tendency I:
       Meanings based in the external described situation > meanings based in the internal (evaluative/perceptual/cognitive) described situation.

       Tendency II:
       Meanings based in the external or internal described situation > meanings based in the textual and metalinguistic situation.

       Tendency III:
       Meanings tend to become increasingly based in the speaker's subjective belief state/attitude towards the proposition.

                                                                 (after Traugott 1989: 34–35)

Tendency I covers cases of pejoration and amelioration, as well as the development of OE *fēlan* 'touch' to perceptual 'feel'. Tendency II involves the development of textual senses, like the use of *while* to link two clauses, and also of metalinguistic meanings; thus, *observe* in the sixteenth century meant 'perceive that', but in the seventeenth century develops the sense 'state that', becoming a speech act verb concerned with the performance of a linguistic act. Finally, by Tendency III, expressive meanings like that of concessive *while* appear. Changes of verbs like *go* into markers of futurity also code the speaker's attitudes and intentions, illustrating the link of Tendency III with grammaticalisation.

Traugott (1989) illustrates increasing subjectivisation using the example of the English modals, arguing that the deontic meanings of the modals (and, she suggests, of verbs universally) precede historically their epistemic meanings, where deontics express will, obligation and permission, and epistemics are concerned with knowledge and belief. Traugott argues that verbs like *sculan, *mōtan (which are asterisked because the infinitives are not actually attested) and *willan* originally had rather concrete meanings, and acquired first evaluative, internal meanings by Tendency I, and then deontic meanings by Tendency II. (5) shows that *willan* could already be used in OE as a deontic of volition, and *mōtan as a deontic of permission.

(5)   *... þā hī tō scipan woldon*
         when they to ships wanted
         'when they wanted to go to their ships'
                    Chronicle E 1009: 38

         ... & þonne rīdeð ælc hys weges mid
         and then rides each his way with
         þan fēo & hyt mōton habban eall.
         the money and it are-permitted to-have all
         'and then each rides his own way with the money and can keep all of it'.
                    Orosius 21.4
                    (after Traugott 1989: 37)

Only later do these verbs gain an epistemic sense, which in encoding the speaker's knowledge and belief is clearly highly subjective and therefore follows from Tendency III. To take *must* as our example, epistemic meanings first develop in ME, when *must* is used with epistemic adverbs like *nedes* 'without doubt' (6).

(6)   *He that dooth goode and doth not goodly ... must nedes be badde.*
         'Whoever does good, but does not do it with good intentions ... must necessarily be bad.'
         Usk, *Testament of Love* 109, 90 (1385)
         (From Traugott 1989: 42)

The epistemic meaning is then transferred from the adverb to the verb, as shown in (7), where *must* clearly means that the speaker believes something to be the case.

(7)   *The fruite muste be delicious, the tree being so beautiful.*
         Middleton, *Spanish Gipsie*, I:i.16 (1623)
         (From Traugott 1989: 42)

Similarly, strongly subjective and epistemic meanings develop for *will* (as in *You'll be going out later, I expect*) and for *shall*, where the original meaning of financial debt shifts to moral obligation. Traugott argues that this development for *shall* is the result of metaphor, whereas for *must* and *will* it involves 'the conventionalising of conversational implicatures' (1989: 50). These implicatures involve principles used in interpreting conversation. For instance, if I ask Sam where Jane is, and Sam replies *There's a blue bicycle outside*, the answer may seem hopelessly opaque;

however, if I invoke the principle of relevance and assume that the reply addresses the question, I will conclude that the blue bicycle is Jane's, so Jane herself is unlikely to be far away, although Sam has not seen her himself, or he could more economically have said so. Traugott argues that the phrase *you must go* involves permission, but also implicates expectation; and from the expectation follows obligation. However, this account is rather sketchy and the processes of strengthening and conventionalising implicatures must await further study.

Traugott (1985) adopts an alternative, typological approach to semantic change, concentrating on conditionals, and specifically equivalents of English *if* in *if A then B* constructions. Traugott establishes that such conditionals come from five main sources cross-linguistically. First, they develop from epistemics, relating to possibility and doubt, and optatives, which involve wishing; thus English *suppose* has become the conditional marker in creoles like Tok Pisin, while the Hittite conditional *mān* earlier meant 'potential'. Second, *if* words develop from copulas and existentials, like Chickasaw *(h)oo* 'be' and Swahili *i-ka-wa* 'it being that'. Third, conditionals come from interrogatives, like Hua *-ve*, which has both meanings; likewise, some etymologies of English *if* trace it to the dative of the noun meaning 'doubt'. The fourth source of conditionals are words which mark certain information as given or known. These may be demonstratives like *given that*, *seeing that*; topic markers like Sanskrit *yád*; or focus markers such as Mokilese *ma*. Finally, and most commonly, conditionals develop from temporal expressions, especially those marking duration, as shown in (8).

(8)   Tagalog *(ka)pag(ka)*, *kung* 'if, then, while'
        Gumbaynggir *-ndi* 'temporal, conditional'
        Lake Miwok *miti* 'when, if'
        Hebrew *kaasher* 'when, consecutive, conditional'
        English *when(ever)*

Traugott (1985) suggests that all these semantic changes involve forms which stand for one aspect of the conditional meaning coming to stand for the whole. For instance, conditionals are concerned with imaginary possible worlds: the notion of possibility would motivate using epistemics as conditionals, while the fact that one is often wishing for the imagined state would explain the use of optatives. Similarly, interrogatives ask about truth and consequently about the reality and possibility of situations, and are therefore appropriate candidates for conditionals. Similar accounts can be given for the other sources. This example again indicates a possibly fruitful approach to semantic change: if we can establish the atoms of meaning within a particular element, we might predict that forms which signal any one aspect of this composite meaning may in time develop the sense of the whole. This hypothesis can be tested by collecting cross-linguistic data on the historical developments of forms like conditionals, and on the occurrence of other meanings for existing conditionals in languages without a written history. Such work, involving pragmatics and typology, indicates ways in which we may in time acquire a greater understanding of semantic change.

7.3   Lexical change: language internal creativity

7.3.1   *Introduction*

Guilbert (1975) distinguishes four classes of neologisms in French which correspond to the four possible sources of new words in any language. Semantic neologisms, or the assignment of novel meanings to existing lexical items, was the subject of the last section; and a second type, borrowing, will be discussed in Chapter 8. This leaves phonological and morphosyntactic neologisms. The former is relatively unimportant, and will be outlined only briefly: our main topic here is the creation of morphosyntactic neologisms by analogical extension of productive rules of the derivational morphology, including compounding. We are not concerned here with the inflectional morphology, since neologisms are new lexemes, or independent words with their own dictionary entries; inflectional processes typically create only new word-forms of existing lexemes. Thus, the plural *trees* is a word-form of the lexeme TREE, whereas HAPPINESS, although derived morphologically from HAPPY, has its own lexical entry (for further discussion see Matthews 1991).

7.3.2   *Phonological neologisms*

Guilbert (1975) notes that all neologism except the semantic type involves phonology, since each introduces new lexical items, or new combinations of phonemes, into the language. However, borrowing and morphosyntactic neologisms are affected by the phonology only insofar as new words must conform to the phonotactic rules of the language concerned. The phonotactics govern the possible combinations of sounds in a language; for instance, in English initial clusters of [pl] and [tr] are permissible, but **[lr], **[bn], **[plr] are outlawed. We would not then expect new formations with these impossible clusters to appear, while loans with unfamiliar phonological structures are liable to be simplified or reformed in accordance with the phonotactics.

Specifically phonological neologisms might include onomatopoeias and formations *ex nihilo*. New onomatopoeias are particularly common in comic books (or, to use the recent latinisation, *graphic novels*). In a single issue of a children's comic *Pif le Chien*, Guilbert (1975: 62) found, among many others, *ha* 'étonnement' (astonishment), *ouf* 'fin d'un travail pénible' (end of a horrid job), *klong* 'coup de poing + étoiles' (punch, followed by seeing stars), and *paf, gnap, clap, touk* 'bruits d'instruments de musique pop' (noises of instruments in pop music). Many onomatopoeias are nonce formations, introduced once and forgotten, but others, like English *tut-tut*, enjoy a more general distribution in the language. Some may even be incorporated into the morphology, as *dring* 'bell ringing' has given the French verb *dringuer* (Guilbert 1975: 62).

Formations *ex nihilo*, which are popularly simply called neologisms, are rather rare, but might include *blurb*, coined in 1907 by Gelett Burgess, and *Kodak*, created by George Eastman. Such neologisms are found primarily in brand and business names; these may also be orthographic rather than strictly phonological formations, with for instance an implausible number of initial ⟨a⟩s designed to give priority in alphabetical listings (my local paper reveals a car dealer called ⟨Aaaardvark⟩). Lewis Carroll produced a number of coinages, some of which, like *chortle*, have become relatively common. However, not all apparently *ex nihilo* formations come quite literally from nothing; for instance, *gas* was coined by the seventeenth century Dutch chemist van Helmont, who might have been influenced by Greek *chaos* (Bloomfield 1935). This possible lexical interference would be particularly apt since the particles in gases are characteristically in unstructured and chaotic motion.

Constant innovation in science and technology must necessitate new terms particularly frequently in these domains. However, we do not often have first-hand accounts of the dissemination of terms into the language in general or into specific registers. One such case *is* reported in Mermin (1990), which begins, 'I know the exact moment when I decided to make the word *boojum* an internationally accepted scientific term' (Mermin 1990: 7). *Boojum* is another of Lewis Carroll's nonce formations, from his poem 'The Hunting of the Snark': a boojum is a particular sort of snark which causes anyone encountering it to 'softly and suddenly vanish away'. In 1976, Mermin, a physicist, was working on what happens at very low temperatures in a liquid called superfluid helium-3. In a spherical drop of this liquid, symmetrical lines of atomic structure radiate out from the centre; but this pattern cannot be maintained, and is gradually usurped by a less symmetrical but more stable pattern in which the lines radiate out from a point at the base of the drop. In a talk, Mermin (1990: 8) found himself 'describing this as the pattern that remained after the symmetric one had "softly and suddenly vanished away." Having said that, I could hardly avoid proposing that the new pattern should be called a boojum.'

A number of alternative terms were also proposed as labels for this new pattern; different scholars began to call it a *flower*, a *bouquet* or a *fountain*, describing its shape rather than its effect. Extensions of the semantic scope of existing words typically meet with less resistance than the introduction of entirely new formations, so that these terms might have been accepted into physics with rather less controversy than Mermin's boojum. Mermin (1990: 8) was conscious of this fact: 'I was not unaware of how editors of scientific journals might view the attempt of boojums to enter their pages; I was not unmindful of the probable reactions of international commissions on nomenclature; nevertheless, I resolved ... to get the word into the literature.'

As a first step, Mermin succeeded in introducing *boojum*, safely enclosed in quotes, into the published proceedings of a conference. Alerting readers to new words by using inverted commas is common with both phonological and morphosyntactic neologisms, and is paralleled in both speech and writing by the habit of introducing new or unfamiliar terms with a phrase like 'what has been called', or French *ce que j'appelle*. A definition or equivalent term may also be provided afterwards; thus, La Landelle introduced the word *aviation* by juxtaposing it with a synonym in its first usage: 'aviation ou navigation aérienne' (Guilbert 1975).

In Mermin's next paper, he 'let loose a flock of boojums' (Mermin 1990: 9), this time quoteless. These were editorially approved, and duly published and indexed in the conference proceedings. Boojums made further appearances in the same year at a summer school in Sicily and a conference in New Hampshire, where the term was introduced to some Russians in the audience. To Mermin's (1990: 10) obvious delight, 'the Russians took to boojums at once, and one even said a boojum or two in his own talk.'

However, Mermin then encountered an obstacle: a paper by another author, but using the term *boojum*, was submitted to the *Journal of Low Temperature Physics*, and accepted subject to the excision of all boojums. Mermin wrote to lobby for the term, pointing out the numerous conference papers in which it had by now appeared, and noting its presence in the second edition of Webster's New International Dictionary. The ultimate accolade for any neologism is inclusion in a dictionary; and of course, dictionaries are seen as authoritative precisely because they are to some extent selective. On this occasion, however, the appeal failed on the grounds that the new term would cause difficulties for the international readership of the journal. As Mermin (1990: 12) notes, 'Only later did I learn that the boojum appears not only in 'The Hunting of the Snark', but also in 'La Chasse au Snark', 'Die Jagd nach dem Schnark', 'La caccia allo Snarco', 'Snarkjakten' and 'Snarkejagten', to name only a few.'

Mermin now aimed to somehow inveigle a boojum into an extremely authoritative physics journal, *Physical Review Letters*. He recognised

(1990: 13) that two problems were involved: 'the first is getting the article into *Physical Review Letters*; the second is getting the boojum into the article'. The first difficulty was quickly resolved, but the second battle was won only after a lengthy telephone conversation with one of the editors, during which, as Mermin (1990: 13) complains, 'he put me through a cross-examination such as I have not had since my PhD qualifying exam. What aspect of the boojum was pertinent? What was it that vanished away? Could the metaphor be construed as mixed? And, perhaps most importantly, if they let me get away with *boojum* would I be back to them with *snark*?' Finally, having settled a small dispute over whether the plural should be *boojums* or *booja*, Mermin was rewarded by the public appearance of his neologism, followed by the first boojum in French, and the first *budzhum* in Russian; the latter appeared complete with a genitive plural *budzhumov* and an instrumental singular *budzhumom*, in a paper acknowledging both Mermin and 'Lyuis Kerrol's "Okhota na Snarka"'.

7.3.3   *Morphosyntactic neologisms*
7.3.3.1   Introduction

Morphosyntactic neologisms, like phonological ones, may be nonce formations which are used only once or catch on briefly and then drop out of use. Guilbert (1975) cites *nouvelle vague* 'new wave', extremely common in the 1950s and 1960s but seldom encountered now, as one of these 'mots dans le vent' ('words in the wind'). Similarly, in present-day English, there is a fashion for *post-*, as in *post-modernism*, *post-feminism* and a host of others, few of which seem likely long-term survivors. Neologisms of any sort also have to struggle against conservative attitudes, and new words often stand more chance of acceptance if they are introduced first by some prominent person or in a more prestigious publication. Finally, new words are most likely to survive, and indeed to be created in the first place, if they are felt to be necessary in the society concerned. This is a difficult notion to formalise, but a well-established one: Matthews (1991: 75) quotes the Roman grammarian Varro, writing in the first century BC, who notes in his treatise *De Lingua latina* that Latin has a word *leaena* 'lioness', but no specifically feminine word for 'crow' because it is rarely necessary to refer to female crows.

   In this section we are concerned largely with analogical formations, or extensions of established techniques of word formation, not with entirely new coinages. We shall first discuss productive rules of derivational morphology, including compounding, and then turn to less predictable processes like clipping, blending and conversion.

7.3.3.2 Productive morphological processes

Derivational morphology, which in English and its relatives generally involves affixation, is the formation of new lexemes on the basis of simpler ones. The resulting, morphologically complex forms are new lexemes, with their own dictionary entries, since they may differ unpredictably from the original input form. For instance, the derived form frequently belongs to a different word class from the base, so that *act* is a verb but *actor* a noun, and *person* a noun but *personal* an adjective. Furthermore, the meaning of derived forms can vary widely from that of the input and of different derived forms with the same suffix: *generation* is clearly related to *generate* when it means 'production', but not so clearly in *within two generations everything had changed*. Likewise the noun *arrival* may be closely linked to its base verb *arrive* in terms of meaning (*I awaited his arrival impatiently*), but can also, less obviously, mean 'new baby' (*I visited my sister and the new arrival*). *Proposal* can mean 'an act of proposing', but also has the more concrete meaning of 'plan'; and a *recital* rarely if ever involves anyone reciting anything: thus we have *'cello recital*, but not **poetry recital*, the meaning being expressed by *poetry reading*. Newly derived forms can therefore go off collecting their own meanings, and so must have lexical entries in their own right.

The productivity of morphological processes varies considerably, not only at a particular period but across dialects and across time. Some affixes are almost entirely restricted to a particular set of words, like Modern English *-th*, which appears only in *truth, warmth, growth, length, breadth* and *width*. Matthews (1991) notes that *coolth*, although listed in the *Oxford English Dictionary*, is not in general usage, and that new, analogical formations like *thickth*, although clearly understandable, are unlikely except in word play. At the other extreme, certain affixes are extremely productive, like English *-able* which can make an adjective from almost any verb, and is increasingly found on phrases like *getatable* and *unputdownable*; similarly, *-er/-or* can be added to a very wide selection of verbs to form derived nouns. Sometimes, we find a selection of derivational formations which are functionally and semantically almost equivalent, but differ in productivity; for instance, English currently has at least five ways of forming negative adjectives, illustrated by *indecent, unkind, non-toxic, disloyal* and *aperiodic* (Matthews 1991). Of these, *dis-* is fairly unproductive, and *in-* is declining in productivity while *un-* is increasing, which has led to the formation of doublets like *intolerant* and *untolerant*. *Non-* is also productive; *a-*, on the other hand, is primarily found in academic terminology, with a few more general additions like *apolitical, amoral* and *atonal*.

Bauer (1983) argues that there are certain general restrictions on morphological productivity. One is blocking (which Aronoff (1976) labels 'preemption by synonymy'), which makes a new form unlikely if an existing item has the same meaning. Thus, *bad, small* block ****ungood*, ****unbig*, while ****dogess* and ****horsess* are blocked by *bitch* and *mare* (Matthews 1991). The phonological characteristics of a base form may also make it unsuitable for a particular word formation process, so that English adverb-forming -*ly*, is typically not added to adjectives ending in -*ly*: ****elderlily*, ****sisterlily* and ****worldlily* are therefore unlikely, while *friendlily*, although listed in the *Oxford English Dictionary*, tends to be avoided.

In many languages, loanwords also behave differently from native ones in morphological terms; in German and Czech, for example, neither foreign bases and native affixes nor native bases and foreign affixes can mix. Finally, there are semantic restrictions on productivity. For instance, English adjectives ending -*ed*, like *blue-eyed, three-legged, red-roofed* are only permissible when the base is inalienably possessed by the noun being modified; someone with blue eyes cannot exchange them for brown ones. Alienable possession rules out these adjectives, as in ****a two-carred man, or *****a black-shoed lady* (where the car could be sold or the black shoes swapped for green ones). Similarly, Italian *grande* 'big' can only modify non-man-made, concrete nouns if they refer to things smaller than human beings; so, *grande* can collocate with *pietra* 'stone', *fiore* 'flower' or *ciòttolo* 'pebble', but not *fiume* 'river', *lago* 'lake' or *vallata* 'valley' (Bauer 1983).

Compounding is also not fully productive; thus English has *blackbird, bluebird* but not ****yellowbird* or ****greenbird*, and *greyhound* but not ****blackhound* or ****brownhound*. Compound lexemes are derived from two or more simple ones, like *blackbird*, which is a noun formed from an adjective and a noun. Compounds behave syntactically like single words, and are typically stressed differently from phrases, having stress on the first element rather than the second in English: thus a *gréenhouse* and a *green hoúse* are quite different things. Compounds may also have unpredictable and idiosyncratic meanings: female *blackbirds*, for instance, are brown; and as Matthews (1991) points out, a *windmill* may be powered by wind, but for the similarly formed *flourmill*, flour is the output rather than the input. Even worse, the meanings of compounds can be entirely opaque; it would be impossible to guess that a *bluebottle* is an insect, or a *nuthatch* or a *titmouse* a bird.

Compounds can in theory be arbitrarily long, but many longer ones are simply nonce formations and do not gain wide currency; Bauer (1983) cites the one-off formation *épaules façon bouteille Perrier* 'shoulders shaped like a bottle of Perrier water', while Norman Lamont's acceptance of financial help to remove an unsuitable tenant from his flat recently inspired 'the Chancellor's now famous *sex therapist eviction legal fees*' (*Today*, Radio 4, 21 January 1993). Bauer (1983) refers to a survey by Thiel of one 1970 issue of *Die Zeit*, in which 62.1 per cent of the compounds were not listed in any dictionary. These nonce compounds may be highly ambiguous, and it is only when they are lexicalised and gain wider acceptance that certain potential meanings are selected – thus *teapot* could be 'a pot for keeping tea in', or 'something for drinking tea out of', but has been restricted by use to mean 'an item with a handle and spout in which tea is made'.

Over time, compounds can become opaque and be reinterpreted as monomorphemic words; as Bauer (1983: 44) puts it, 'very few speakers of contemporary English think of a *hedgehog* as a pig which lives in a hedge.' Signs of reanalysis include phonological reduction, which has affected *day* in *Monday* and *Teil* 'part' in German *Viertel* 'quarter'; and loss of compositional meaning, as with *understand*, which now lacks any trace of the meanings of either *stand* or *under*. There are indeterminate cases, like English *pullover* which is somewhere between a compound and a single lexeme. However, many formerly transparent compounds are now completely unanalysable: Old English **hlāf-weard* 'loaf-keeper' became *hlāford* and is now *lord*, while *lady* comes from OE *hlǣfdige*, itself from **hlāf-dige* 'loaf-kneader'.

Finally, just as the boundary between compounds and simplex lexemes is rather fluid, so too is the division between compounding and affixation: neo-classical compounding in Modern English (Bauer 1983) involves elements which may or may not be prefixes and suffixes. These forms are generally of Latin or Greek origin, and include *astro-*, *electro-*, *-naut*, *-phile* and *-phobe*. The problem with calling these compound elements is that compounds are generally composed of independent lexical items, whereas these cannot stand alone; the argument against seeing them as affixes is that they can form entire words, like *astronaut* and *electrophobe*. Words composed of prefix plus suffix, without an intervening stem, are not otherwise permissible – compare ***unhood* or ***disness*.

7.3.3.3 Less productive formations

Affixation and compounding are undoubtedly the most common techniques for making neologisms, in English and its relatives at least, but there are also various less productive formations, which are surveyed for English by Bauer (1983, Chapter 7), and for French by Guilbert (1975). These include conversion, back formation, clipping, acronyming, and blending.

Conversion is perhaps the most straightforward, since it involves a

8   Language contact

8.1   Introduction

In the first seven chapters of this book, we have mostly been treating languages as isolated and self-contained, and linguistic changes as internally motivated. This, of course, is downright misrepresentation, since the majority of the world's speakers are probably at least bilingual, if not trilingual or multilingual: and bilingualism necessarily means linguistic contact. In contact situations, elements can be transferred from one language to another; and in this chapter, we shall examine the effects of such transference. Section 8.2 will focus on lexical borrowing; structural features other than words can also be borrowed, as we shall see in 8.3. Finally, in 8.4, we shall consider convergence, the mutual sharing of features among members of an areally defined set of languages, whose speakers tend to be in a state of stable bilingualism.

8.2   Lexical borrowing

The term <u>borrowing</u> is a fairly recent label for what used to be called 'mixing of languages' (see 8.4 below). We shall follow Haugen here in using the term borrowing for 'the attempted reproduction in one language of patterns previously found in another' (1950: 212), restricting ourselves at present to the lexicon. Of course, as Haugen notes, the donor need not be aware of the loan and does not consent to it, while the recipient need not repay it; but since alternative metaphors, like stealing or adoption, are at least equally absurd, we shall stick to borrowing.

We must begin by emphasising that language contact, and therefore borrowing, relies on bilingualism. As Lehiste (1988: 1) notes, 'the theoretical limits to bilingualism might be drawn to encompass the range between the person who uses one nonintegrated loanword and the so-called perfect bilingual who can pass for a monolingual in more than one language'. Here, I shall simply define a bilingual speaker as a person with some knowledge of two or more languages. Larger numbers of more

simple transfer of a lexeme from one word class to another, with no overt morphological signal. Thus, nouns may become verbs quite readily in English, with *a bottle* giving *to bottle*, and *a hammer*, *to hammer*. Verbs can also, conversely, be used as nouns, giving *a transfer*, *an import*, *a refill*, and so on. Adjectives convert to verbs in *to better*, *to dirty*, *to open*, and even prepositions can yield nouns and verbs, as in *to up prices*, *he downed the beer*, and *the hereafter*. Similarly, in French, nouns like *fantôme* 'ghost' become adjectives, as in *une armée fantôme* 'a phantom army'; while verbs like *dîner* 'to dine', *pouvoir* 'to be able' have yielded the nouns *le dîner* 'dinner' and *le pouvoir* 'power'.

A much less productive technique is back formation (see Chapter 4 above), which creates new forms by the removal of affixes or supposed affixes. For instance, speakers of English are used to deriving nouns from verbs by adding *-er/-or*; consequently, when they hear an unfamiliar noun with this suffix, they may produce a related verb by removing it, although this verb may not have formed the base historically. Thus, *editor* and *lecher* have given *to edit* and *to lech*. Similarly, *paramedic* comes from *para-medical*; *surreal* from *surrealist*; and *transcript* from *transcription*. Clipping is also characterised by shortening, but this time the element which is removed is not an affix, but part of the lexical item itself. The element removed may be a distinct morphological unit – so, when *bisexual* is shortened to *bi*, the residue still forms an English word. But more frequently, this is not the case; indeed, the shortening process is often based on a missegmentation. For instance, *delicatessen* is frequently clipped to *deli*, whereas the boundary, if we are guided by the original German, should fall between *delicat-* and *-essen*. The clipped form will usually be the first syllable or two of the original, as with *porn* from *pornography*, *fan* from *fanatic* and *loony* from *lunatic*; but the technique is rather unpredictable, and does not always follow this course, as can be seen from *stroppy*, a clipping from *obstreperous*.

Blending also in a sense involves clipping, since it can be defined as 'compounding by means of curtailed words' (Marchand 1969: 451). Lewis Carroll's *slithy*, composed of part of *slimy* and part of *lithe*, *smog* from *smoke* and *fog*, *brunch* from *breakfast* and *lunch*, and the recent *chunnel* from *channel* and *tunnel*, are good examples of the technique. Both words may be shortened, as in *Amerind*, from *American Indian*, or only one, as in (American English) *happenstance* or *animule*. It can be rather hard to predict what the outcome of blending will be for particular words; for instance, Bauer (1983) cites *ballute* from *balloon* plus *parachute*, but notes that *paroon*, *balachute* and *paraloon* would all have been possible alternatives, all being readily spellable and pronounceable. In some cases, both input words may be unclipped; this seems to happen predominantly when there is an overlap between the last syllable of the first and the initial syllable of the second, as in *guestimate*, or *slanguage*.

While it is almost certainly going too far to surmise, as Hockett (1973) did, that early man extended his original closed-call system of communication, with a fixed number of calls or words, to an open system solely through blending, blends may be a useful source of new affixes in languages. It is relatively common for nouns in particular to become compound elements and then affixes over time – thus Modern English *-dom* in *wisdom* and *-hood* in *childhood* are from Old English *dōm* 'judgement, doom' and *hād* 'state, rank, condition' respectively. However, new suffixes may also arise from blend elements; this might perhaps be a way of dealing with the awkward class of neo-classical compounds, which may be composed of units which were historically part of blends, and are now becoming affixes.

A similar story can be told for the elements *-eteria* and *-oholic*. The former was briefly extremely productive in the first half of this century, in American English; Mencken (1936) gives 34 examples of *-eteria* words which he clearly considers to be fairly well established. However, *-eteria* words have rather declined in popularity since, and never really caught on in British English. The form seems (Bauer 1983, Soudek 1978, Marchand 1969) to have come into English from Spanish in the word *cafeteria*; presumably, as *cafe* began to be used alone, *-eteria* was interpreted as a separable unit meaning roughly 'place where you can buy X', and became first a blend element, being seen as a shortened form of *cafeteria*, and then a relatively productive suffix. The form of this suffix was variable, with the relevant condition apparently being that the output word should have the same stress pattern and number of syllables as the original form *cafeteria*: thus, if added to a monosyllabic word, the form *-eteria* was used, as in *scarfeteria*, *caketeria*, *washeteria*, while the reduced form *-teria* or *-eria* was affixed to disyllabic forms to give *basketeria*, *chocolateria*, *honeyteria*.

The new suffix *-oholic* has a very similar history, arising from a missegmentation of *alcoholic*. This formation is becoming relatively common in British as well as American English: Soudek (1978: 465) refers to it as 'a developing suffix with the semantic load of "addicted to something"', and Kolin (1979) gives 23 examples, including *beeroholic*, *chocoholic*, *foodaholic*, *workaholic*, *talkaholic* and *shopaholic*. Again, the output forms seem generally to share the stress pattern and number of syllables of *alcoholic*, presumably because analogical formations rely on formal resemblance, so that the model, and consequently the sense of the new suffix, remains clearer if these conditions are adhered to. The transitory nature of many new affixes means, however, that the longevity of such formations is unpredictable.

A final source of neologisms involves acronyms, or words formed from

abbreviations. Thus, the *Strategic Arms Limitation Treaty* is redu[ced] orthographically to *SALT*, and pronounced [sɒlt], while *White An[glo] Saxon Protestant* gives *WASP* [wɒsp]. Not every combination of ini[tial] letters which could be pronounced in a particular language actu[ally] becomes an acronym – *VAT* (for *Value Added Tax*) is pronounced ma[inly] as [vi ei ti], not [væt], for instance. Other abbreviations contravene [the] phonotactics, or lack vowels, like *BBC*, and are not therefore candida[tes] for acronyming. Acronyms do, however, seem to be becoming m[ore] common, with organisations selecting names which will form semantica[lly] appropriate acronyms, like the anti-smoking pressure group *ASH*, [for] *Action on Smoking and Health*. Eventually, accepted and familiar acrony[ms] lose their orthographic capitalisation; many speakers then cease to perce[ive] them as acronyms. For example, *laser* was originally an acronym for *Li[ght] Amplification by Simulated Emission of Radiation*; its source as an acron[ym] is now rather opaque, and it has been borrowed into French (Guilb[ert] 1975: 276), where it is regarded as a simple, unanalysable word.

In any language, there will then be numerous ways of creating n[ew] words. Some of these will be purely phonological; others will invo[lve] rather unpredictable techniques like clipping and blending; and yet oth[ers] will correspond to analogical extension of the more productive processes [of] the derivational morphology. Once formed, each neologism has its ow[n] lexical entry and will acquire its own senses; and it will be liable to meani[ng] changes of all the types described above, so that its etymological sourc[e] may in time become considerably obscured. However, creativity of th[is] sort is not the only way in which the lexical resources of a language can [be] renewed or extended, and in the next chapter we turn to the alternati[ve] method, lexical borrowing, and to the further and more extreme cons[e-] quences of language contact.

actively bilingual speakers indicate closer contact between their languages; borrowing is then likely to be more common and more far-reaching in its effects.

The unifying factor underlying all borrowing is probably that of projected gain; the borrower must stand to benefit in some way from the transfer of linguistic material (Winter 1973: 138). This gain may be social, since speakers often borrow material from a prestigious group; or it may be more centrally linguistic, in that a speaker may find a replacement in her second language for a word which has become obsolete or lost its expressive force. However, the most common and obvious motive for borrowing is sheer necessity: speakers may have to refer to some unfamiliar object or concept for which they have no word in their own language. This need may be a function of new information or technology, or contact with foreign flora, fauna and culture, as with the loans into English listed in (1). Bloomfield calls this cultural borrowing – one group of speakers borrows an object or concept from another, and its name tends to come along too. After all, 'using ready-made designations is more economical than describing things afresh. Few users of language are poets' (Weinreich 1953: 57).

(1)   Cultural borrowing into English:
         apartheid   (Afrikaans)
         perestroika   (Russian)
         pyjamas   (Hindi)
         quay   (Gaulish via French)
         gala   (Arabic via French or Italian)
         garnet   (Middle Dutch)
         flannel   (Welsh)
         hammock   (Taino via Spanish)
         lama   (Tibetan)
         potato   (Taino via Spanish)
         aardvark   (Afrikaans)
         arrowroot   (Arawak)
         artichoke   (Arabic via Spanish or Italian)
         banana   (Wolof via Spanish)

Different phases of loans may reflect the importance of particular semantic fields at different periods. For instance, English has borrowed heavily from Latin (and from Greek via Latin) at four different periods at least, as shown in (2). These spates of borrowing reflect the continental Germanic acquisition of basic commodities and terminology from the Romans; the coming of Christianity; the rise of literary language; and the scientific revolution. They might also be joined by a fifth class indicating current technological neologisms, again normally formed from latinate elements.

(2)   Basic: continental Germanic
        wine, street, mile, butter, cheese ...
        Religious: sixth to seventh century
        mass, monk, bishop, abbot, altar, angel ...
        Literary: Renaissance
        democratic, enthusiasm, pernicious, dexterity, imaginary,
        allusion ...
        Scientific: seventeenth to eighteenth century
        nucleus, formula, atomic, molecule, carnivorous ...
                (after Hughes 1988: 4)

The second major motivation for borrowing is essentially social, and depends on perceptions of prestige. Cultural borrowing is frequently bidirectional; English, for instance, has borrowed from various African languages, which have in turn borrowed technological vocabulary from English. However, in cases of close contact, two languages may not be perceived as equivalent in status within their speech communities: typically, the language with more powerful speakers will be regarded as more prestigious.

In such linguistic relationships of unequal prestige, borrowings generally move from the more to the less prestigious language, and will be concentrated in the semantic fields where the more prestigious speakers wield the greatest influence. For instance, after the Norman Conquest, we find a huge influx of French vocabulary into English, mainly connected with the Church, warfare, the arts and administration. These lexical items reflected the interests of the French-speaking ruling group, and had prestigious connotations. Borrowed and native words consequently come to occupy different registers (Hughes 1988): for instance, in the sequences *leech – doctor – physician* or *ask – question – interrogate*, the words further right are more literary and formal; in each case, the first is Germanic, the second French and the third Latin or Greek. As we saw in Chapter 7, the existence of such register differences provides a useful source of euphemisms. Translating between registers can also produce humorous or peculiar effects, as elevated terms are used for workaday concepts and *vice versa* (thus, Hughes (1988) suggests that *skipping* might be latinised as *bipedal saltatorial locomotion*).

If borrowings are particularly numerous, speakers of the recipient language may argue that it is being contaminated or overwhelmed. For instance, Guilbert (1975) notes that occupied France during the Second World War fell behind in science and technology; after the War, France therefore borrowed terms for technological innovations from American English. The increasing impact of American culture resulting from music, films, the media and reciprocal tourism then led to a large batch of further loans, including *shopping*, *gadget* and *parking*. The Académie Française simple transfer of a lexeme from one word class to another, with no overt morphological signal. Thus, nouns may become verbs quite readily in English, with *a bottle* giving *to bottle*, and *a hammer, to hammer*. Verbs can also, conversely, be used as nouns, giving *a transfer, an import, a refill*, and so on. Adjectives convert to verbs in *to better, to dirty, to open*, and even prepositions can yield nouns and verbs, as in *to up prices, he downed the beer*, and *the hereafter*. Similarly, in French, nouns like *fantôme* 'ghost' become adjectives, as in *une armée fantôme* 'a phantom army'; while verbs like *dîner* 'to dine', *pouvoir* 'to be able' have yielded the nouns *le dîner* 'dinner' and *le pouvoir* 'power'.

A much less productive technique is back formation (see Chapter 4 above), which creates new forms by the removal of affixes or supposed affixes. For instance, speakers of English are used to deriving nouns from verbs by adding *-er/-or*; consequently, when they hear an unfamiliar noun with this suffix, they may produce a related verb by removing it, although this verb may not have formed the base historically. Thus, *editor* and *lecher* have given *to edit* and *to lech*. Similarly, *paramedic* comes from *paramedical*; *surreal* from *surrealist*; and *transcript* from *transcription*. Clipping is also characterised by shortening, but this time the element which is removed is not an affix, but part of the lexical item itself. The element removed may be a distinct morphological unit – so, when *bisexual* is shortened to *bi*, the residue still forms an English word. But more frequently, this is not the case; indeed, the shortening process is often based on a missegmentation. For instance, *delicatessen* is frequently clipped to *deli*, whereas the boundary, if we are guided by the original German, should fall between *delicat-* and *-essen*. The clipped form will usually be the first syllable or two of the original, as with *porn* from *pornography, fan* from *fanatic* and *loony* from *lunatic*; but the technique is rather unpredictable, and does not always follow this course, as can be seen from *stroppy*, a clipping from *obstreperous*.

Blending also in a sense involves clipping, since it can be defined as 'compounding by means of curtailed words' (Marchand 1969: 451). Lewis Carroll's *slithy*, composed of part of *slimy* and part of *lithe, smog* from *smoke* and *fog, brunch* from *breakfast* and *lunch*, and the recent *chunnel* from *channel* and *tunnel*, are good examples of the technique. Both words may be shortened, as in *Amerind*, from *American Indian*, or only one, as in (American English) *happenstance* or *animule*. It can be rather hard to predict what the outcome of blending will be for particular words; for instance, Bauer (1983) cites *ballute* from *balloon* plus *parachute*, but notes that *paroon, balachute* and *paraloon* would all have been possible alternatives, all being readily spellable and pronounceable. In some cases, both input words may be unclipped; this seems to happen predominantly when there is an overlap between the last syllable of the first and the initial syllable of the second, as in *guestimate*, or *slanguage*.

While it is almost certainly going too far to surmise, as Hockett (1973) did, that early man extended his original closed-call system of communication, with a fixed number of calls or words, to an open system solely through blending, blends may be a useful source of new affixes in languages. It is relatively common for nouns in particular to become compound elements and then affixes over time – thus Modern English *-dom* in *wisdom* and *-hood* in *childhood* are from Old English *dōm* 'judgement, doom' and *hād* 'state, rank, condition' respectively. However, new suffixes may also arise from blend elements; this might perhaps be a way of dealing with the awkward class of neo-classical compounds, which may be composed of units which were historically part of blends, and are now becoming affixes.

A similar story can be told for the elements *-eteria* and *-oholic*. The former was briefly extremely productive in the first half of this century, in American English; Mencken (1936) gives 34 examples of *-eteria* words which he clearly considers to be fairly well established. However, *-eteria* words have rather declined in popularity since, and never really caught on in British English. The form seems (Bauer 1983, Soudek 1978, Marchand 1969) to have come into English from Spanish in the word *cafeteria*; presumably, as *cafe* began to be used alone, *-eteria* was interpreted as a separable unit meaning roughly 'place where you can buy X', and became first a blend element, being seen as a shortened form of *cafeteria*, and then a relatively productive suffix. The form of this suffix was variable, with the relevant condition apparently being that the output word should have the same stress pattern and number of syllables as the original form *cafeteria*: thus, if added to a monosyllabic word, the form *-eteria* was used, as in *scarfeteria*, *caketeria*, *washeteria*, while the reduced form *-teria* or *-eria* was affixed to disyllabic forms to give *basketeria*, *chocolateria*, *honeyteria*.

The new suffix *-oholic* has a very similar history, arising from a missegmentation of *alcoholic*. This formation is becoming relatively common in British as well as American English: Soudek (1978: 465) refers to it as 'a developing suffix with the semantic load of "addicted to something"', and Kolin (1979) gives 23 examples, including *beeroholic*, *chocoholic*, *foodaholic*, *workaholic*, *talkaholic* and *shopaholic*. Again, the output forms seem generally to share the stress pattern and number of syllables of *alcoholic*, presumably because analogical formations rely on formal resemblance, so that the model, and consequently the sense of the new suffix, remains clearer if these conditions are adhered to. The transitory nature of many new affixes means, however, that the longevity of such formations is unpredictable.

A final source of neologisms involves acronyms, or words formed from abbreviations. Thus, the *Strategic Arms Limitation Treaty* is reduced orthographically to *SALT*, and pronounced [sɒlt], while *White Anglo-Saxon Protestant* gives *WASP* [wɒsp]. Not every combination of initial letters which could be pronounced in a particular language actually becomes an acronym – *VAT* (for *Value Added Tax*) is pronounced mainly as [vi ei ti], not [væt], for instance. Other abbreviations contravene the phonotactics, or lack vowels, like *BBC*, and are not therefore candidates for acronyming. Acronyms do, however, seem to be becoming more common, with organisations selecting names which will form semantically appropriate acronyms, like the anti-smoking pressure group *ASH*, or *Action on Smoking and Health*. Eventually, accepted and familiar acronyms lose their orthographic capitalisation; many speakers then cease to perceive them as acronyms. For example, *laser* was originally an acronym for *Light Amplification by Simulated Emission of Radiation*; its source as an acronym is now rather opaque, and it has been borrowed into French (Guilbert 1975: 276), where it is regarded as a simple, unanalysable word.

In any language, there will then be numerous ways of creating new words. Some of these will be purely phonological; others will involve rather unpredictable techniques like clipping and blending; and yet others will correspond to analogical extension of the more productive processes in the derivational morphology. Once formed, each neologism has its own lexical entry and will acquire its own senses; and it will be liable to meaning changes of all the types described above, so that its etymological sources may in time become considerably obscured. However, creativity of this sort is not the only way in which the lexical resources of a language can be renewed or extended, and in the next chapter we turn to the alternative method, lexical borrowing, and to the further and more extreme consequences of language contact.

8   Language contact

8.1   Introduction

In the first seven chapters of this book, we have mostly been treating
languages as isolated and self-contained, and linguistic changes as
internally motivated. This, of course, is downright misrepresentation, since
the majority of the world's speakers are probably at least bilingual, if not
trilingual or multilingual: and bilingualism necessarily means linguistic
contact. In contact situations, elements can be transferred from one
language to another; and in this chapter, we shall examine the effects of
such transference. Section 8.2 will focus on lexical borrowing; structural
features other than words can also be borrowed, as we shall see in 8.3.
Finally, in 8.4, we shall consider convergence, the mutual sharing of
features among members of an areally defined set of languages, whose
speakers tend to be in a state of stable bilingualism.

8.2   Lexical borrowing

The term borrowing is a fairly recent label for what used to be called
'mixing of languages' (see 8.4 below). We shall follow Haugen here in
using the term borrowing for 'the attempted reproduction in one language
of patterns previously found in another' (1950: 212), restricting ourselves
at present to the lexicon. Of course, as Haugen notes, the donor need not
be aware of the loan and does not consent to it, while the recipient need not
repay it; but since alternative metaphors, like stealing or adoption, are at
least equally absurd, we shall stick to borrowing.

We must begin by emphasising that language contact, and therefore
borrowing, relies on bilingualism. As Lehiste (1988: 1) notes, 'the
theoretical limits to bilingualism might be drawn to encompass the range
between the person who uses one nonintegrated loanword and the so-
called perfect bilingual who can pass for a monolingual in more than one
language'. Here, I shall simply define a bilingual speaker as a person with
some knowledge of two or more languages. Larger numbers of more

actively bilingual speakers indicate closer contact between their languages; borrowing is then likely to be more common and more far-reaching in its effects.

The unifying factor underlying all borrowing is probably that of projected gain; the borrower must stand to benefit in some way from the transfer of linguistic material (Winter 1973: 138). This gain may be social, since speakers often borrow material from a prestigious group; or it may be more centrally linguistic, in that a speaker may find a replacement in her second language for a word which has become obsolete or lost its expressive force. However, the most common and obvious motive for borrowing is sheer necessity: speakers may have to refer to some unfamiliar object or concept for which they have no word in their own language. This need may be a function of new information or technology, or contact with foreign flora, fauna and culture, as with the loans into English listed in (1). Bloomfield calls this cultural borrowing – one group of speakers borrows an object or concept from another, and its name tends to come along too. After all, 'using ready-made designations is more economical than describing things afresh. Few users of language are poets' (Weinreich 1953: 57).

(1)   Cultural borrowing into English:
     apartheid   (Afrikaans)
     perestroika   (Russian)
     pyjamas   (Hindi)
     quay   (Gaulish via French)
     gala   (Arabic via French or Italian)
     garnet   (Middle Dutch)
     flannel   (Welsh)
     hammock   (Taino via Spanish)
     lama   (Tibetan)
     potato   (Taino via Spanish)
     aardvark   (Afrikaans)
     arrowroot   (Arawak)
     artichoke   (Arabic via Spanish or Italian)
     banana   (Wolof via Spanish)

Different phases of loans may reflect the importance of particular semantic fields at different periods. For instance, English has borrowed heavily from Latin (and from Greek via Latin) at four different periods at least, as shown in (2). These spates of borrowing reflect the continental Germanic acquisition of basic commodities and terminology from the Romans; the coming of Christianity; the rise of literary language; and the scientific revolution. They might also be joined by a fifth class indicating current technological neologisms, again normally formed from latinate elements.

(2)   Basic: continental Germanic
        wine, street, mile, butter, cheese ...
        Religious: sixth to seventh century
        mass, monk, bishop, abbot, altar, angel ...
        Literary: Renaissance
        democratic, enthusiasm, pernicious, dexterity, imaginary,
        allusion ...
        Scientific: seventeenth to eighteenth century
        nucleus, formula, atomic, molecule, carnivorous ...
                (after Hughes 1988: 4)

The second major motivation for borrowing is essentially social, and depends on perceptions of prestige. Cultural borrowing is frequently bidirectional; English, for instance, has borrowed from various African languages, which have in turn borrowed technological vocabulary from English. However, in cases of close contact, two languages may not be perceived as equivalent in status within their speech communities: typically, the language with more powerful speakers will be regarded as more prestigious.

In such linguistic relationships of unequal prestige, borrowings generally move from the more to the less prestigious language, and will be concentrated in the semantic fields where the more prestigious speakers wield the greatest influence. For instance, after the Norman Conquest, we find a huge influx of French vocabulary into English, mainly connected with the Church, warfare, the arts and administration. These lexical items reflected the interests of the French-speaking ruling group, and had prestigious connotations. Borrowed and native words consequently come to occupy different registers (Hughes 1988): for instance, in the sequences *leech – doctor – physician* or *ask – question – interrogate*, the words further right are more literary and formal; in each case, the first is Germanic, the second French and the third Latin or Greek. As we saw in Chapter 7, the existence of such register differences provides a useful source of euphemisms. Translating between registers can also produce humorous or peculiar effects, as elevated terms are used for workaday concepts and *vice versa* (thus, Hughes (1988) suggests that *skipping* might be latinised as *bipedal saltatorial locomotion*).

If borrowings are particularly numerous, speakers of the recipient language may argue that it is being contaminated or overwhelmed. For instance, Guilbert (1975) notes that occupied France during the Second World War fell behind in science and technology; after the War, France therefore borrowed terms for technological innovations from American English. The increasing impact of American culture resulting from music, films, the media and reciprocal tourism then led to a large batch of further loans, including *shopping*, *gadget* and *parking*. The Académie Française has attempted to oust these terms, or at least make them conform more closely to French orthography and morphology, suggesting *parc* or *parcage* for *parking* and *campement* or *campisme* for *camping* – but in vain.

An English Academy along the lines of the Académie Française has been mooted at various periods, most notably in the famous 'Inkhorn Controversy' of the sixteenth and seventeenth centuries. Hughes (1988: 102–3) notes that approximately 50 new words and senses were being introduced into English annually around 1500, but nearer 350 per year by 1600. This widespread borrowing largely resulted from the new technology of printing, which involved translation and wide dissemination of classical literature. Opponents of the new loans called them 'inkhorn terms', to indicate their literary character, and argued that they were obscure and difficult for English speakers – an opinion perhaps borne out by the evidence of malapropism in the period. Sir John Cheke, the first Professor of Greek at Cambridge but nonetheless one of the leading linguistic purists, wrote that: 'I am this opinion that our own tung should be written clene and pure, vnmixt and vnmangeled with borrowing of other tunges, wherein if we take not heed by tijm, euer borrowing and neuer payeng, she shall fain to keep her house as bankrupt' (quoted Hughes 1988: 103). *Pure* and *bankrupt* are, of course, loans from an earlier period. The purists suggested that neologisms using native forms and strategies should replace borrowings: Cheke, in his translation of Matthew's Gospel, coined *gainrising* 'resurrection', *groundwrought* 'founded' and *moond* 'lunatic', among others. However, these are arguably no more readily comprehensible than the loans; and the existing latinisms had created a momentum which meant new introductions would seem familiar and be more readily accepted.

Sometimes loans do enter the more prestigious from the less prestigious language, but these often have rather derogatory connotational meanings. For instance, Scots Gaelic has been under pressure from Scots and English since the Old English period. Its use has often been discouraged or even suppressed, and it has come to be regarded as an inferior language, even by its own speakers. It is now dying (see Chapter 11). English has borrowed lexical items from Gaelic, but these are few, and are concentrated in the domains of placenames, indigenous flora and fauna, and native life and culture, as shown in (3).

(3)   English loans from Scots Gaelic
    a.   Placenames:
          Auchinleck, Auchencrow, Auchendinny
            (< *achadh* 'field')
          Balmuir, Ballantrae, Balintore
            (< *baile* 'town')

b.   Topography/landscape:
       glen, ben, loch, strath, craig

c.   'Local colour':
       capercaillie, ptarmigan, banshee, clan, caber

Some words also seem to be more borrowable than others: specifically, basic vocabulary (including words for body parts, weather, universal experiences like birth and death, natural phenomena like rivers and mountains, and small numerals) is only infrequently affected, and then almost always in situations where neither of the languages involved is perceived as more prestigious than the other. English borrowed a good deal of basic vocabulary, including *skin, sky, get* and the pronouns *they, them, their*, from Norse in the late Old and early Middle English period, when the two languages were in close contact in areas of the north of England settled by the Viking invaders. Since English and Norse were probably mutually intelligible at this time, we are dealing with an even closer relationship, one of dialect borrowing.

Lexical borrowing requires only very restricted bilingualism; for instance, Spanish borrowed the Wolof word *banana* along with the object, and we need only imagine a puzzled Spanish speaker pointing to the object in question with an enquiring look, and receiving the one-word answer 'banana' from a co-operative Wolof speaker. The only requirement is that the borrowing speaker must understand, or believe he understands, the meaning of the items he is learning.

In the next section, we shall consider more far-reaching cases of structural borrowing. However, even lexical borrowing may affect the structure of the recipient language, depending on the degree to which loans are integrated into its system. A bilingual speaker's two languages will not match completely in phonology and grammar: one may have sounds which are absent from the other; the same sound may be allophonic in one but phonemic in the other; or one language may express grammatical categories, such as aspect or gender, which the other does not. This means that the bilingual speaker has a choice. She can borrow a word in its donor-language form, maintaining features foreign to the borrowing language: this is adoption, or importation. On the other hand, she may nativise the loan, attempting to fit it into the patterns of the borrowing language: this is adaptation, or substitution. For instance, the noun *croissant* has been borrowed into English from French. The French pronunciation is [kʁwasɔ̃], which has various un-English features, including the uvular trill and the final nasal vowel. English speakers with more knowledge of French will reproduce the French pronunciation, adopting these features. However, those who speak little or no French are apt to adapt the loan, substituting native English elements for the foreign ones and producing [kɹwasənt], [kwasɒŋ], [kɹasɒn], or some similar string.

The choice of adoption versus adaptation is not, however, an all-or-nothing one. Speakers may produce more adoptions when they are trying to impress someone, or when the vocabulary involved has particularly prestigious connotations, as French loans in the domains of food, wine and cooking currently do in English. An initial act of borrowing is more likely to be an adoption, since the borrower will almost certainly have some knowledge of the donor language; however, if he repeats the loan in the company of monolingual speakers of the recipient language, he may introduce some adaptations. This process of adaptation will persist as the monolinguals themselves acquire the loan (Haugen 1950).

Some languages seem to be predominantly adopters, while others generally adapt. It is unclear whether these tendencies are predictable, but Hock (1986) attempts to connect them with linguistic nationalism in the speech community. In Iceland, for example, borrowing is actively discouraged as it is thought that this might alienate speakers from their much-revered native culture and literature, and the speech of Reykjavik, which as the capital is inevitably more cosmopolitan, is frowned on as 'corrupted' by loans. Any loans are adapted to Icelandic patterns; but frequently, obsolete Old Norse words are instead revived and given new meanings.

The degree of adaptation also depends on the quantity of loans from the same source already in the recipient language, and the degree of bilingualism: if the speakers of the recipient language are familiar with the donor language, they are less likely to adapt words borrowed from it. To illustrate this point, Thomason and Kaufman (1988: 33) give examples of loans from Russian into Asiatic Eskimo from the pre-Soviet period when there was very little bilingualism, and the later Soviet phase when Russian was a second language for the Eskimos, who were taught in Russian schools. As (4) shows, in the first set Russian sounds were replaced by the closest equivalent Eskimo ones; the amount of adaptation is much smaller in the second set. To predict these substitutions, we must therefore know about the phonological structure of both languages, *and* such social factors as the degree of bilingualism in the community.

(4)   Russian   Early loan   Later loan
         [blʲutcə]   [pljusa]   [bljutca]   'saucer'
         [tʃaj]   [saja]   [tʃaj]   'tea'
         [tabak]   [tavaka]   [tabak]   'tobacco'
         [patʃka]   [paskaq]   [patʃka]   'bundle'

This sort of phonic substitution (Weinreich 1953), whereby a speaker attempting to produce a sound of her secondary language replaces it with a sound or sequence of sounds from her primary language, is one of the most obvious types of adaptation. For instance, English speakers often 'unpack' French nasal vowels into sequences of vowel plus nasal, as in the pronunciation of *croissant* with final [− ɒŋ]/[-ɒn], while German speakers in Switzerland use [tʃ] for Romansch [c], and [lj] for [ʎ] (Weinreich 1953: 14). Speakers are said to substitute the closest possible sound from their native language, but it is not easy to define closeness: both French and German lack the dental fricatives /θ ð/, which exist in English, and all three languages have the alveolar stops /t d/ and the alveolar fricatives /s z/, but French speakers tend to substitute /s z/ for the dentals, pronouncing the name of the former Prime Minister, Mrs Thatcher, with an initial [s], while German speakers favour /t d/ and give Mrs Thatcher an initial [t]. Adapted loans will also fit into the phonotactic patterns and follow the phonological processes of the recipient language. Consequently, English nouns with final voiced stops, like *job*, are borrowed into German with a final voiceless stop, giving [jɒp], to conform to the rule of Final Devoicing. Furthermore, languages which permit only CV syllables may delete consonants from loans, or insert vowels; thus, New Guinea Tok Pisin borrows English *parliament* as *palamen*, while *Scotsman* appears in Maori as *kotimani*. It follows that those languages with more rigid phonotactic restrictions and syllable structure constraints will be those where phonological adaptation is most extreme. For instance, an English loan into French, or *vice versa*, is likely to be altered very little, with the overall structure remaining broadly the same. However, a loan from English into Japanese will be changed profoundly, to fit into the rigid CVCV structure: this can lead to considerable lengthening of forms, as *tractor* becomes [torakuta], or clipping, as in the recent loan *seku-hara* (*The Independent*, 20 April 1992) from *sexual harassment*.

Phonological adaptation will also depend on spelling, in the numerous cases where a loan is initially seen but not heard. The orthographic conventions of the donor and recipient languages may give entirely different pronunciations, as with *Don Quixote*, who is [don kihote] in Spanish but [dɒn kwɪksɒt] for many English speakers.

Adaptation can be grammatical as well as phonological; for instance, English nouns must be assigned grammatical gender when they are borrowed into German or Norwegian. Syntactic modifications may also occur, and Lehiste (1988: 21) cites speakers of Pennsylvania German who import the German order of modifiers into English, giving constructions like *throw the baby from the window a cookie*. Misanalyses may also occur during adaptation. For example, suffixes may be interpreted as part of the stem, as in American Norwegian *kars* 'car', *karsar* 'cars', from English *cars*. Conversely, English final *-n* may be reinterpreted as the Norwegian postposed definite article: *pumpkin* is therefore segmented as *pumpki+n*, giving the adapted loan *panki* 'pumpkin', *pankin* 'the pumpkin', with the new plural *pankiar* (Lehiste 1988: 15). A particularly complex case of this type is reported by Whitely (1967). In Swahili, nouns fall into a number of classes, depending on the plural prefix. This prefix corresponds to a different prefix, or zero, in the singular, and is copied onto the verb, and adjectives and other modifiers in the sentence, for agreement. Swahili has borrowed English *keep left* to mean 'roundabout', and the adapted loan is *kiplefiti*. Since Swahili nouns with *ki-* in the singular have *vi-* in the plural, we have the corresponding plural *viplefiti* 'roundabouts'. Similarly, *madigadi* 'mudguards' and *maching'oda* 'marching orders' fit into the Swahili class of *ma-* plurals, which delete *ma-* in the singular, producing *digadi* 'mudguard' and *ching'oda* 'marching order'.

Finally, adaptation may involve a new meaning being expressed by native lexical material in a calque, or loan translation. The most famous example is probably English *skyscraper*, which has yielded the calques in (5).

(5)   skyscraper
         French *gratte-ciel*   German *Wolkenkratzer*
         Spanish *rascacielos*   Russian *nebo skrjób*

Another example is Latin *paeninsula*, which has given French *presqu'île* and German *Halbinsel*, although English has borrowed the Latin word as *peninsula*. Similarly, Greek *sympátheia* is calqued as Latin *compassio*, German *Mitleid*, Danish *Medidenhed* and Russian *soboleznovanie*, all combinations of 'with' and 'suffering' (Haugen 1950): in this case, English has borrowed both the Greek and the Latin forms, as *sympathy* and *compassion* respectively.

Adaptation strategies within a particular language do not seem to be entirely sporadic. Instead, speakers will generally adhere to particular methods of borrowing, or routines, 'productive processes by which speakers with at least some bilingual competence introduce new borrowings from L2 into L1' (Heath 1984: 372). For instance, verbs borrowed into a language often have a particular native suffix added; in German, this is *-ieren*, in Russian *-irovat'*, and in French *-er*, as in *bluffer* from English *to bluff*. Rumanian used the suffix *-isi* for early borrowed verbs from Greek, and later attached *-arisi* to verbs from Spanish and Italian borrowed via Greek, the *-ar* element coming from the Romance infinitive marker *-ar(e)*. Later, *-arisi* was extended also to loans from French, like *amuzarisi* 'to amuse, entertain' from *amuser*. Alternatively, borrowed verbs may be marked using an auxiliary; thus, Turkish borrows Arabic nouns and makes them verbal by adding the verb *etmek* 'to make, do', giving for instance *tešekkür etmek* 'to thank' (Heath 1984). This sort of strategy is extremely common: verbs are relatively hard to borrow, and languages often borrow a nominal or adjectival form and verbalise it by adding an all-purpose verb like 'make' or 'do'. The majority of loanwords within the non-basic vocabulary seem to be nouns, as emerges clearly from the percentage of loans into American Norwegian in various lexical categories reported by Haugen (1950: 224): 75.5 per cent were nouns, 18.4 per cent verbs, 3.4 per cent adjectives, and only 1.2 per cent adverbs or prepositions. Guilbert (1975) comes to a similar conclusion: in a dictionary of new French words, he found 23 English loans under <s>, of which all were nouns except one, which was an adjective.

Routines are also found for borrowing and adapting nouns. Borrowed nouns often fit into the weak, unmarked class in the recipient language; the majority of nouns borrowed into English therefore take the regular *-s* plural rather than *-en* or vowel mutation (as in *foot – feet*). However, a common routine in noun adaptation involves the reinterpretation of a plural form as singular; this is then equipped with a new plural form using a native pluralising strategy. We have already encountered this routine in American Norwegian, where the singular 'car' is *kars*, with plural *karsar*; and a similar strategy affects Spanish loans in Tagalog, where Spanish *zapatos* 'shoes' becomes *sapatos* 'shoe', with the new plural *mga sapatos* 'shoes'. Routines are also in operation for other grammatical categories, such as gender, and frequently one gender class becomes the unmarked option for loans. For instance, borrowed nouns are typically assigned masculine gender in Natal (South African) German, but feminine in Australian German (Heath 1984).

Heath (1984) argues that these routines are essentially analogical, that they are based partially on earlier borrowings from the same source, and that they indicate that speakers can recognise a foreign lexical stratum in the vocabulary of their native language. However, this stratum may be layered, since routines can change over time: early Greek and Romance verbs borrowed into Rumanian have the endings *-isi* and *-arisi*, while more recent ones may have *-izà* and *-à*; and Philippine languages have two sets of loans from Spanish verbs, older ones with *-al* for infinitival *-ar*, and newer ones with *-ar*. If older loans are still recognisably foreign at the time when the routines change, they may be reshaped to fit the new pattern; for instance, current Moroccan borrowings from French have /p/ for French /p/, while earlier ones had /b/ – *épicerie* 'grocery' was initially borrowed as /bisri/, and has now been reshaped as /pisri/ (Heath 1984).

So far, we have seen that lexical items borrowed from some L2 into L1 may undergo adaptation to make them adhere more closely to the structure of L1. Loans may alternatively be adopted, maintaining the patterns of L2 with minimal interference from L1. Such adopted loans tend to be seen as foreign for a time, but are then accepted and behave subsequently like native elements. For instance, a borrowed word will regularly undergo all sound changes which begin after its adoption, just as a native word would.

Guilbert (1975) suggests that adoption occurs in several stages. At first, loans are 'xénismes', foreign words normally italicised or enclosed in quotes in a text, and generally translated. These may be nonce forms, or may enter a second stage of 'pérégrinisme', or true adoption, in which they begin to be used more widely, partly by non-bilinguals; at this stage, loans are still seen as foreign. At the third stage, some proto-loans will be rejected, perhaps because they are phonologically or orthographically out of step with the borrowing language; in French, for instance, *lobby* has been replaced by *groupe de pression*, and *computer* by *ordinateur*. Others, like *gadget* and *shopping* are accepted and integrated morphosyntactically and semantically into the recipient language. Crucially, these types of integration do not always require prior phonological integration. Thus, English *sprint* gives French [sprint], although an orthographic sequence would normally be pronounced [ɛ̃] in French: however, it now has a regularly derived verb *sprinter* and an agent noun *sprinteur*. Similarly, *lock-out* has been borrowed and given rise to the verb *lockouter*, which is variously pronounced [lokaute] or [lokute], but is now integrated into the morphology and is therefore seen as French. In the semantic domain, *black-out*, which has a similar, non-adapted pronunciation, has acquired the new, figurative sense of 'wall of silence' in French (Guilbert 1975).

If adoption rather than adaptation takes place, and especially if borrowing is relatively intense, the impact on the borrowing language can be far wider than the simple addition of a few words, affecting the phonology, morphology and syntax as well as the lexicon. Examples of such structural borrowing will be given in the next section.

8.3   Structural borrowing

According to Winter (1973: 144), 'no component of a natural language is totally immune to change under the impression of outside languages. However, not all components appear to be equally susceptible to such changes.' In general, the lexicon is most easily and radically affected, followed by the phonology, morphology and finally the syntax. It is harder to formulate acceptable constraints on what can be borrowed within a particular component, or when it is feasible to propose an external source for a particular linguistic innovation. One possibility is that structural loans are only possible between two very similar systems; but the concept of similarity is not easily defined. A weaker version states that 'a language accepts foreign structural elements only when they correspond to its own tendencies of development' (Thomason and Kaufman 1988: 17); but as Thomason and Kaufman note, this argument is circular and therefore vacuous, since we can always claim that, if a language has accepted a loan, it must have been drifting in that direction anyway. It seems more likely that the extent and type of structural borrowing, like lexical borrowing, will depend largely on rather unpredictable social attitudes, although in cases of light or moderate structural borrowing, the features borrowed are typically those that fit typologically into the borrowing language.

As for the question of when external influence is an appropriate explanation for a change, we must recall that many changes have multiple causes: these may be solely internal, or involve influence from other languages. It is sometimes argued that a change in a certain language cannot be due to contact so long as there is a case somewhere of the same change being internally motivated; but since the same change can happen under different circumstances for different reasons, this argument is flawed (Thomason and Kaufman 1988). One possible constraint is that external causation should be invoked only when the allegedly borrowing language has undergone changes in more than one grammatical system; Thomason and Kaufman (1988) found no cases of non-lexical, structural borrowing in only a single subsystem. So, for feature x in the phonology of language A to be from language B, there must also be some feature y in another subsystem, say the morphology, which is also demonstrably from B. This condition is useful as a guiding principle, although it requires further testing and refinement.

In terms of phonology, widespread borrowing may introduce new phonemes into the borrowing language, or alter the distribution of existing ones. For instance, the Mexican Mayan language Huastec has borrowed the phonemes /d g/ from Spanish (Thomason and Kaufman 1988); while English /ʒ/ arose from medial combinations of /z/ and /j/ in words like *measure* and *treasure*, but then had its distribution extended by French loans like *rouge* and *beige* with final /ʒ/. Sometimes, such a change in the distribution of a sound can cause an allophone to become phonemic. In Old English, there was a phoneme /f/, with allophones [f] initially, finally and adjacent to other voiceless sounds, and [v] medially between voiced sounds. However, a number of Norman French loans, like *veal, verve* and *virtue*, have initial [v], which introduced [v] into contexts where it had not previously appeared, establishing a contrast with [f], and giving us the two Modern English phonemes /f/ and /v/.

Morphological material can also be borrowed, but it seems easier to borrow derivational affixes than inflectional ones. English has borrowed a number of Latin derivational affixes: for instance, words like *edible* and *visible* containing *-able/-ible* were borrowed from Latin or French, and were then reanalysed to allow the affix to attach to other Romance stems, as in *legible* and *palatable*. *-Able* now also attaches freely to native Germanic stems, such as *readable* and *eatable* (and increasingly, *unputdownable*). However, the few inflectional affixes which have been introduced into English are restricted to small sets of borrowed words, as in (6), and are not generalised. Most loans have instead been assimilated to the productive English pattern, and even the items in (6) are in some cases losing their foreign suffixes, as with *indexes*, *cactuses* and *formulas*. Similarly, some items with borrowed suffixes, like *data*, are sometimes regarded as singular and sometimes as plural, and may well be regularised in the future.

(6) criterion – criteria   phenomenon – phenomena
     cactus   – cacti   index   – indices
     formula – formulae

Situations with more widespread bilingualism may be conducive to much more widespread structural borrowing. Thomason and Kaufman (1988: Chapter 4) propose a hierarchy of types of borrowing, beginning with borrowing only of non-basic vocabulary and progressing to slight structural borrowing, which would encompass the cases reported above. There are two further categories, the first of which is intense structural borrowing, and Thomason and Kaufman here consider the Dravidian language Brahui.

Brahui has borrowed extensively from the Iranian language Balochi, and this has affected all areas of the Brahui grammar, as well as the lexicon. For instance, Dravidian languages typically have the vowels /e/ and /o/, which do not occur in Balochi and have been lost from Brahui. Balochi has lost its gender system, which has subsequently disappeared from Brahui; and Brahui has also dropped the inclusive versus exclusive 'we' distinction, which never occurred in Balochi. Although Dravidian languages are characteristically suffixing, Brahui has locative verbal prefixes based on a Balochi pattern. Furthermore, Brahui is the only Dravidian language to have suffixed pronouns that become possessives on nouns and objects on verbs, again a characteristic of Balochi. Finally, Brahui has borrowed the Balochi subordinating conjunction *ki*.

However, there are cases of even more widespread structural borrowing, which Thomason and Kaufman consider as a separate category. In such cases, there is so much borrowing that languages become 'nongenetic'; that is, they can no longer be plausibly regarded as related to the rest of their previous language family. One example is the language Ma'a (also known as Mbugu).

Ma'a is spoken in Tanzania, and is historically a Cushitic language. It retains around 50 per cent Cushitic vocabulary, including its basic vocabulary, and a few residual elements of Cushitic structure, but the rest has been borrowed from Bantu. All the phonology of Ma'a is now arguably Bantu, with the only clearly Cushitic features a few segments including the glottal stop, which are not common in the Bantu languages. Ma'a has borrowed various un-Cushitic phonological features, including implosives and prenasalised voiced stops, and /v/, and has lost syllable-final consonants in keeping with the Bantu pattern. In morphology, Ma'a retains Cushitic suffixed pronominal possessives, but all other productive inflectional morphology is Bantu. Cushitic is inflecting, while Bantu and Ma'a are agglutinating; Cushitic is suffixing, while Bantu and Ma'a are mainly prefixing. Cushitic languages have natural masculine-feminine gender, but Bantu languages instead have matching singular and plural prefixes on nouns, and Ma'a has borrowed this system. Finally, Cushitic is SOV with postpositions, but Bantu and Ma'a are SVO with prepositions.

Thomason and Kaufman (1988) use the term 'language mixing' for situations like that of Ma'a. As we saw at the beginning of this chapter, borrowing was previously referred to as language mixing; Haugen (1950) rejects this earlier term, on the grounds that 'the introduction of elements from one language into the other means merely an alteration of the second language, not a mixture of the two. Mixture implies the creation of an entirely new entity and the disappearance of both constituents; it also suggests a jumbling of a more or less haphazard nature' (1950: 211). These connotations are inappropriate in cases of lexical or slight structural borrowing, where certain constraints can be placed on the transfer of linguistic elements, but make the reference to mixing rather apt for the situation of Ma'a, where such widespread borrowing has occurred that the grammar and vocabulary of the language concerned are no longer from the same source. We shall therefore use the term 'mixed languages' solely for Thomason and Kaufman's category of nongenetic languages, which involve extreme cases of external influence and consequently abnormal transmission from generation to generation. Other languages alleged to have a similarly nongenetic development are pidgins and abrupt creoles, which we shall examine in Chapter 10.

Thomason and Kaufman (1988) also argue that particularly intense structural borrowing is subject to sociolinguistic constraints in that the borrowers' attitude to the donor language and its speakers may facilitate or inhibit the borrowing. In the case of Ma'a, there has been close contact with speakers of the Bantu languages Pare and Shambaa for around 300 years, and part of the Ma'a group has become Pare-speaking, although maintaining contact with the rest of the Ma'as. These conditions are likely to be conducive to the transfer of linguistic features from Bantu to Ma'a. We shall examine the sociolinguistic context of change further in the next chapter, but must first consider cases of contact-induced change which are not unidirectional – the phenomenon of convergence.

8.4   Convergence

8.4.1   *Definitions*

We shall now examine a second type of contact-induced linguistic change which, in some senses, is the inverse of borrowing: this is the phenomenon of convergence. While borrowing requires only very limited bilingualism, and often involves influence of a more prestigious on a less prestigious language, convergence occurs only in cases of widespread and stable bilingualism and requires the participating languages to be perceived as socially equal, since if one gains significantly in prestige it is likely to cause the death of the others (see Chapter 11); the situation of bilingualism will then not last long enough for convergence to occur. While borrowing affects primarily the vocabulary, convergence has its greatest effect on the syntax and morphology, and relatively rarely involves lexical items. Finally, while borrowing is typically unidirectional, convergence is mutual, with features being shared among converging languages; and it is not always possible to identify the source of a particular feature.

Convergence takes place within a convergence area, linguistic area, or Sprachbund, 'which includes languages belonging to more than one family but showing traits in common which are found not to belong to the other members of (at least) one of the families' (Emeneau 1956: 16). In other words, in a convergence area, 'genetic heterogeneity is gradually replaced by typological homogeneity' (Lehiste 1988: 59). The motivation for such developments may involve ease of learning, and communicative efficiency. Convergence typically occurs in situations where communication between linguistic groups is essential, and all, or the majority of speakers must learn and use two (or more) languages. Individuals in such communities will therefore have two (or more) grammars, each with its own lexicon and set of rules. It will clearly be easier for an individual to learn the grammars, and therefore master the languages, if the grammars are similar. What seems to happen in extreme cases of convergence is a gradual ap-proximation of the rules that generate the two languages over time, so that the structures generated correspondingly become more and more similar. However, there is usually little effect on the lexical material; the languages retain their own words and morphemes, but become markedly similar in structure, producing ultimate intertranslatability with effectively a single set of syntactic rules and two sets of lexical items. Children can then learn second and further languages by learning further sets of vocabulary and performing direct morpheme-for-morpheme translation. Retaining different vocabulary allows the languages involved to retain their status as distinct systems, which may be sociolinguistically helpful where national or group identity coincides with linguistic identity, while the loss of discrepancies in the rule component may facilitate acquisition and communication.

In the following sections, we shall examine three cases of convergence, the first involving a small community where direct intertranslatability has virtually been achieved, and the others illustrating less comprehensive and clear cases of convergence, where the source language for certain features may not always be identifiable, and where similarities but not intertranslatability have developed.

8.4.2   *Kupwar*

Kupwar (Gumperz and Wilson 1971) is a village with around 3,000 inhabitants in the Sangli district of Maharashtra province in India. The population consists of four groups, based on caste and language. The majority are Jains, land-owners who speak the Dravidian language Kannada. A second group of land-owners are Urdu-speaking Moslems; Urdu is Indo-European and therefore unrelated to Kannada. Another Indo-European language, Marathi, is spoken by the untouchables; and finally, the caste of rope-makers speak Telugu, which is Dravidian; however, Gumperz and Wilson do not consider Telugu in much detail, since it is rather peripheral in Kupwar, and we shall therefore concentrate on Kannada, Urdu and Marathi.

Almost all men in Kupwar are bilingual or multilingual. There is some literacy, mainly in Marathi, which is also the dominant language of Sangli, the district capital, and in Urdu; few read or write Kannada. Marathi is also dominant in inter-group communication, being seen as a neutral language since it is *not* the native language of any of the land-owners.

Although society is caste-based in Kupwar, the languages involved are in a relationship of broadly equal prestige: Urdu and Kannada are spoken natively by the land-owning castes, and Marathi, the native language of the lower-caste untouchables, is used by all castes in interactions with other groups. Furthermore, the caste system means that no single language is likely to become dominant, since speech within the home involves exclusively the caste language; family life is rigidly caste-based, and each group uses its language as a marker of identity. This facilitates stable bilingualism; and indeed, Marathi and Kannada have both been spoken in Kupwar for more than 600 years, and Urdu also for at least 300.

Although standard Urdu, Marathi and Kannada are very different from one another, convergence among the Kupwar varieties of the three languages has produced virtual intertranslatability. The structural convergence involved is clear from the example in (7), as is the tendency for each language to retain its own lexical material. Some lexical similarities do appear for Urdu and Marathi, but this is due to genetic relationship rather than convergence: both are Indo-European.

(7)   Kupwar Urdu   o   gae t-a   bhaes carn-e-ko
         Kupwar Marathi   tew gel hot-a mhaes car-ay la
         Kupwar Kannada   aw hog id-a yəmmi mes-Ø-k
                          he go past buffalo graze + oblique + dative
                          'he went to graze the buffalo'
                          (after Gumperz and Wilson 1971: 156)

By comparing the standard and Kupwar varieties of Urdu, Kannada and Marathi, we can assess the changes which have occurred during convergence. Each of the three languages acts as the model for some changes, but Kupwar Urdu and Kannada have changed more than Kupwar Marathi. In two of the three following examples, Kupwar Kannada alters to fit the pattern established by Urdu and Marathi; in the third, Urdu is the innovator.

1   *Demonstratives and possessives*

In all three languages, demonstratives and possessives can either modify the head noun (as in English *That is her dog*) or occur as predicates (as in *That dog is hers*). In Standard and Kupwar Urdu and Marathi, the demonstrative or possessive will have a suffix in both cases, but in Standard Kannada the suffix appears only in the predicative uses. In Kupwar Kannada, however, the suffix has been generalised to modifier position, as shown in (8). Kupwar Kannada also uses the copula verb 'be' which Standard Kannada lacks.

(8)a.   Kannada   ii   məne nim-də
         Kupwar Kannada   id   məni nim-d   eti
         Kupwar Marathi   he   ghər tumc-ə   hay
         Kupwar Urdu   ye   ghər tumhar-a həy
                            this-one house yours is
                            'This house is yours'

b. Kannada   i-du nim   mənə
    Kupwar Kannada   id   nim-d   məni eti
    Kupwar Marathi   he   tumc-ə   ghər hay
    Kupwar Urdu   ye   tumhar-ə ghər həy
                         this-one your house is
                         'This is your house'
            (Gumperz and Wilson 1971: 158)

2   *Dative and accusative postpositions*

Standard Kannada has both an accusative and a dative postposition,
while Urdu and Marathi have only a dative postposition for human
objects. Kupwar Kannada similarly lacks the accusative, as shown in (9).

(9) Kupwar Urdu   gərib manus-ko dekh   ke die ta
     Kupwar Marathi   gərib mansa-la bəgun   dil hota
     Kupwar Kannada   gərib mansys-gə nod   i kwatt ida
                      poor man-to having seen he gave
                           'Seeing the poor man, he gave'

3   *Purposive sentences*

As shown in (7) above, all the Kupwar varieties use a construction with
Verb + oblique + dative to mean 'in order to do something'. Standard
Urdu uses the construction *ke liye* with the same meaning, but Kupwar
Urdu follows the Marathi and Kannada pattern. The relevant sentences
from (7) are repeated as (10), along with the Standard Urdu equivalent.

(10) Standard Urdu   wo bhəys   car-n-e ke liye gəy-a
      Kupwar Urdu   o   gae t-a bhaes carn-e-ko
      Kupwar Marathi   tew gel hot-a mhaes car-ay la
      Kupwar Kannada   aw hog id-a yəmmi mes-Ø-k
                        he go past buffalo graze + oblique + dative

These examples illustrate the scope of convergence in Kupwar. All the
languages have undergone structural changes, while maintaining their own
lexical items, and in each case the source of innovations is clear. We shall
now consider two further cases of convergence, in larger linguistic areas,
where the similarities produced are less marked and comprehensive, and
the direction of change cannot always be established: these involve the
languages of India, and the Balkan Sprachbund.

8.4.3   *The Indian linguistic area*

The vast majority of Indian languages belong to one of three families: just
less than three-quarters are Indo-European, around a quarter are
Dravidian, and a small minority are Munda. We have good written records
for the two larger families, and although the dozen or so Munda languages
are not generally written, some earlier descriptions of them by members of

other linguistic groups do exist. Emeneau (1956) argues that, if we compare our knowledge of previous stages of these languages with their current structure, we find that a general 'Indianisation' has occurred, producing gradual convergence among the families. Certain traits now appear in contiguous languages, irrespective of their genetic affiliation, although the source of these features cannot always be ascertained.

Although there has been some inter-borrowing of vocabulary, many of the convergence features are non-lexical. In the domain of phonology, Indo-Iranian, Dravidian and Munda languages all have retroflex consonants. There is evidence that Sanskrit had retroflexes, but they are not generally reconstructed for Proto-Indo-European; and since So.ra, a particularly archaic Munda language, lacks retroflexes, we can assume that they are not Proto-Munda. However, they are usually reconstructed for Proto-Dravidian, so that in this case we can establish that these consonants have spread from Dravidian to the other families.

Another phonological feature characteristic of this convergence area is affrication. Marathi, an Indo-European language, has the palato-alveolar affricates [tʃ dʒ] before front vowels and the alveolar affricates [ts dz] before back vowels as reflexes of the old Indo-European palatal stops. The same sounds with the same distribution appear in Oriya, which is also Indo-European; the Dravidian languages Telugu and Kannada; and the Munda language Kurku. These languages form a geographical band across central India, and Emeneau hypothesises that the affricates must have diffused across this area, but their source is unknown.

Other convergence features involve the syntax. For instance, Dravidian, Munda and Sanskrit have a construction consisting of a series of verb stems with a final finite verb. Sanskrit is the only Indo-European language to have this construction, so we can assume that it has spread from either Dravidian or Munda, but cannot establish which. Similarly, Indian languages from all three families have an echo-word, constructed from any CVX word, which is followed by a sequence of gi-X (or u-X or m-X, depending on the language); the echo-word means 'and the like'. For instance, if *puli* means 'tigers', and is echoed, the resulting *puli gili* means 'tigers and the like'. Again, we know that this feature is non-Indo-European in origin, but we do not know its source.

Although we cannot always establish the source and direction of spread of these innovations, there are arguably enough of them to justify Emeneau's (1956) assertion that India is a single linguistic area. We shall now consider a final example of a convergence area, probably the most famous case, which again involves innovations crossing linguistic and political boundaries: this is the Balkan Sprachbund (Sandfeld 1930, Weinreich 1953, Joseph 1983).

8.4.4   *The Balkans*

The principal languages involved in the Balkan convergence area are Rumanian, Bulgarian, Serbo-Croat, Macedonian, Albanian and Greek. All are Indo-European, but from different subfamilies: Albanian and Greek each form a minor subgroup, Rumanian is Romance, and the others are Slavic. Sometimes Turkish and Hungarian are included in the Sprachbund, adding representatives of the Ural-Altaic and Finno-Ugric families to the Indo-European core.

From written records, we can assume that the Balkan Sprachbund was fairly well established by the seventeenth century. As in the other cases of convergence we have considered, there is some transfer of lexical items (mainly from Greek and Turkish), but in the main we see the spread of linguistic patterns rather than units; each language then instantiates these patterns using its own lexical material. We shall now consider a subset of these Balkanisms.

1   Many of the Balkan languages have the definite article postposed, or following the noun, as shown in (11).

(11)	Rumanian	*om* 'man'	*omul* 'the man'
	Bulgarian	*kniega* 'book'	*kniegata* 'the book'
	Albanian	*mik* 'friend'	*miku* 'the friend'

Each language retains its native morphology, however; for instance, the Bulgarian postposed *ta* is from the Old Church Slavonic demonstrative pronoun 'that', while in Rumanian *-ul, -l* reflects Latin *ille* (and *-u* is the masculine ending), as do the definite articles of French, Italian and Spanish, although in these other Romance languages the article is preposed.

2   Balkan languages have undergone certain case-mergers in the nominal morphology, including a merger of the dative and genitive. Thus, Bulgarian *na starikut* means both 'to the old man' and 'of the old man', while Rumanian *omuloi* means 'to / of the man'.

3   A mid central vowel, like schwa [ə], has developed in a number of Balkan languages; this is variously represented orthographically as Rumanian ⟨a⟩, Albanian ⟨ë⟩ and Bulgarian ⟨ъ⟩.

4   The numerals eleven to nineteen in the Balkan languages are frequently of the form 'one on ten', 'two on ten', and so on; some examples are given in (12).

(12)	eleven, twelve		
	Rumanian:	*un-spre-zece*	*doi-spre-zece*
	Bulgarian:	*edin-no-deset*	*dva-na-deset*
	Albanian:	*njëm-bë-dhjetë*	*dym-bë-dhjetë*
		'one-on-ten'	'two-on-ten'

5   The future tense in Balkan languages has often become periphrastic, and is formed using a verb of volition, such as 'will', as the auxiliary. For instance, Greek *θa fígo* 'I will leave' is diachronically derived from *thélei nà phúgo*, literally 'it-will that I-leave'.

6   Various Balkan languages have an analytical comparative form of the adjective rather than a synthetic one; that is, comparatives are of the form *more lucky* rather than *luckier*. In Rumanian, 'better' is *mai bun* 'more good' (although, of course, all other Romance languages have an analytic comparative: compare French *plus bien*). Macedonian and Bulgarian use comparative *po*.

7   Balkan languages have characteristically lost the infinitive, replacing it with a finite subordinate clause, as shown in (13).

(13)   Bulgarian: *daj mi da pija*
        Modern Greek: *dos mou na pio*
        Albanian: *a-më   të pi*
                            give me that I-drink
                                (Lehiste 1988: 59)

8   Many common idioms and calques exist in the Balkan languages. For instance, all use the phrase *to be left without a mouth* to mean 'to commit suicide', and *may you find it from God* for 'may God punish you' (see (14)).

(14)   Arumanian: *S-tǐ-o-afli dila Dumnidäu!*
        Albanian: *E gétš nga Perendia!*
        Greek: *Apò tò theò tobrẽs!*
        Bulgarian: *Ot Boga da mu se naměri!*
        Serbo-Croat: *Da ot Boga nadješ!*
                        'may you find it from God'
                            (Weinreich 1953: 50)

These shared linguistic patterns and strategies are not unique to the Balkans: other languages have lost infinitives, innovated periphrastic future tense constructions (as English has), and undergone case-mergers. However, the particular combination of features found in the Balkan languages, and the fact that they are not characteristic of non-Balkan languages from the same families, establishes the existence of a Balkan convergence area.

It is harder, however, to establish the source of the Balkanisms. They cannot all be from the same source, since no single Balkan language contains all the features: for instance, the Greek definite article is preposed rather than postposed; Macedonian has not developed a schwa vowel; and Serbo-Croat has not undergone the genitive-dative case-merger. One hypothesis is that the Balkanisms reflect the influence of the Byzantine civilisation and the Greek church, which pervaded the Balkans; the source of most innovations is therefore generally held to be Greek. This clearly cannot be so for the postposed article and the structure of the -*teen* numerals, which are not found in their Balkanised form in Greek; but Joseph (1983) also argues that other Balkanisms, like infinitive loss, cannot be traced to Greek with any confidence.

The replacement of infinitives by subordinate clauses in Greek does seem to be internally motivated; the final nasal of the Greek infinitive ending -*ein* was lost, leaving it identical with the third person singular suffix -*ei*. This led to reinterpretation as a finite form, which then spread, propelled by Byzantine influence, through the Balkans. Joseph (1983), however, points out that infinitive loss is by no means a uniform feature of the Balkan languages, Greek included. For instance, Macedonian has entirely lost the early Slavic infinitive, while Bulgarian retains it residually; Greek retains the infinitive in perfect constructions formed with *éxo*; Rumanian and Serbo-Croat have a partially productive infinitive; and finally, Albanian infinitives were partly replaced by finite forms, but have subsequently been reinstated. The 'traditional' idea of a Greek source for infinitive loss predicts south-to-north diffusion, and consequently more residual infinitives in those languages farthest away from Greek. However, the facts seem more consistent with Joseph's (1983) hypothesis that infinitive loss is a central Balkan innovation, begun in Macedonian, Bulgarian and Greek and spreading partially to peripheral languages like Rumanian, Serbo-Croat and Albanian. The retention of the infinitive in Greek perfectives is ascribed by Joseph to the fact that Greek is also geographically peripheral, extending beyond the other Balkan languages to the south.

8.4.5   *Alternative explanations*

Although some Balkanisms can be traced to a source in a particular language or group of languages (albeit several sources have been suggested for certain phenomena), the direction of diffusion for others cannot be readily established; and, as we have seen, this is also true of other convergence areas. Dissatisfaction with this aspect of contact-induced change has provoked alternative explanations for apparent convergence; two of these, which are ultimately rather less enlightening, will be discussed below.

8.4.5.1 Substrate theory

Bynon (1977: 252) defines a linguistic substrate as 'the survival of features typical of a language formerly spoken in an area in that language which has replaced it'. Such relics are often particularly numerous in placenames; for instance, we know virtually nothing of the Pictish language (or languages) spoken in Scotland before Gaelic, but one placename element *pit* 'a field' survives in *Pitlochry, Pittenweem*, and others, giving us some clues as to the area which the Picts originally inhabited. However, substrate theory becomes increasingly speculative and dubious when used to account for the transfer of larger-scale linguistic features. For instance, given the difficulty of pinpointing the source of the Balkanisms, they have been attributed to an Illyrian substrate; the features which characterise the Balkan languages are then precisely those which happen to have survived from Illyrian. Unfortunately, since the Illyrian language vanished in the prehistoric period, so that we have no records of it or of the area in which it was spoken, this hypothesis can neither be verified nor falsified.

Numerous linguistic features have been attributed to substrate influence; but many such cases can be argued against more easily than the Illyrian one. For instance, in Spanish /f/ became /h/, which has now deleted in many cases, so that Latin *filius* 'son' has given *hijo* (compare French *fils*). This change has been ascribed to a Basque substrate, since Basque had no /f/ at the time of the Spanish change. Unfortunately, the same change also affected northern Italian dialects, which lie well outside the area in which Basque is likely to have been spoken. Similarly, Latin /u/ fronted to /y/ in French, Provençal, and some northern and western German dialects – that is, roughly the region once inhabited by Celtic speakers. This fronting has been explained on the basis of a Celtic substrate (see Brosnahan 1961), since Welsh *u also fronted, and Gaulish was related to Welsh. Again, however, there are objections to this idea. For instance, although Welsh *u did front, it also unrounded; and there is no evidence that even the fronting happened in continental Celtic. Furthermore, the French change is late, occurring after the loss of Celtic in the area. Finally, the domain of [y] is similar but not identical to the Celtic-speaking region; [y] did not develop in ex-Celtic southern Germany, but did in parts of Holland, which was not Celtic- but Germanic-speaking at the appropriate period.

We must conclude that these changes do not benefit from, and do not even require, the proferred substratal motivation. The loss of /f/ and fronting of /u/ are relatively common sound changes which might be better explained with reference to articulatory or acoustic factors; and the Balkanisms already have a satisfactory explanation in terms of contact, even though it is incomplete, since we cannot establish a source for every feature involved. Incomplete explanations, however, are a way of life for historical linguists, and we do ourselves no favours by rejecting them and substituting even less complete ones which are unfalsifiable into the bargain.

This is not to say that substrate theory is useless by definition, but rather that, to produce decent hypotheses, 'we must be able to identify a substratum language or language group (some of) whose speakers shifted to the target language at the relevant time period; we must have information about its structure; and we must have information about the structure of the target language before the shift' (Thomason and Kaufman 1988: 111). None of the cases of alleged substrate influence mentioned above can meet all these requirements, although the Basque case arguably comes closest. A substrate theory adhering to these criteria could provide powerful explanations of change; but without them, hypotheses invoking substrates become tenuous, unsubstantiable, and ultimately unconvincing.

8.4.5.2 Genetic factors

Brosnahan (1961) adopts a hypothesis made by the geneticist Darlington, who held that the sounds found in a given language reflect the speakers' preference for particular articulations. Our genetic inheritance, claimed Darlington, may influence the shape and structure of our vocal organs; these obviously differ from individual to individual, but certain characteristics will also be statistically more common within groups. Each group, with its particular vocal tract configuration, will find some sounds easier to produce; these will be favoured, while others are lost.

Brosnahan illustrates Darlington's hypothesis using the example of dental fricatives. These sounds are now found, within Europe, in Icelandic, Danish, some varieties of Norwegian, English, Welsh, Basque, Spanish, Greek and Albanian, but probably had a wider distribution at an earlier period, occurring across almost all of western Europe. However, they have been gradually lost in all but the peripheral western and southern languages named above.

Brosnahan asserts that, since the dental fricatives have been lost principally from eastern areas of Europe, the pattern of loss must have spread from east to west, and consequently looks for some change in genetics which also arose in the east and might conceivably disfavour dental fricatives. His choice is the gene producing blood group O.

The proportion of blood group gene O in the European population increases from east to west, with around 50 per cent in Eastern Russia and 75 per cent in Iceland, correlating with the prevalence of dental fricatives in the North Germanic languages and their absence from the Slavic group. Brosnahan suggests that the early population of Europe had a high percentage of blood group O, but that this has been diluted by the migration from eastern areas, and notably from Asia, of peoples with a lower frequency of the O gene. For some reason, the decrease in frequency of blood group O disfavours dental fricatives, which are retained only in peripheral areas where genetic change has been minimal.

Brosnahan notes that this theory does encounter certain difficulties; for instance, Ireland, Holland and France have relatively high percentages of blood group O, but have no dental fricatives. However, he produces figures which indicate a strong statistical correlation of blood group O and the presence of dental fricatives.

However, it should be noted that the problems Brosnahan recognises are the very least his hypothesis faces. First, his correlation does not extend beyond Europe, since, as Allen (1961: 152) points out, the western Caucasian region has a high concentration of blood group O, but no dental fricatives whatsoever, even though some north-western Caucasian languages have highly complex consonant systems with upwards of seventy phonemes. Furthermore, we might agree that genetic factors could influence physiology, and therefore prohibit certain articulations, but Brosnahan does not indicate that speakers in a community with a decreasing proportion of blood group O suddenly become unable to pronounce dental fricatives; rather, they *prefer* not to use such sounds. Here we are on the horns of a dilemma. If we claim that the dental fricatives were lost due to physiological restrictions, we can use genetic explanations for phonetic and phonological change, but it is unclear how these could extend to change in the morphology, syntax or semantics; we also seem to have returned to the pre-Neogrammarian days of ascribing differential sound change to racial characteristics, motivating Grimm's Law, for instance, with reference to the adventurous spirit of the Germanic peoples. If, on the other hand, the loss of the dental fricatives was not physiological, then why exactly were they lost at all? Is the effect of the O gene on the brain rather then the vocal tract? It should be noted that, although some genes may have more than one effect, the gene determining blood group has not been shown to have direct physiological consequences for the shape of the vocal organs. In fact, the blood group gene simply relates to the presence of one of a subset of possible proteins on the surface of each cell, so that the immune system can recognise cells belonging to its own body and distinguish them from foreign bodies. Brosnahan further suggests that other linguistic changes might be correlated with the frequency of genes determining fingerprint shape and the ability to taste phenylthiocarbamide (a particularly bitter substance), and in these cases the putative causal connection seems even more tenuous.

Finally and most importantly, we must realise that at best Brosnahan succeeds only in establishing that there is a statistical correlation between the percentage of blood group O in a population and the presence of dental fricatives. In statistical terms, a correlation of A with B does not mean that A causes B or B causes A, nor that one property can be predicted from the other outside the population within which the correlation was observed.

A correlation of two properties <u>may</u> indicate causality; on the other hand, it may indicate that some third property exists which explains both, or that there is no relationship beyond chance. For instance, the crime rate in America seems to correlate with the number of church-goers (Moroney 1951): that is, the more people attend church, the higher the incidence of crime. It seems unlikely that this correlation reflects direct causation; however, there may be a third factor underlying both. In this case, this seems likely to be the incidence of large families from deprived backgrounds, which has been shown to produce both a large proportion of churchgoers and an elevated crime-rate, both reactions, albeit of different kinds. Similarly, a story which may be apocryphal but deserves to be true involves research in an Austrian village in the 1960s, which indicated a statistical correlation between the number of storks nesting and the birthrate: during the relevant period the town was expanding, producing a contemporaneous increase in families and in rooftops congenial to storks.

In Brosnahan's case, the prevalence of blood group O is unlikely to cause a change in the incidence of dental fricatives for the reasons given above. There may be an underlying common cause, unique to the European speech community, but this is unknown and perhaps, given the time depth involved, unknowable. Under these circumstances, we should reject such hypotheses in favour of explanations invoking linguistic contact, at least until they can be better tested and evaluated: at present we can only conclude that Brosnahan is violating Occam's Razor by introducing an extraneous additional factor.

8.5   Conclusion

In this chapter we have seen that language contact and bilingualism may precipitate the transfer of linguistic units and patterns from one system to another. The more stable and prolonged such contact is, the more likely the resulting influence is to be grammatical as well as lexical, and mutual rather than unidirectional, distinguishing convergence from borrowing. However, all these cases of linguistic contact may be modified by social factors; thus, languages roughly equal in prestige are likely to show mutual influence, while a less prestigious language is more likely to borrow from a more prestigious one than vice versa. In the next chapter, we shall explore the social context of language change, and the connections of change with variation.

9 Linguistic variation

9.1 Introduction

In this chapter, we return to the problems of the actuation (or initiation) and implementation (or transmission) of change which have been at least a background concern throughout this book. In Chapter 3, we considered a partial solution to the implementation problem, namely the model of lexical diffusion which assumes that at least some changes spread gradually across the set of eligible lexical items. However, this still does not resolve the issue of how or why changes move from speaker to speaker. We have also failed so far to find any satisfactory account of actuation; the schools of theoretical linguistics we have studied have all attempted, more or less successfully, to explain why changes take the particular courses they do once they have begun, but none is able to explain that beginning. For instance, the Structuralist notions of function and structure may tell us why the Great Vowel Shift proceeded through the vowel system in the way it did, but not why the first vowel shifted in the first place. In this chapter, we shall attempt to solve these problems by invoking linguistic variation, which many historical linguists now see as inextricably linked with language change. Our conclusion will be that studies of variation do enlighten us as far as transmission is concerned: the actuation problem, sadly, will remain as mysterious as ever, and we shall consider arguments that this issue may even be outside the domain of historical linguistics.

The issue of variation has until relatively recently been rather neglected within linguistic theory, which has been concerned predominantly with idealised synchrony; variability is generally consigned to the tray marked 'future research'. This kind of temporary evasion may be unobjectionable enough in itself – we cannot, after all, expect to produce a Theory of Everything instantaneously, and must therefore operate with a certain list of priorities – but it becomes dangerous when it is enshrined as an unstated principle; variation studies have become a neglected and perhaps unfashionable area of linguistics, and this has had profound consequences for historical linguistics, as we shall see.

Different schools of linguistics have factored out variation in different ways. Paul, for instance, assumes that change can only be considered with respect to the individual idiolect, while Saussure idealises, seeing languages as essentially homogeneous entities. Bloomfield and the Descriptivists showed more interest in variation, partly because one of their central tenets was the assumption that languages could differ in unpredictable and unconstrained ways; but their interest was primarily cross-linguistic rather than intra-linguistic, and in any case they lacked the theoretical apparatus to tackle problems of variation. Finally, Chomsky made assumed homogeneity a central and explicit part of Generative theory. Since the goal of linguistics in his view is to describe competence and not performance, 'Linguistic theory is concerned with an ideal speaker-listener, in a completely homogeneous speech-community, who knows its language perfectly and is unaffected by such grammatically irrelevant conditions as memory limitations, distractions, shifts of attention and interest, and errors (random or characteristic) in applying his knowledge of the language in actual performance' (Chomsky 1965: 3–4). Variation, in the speaker or in the speech community, is seen as a peripheral performance factor.

We shall see below how the re-centralising of linguistic variation may affect the study of language change; and rather than considering variation as random, inexplicable and dangerous, we shall adopt Weinreich, Labov and Herzog's picture of language as a system containing 'orderly heterogeneity' (1968: 100). That is, variation is not random but strictly controlled, often by extra-linguistic factors, and the specification of these factors may help us account for change. Dialectological and sociolinguistic studies, which we shall consider in 9.2 and 9.3 respectively, reveal correlations of language variation with geographical region, sex, age, social class and ethnic group; and shifts in these correlations may tell us why linguistic features spread through the speech community, and conceivably how this spread begins. We may thus escape from the pessimism regarding the discovery of causes of change which prevailed before the advent of sociolinguistics, neatly summed up by Paul Postal (1968: 283) in his assertion that 'there is no more reason for language to change than ... there is for jackets to have three buttons one year and two the next'.

9.2   Dialectology

The observation of dialect differences within a language is by no means new, and by the mid nineteenth century there were already numerous studies, for instance in Romance linguistics, for which the Neogrammarians attempted to provide a theoretical framework. The Neogrammarian regularity hypothesis, claiming that sound change is regular and exceptionless, was first promoted in 1876; but it clearly had to remain a hypothesis until some way of testing it could be found. A possible experiment was attempted by Georg Wenker, a young German scholar working on West Germanic consonants, also starting in 1876. Wenker's work marks the beginning of the systematic study of the regional distribution of language variation, using the methods of dialect geography.

Grimm's and Verner's Laws (see Chapter 2) together form the First Germanic Consonant Shift. A second, and chronologically later Second Germanic Consonant Shift also operated in German around AD 500. It affected only Proto-Germanic voiceless stops, as shown in (1), and split German into two sets of dialects, Low German in the north, where the change did not take place, and High German further south, where it did operate.

(1)   Proto-Germanic *p *t *k in Low German remain /p t k/

          Proto-Germanic *p *t *k in High German:
          a. remain /p t k/ after a fricative
          b. shift to affricates ([pf ts kx]) initially, after consonants other than fricatives, and
             when geminate ([kx] later becomes [kx], [k] or [x] dialectally)
          c. shift to fricatives /f s x/ after vowels and finally.

Some examples of the results of this change, specifically as it affected medial and final reflexes, are given in (2).

(2)   Low German   High German
          Dor[p]   Dor[f]   'village'
          da[t]   da[s]   'the'
          ma[k]en   ma[x]en   'make'

Wenker's approach to the regularity hypothesis relies on the assumption that sound change is instantaneous as well as exceptionless, operating for all speakers in a speech community, and in all words with the appropriate phonetic environment, at the same time. Consequently, if the regularity hypothesis is to be upheld, a sound change which has operated in one dialect but not another should have left a clear and definite boundary between the affected and unaffected varieties. Wenker therefore set out to find the boundary created by the Second Germanic Consonant Shift between High and Low German.

Wenker developed a questionnaire consisting of approximately forty sentences, each containing large numbers of Proto-Germanic voiceless stops – the diagnostic words are easily recognisable in an example like *Im Winter fliegen die trocknen Blätter durch die Luft herum* ('in winter the dry leaves fly around through the air'). He sent these, written in conventional Standard German orthography, to schoolteachers in every village along the supposed High/Low German boundary; an initial pilot study was conducted around Düsseldorf, but between 1877 and 1887 around 50,000 localities were covered. The schoolteachers were asked to transcribe the sentences into the local dialect; and equipped with these results, Wenker sat down to trace the boundary and to prove the regularity hypothesis.

Unfortunately, 'from the beginning, the findings of linguistic geography have been used by historical linguists to bolster their theoretical viewpoints, but seldom has the evidence provided the proof that was desired' (Weinreich, Labov and Herzog 1968: 151). Wenker's goal was to find a single isogloss, or bundle of coincident isoglosses, dividing High from Low German, where an isogloss is an imaginary line on a map marking the boundary between two linguistic variants. This is precisely what he found for most of the way across Germany; however, in the area of the Rhine, all the isoglosses for individual eligible lexical items seemed to go their separate ways, so that the *dat/das* isogloss crosses the Rhine south of Koblenz, *Dorp/Dorf* south of Bonn, *maken/machen* between Düsseldorf and Köln, and *ik/ich* a good deal further north at Urdingen.

The discovery of this so-called Rhenish Fan, and its theoretical implication that isoglosses reflecting the same sound change could part company, seemed to indicate that the regularity hypothesis was entirely misconceived, and for a while it was rivalled by the opposing maxim that 'every word has its own history'. However, this return to atomism was too extreme a reaction, and regularity can be discerned in the pattern of the Rhenish Fan, which in fact tells us two rather important things.

First, 'the network of isoglosses which proceeds from a study of dialect geography often represents the synchronic equivalent of the *transition* problem – that is, the route by which a linguistic change is proceeding to completion' (Weinreich, Labov and Herzog 1968: 153). In other words, the synchronic distribution of the isoglosses, revealed by dialect geography, presents a picture of the stages of the change, showing its spread in space and time. It seems that the Second Germanic Consonant Shift moved from south to north, affecting certain categories of sounds and certain words earlier than others. This means that the regularity hypothesis need not be discarded, but only modified; we can no longer make the claim that all sound changes are instantaneous, phonetically gradual and lexically abrupt – instead, we must allow some changes to operate by gradual diffusion. Diffusion theory (see Chapter 3) then gives some theoretical status to the widely separated isoglosses found in cases like the Rhenish Fan.

Secondly, this kind of distribution of isoglosses begins to indicate that linguistic change is not purely linguistic, but instead may depend on social, political and environmental factors. For instance, the individual isoglosses in the Rhenish Fan reflect to some extent the political boundaries of the city-states which existed at the time of the shift. Sound changes seem to originate in cultural centres or areas of political dominance, which we might call focal areas. Changes diffuse outwards from these focal areas, but may not affect relic areas, which are isolated for social or geographical reasons. Finally, between focal areas there are transition areas, which may be subject to pressure from more than one direction; and it is in areas like these, which have also had a long history of settlement, that complex patterns of isoglosses like the Rhenish Fan are characteristically found. Areas which have been settled more recently will tend to have fewer dialect differences; it follows that dialectal variation in British English is far more pronounced than in American English.

The recognition that sound changes take time to operate and can diffuse from one area, speaker or word to others also required a fundamental revision in historical linguistic theory. The Neogrammarians had traditionally represented linguistic relationships and language history by means of family trees (3), introduced into linguistics by Schleicher in 1871.

(3)

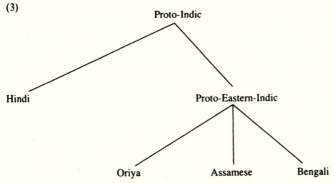

Family trees, like the one in (3), represent languages as uniform entities, and show splits of languages as clear-cut and immediate. If we are to accept Wenker's results, and incorporate notions like diffusion, gradual sound change, and influence of one variety on another into our theory, then these simplistic assumptions are untenable, certainly if we take trees literally and perhaps even if we are careful to see them as no more than shorthand.

The alternative model introduced to supplement or supplant family trees is the wave model, suggested by Schmidt in 1872. Wave theory recognises that innovations may arise in one variety and spread to others to which it may or may not be related, accounting for the influence of one dialect on another within a language, as well as borrowing and convergence (the topic of the last chapter). Innovations can spread over dialect and language boundaries, but may be constrained by socio-political factors, allowing both for the development of new isoglosses which may follow the creation of a new political or cultural centre, and the levelling of dialects which may result from the removal of a political boundary.

Isogloss maps are used in wave theory to indicate the features shared by particular varieties, but may become extremely clumsy and hard to read if large numbers of features are included, and are essentially synchronic rather than diachronic – a map reflects the situation at a particular point in time, and further description will be required to ascertain how that situation arose. Although the family tree incorporates problematic assumptions, it is accessible, convenient and clearly shows the historical dimension. One solution might be to find a way of combining the two (Hock 1986, Southworth 1964), or alternatively one might supplement a tree diagram with an isogloss map in cases where the spread of a particular feature rather than the broad historical perspective is at issue.

Wenker's techniques of data-gathering were also problematic in several respects. First, he used postal questionnaires, so that answers were not collected in person. Secondly, the sentences were written in standard German orthography; Wenker's informants obviously had no knowledge of any form of phonetic transcription, so this is inevitable, but it is notoriously difficult to represent dialect and accent differences using a standardised spelling system, and the methods of transcription used must have varied from person to person, leading to inconsistency. Finally, Wenker sent his questionnaires to schoolteachers, who are often seen as the arbiters of 'good' language use in a community. It is certainly conceivable that such people might be unwilling to accept the existence of non-standard linguistic behaviour in their villages, or at least inclined to modify it in the direction of the standard in their written responses.

Dialect surveys following Wenker have attempted to address these difficulties, generally by introducing personal interviews by a trained fieldworker using the International Phonetic Alphabet or some other form of phonetic transcription, to replace or supplement written questionnaires. The first work of this kind was the Linguistic Atlas of France, co-ordinated by Jules Gilliéron from 1896 onwards. Gilliéron employed as his principal fieldworker one Edmond Edmont, a grocer by trade, who was trained in phonetic transcription and spent some years cycling around France, interviewing villagers, and sending the results back to base. From these results Gilliéron discovered a bundle of coincident isoglosses separating French and Provençal, of the sort Wenker had looked for in vain with respect to High and Low German. This bundle runs from the west, north of Bordeaux, around Clermont-Ferrand and off to the east, and again correlates with non-linguistic features. For instance, houses to the north of this line generally have pitched roofs, while those to the south have the flat roofs characteristic of Mediterranean areas; and agricultural practices differ markedly between the two sectors.

Gilliéron's main interest was in what he called phonetic etymologies. He applied to Latin forms the changes he knew should have operated between Latin and modern French, then checked various modern dialects to see whether they exhibited the expected outcome. If a form in a particular dialect was different from that predicted from Gilliéron's knowledge of historical developments, then this discrepancy had to be explained. For instance, the word for 'cockerel' in modern French should be a descendent of Latin *gallus* 'cockerel'. In Gascony, however, we find instead the words *faisan* (usually 'pheasant') or *vicaire* (usually 'curate'). Gilliéron pointed out that *gallus* should have undergone certain changes specific to Gascon, becoming **gat; however, this is also the expected reflex of Latin *cattus* 'cat', and in fact Gascon *gat* 'cat' does occur. Gilliéron's suggested explanation involves homonymic clash; that is, homophony involving items from the same semantic field is not permitted, since unacceptable confusion might result. Since 'cat' and 'cockerel' are both farmyard animals, and since the expected developments in Gascon would leave *gat* for both, this item has been restricted to mean 'cat', and an alternative has been substituted for 'cockerel' - although it is not clear why the particular substitutes we find have been selected, or why 'cockerel' should have been replaced rather than 'cat'.

Since these initial dialect surveys in Germany and France, many others have been carried out, in England, Scotland, Italy, the USA and elsewhere. They all involve essentially the same methods of dialect geography, using direct interviewing, questionnaires or a combination of the two, and the results are usually published in atlas form, with each map showing the particular variants of a word used in different areas of the country. These are frequently of limited interest, notably because data are often presented without analysis or attempts at explanation, and especially because of their emphasis on 'purity' - the recording of a dialect before it becomes corrupted by the young or by incomers from other areas. To obtain information on this unsullied state, early dialect surveys concentrated on only one type of informant, the NORMS (Chambers and Trudgill 1980) or Non-mobile, Older, Rural Males. Speakers falling into this category were generally thought to speak a 'purer' version of the dialect than mobile individuals, who might have had their speech contaminated by other varieties; young people, who more easily incorporate innovations into their language; urban informants, who are surrounded by speakers of different varieties; and women, who, as we shall see in 9.3, tend to produce more standard speech than men. We shall see in the next section what attempts have been made to redress the balance and include a wider range of informants in sociolinguistic studies.

There are also bodies of dialectological work within the Structuralist and Generativist paradigms, which we can safely bypass here since they are of no particular consequence for historical linguistics. The Structuralist approach (Weinreich 1954; Moulton 1960) relies on the independent establishment of a phoneme system for each of the varieties being examined; from these individual systems, a single, higher order comparative system is constructed. Such so-called diasystems allow dialects to be compared, but can really only indicate differences of phoneme inventory. On the other hand, the Standard Generative approach to dialectology rests on an assumption of identity: dialects of one language are said to share the same underlying representations, and differ only in the form, ordering and/or inventory of rules. The underlying representations may be supplied by a single dialect (Brown 1972), or be neutral between the various dialects (Thomas 1967). However, this model is again inadequate, since the status of these basal forms for speakers is unclear. Furthermore, the view that dialects of a single language share common underlying forms whereas different languages differ at this level prevents us from seeing dialect and language variation as the continuum which geographical and social investigation have shown it to be. The change from shared underliers to discrepant ones would have to be sudden and catastrophic, conflicting with the growing body of evidence that suggests language change is predominantly gradual. In view of these difficulties, we shall not pursue Structuralist and Generative dialectology further here, turning instead to the impact of sociolinguistics on the study of language change.

9.3   Sociolinguistics

9.3.1   *The methodology of sociolinguistic investigation*

'The study of language change in its social context has been described by some as a virgin field; by others, as a barren territory. A brief examination of what has been written in the past on this subject shows that it is more like an abandoned back yard, overgrown with various kinds of tangled, secondary scholarship' (Labov 1972: 260).

Labov is quite right in his observation that some weird and wonderful work has been done in sociolinguistics. In this section, we shall concentrate on the relevance of some better-substantiated sociolinguistic studies for historical linguistics, and will refer in particular to the work of Labov in America, and Trudgill and the Milroys in Britain, describing their techniques and findings and their contribution to the actuation and transmission problems. The historical consequence of this work arises from the assumption that variation in the speech community is not random, but structured, and that it may in some cases represent change in progress. Since the social context of ongoing change is clearly observable, its mechanisms and causes may be easier to perceive than those of completed changes, for which the context is often not recoverable. Findings may then be generalised from changes in progress to completed changes, provided that we accept the Uniformitarian Principle, ' ... the claim that the same mechanisms which operated to produce the large-scale changes of the past may be observed operating in the current changes taking place around us' (Labov 1972: 161).

Of course, sociolinguistics was not always such a lively field; as we saw in the last section, studies of variation before the 1960s, when they were done at all, focussed on regional, and specifically rural dialectology. By the middle of this century, 'some dialectologists began to recognise that the spatial dimension of linguistic variation had been concentrated on to the exclusion of the social dimension' (Chambers and Trudgill 1980: 54). The emphasis on rural investigations followed from the early dialectological preoccupation with 'pure' varieties, since rural areas tend to be more linguistically uniform than urban ones, and older rural speakers in particular are likely to have been in contact with fewer other varieties than their town-dwelling counterparts. However, with the advent of descriptive rather than prescriptive linguistics, and the recognition that the majority of potential informants in America and Europe now live in the cities, it was realised that a great deal of potentially interesting data was simply being ignored. In the 1960s, urban dialectology, or sociolinguistics, was born.

The earliest work on urban variation simply represented a transfer of dialectological methodology to the towns – for instance, Eva Sivertsen's *Cockney Phonology* (1960), although ostensibly dealing with a variety spoken by thousands of speakers, drew all its data from four old ladies living in Bethnal Green (Chambers and Trudgill 1980). However, various strategies for achieving a wider distribution of data, from a good range of speakers, have been developed since, and are now generally used in sociolinguistic investigations. Notably, it is essential not to select informants in a subjective way, since the experimenter's own prejudices could have an unwelcome influence on the results. Instead, random, representative samples are required. Of course, it is impossible to interview every member of a speech community, especially one as large as the Lower East Side of New York City (Labov 1972), Norwich (Trudgill 1974) or Belfast (Milroy and Milroy 1985), but every speaker must have an equal chance of being chosen. Frequently, random sampling is achieved by selecting every hundredth, or thousandth name from the electoral register or some similar list.

Once the informants have been selected, they are interviewed. At this point, experimenters encounter the problem of eliciting natural, informal speech (which may well be where changes begin) from their informants, who may be made nervous by the presence of an unfamiliar interviewer and a taperecorder; this may cause them to concentrate on speaking 'correctly', and therefore formally. The difficulty this presents is summed up in the Observer's Paradox: sociolinguists would like to know how speakers speak when they are not being observed, but the only way to find out is by observing them. To use Labov's analogy, everybody knows that the light inside the fridge is on when the door is open, but how do we find out whether it is on or off when the door is closed, when checking might itself interfere?

Various techniques have been developed to deal with the Observer's Paradox, including recording informants in a group and observing speech which is strictly outside the interview situation. The most common technique in earlier sociolinguistic studies (see Trudgill 1974) is the structured interview, which involves asking the informant to perform various tasks at decreasing levels of formality. First, the informant reads a list of minimal pairs, a word list and a short passage. Next comes a question and answer session, and finally the interviewer encourages the informant, who by now has probably relaxed a little, to produce informal conversational speech by asking about childhood rhymes and sayings, encouraging diversions to make the informant talk for longer continuous periods, and perhaps asking questions which are likely to elicit an emotional response. This structured interview technique therefore enables a comparison of formal and casual styles within the same speaker.

Later experimenters have often followed Milroy (1980), who argues that it is easier to gain access to the vernacular if the informant feels at ease, and that this can be achieved by using an interviewer who is integrated into the speech community. This technique is known as participant observation, or more colloquially, as the 'friend-of-a-friend technique'. Milroy, investigating the speech of three housing-estates in Belfast, integrated herself into the various communities by making friends with one person, and having that person introduce her to other contacts. After visiting the communities over a certain period of time, making herself known and doing various favours for her potential informants (such as giving them lifts in her car), she succeeded in recording a good deal of high-quality informal speech.

The recorded data next have to be analysed. In general, the experimenter will have had a fairly good idea to start with of the features which are in variation, and therefore perhaps changing, and the interview is designed to elicit plentiful examples of these features. Sociolinguistic research is centred on the notion of the linguistic variable, an element which has a number of realisations, or variants, in speech, but a constant meaning. For instance, some English speakers pronounce the word *hat* as [hæt], and others as [æt], but the meaning is the same in both cases. The variants of each variable are typically not randomly distributed, but instead correlate with extra-linguistic factors like the age, sex and social class of the speaker, and the level of formality. To pursue the example of [h]-dropping, a sociolinguistic investigation would recognise a variable, written (h), with two variants, (h):[h] and (h):Ø. When analysing the data, the experimenter would assign a particular score to each occurrence of each variant, perhaps giving 1 for (h):[h] and 0 for (h):Ø. The resulting figures are then plotted against age, sex and so on, to see whether any significant pattern emerges. This kind of quantitative, statistical approach is necessary because most speakers will use both variants; however, their frequency of use will differ from speaker to speaker on the basis of non-linguistic factors. Most variables investigated have been phonological, and the examples discussed below will follow this trend, although it is certainly possible to study syntactic variables. For instance, the variation between single and multiple negation in English might be one such example; Labov (1972) also includes studies of the presence or absence of *be* in Black Vernacular English in sentences like *She's real nice* versus *She real nice*, and of negatives with *no* and *any* in the same dialect, as in *I ain't got no money* versus *I don't have any money*.

One rather common type of variation can be illustrated with Trudgill's (1974) results on the (ng) variable in Norwich. (ng) is the final consonant in words ending *-ing*, such as *seeing*, *helping*, *sitting*, and has two variants, (ng):[ŋ] with the velar nasal, and (ng):[n] with the alveolar. In (4), the score 100 indicates consistent use of [n], while 0 shows consistent use of [ŋ].

(4)   (ng) plotted against class and style
        (after Trudgill 1974: 92)

| | | Style | | |
Class	Word list	Reading passage	Formal speech	Casual speech
Middle Middle Class	0	0	3	28
Lower Middle Class	0	10	15	42
Upper Working Class	5	15	74	87
Middle Working Class	23	44	88	95
Lower Working Class	29	66	98	100

The occurrence of the two variants clearly correlates with two non-linguistic factors: one is style, with all speakers producing progressively more instances of [n] as formality decreases, and the other is social class; the higher the class to which an informant belongs, the more instances of [ŋ] he or she will produce in all styles. Of course, the concept of social class is a notoriously difficult one to define, and correlations of linguistic variation with class must therefore be treated with some care; but even so, the pattern revealed by Trudgill's data is striking.

It should also be borne in mind that tables like (4), where speakers are treated as representatives of a particular group, do not reveal what individuals are doing; they simply indicate trends in the speech community. Furthermore, a given individual may belong to more than one group. For instance, if we further split Trudgill's informants according to gender as well as social class, we find (see (5)) that quite consistently, across classes and styles, women use more of the higher-status variant [ŋ] than men. The anomalous LMC figures for casual speech arise from the small number of cases of this variable Trudgill succeeded in recording for this group and context; small amounts of data can therefore skew experimental results. We shall return in 9.3.2 to the general claim that women typically produce more high-prestige variants than men of the same class.

(5)   (ng) plotted against class, sex and style
        (after Trudgill 1974: 94)

| Class | | Word list | Style | | |
			Reading passage	Formal speech	Casual speech
MMC	M	0	0	4	31
	F	0	0	0	0
LMC	M	0	20	27	17
	F	0	0	3	67
UWC	M	0	18	81	95
	F	11	13	68	77
MWC	M	24	43	91	97
	F	20	46	81	88
LWC	M	66	100	100	100
	F	17	54	97	100

Linguistic variation may also correlate with the speaker's age. Labov (1972: Chapter 1) reports a study of vowel centralisation of the diphthongs (ai) and (au) on the island of Martha's Vineyard, off Massachusetts. Some of his results are shown in (6).

(6)   Centralisation plotted against age
        (after Labov 1972: 22)

Age	(ai)	(au)
75–	25	22
61–75	35	37
46–60	62	44
31–45	81	88
14–30	37	46

Levels of centralisation for both diphthongs clearly increase as age decreases, reaching an apparent peak in the 31- to 45-year-olds, with less centralisation in the youngest age group. We shall return to this example, and to the link between age variation and linguistic change, in the next section.

Finally, it should be stressed that linguistic features may also correlate with ethnic or religious group, and with other, less easily definable characteristics like the speaker's level of ambition, for instance. Furthermore, the recognition that some linguistic variation may be conditioned by social factors does not mean that linguistic factors cease to be important. For example, the two diphthongs in (6) pattern in slightly different ways, and this is likely to have a linguistic rather than a social explanation. Similarly, the Milroys' work in Belfast revealed that the variable (u) has a variant [ʌ], characteristic of lower-class speech. However, the percentage of [ʌ] found varied quite noticeably from word to word, as shown in (7).

(7)   Percentage of [ʌ] in Belfast
               (after Hudson 1980: 169)

pull	74 %
put	39 %
look	27 %
should	8 %

This variation may be a function of linguistic context, or may show that [ʌ] is spreading by lexical diffusion. In other words, linguistic changes in progress do not only spread from speaker to speaker or from group to group; they may also spread from word to word or from context to context.

Figures like those given above seem to indicate that speakers are, consciously or subconsciously, obeying certain fixed norms of behaviour; indeed, Labov (1972) defines a speech community as a group of speakers sharing a set of norms. Certain follow-up tests can be carried out after the primary data from a sociolinguistic experiment have been analysed, to check for the existence of, and informants' adherence to, these norms. First, speakers can be asked to participate in self-evaluation tests, during which they are played recordings of sentences containing the variants under investigation, and asked to assess which they would tend to produce themselves. In general, 'their answers reflect the form which they believe has prestige or is 'correct' rather than the form they actually use' (Labov 1972: 213). Only working-class men tend to under-report their level of use of prestige variants; men wishing to stress their membership of lower-class, urban male groups are unlikely to publicly assert their adherence to values, in language or other aspects of behaviour, largely determined by the middle class.

A second option is a matched guise test (Lambert *et al.* 1967), in which one speaker who is able to use two (or more) accents is recorded twice, once using each variety. These recordings are played to the informants, who are asked to evaluate 'Speaker A' and 'Speaker B' according to a number of criteria, including the speaker's occupation, likely level of education, salary, family background, leadership qualities, degree of honesty, and so on. It seems that most informants judge the voice with the higher percentage of prestige variants as belonging to a more educated speaker from a higher social group, who is likely to have a higher-status job – although speakers with regional accents, especially rural ones, are sometimes judged to be more honest and friendly! Such tests again evidence the existence of shared norms of linguistic behaviour, which govern informants' judgements of other speakers as well as their own actions.

Finally, the results obtained from sociolinguistic experiments may be skewed by the Observer's Paradox. It can be useful, therefore, to conduct a follow-up experiment using the technique of rapid anonymous observation: here, very short interviews are conducted with a number of informants who did not form part of the original survey, who will be encountered by chance (maintaining the random nature of the experiment) and who really will <u>not</u> know that their speech is being observed, so that the Observer's Paradox should not come into play. If the results are comparable with those from the main experiment, it can be concluded that the Observer's Paradox did not have too detrimental an effect on the original interviews. The best-known rapid anonymous survey is Labov's (1972) New York department store experiment. As part of his sociolinguistic survey of the Lower East Side, Labov examined the (r) variable, which has variants (r):[r] and (r):Ø before consonants and pauses; his results for (r) were generally comparable to Trudgill's figures for (ng) in Norwich (see (4) above). To verify these results, Labov selected three New York department stores, one high-class, one middle-class and one lower-class. Labov assumed that sales assistants in these stores were likely to imitate or accommodate linguistically towards their customers, in order to 'fit in': staff at the higher-class store should therefore be predicted to produce most occurrences of the prestige variant (r):[r], and those in the lower-class store should produce fewest. Labov approached shop assistants in all three stores and asked the location of particular goods, selected to elicit the phrase *fourth floor*, which contains two instances of (r). The results showed exactly the predicted variation, if the staff at the three stores are compared with the classes of informants from Labov's main experiment. A further example of rapid anonymous observation, again designed by Labov and again rather ingenious, involved the variation between [s] and [ʃ] in *str-* clusters in Philadelphia. Labov and his co-experimenters stopped people at random around Philadelphia and asked 'Can you tell me how to get to X Avenue?' The answer was generally 'X <u>Street</u>?', allowing observation of the required variable (L. Milroy 1987: 74).

9.3.2   *Sociolinguistics and language change*
9.3.2.1   Introduction

We now return to the question of how the results of sociolinguistic surveys can enlighten us on the subject of linguistic change in progress. Just as separated isoglosses in dialectology could be taken as showing the spread of a change in space and time, so the correlations of linguistic features and social factors, if they are seen not as fixed but as shifting, can indicate the spread of an innovation through the speech community. It may be that our quantitative data can even tell us which group has started the spread of the change.

9.3.2.2   Real and apparent time

Let us begin our investigation by returning to the variable centralisation of the diphthongs /ai/ in words like *fire, high, sight* and /au/ in *loud, mouth, how* among inhabitants of Martha's Vineyard, a small island with a population of around 6,000, off Massachusetts. Some data from Labov's (1972, Chapter 1) investigation were given above as (6), and are repeated for convenience as (8).

(8)   Centralisation plotted against age
          (after Labov 1972: 22)

Age	(ai)	(au)
75–	25	22
61–75	35	37
46–60	62	44
31–45	81	88
14–30	37	46

It is clear from (8) that younger people, with the exception of the very youngest group, show a higher degree of centralisation of both diphthongs than older ones. Labov hypothesises that this distribution of variation indicates a change in progress, and moreover a change which is being introduced by middle-aged speakers and being adopted strongly by 31- to 45-year-olds, and variably by younger speakers. However, Labov's proposal relies on the validity of studies in apparent time.

The ideal historical linguistic survey would take place in real time; a representative sample of informants would be interviewed, then re-interviewed at ten or twenty year intervals, with the resulting data tracing the movement of ongoing changes through the community. There are all kinds of obvious difficulties with this procedure: informants will die, or move away, or refuse to be interviewed again; the experimenter may have to be replaced, perhaps with consequences for the methodology; and results will not be available for many years. Real-time studies using comparable populations at the different stages rather than precisely the same set of informants would not be restricted to the life-span of individual speakers, but the other problems would remain. Consequently, Labov and his followers have introduced apparent time studies, in which only one set of interviews is done, at one point in time. The set of speakers interviewed is selected to be representative of all age groups in the community, and correlations of linguistic variants with age are calculated. Variation in these correlations is interpreted as indicative of ongoing change, and the speech of older people is therefore seen as characteristic of earlier stages of the language. In other words, 'the validity of such a study hinges crucially upon the hypothesis that the speech of, say, 40 year olds today directly reflects the speech of 20 year olds twenty years ago and is thus comparable for diffusion research to the speech of 20 year olds today. Discrepancies in the speech of 40 year olds and 20 year olds are attributable to the progress of a linguistic innovation in the twenty years that separate the two groups' (Chambers and Trudgill 1980: 165). In short, apparent-time studies do not involve 'real' diachronic work at all, in the sense of explicitly comparing different periods in the history of a language; instead, they involve looking at synchrony and attempting to perceive the seeds of diachrony in it.

Various difficulties are also inherent in apparent-time work. For instance, we must assume that adult speakers maintain their language from age twenty or so throughout their lives, unless they are subject to some sound change, and this seems over-simplistic. Furthermore, and perhaps even more seriously, it is in principle impossible to distinguish age variation in apparent time which signals a change in progress, from some linguistic feature which simply varies with age, becoming apparent in the speech of people of a certain age. Younger people sometimes behave differently from older ones in other respects; why should certain linguistic features not also be restricted to particular age groups?

One compromise is to attempt to find some early survey, perhaps of a dialectological nature, relating to the variety being investigated or a closely related variety. This can then be used to confirm the apparent-time data by providing a partial real-time comparison, albeit conducted by a different investigator, using different informants and a different methodology. For instance, in the case of Martha's Vineyard, Labov was able to refer to interviews with islanders conducted in the 1930s as part of the fieldwork for the

Linguistic Atlas of New England (LANE). These revealed that, at that time, inhabitants of Martha's Vineyard did centralise (ai) to a moderate extent, but scarcely if ever centralised (au). Comparing these LANE records with Labov's findings therefore indicates clearly that a change is under way.

Such cases, where apparent-time experiments can be checked against earlier dialectological records, may predispose us more favourably towards accepting the results of surveys conducted in apparent time, even when no real-time back-up is available. We can then identify the distribution of variants we would expect to find in a speech community when some linguistic change is in progress. The 'normal' distribution, expected when change is not affecting the variable under consideration, would be roughly that shown in (9), where young and old speakers characteristically use higher proportions of lower-status variants. Chambers and Trudgill (1980) suggest that this may be because 'middle-aged' speakers are generally trying to succeed in their careers, and may be in contact with a wide range of contacts who they wish to impress: speakers in this central age band are therefore most likely to be responsive to the norms of linguistic behaviour in their speech community.

(9)

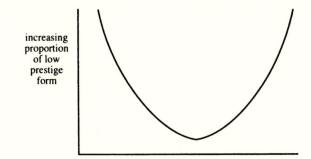

increasing
proportion
of low
prestige
form

increasing age

However, when a change is in progress, the variable investigated will tend to show one of the patterns of distribution in (10) or (11).

(10)

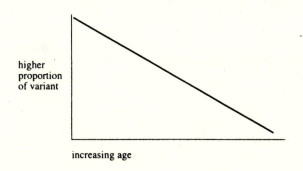

higher
proportion
of variant

increasing age

(11)

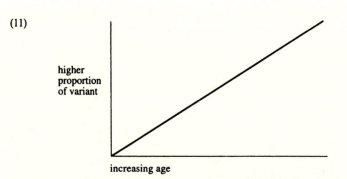

A variant being introduced by linguistic change will occur much more frequently in the speech of younger people, as in (10). However, a variant being lost will conform to the pattern in (11), with many more occurrences in older informants.

The centralisation change in Martha's Vineyard seems to conform broadly to the pattern in (10), since the amount of centralisation is increasing from generation to generation. Labov also attempts to consider the social meaning of this change by taking into account the social context: 'no change takes place in a social vacuum' (Labov 1972: 2). He points out that Martha's Vineyard, although widely regarded as a pleasant place to live, had by the 1960s lost most of its traditional industries; many islanders had therefore left to work on the mainland, and those remaining often found it hard to make a living. Furthermore, property on the island was increasingly being bought by mainlanders, who flocked to Martha's Vineyard in the summer. Those islanders remaining understandably became resentful of this influx of wealthy summer visitors, and sought to affirm their identity as islanders. It is entirely plausible that they should have done so partly through their language; on this view, the centralisation of diphthongs is the linguistic equivalent of wearing a T-shirt which says 'I'm not a tourist, I live here'.

The next question is where this tendency towards centralisation originated. Labov's data indicated that fishermen from Chilmark, in the rural up-island, exhibited the highest amount of centralisation, which seems to have spread from their dialect. This accords well with the general island attitude towards the Chilmark fishermen, who are seen as almost emblematic of the island's history and culture, especially given their independence and the courage needed for their occupation. The feature of centralisation has therefore been adopted and exaggerated, albeit unconsciously, on the basis of their speech. It also follows quite naturally that most centralisation should be found, in Labov's survey, in the 31- to 45-

year-olds, who have generally been away at College, then made a positive decision to return to Martha's Vineyard despite the island's economic problems. This positive commitment to the island is reflected in their language.

Labov's final concern is to explain the ostensibly discrepant figures for the youngest category of speakers. In fact, young informants who wish ultimately to leave the island characteristically have very low indexes of centralisation, while those who intend to remain have extremely high levels of centralisation, rather more indeed than the average for the 31- to 45-year-olds, showing that the change is still proceeding. However, combining these two opposing groups of younger speakers produces average figures for the age group which are lower than those for the 31- to 45-year-olds, misleadingly suggesting that the change is reversing itself.

Labov's study of Martha's Vineyard, then, shows the importance of apparent-time studies in tracing change in progress, and also indicates that taking into account the social meaning of linguistic variation can allow us to pinpoint the source of the change. However, we are still really no nearer solving the actuation problem; we know that the Vineyarders adopted centralisation of diphthongs from the Chilmark fishermen, but we still have no idea why this particular feature was adopted, or why the fishermen produced centralised diphthongs in the first place.

9.3.2.3 Overt and covert prestige

Apparent-time studies based on age do not provide the only indication of ongoing change, since 'ongoing linguistic changes may often be reflected in unusual patterns of social class differentiation' (Chambers and Trudgill 1980: 95). Such unexpected patterns can also suggest which group might be at the forefront of the change. For instance, the data in (12), again from Trudgill's Norwich survey, show scores for speakers from five social classes for the variant [ʌ] of the variable (e), found in words like *hell*. The table shows that the amount of [ʌ] increases gradually from the middle middle class (MMC) to the lower working class (LWC), except that the Upper Working Class informants have far higher levels of [ʌ] than would be expected. It may well be that the Upper Working Class speakers are therefore the initiators of this change.

(12) Norwich (e):[ʌ]
MMC	2
LMC	42
UWC	127
MWC	87
LWC	77

Many unusual patterns of class-conditioning are specific to particular changes, but one such pattern has been frequently reported in the literature; this involves the phenomenon of hypercorrection. In New York City, Labov discovered that more instances of the higher-prestige variant (r):[r] were found in all speakers in formal speech, and that working-class speakers had less [r] than upper-middle-class speakers in all styles. In casual speech, the lower-middle-class informants, as might have been expected, produced levels of (r):[r] intermediate between the upper-middle-class and working-class levels; but in more formal styles, the lower-middle-class informants produced significantly higher levels of (r):[r] than those from the upper middle class. This exaggerated level of [r] production is achieved by inserting [r] even in environments where it is not historically appropriate; for example, some of Labov's lower-middle-class informants pronounced *God* as [gɑ:rd]. An equivalent case of hypercorrection involves some British English speakers who characteristically use (h):Ø – these '[h]-droppers' may in formal situations attempt to speak 'correctly' by inserting [h], but are unsure of the appropriate environments and therefore overshoot, producing hypercorrect forms like [hæt] for the preposition *at*. Furthermore, matched guise and self-evaluation tests indicate that lower-middle-class speakers are characteristically hypersensitive to lower-status variants, claiming virtually never to use these themselves and evaluating other speakers who do produce them extremely adversely.

It seems that members of the lower middle class tend to be socially and linguistically insecure, perhaps due to their position between the norm-setting upper middle class, to which they aspire, and the working class, from which they may wish to distance themselves. This leads to a careful adherence to norms imposed by the upper middle class, which may become exaggerated, resulting in hypercorrection. However, lower-middle-class hypercorrection will result in a greater number of prestige variants being heard and perhaps ultimately produced by the lower classes. Because of their insecurity and social mobility, the lower middle and upper working classes are therefore of some importance in the spread of change, whereas the upper and lower extremes of the class scale are relatively conservative.

Many sociolinguistically motivated changes do involve the progressive adherence of other speakers to norms set by the upper middle classes. Such changes are often changes from above (Labov 1972), so-called because they operate above the level of conscious awareness (speakers are conscious of phenomena like pronunciation versus lack of [r]), not because they involve prestige pronunciations. Such changes characteristically involve variation correlating both with style and with some other social factor such as social class or sex. Most of the variables discussed above have been of this doubly-conditioned type, which are known as markers; the general pattern of distribution for a marker is shown in (13).

(13)

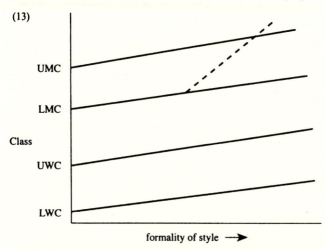

There are also variables which are conditioned by class or sex, for instance, but not by style, giving the typical pattern in (14): these variables are indicators.

(14)

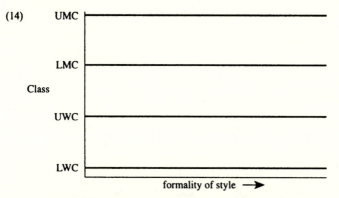

The great majority of changes involve markers, but occasional changes proceed on the basis of an indicator. These are called changes from below, to suggest that the change begins below the level of conscious awareness, not that the source is a variant characteristic of a lower class, although this is often the case. The spreading medial glottal stop in words like *butter*, *letter* seems to have started as an indicator, as does the pronunciation of *bird*, *heard* in New York with a diphthong [ɜɪ]. The variants involved in changes from below are liable to become stereotyped; that is, speakers begin to notice them and to associate them with particular groups in the speech community. If they are stigmatised, or regarded as indicative of low status or lack of education, they may then be lost, so that the ongoing change is reversed from above the level of conscious awareness. For example, speakers are frequently told not to say [bʌʔə] and so on, although whether this is actually reducing the incidence of the glottal stop is open to debate. Similarly, [ɜɪ] in New York is both stigmatised and stereotyped, even being represented in writing with spellings like *boid*, and this change does indeed seem to be reversing. Interestingly, not only those variants which are stereotyped as indicative of low class membership tend to be lost, but also those which are seen as characteristic of the upper class, or more accurately, of would-be members of the upper class. For instance, a pronunciation of *house* as [haɪs] surfaced briefly in the 1980s among workers in the City of London, was stigmatised as a feature of the then-prevalent 'yuppie' culture, and seems to have all but gone. In cases where indicators are involved in language change, and are not stigmatised and lost, they seem to become markers and begin to vary with style before the change is completed (Chambers and Trudgill 1980).

Most of the changes discussed above involve an attempt to emulate the highest-status group, whose behaviour and language are seen as prestigious. Prestige based on norms set by the upper classes is known as overt prestige, and is reflected in the actions and attitudes of all classes in the speech community. However, not all linguistic behaviour or change is dictated by overt prestige; if it were, we would all speak similarly, using high-status variants, and language change would presumably take the form of a spiral of hypercorrections. Of course, lower-class varieties and variants are also maintained, and inspire some changes. Sociolinguists have introduced the notion of covert prestige to account for these phenomena.

Just as there are norms of upper-class usage, there are also lower-class norms; these generally have less impact on the speech community as a whole, since the speakers of low-status dialects tend to be less socially influential. These norms can also be enforced, and will tend to be adhered to by speakers wishing to emphasise their group membership; we have already seen that this is the case for lower-class males, who characteristically evaluate low-status forms favourably and are thus influenced by a second, covert type of prestige.

In their Belfast studies, the Milroys (L. Milroy 1980, J. Milroy 1992) used the notion of social network to account for the maintenance of lower-class variants. Each speaker has a social network, which is the sum of all contacts he or she has with other speakers – family, friends, acquaintances and once-met strangers at the bus-stop included. Every personal network will be unique, but some share particular characteristics. Notably, social networks can be placed on scales of denseness and multiplexity, where a dense network is one in which any third party mentioned by a speaker is likely also to be known to her hearer, and a multiplex network includes many members who know one another in several different social spheres; for instance, two speakers might be neighbours, work for the same company, socialise together and worship in the same church. The Milroys devised various tests for denseness and multiplexity, and applied these to give a strength score for each social network. The higher this network strength score, the more integrated the speaker is likely to be into his or her community. Well-integrated, central speakers in closeknit networks are most susceptible to norm-enforcing mechanisms; although they may passively share the more overtly prestigious norms determined by upper-middle-class speech, they do not themselves produce such speech, since these norms are outweighed by conflicting standards set by peer pressure and covert prestige. Thus (L. Milroy 1987: 106), 'individuals in Belfast whose personal networks were closeknit tended to approximate closely to the stigmatized vernacular norms characteristic of the locality, which like other 'in-group' norms powerfully symbolized values of solidarity, reciprocity and to some extent opposition to standardized norms along with *their* associated values'.

This notion of degree of integration into a closeknit network may also account in part for our observation that men seem most influenced by covert prestige. In many working-class communities, men have tradition-ally gone out to work while women remained at home. Since there is often one major employer like a factory or a shipyard for a single community, men will contract relationships in the workplace which supplement ties with neighbours, producing higher network strength scores. Men will therefore lead changes inspired by features of the vernacular. Women, however, with their more looseknit social networks, will be more open to external norms set by the upper classes, so that women are charac-teristically in the forefront of changes based on overt prestige. These tendencies do not seem to hold in communities like India and Iran, where women have a fixed and clearly subordinate role; women seem to lead change towards the standard only where they play some part in public life (Holmes 1992: 234).

In fact, the crucial factor determining who leads changes based on vernacular norms does not seem to be gender per se. There is a tendency in Belfast (Milroy and Milroy 1985) for /a/ to be backed, and this variant is especially characteristic of casual speech and inner city areas; it is a core feature of the Belfast vernacular. In the Ballymacarrett area of the city, the backed variant is found predominantly in working-class men, as would be predicted in the social network model. However, in the Clonard district, young women aged 18–25 have a far higher network strength score than young men; the closure of traditional industry in the area means that many men are unemployed, while young women typically do have jobs. These women also produce the backed variant of /a/ far more than their male counterparts, although the expected, reverse pattern is found in other age groups, showing that network strength may indeed be relevant in explaining the propagation of change and the maintenance of vernacular features.

9.3.3   *Actuation*

Thus far, we have largely been tacitly ignoring the problem of actuation or initiation of change, concentrating instead on its transmission through the speech community. Although variation studies do seem to produce enlightening accounts of the spread of variants, a large question mark continues to hover over the genesis and selection of the variant itself: for instance, Labov's study of Martha's Vineyard revealed that centralisation of diphthongs probably spread from the Chilmark fishermen, but not why the fishermen centralised *their* vowels or why this feature in particular should have been adopted by other islanders.

Labov (1972) provides a certain amount of encouragement on this matter, claiming that historical linguists do not fail to account for the ultimate actuation or birth of a variant, since this is simply beyond our remit. A huge number of sources for variation exist; 'variations may be induced by the processes of assimilation or differentiation, by analogy, borrowing, fusion, contamination, random variation, or any number of processes in which the language system interacts with the physiological or psychological characteristics of the individual' (Labov 1972: 1–2). However, these possible explanations are not part of our problem: the real actuation question is why some of these innovations die out and others catch on, spreading through the community, or why certain instances of variation become changes while others don't.

In fact, Labov argues that it is not meaningful for us to distinguish actuation from transmission. An idiosyncratic speech habit, or a slip of the tongue certainly introduces variation, but *change* is only initiated when the new variant is adopted by a group of speakers, becomes systematic and acquires some social significance. As Labov (1972: 277) puts it, we may 'assume that a certain word or pronunciation is indeed introduced by one individual. It becomes a part of the language only when it is adopted by others, i.e. when it is propagated. Therefore the origin of a change is its 'propagation' or acceptance by others.'

However, it seems that we cannot (yet?) predict with any accuracy which instances of variation will lead to change (see also Chapter 12). Labov accepts that this is a function of the influence of social context on language; since every social situation is unique, linguistic behaviour in such situations is bound to be to some extent unpredictable. He does accept that variants will start off as characteristic of particular social groups and will then spread out to others, gradually acquiring some systematic social value; however, the fate of the variant, and consequently the rate, extent and direction of the change, will depend on that social value and the prestige of the group first using the form in question. Only a few tentative generalisations can be made: for instance, Labov claims that women are more active in spreading overtly prestigious variants; that the upper working and lower middle classes are most active in initiating change as their linguistic insecurity causes them to imitate upper-class speakers; and that innovating speakers will tend to be the central members of their groups, with high status within their communities and also many contacts outside them.

The Milroys (Milroy and Milroy 1985; J. Milroy 1992) adopt a subtly different approach to the problem of actuation. They see the essential goal as the explanation of why language is sometimes changed and sometimes maintained, even in very similar sets of circumstances. They note that the answer to this question has generally been sought in the dynamics of the language system but argue that we might make more progress by considering the role of the speaker, and distinguishing speaker innovation from language change. In other words, 'it is not languages that innovate; it is speakers who innovate. The reflexes of speaker-innovations are then observed in language states, where they appear as systematic and rule-governed linguistic change' (Milroy and Milroy 1985: 345). Of course, linguistic structure is still important; speaker innovation may start a change, but a chain reaction may then begin, with subsequent steps being motivated by the system. Thus, we maintain the Structuralist notions of the structure and function of linguistic systems as influences on change.

However, although 'we can describe speaker-innovation as an act of the speaker which is capable of influencing linguistic structure' (J. Milroy 1992: 169), not all innovations lead to change. Some may remain idiolectal features of the innovator; others may reach the speaker's immediate community but go no further; but some innovations will spread into other communities via some mediator who is connected to all the networks involved – and this is linguistic change.

The Milroys argue that dense, multiplex social networks typically retard or resist language change, instead maintaining vernacular norms. Furthermore, central, well-integrated members of such networks are liable to be more sensitive to their normalising influences, and will therefore be less likely to innovate. This is a problem for Labov's hypothesis that innovators in language change are likely to be those with strong ties inside and outside their social group. Milroy and Milroy (1985) suggest an alternative solution: if closeknit networks and strong interpersonal ties lead to language maintenance, might not looseknit networks and weak interpersonal ties promote language change? Innovators might then be sought among speakers contracting large numbers of weak links with other groups without occupying a central position in their own, while a loosening of network structure could signal a volatile situation conducive to change.

Strong interpersonal ties might be roughly defined as those between friends, while weak ties connect acquaintances; the measurement depends on the intensity and intimacy of the relationship, and the time the two people spend together (J. Milroy 1992: 178). Characteristically, people draw their friends from their own social group, while their acquaintances may have widely differing social backgrounds; it follows that 'weak ties BETWEEN groups provide bridges through which information and influence are diffused, and ... weak ties are more likely to link members of DIFFERENT social groups than strong ones, which tend to be concentrated WITHIN particular groups' (Milroy and Milroy 1985: 364). Furthermore, since a person will generally have more acquaintances than friends, weak ties reach more people and are more numerous. Consequently, 'weak intergroup ties ... are likely to be critical in transmitting innovations from one group to another, despite the commonsense assumption that STRONG ties fulfil this role' (ibid.: 365).

The innovators crucial to linguistic change, who start the movement of a variant through society, are therefore highly likely to be socially mobile individuals who are not central enough in any group to be constrained by its norm-enforcing mechanisms, but who have weak links with enough groups to pass the variant on to their members. They are consequently liable to be members of the more mobile upper working or lower middle class, as Labov hypothesised. For the change to be successfully transmitted, however, it must be passed from these peripheral innovators to the so-called early adopters. These will be central in their social group, and subject to its norms. However, they may adopt the crucial variant from the innovators due to its (covert or overt) prestige, and because, although change is 'risky' and could lead to rejection, it bears less risk if the variant involved is already characteristic of speakers on the fringes of the group. Once the socially central, influential early adopters have begun to use a variant, other members of the group who may regard them as role-models are likely to follow suit. On this analysis, Labov fails adequately to account for the early stages of change because he does not distinguish innovators from early adopters – although, as the Milroys note, this distinction may only be possible in principle; in the case of a particular change, a given group of speakers may not be identifiable as innovators or early adopters.

The Milroys' theory has a number of advantages. Notably, it makes the strong claim that 'linguistic change is slow to the extent that the relevant populations are well established and bound by strong ties, whereas it is rapid to the extent that weak ties exist in populations' (Milroy and Milroy 1985: 375). This may account for the existence of conservative and innovating languages, such as Icelandic and English respectively, and for periods of rapid and slow change in the history of one language. By extension, it may also explain the more innovatory nature of urban dialects as compared with rural ones (and the preoccupation of traditional dialectology with the latter). Finally, this hypothesis predicts that language contact, migration and invasion should promote linguistic change, and (as Chapters 8, 10 and 11 show), this does seem to be the case.

However, there is also a considerable drawback: weak ties, by their very nature, are hard to investigate, and the initial spread of a variant from one group to another by a mediating innovator, the real actuation of the change, may therefore not be observable; we now know where to look, but can't see anything. That is, 'for the very reason that persons who actuate linguistic change may do so in the course of fleeting, insignificant encounters with others occupying a similarly marginal position in their social groups, direct observation of the actuation process may be difficult, if not impossible. What we most probably CAN observe is the take-up of the innovation by the more socially salient EARLY ADOPTERS' (Milroy and Milroy 1985: 370). For instance, as we saw above, the speakers in the Clonard area of West Belfast with the highest instances of backed /a/ are the young women. These also have a very high network strength score, are part of a closeknit community, and are therefore unlikely to be innovators; this is supported by the fact that backing of /a/ seems to be spreading from the East of the city. However, the young Clonard women may well be early adopters. They tend to be employed as shop assistants in a store with customers from East and West Belfast, and are therefore in contact with many speakers who have only weak ties to their community and to others. These weak ties can act as channels down which innovations pass; through them, the young Clonard women have adopted backed /a/ and are now passing it on to other members of their own community.

Thanks to Labov and the Milroys, we now have a general theory of the transmission of change, and at least an idea of where actuation fits in. First, variation arises, constrained by perceptual, acoustic and other general linguistic conditions on possible innovations (Harris 1986). This is not yet actuation, but speaker innovation. Some innovations spread, while others do not, at least partly for reasons of prestige; the projected link of network theory with a general theory of social structure (J. Milroy 1992) may help us understand which changes are likely and why. Change is then actuated as it spreads from the innovator to other social groups, where it will be accepted by the early adopters, then diffuse to the other members. Gradually, the variation involved becomes orderly, the variants acquire social meaning, and change becomes apparent in the system – at which rather late stage it becomes detectable by sociolinguistic observation. Earlier stages are not yet observable or altogether explicable, and previous studies claiming to observe actuation have probably, at best, been noticing early adoption. We have, then, a framework for the transmission of gradual, socially motivated language change, and can observe and measure its progress. Actuation, the initial spread of an incipient change by innovators through weak ties with other groups, remains almost as mysterious and unattainable as ever.

10 Pidgins and creoles

10.1 Introduction

> The pidgin English as spoken in these days is about the most atrocious
> form of speech perhaps one could find in any corner of the globe. It is
> neither one thing nor the other. Consisting of a mixture of Samoan and
> Chinese here and there, with an occasional word of Malayan, it is
> conglomeration truly worthy of the Tower of Babel
>
> (*Rabaul Times*, 16 October 1925; quoted Romaine 1988: 10).

This quotation, taken from a newspaper published in Papua New
Guinea, specifically involves Tok Pisin, the pidgin language of New
Guinea which is now becoming a creole and which has been recognised as
one of the official languages of the country. However, the criticisms
contained in it are characteristic of earlier attitudes to pidgin and creole
languages, both inside and outside linguistics. Popularly, pidgins and
creoles are often still written off as 'inferior, haphazard, broken,
bastardized versions of older, longer established languages' (Todd 1990:
1); and although the first systematic studies of pidgins and creoles were
carried out in the 1880s by Hugo Schuchardt, these languages were
subsequently shunned by linguists, who saw them as aberrant and
uninteresting, for the best part of a century. The first conference on pidgin
and creole studies took place only in 1959, and most of the key ideas in the
field date from this time or later. The study of language birth is therefore
a new, expanding, and often controversial one.

It may be useful to begin with some preliminary definitions. Approximately 200 pidgin and creole languages are spoken today, mostly in West
Africa, the Caribbean and the South Pacific. A pidgin is essentially a
contact language, developed in a situation where different groups of people
require some means of communication but lack any common language.
Crucially, a pidgin is nobody's first language; all its speakers learn it as
adults as a second or further language, and all have native languages of
their own. Pidgins are typically restricted in function, since they are used
only in contact situations; for instance, in communication between masters

253

and slaves on former European-owned plantations in the Caribbean, or between the slaves themselves, who were often separated from others of their own linguistic group to lessen the chance of revolt. In more modern times, pidgins often arise in areas where many disparate languages are spoken – Papua New Guinea has one of the densest concentrations of indigenous languages of any area, and Tok Pisin has become very successful there as a lingua franca. Along with this restriction in function goes a restriction in form, as we shall see in the next section. Finally, pidgins will generally have at least three parent languages. One will typically be a European language, since pidgins arose predominantly in the context of European colonisation; this language is known as the superstrate, and was typically spoken by the dominant social group, and consequently more socially prestigious in the community. Two or more substrate languages will also be involved: these are typically less prestigious and are often indigenous, although in the Caribbean, for instance, they were typically introduced to the area by the slave population.

It is probably worth emphasising here that pidgins are not lazy, corrupted or debased forms of either the superstrate or the substrate languages, nor are they haphazard mixtures. It is quite possible for *ad hoc*, mixed and highly simplified systems to arise given a particularly pressing need for communication; these can be heard, for instance, in exchanges between taxi drivers and foreign tourists. However, these one-off, unsystematic varieties are not pidgins, but jargons, which lack fixed norms; pidgins represent a later stage in the process and have acquired rules of their own and a degree of systematicity. They can be learned as languages in their own right, albeit rather restricted ones. Pidgins therefore do not only simplify the grammars of their superstrate and substrate languages, but also restructure them to produce a new linguistic system.

A pidgin becomes a creole when it is adopted as the native language of a speech community. For instance, children may be born to parents who have no common language other than the pidgin; or perhaps to slaves who had been separated from others of their own linguistic group, and therefore had to rely on the pidgin to communicate. Such children would be exposed to the pidgin as their first linguistic input, and would acquire it as a native language. Under these circumstances, the new creole will have to fulfil many more functions than its pidgin ancestor, which was used only in particular situations by speakers who had a native language to fall back on; and creoles very quickly become expanded and elaborated in all areas of their grammar. Quite where these new, expanded structures come from is one of the most interesting and controversial areas of current 'creolistics', to which we shall return in some detail in 10.5.

Before going on to consider the structures of pidgins and creoles in more depth, readers should be warned that there is no real agreement in the current literature as to exactly what pidgins and creoles are, or even whether it is profitable to make a distinction between them (Mühlhäusler 1986). For present purposes, I shall accept the pidgin versus creole dichotomy as a useful working definition, with the added notion of a pidgin-creole 'life-cycle'; that is, I assume that systems may proceed along a continuum from jargon to stabilised pidgin to expanded pidgin, and that creolisation may affect a pidgin at any stage, or not at all.

10.2   Pidgins

10.2.1   *Theories of origin*

There is considerable disagreement in the literature over how pidgin languages arise, the five most popular theories probably being nautical jargon, independent parallel development, substratum theory, monogenesis with relexification, and baby talk / foreigner talk. I shall review these hypotheses very briefly.

The nautical jargon theory assumes that pidgins are derived from the lingua franca used by the crews of ships, presumably through trading and other contacts. This hypothesis might explain some lexical similarities among pidgins; but it is hard to extend this to cover the numerous structural similarities. Furthermore, as Romaine (1988) notes, it is hardly surprising that pidgins have nautical elements in their lexicon, since the majority are spoken near the sea.

On the other hand, as Hall argues, each pidgin might have evolved independently; they are similar in structure because they are restructurings of similar languages, with predominantly European superstrates and African substrates, which develop in similar social and physical conditions. As we shall see in 10.5, Aitchison (1987, 1989a) views creolisation similarly, arguing that particular types of expansion are characteristic of creoles because pidgins are such simple systems: 'given a very simple initial state, there are only a few logically possible ways of extending it. Faced with this limited choice, different pidgins are likely to choose similar options' (1987: 22).

An early account of pidgin origins, which is currently undergoing something of a revival, is the idea that the superstrate or lexifier language contributes the vocabulary to a pidgin, while its grammar comes directly from the substrate(s). Mühlhäusler (1986) argues that this view is partly politically motivated; for instance, it is important for present-day Black Caribbeans to recognise and affirm their linguistic and cultural heritage from their African ancestors. However, substrate influence on pidgins rarely involves all and only the grammar. For instance (Romaine 1988), constructions in various French-based pidgins and creoles attributed to African languages could also be traced to seventeenth century dialects of French, or might be quite natural developments from earlier French. In fact, many pidgin constructions and lexical items have two or more possible sources, which may not have conflicted, but rather conspired to include the particular structure in the pidgin. Thus, for Tok Pisin *meri* 'woman', we have English *Mary* and *marry*, and also *mari* 'pretty' from the indigenous language Tolai; while Jamaican Creole *doti* 'dirty' may be derived from English *dirty*, West African Twi *doti* 'dirty', or both, with each source reinforcing the other (Mühlhäusler 1986, and see 10.5 below).

The fourth theory, monogenesis, holds that all current pidgins are descended ultimately from Sabir, a fifteenth century proto-pidgin with a Portuguese superstrate which was used in trading and in the first Portuguese colonising expeditions to India, West Africa and the Far East. Sabir itself is sometimes said to be a relic of the original Lingua Franca, a medieval language used by Mediterranean traders and by the Crusaders. Sabir was supposedly acquired by the indigenous populations in trading areas; if later colonisation occurred, it would be relexified, with words from the locally dominant language replacing the original Portuguese forms. There is certainly some evidence for relexification: for instance, many Romance loans in English have supplanted inherited Germanic forms, while Voorhoeve (1973) claims that two of the creoles of Surinam, Sranan and Saramaccan, show varying degrees of relexification from Portuguese and towards English. However, the possibility of relexification does not prove monogenesis. This hypothesis does have the advantage of accounting for the Portuguese-derived words which occur very regularly in almost all pidgins and creoles, two examples being the verb 'to know', often of the form *sabi* or *savi*, and the word for 'small' or 'a child', which is frequently *pikin*, *pikni* or *pikinini*. On the other hand, French and Spanish influence on West Indian creoles might equally well account for the presence of *savvy* in Early Trinidadian Creole, for instance; and structural similarities are not so readily explained as lexical ones. Finally, this theory cannot account for the existence of non-European-based pidgins which nonetheless share structural similarities with pidgins which do have European superstrates. In the absence of positive evidence for the spread and relexification of Sabir, we must treat this explanation with some caution.

Finally, the baby talk and foreigner talk accounts both relate pidgin origin to second language acquisition; either non-European, indigenous people learned an imperfect version of the target, superstrate language, or the European colonisers simplified their own language to make it easier for the substrate speakers to learn. These entirely compatible explanations may be rather enlightening, provided that we dispose of the unjustified racist notion, thankfully becoming rarer now, that non-Europeans are intellectually incapable of mastering the subtleties of a European language. It is overwhelmingly likely that substrate speakers acquire a pidgin simply because they are not exposed to the superstrate sufficiently often or for sufficiently long for it to serve as an adequate model: 'pidginization is second-language learning with restricted input' (Bickerton 1977: 49). Access to the superstrate is generally restricted for socioeconomic reasons. For instance, slaves arriving on plantations early may have had more opportunity to acquire the superstrate, since there would be a higher proportion of Europeans to non-Europeans; but gradually, the substrate population would outnumber the superstrate speakers, diluting access to the superstrate (Muysken and Bickerton 1988). Alternatively, the super-strate speakers may not wish their language to be learned by outsiders: thus, the Chinook Indians produced a simplified version when talking to non-Chinooks (Foley 1988); the resulting Chinook Jargon is a pidgin with Chinook, Nootka, French and English as its sources. Naro (1978) provides a further example of deliberate simplification by superstrate speakers, claiming that Portuguese speakers in the sixteenth century taught a simplified version of Portuguese to Africans they brought back from early voyages to train as interpreters. However, this account is controversial (see Thomason and Kaufman 1988).

Simplifications initiated by superstrate speakers may therefore be a contributing factor in pidginisation. Pidgins and temporary foreigner-talk systems used in communicating with speakers of other languages frequently show radical simplifications of very similar kinds, which might result from universal, innate rules for simplifying grammars. It is certainly true that we all have the capacity for simplifying our native language structures, and that we do so by using sub-conscious, recurrent strategies; this is obvious when, say, an English-speaker addresses someone with a very limited command of English, or in 'motherese', the simplified language which carers use to babies and young children. This phenomenon is not restricted to Indo-European languages; for instance, in Lamso, spoken in Cameroon, there is special vocabulary used only to and by children, and tonal contrasts are reduced when addressing a child (Todd 1990). Such pre-programmed simplification strategies represent one possible explanation of the structural features shared by so many pidgins. However, Bickerton (1977: 55) denies the involvement of universals in pidginisation, pointing out that 'pidgins are usually described as lacking inflections, lacking articles, lacking markers of tense and aspect, lacking sentence-embedding, nominalization, allomorphic variation etc., etc., and people conclude from such definitions that all pidgins are more or less the same; it would, in fact, be as reasonable to suppose that a brick is the same as a cabbage because neither has legs, wings, fur, feathers, independent locomotion, etc., etc.' We now proceed to consider some of these supposed similarities.

10.2.2   *Pidgin structure*

As we have already seen, the term 'pidgin' is in fact a cover-term for languages at various points on a continuum. The first phase involves the formation of jargons, which are extremely simple, *ad hoc* systems of communication, with very restricted structural resources, great variation, and sentences generally no more than one or two words long. These may in time acquire particular norms, become rather more complex, and extend into other domains of usage, whereupon they become stable pidgins. Finally, stable pidgins may expand, acquiring more morphology and more complex syntax, and a characteristically faster tempo of speech; such expanded pidgins are already partly creolised in linguistic terms, although they are not yet properly creoles since they lack native speakers. In what follows, I shall primarily be discussing stable pidgins.

'A pidgin represents a language which has been stripped of everything but the bare essentials necessary for communication' (Romaine 1988: 24). In other words, pidgins are characteristically used only in particular domains and to fulfil certain restricted linguistic functions. To be more precise, they are frequently used in the directive function, to get people to perform particular tasks, and in the referential function, which involves describing some situation to achieve a particular end. However, they are rarely if ever used in the interactional function, which involves the promotion of social cohesion; expressively, to indicate inner states or abstract ideas; poetically, in the creation of literature; or metalinguisti-cally, to talk about language (Foley 1988). These restrictions mean that pidgins typically lack stylistic options, puns and metaphors, and have few sociolinguistic markers, such as politeness phenomena. These restrictions in function and in context typically accompany a restriction in linguistic form, which itself falls into two categories: pidgins are reduced, in that they have a curtailed referential capacity, making certain meanings difficult or impossible to convey; and they are simplified, in that regularity in the grammar is increased (Mühlhäusler 1986).

First, the lexicon of a pidgin is characteristically reduced by comparison with the superstrate and substrate languages; Romaine (1988: 34) estimates that 'normal' languages have approximately 25–30,000 lexical items, while Tok Pisin has around 1,500. However, each word in the pidgin will have a wider range of meanings than is the case in the superstrate or substrates, or will cover a larger semantic domain. Thus, Cameroon Pidgin has two words for the semantic field of animals, *bif*, which is edible, and *bushbif*, which is likely to eat you; each has generic rather than specific reference. In Tok Pisin, *gras* means 'grass', but also more generally 'something which grows somewhere', as shown in (1).

(1)   *gras bilong het*
        grass belong head = 'hair'
        gras bilong maus
        grass belong mouth = 'moustache'
        gras bilong pisin
        grass belong bird = 'feathers'
        gras bilong solwara
        grass belong saltwater = 'seaweed' ...

Words are often multifunctional, acting as nouns, verbs and adjectives; and there is no compounding, so that the expression of complex ideas requires a good deal of circumlocution and periphrasis, as shown in (1) and (2).

(2)   *liklik brum bilong klinim tit* = 'toothbrush'
        bikpela box yu faitim i singaut = 'piano'
        (possibly apocryphal; see Mühlhäusler 1986: 26)

Pidgins rarely exhibit any inflectional morphology, so that no marking for gender, case, number, tense and so on generally occurs. For instance, Yimas is a Papua New Guinean language, which has given rise to a pidgin Yimas, used in trading with the neighbouring Arafundi tribe (Foley 1988). Yimas is inflecting, while Yimas Pidgin is virtually isolating: Yimas has seven tense distinctions, while Yimas Pidgin has two; Yimas has three numbers and more than a dozen noun classes, while Yimas Pidgin has no inflectional marking for either category and marks plurality using *kundammin* 'two' or *manba* 'many' after the noun; Yimas verbs have affixes indicating the person, number and noun class of the subject and the direct and indirect object, while Yimas Pidgin has no such inflections and marks only the indirect object using the postposition *namban* 'towards'. Yimas Pidgin is now dying out under the influence of the more successful and socially prestigious Tok Pisin (Foley 1988), which also lacks inflections for number, as shown in (3), again using numerals and quantifiers.

(3)   *pik* 'pig' / 'pigs'
        tripela pik 'three pigs'
        planti pik 'many pigs'

Since pidgins lack inflectional morphology, words will typically be invariant, with no allomorphy and no irregular forms; this maximises iconicity, making the connection of form and meaning as transparent as possible, and is probably of considerable assistance to the non-native second-language learner. In short, the hearer will find it relatively easy to decode the language, since exceptions and variation need not be coped with (although she may have to rely on context for certain cues as grammatical categories will not be made linguistically overt); while the speaker will also benefit from the minimal grammar and maximal reliance on vocabulary, since words are easier to acquire than grammar (Foley 1988).

Pidgins also tend to have a fixed, invariable word order, which is characteristically SVO. For instance, although German has SVO order in main clauses and SOV in subordinate clauses, Rabaul Creole German, also spoken in Papua New Guinea, has consistent SVO, as in (4).

(4)   *Wenn der Baby weinen, der Mama muss aufpicken.*
        'when the baby cry,   the mother must pick up'
        (Romaine 1988: 30)

The example in (4) also illustrates the earlier points on morphology; the verbs *weinen* and *aufpicken* appear in the infinitive, and the nouns *Baby* and *Mama* appear with the invariable article *der*, which does not alter as its German equivalent does according to gender, number and case. Syntax is also extremely simple in pidgins, with invariant word order for statements, questions and negatives, and no complex syntactic phenomena such as embedding or relative clauses.

Finally, the phonology of pidgins is rather simple, with usually five vowels, typically /i e a o u/, or fewer, and no length distinction. The consonant system is also fairly small; for example, Pidgin Zulu, or Fanagalo, has reduced the three clicks of Zulu to [k], while Tok Pisin has replaced English /s ʃ tʃ/ with the single fricative [s]. Pidgins also tend to have rigidly CV syllable structure, so that loans from English into Tok Pisin, such as *salt* and *parliament*, emerge as *sol* and *palamen*. In African pidgins, tonal distinctions are also characteristically simplified or lost. Finally, words are short, usually mono- or bi-syllabic, and speech tempo is very slow.

10.3   Creoles

10.3.1   *Introduction*

Creolisation is the linguistic inverse of pidginisation: while pidginisation involves reduction and simplification, creolisation is characterised by expansion and elaboration. A pidgin becomes a creole when it acquires native speakers; these will generally be the children of pidgin speakers who are exposed to the pidgin as the medium of communication in the home, and who therefore have the pidgin as their primary linguistic input.

Although the pidgin was adequate for the parental generation, who used it only in specific circumstances and otherwise had recourse to a non-pidgin native language, it appears to be too restricted a system for the children, who need a native language to fulfil not only the directive and referential functions of language, but also the interactional, expressive, poetic and metalinguistic roles which pidgins do not play. Functional and linguistic expansion then typically go together; as the creole becomes the native language of a community, and is gradually extended into new domains, its linguistic resources also increase (Foley 1988). The degree of expansion and elaboration varies from creole to creole, and depends on the status of the pidgin when creolisation begins to take place: most expansion will be necessary when a creole develops from a jargon, as with Hawaiian Creole English; rather less is required for a stable pidgin, which already has certain norms of usage, like Torres Straits Creole English; and least expansion is typical of creoles which develop from expanded pidgins, which are already well on their way to creoles in the linguistic sense – this is probably the most common type of creolisation, examples being Tok Pisin, and Bislama, a creole spoken in Vanuatu and previously called Beach-la-Mar (Crowley 1991). We shall return in 10.5 to the vexed question of where these additions, expansions and elaborations come from, and quite how they become available to creole-acquiring children; first, however, we need a better idea of the types of processes characteristically involved in creolisation. Just as there are numerous characteristics which seem to be common to most or all pidgins, so unrelated creoles also share certain features and processes, some of which will be outlined below. In general, these contribute to the flexibility of the language, creating stylistic options and increasing variation in the system.

10.3.2   *Phonology*

Relatively little attention has so far been paid to phonological creole universals, although Romaine (1988: 63) suggests that creoles typically have CV structure with few or no consonant clusters, and select their vowels from the restricted set /i e a o u/ and their consonants from the set /p t k b d g f s m n l-r w j/. The speed of speech tends to increase, and fewer words in the sentence carry stress, so that pidgin *Mì gó lòng háus* ('I go to the house' / 'I go home'), with main stresses on the verb and noun and secondary stresses on the pronoun and preposition, becomes creole *Mì gò l:áus*, where the preposition *long* has been significantly reduced and only one main stress remains, on the final noun (Sankoff and Laberge 1974). This phonological reduction contributes to the formation of morphology; for instance, Tok Pisin *baimbai*, from English *by and by*, is reduced in the creole to *bai*, which is placed before the main verb of the sentence and typically lacks stress, and which is increasingly interpreted as a prefix (Sankoff and Laberge 1974).

10.3.3 *Lexicon*

Hancock (1980) identifies twelve processes by which the lexical resources of creoles and other languages can be increased, arguing that 'there is a universality of lexical process shared by all languages; the difference between these in creole and non-creole languages is one of degree' (Hancock 1980: 84). For instance, all languages seem to coin words, although none do so very frequently; English has examples like *gobbledigook*, while Trinidadian Creole English has [bobolups] 'fat, ungainly'. A strategy used more in creoles than in non-creole languages is reduplication. The phonological reduction typical of pidgins can lead to widespread homophony, for instance in Krio where *was* meant both 'wash' and 'wasp', and *san* both 'sun' and 'sand' (Todd 1990); this is resolved in the creole using reduplication, which gives *was* 'wash' and *waswas* 'wasp', *san* 'sun' and *sansan* 'sand'. Also in Krio, *tu* means 'two' but *tutu*, 'by twos'; while in Pitcairnese, *drai* is 'dry', but *draidrai* describes unpalatable food.

Words may also undergo semantic extension (see Chapter 7), adding a new meaning, so that Trinidadian Creole English [bʌtn] means 'button' and 'pimple'; or may shift their meaning, losing an older one and gaining a new one, as with English *computer*, which in the seventeenth century meant 'clerk, accountant', and Krio [tomɔk] 'chest', which derives from English *stomach* – in Krio, 'stomach' is [bɛlɛ]. Finally, creoles, like other languages, may borrow words; for instance, Trinidadian Creole English has borrowed [susu] 'mutual savings system' from Yoruba [ɛsúsú].

10.3.4 *Morphology*

As we saw in 10.2, pidgins typically lack morphological marking; for instance, Tok Pisin nouns may be recognised as plural according to the context, or by the addition of a numeral or quantifier, but have no overt plural marker. In creolised Tok Pisin, however, speakers productively insert *ol* before a noun to indicate plurality, increasing redundancy when a numeral or quantifier also appears (Mühlhäusler 1986). Similarly, pidgin Tok Pisin has periphrastic causative constructions formed using the auxiliary verb *mekim*, as in *Yu mekim sam wara i boil* 'You make some water boil', which are now being replaced in the creole by shorter constructions with a transitive / causative suffix *-im* on the main verb, giving *Yu boilim wara* (Foley 1988: 178). Very frequently, new affixes are the result of grammaticalisation: for example, as we saw in Chapter 6, Tok Pisin *save* 'to know' has become a habituality marker *sa* (Aitchison 1989b). This particle now frequently coalesces with the main verb, which it often immediately precedes, being increasingly interpreted as a prefix.

Earlier circumlocutions also give way to compounding in creoles. Pidgin Tok Pisin relied on circumlocutions like *man bilong save* 'man belong know', hence 'expert' and *meri bilong hambak* 'woman belong handbag', 'promiscuous woman', which have now been replaced in the creole by *saveman* and *hambakmeri*. Similarly, *ai bilong mi i laik slip* 'my eyes like sleep' = 'I'm sleepy' becomes *mi aislip nau*, and *yau bilong em i pas* 'his ears are closed' = 'he's deaf' becomes *em i yaupas* (Foley 1988: 177). This process reduces iconicity, as single words no longer necessarily express single concepts, reversing the trend towards maximal iconicity found in pidginisation.

10.3.5 *Syntax*

While pidgins lack sentence-embedding, and have only main clauses, constructions with embedded subordinate clauses tend to develop in creoles. For instance, as shown in (5), creolised Tok Pisin introduces complement clauses using *olsem*, best translated as 'that'.

(5)   Pidgin Tok Pisin:
         Mi no save. Ol i wokim dispela haus.
         Creole Tok Pisin:
         Mi no save olsem ol i wokim dispela haus.
         'I didn't know that they built this house'
                (Foley 1988: 179)

However, embedding is by no means the only syntactic innovation characteristic of creolisation: Bickerton (1981) gives a list of twelve features of grammar common to many creoles, although this set of properties is not exhaustive, and additional or rival features have been suggested (see Romaine 1988, Chapter 2). For instance, many creoles have the same lexical item for the existential, meaning 'there is', and the possessive, meaning 'have' (it is *get* in Hawaiian and Guyanese Creole, and *ge* in Haitian Creole), although apparently none of the superstrate languages have this feature. Creoles have no syntactic difference between statements and questions, although they do have question words, which tend to be bipartite, with the first part derived from a superstrate question word: for example, Guyanese Creole has *wisaid* 'which side' = 'where', and *wa mek* from 'what makes' = 'why'; Haitian Creole has *ki koté* from French 'which side' = 'where'; and Tok Pisin has *wanem* 'what name' = 'what'. Creoles also rarely use passive constructions, and those that do exist, like the *get* passive of Guyanese Creole, tend to be extremely marginal, or are recent borrowings from the superstrate, or both.

All creoles seem to have a system, as shown in (6), whereby a definite article is used for presupposed-specific Noun Phrases (which refer to a particular entity which the speaker assumes the hearer knows about); an indefinite article for asserted-specific Noun Phrases (which have a particular referent which the speaker is introducing to the hearer); and zero to mark non-specific Noun Phrases.

(6)   Papiamentu (Bickerton 1981: 53)
        mi tin e buki   'I have the book'
        mi tin e bukinan   'I have the books'
        mi tin un buki   'I have a book'
        mi tin buki   'I have books'
        buki ta caru   'books are expensive'

The majority of creoles also have three preverbal particles to express distinctions of tense, mood and aspect, which appear in the order TMA. The tense marker typically means [+ anterior], or roughly speaking past tense, while the unmarked verb stem means non-past; the mood marker expresses [+ irrealis], marking phenomena which have not yet happened, either because they are imaginary or conjectural, or in the future or conditional, while the verb stem indicates realised predicates; and the aspect marker signals [+ non-punctual], marking progressive or habitual actions, while the verb stem alone shows completed events. The forms used as particles differ from creole to creole, with Hawaiian Creole *bin, go, stei*, Guyanese Creole *bin, sa/go, a*, Haitian Creole *te, ava, ape*, but the order of particles and their meaning, both alone and in combination, is remarkably consistent.

Creoles tend to mark unrealised complements using a particular particle, while realised complements, which describe an action which actually took place, are marked by zero or a different complementiser. In Sranan (see (7)), unrealised complements are introduced with *foe*, and realised ones with zero; in Mauritian Creole, realised complements have *al* and unrealised ones, *pu al*. This distinction is realised in few if any non-creole languages.

(7)   Sranan (Bickerton 1981: 60)
        a teki a nefi foe koti a brede, ma no koti en
        'he took a knife to cut the bread, but he didn't cut it'
        **a teki a nefi koti a brede, ma no koti en*

Finally, creoles seem to be developing relative markers, although some, including Hawaiian Creole English, currently lack them. Creole Tok Pisin, for instance, is reported (Sankoff and Brown 1976) as using *ia* to bracket relative clauses, as shown in (8).

(8)   *Dispela man ia, lek bilong en idai ia,*
        'this man, whose leg was injured,
        em istap insait nau.
        stayed inside'
                (Sankoff and Brown 1976: 632)

Ia is derived from English *here*, and seems to have been used first as a place
adverb, then as a demonstrative equivalent to English *this, that*, and finally
in relative clauses. Sankoff and Brown (1976) also suggest that, although
the lexical material involved is from English, some substrate reinforcement
may have occurred, since the indigenous Austronesian language Buang has
a particle *ken* which is used as a place adverb, a demonstrative, and a
relativiser; and similar patterns recur in other Melanesian languages
including Iai, Nguna, Tasiko, Uripiv and Tangoa. Again, as with
pidginisation, we see a mixture of substrate and superstrate influences.

10.4   The general relevance of pidgins and creoles

> Pidgins and creoles were for a long time considered 'marginal' or
> 'special' languages. To call them this was to label them and the processes
> by which they developed as marginal to linguistic theory.
>
> > (Traugott 1977: 70)

If we accept this earlier point of view, we might see pidgins and creoles as
interesting objects of study in their own right, more because of their unique
(and, in some opinions, freakish) characteristics than despite them; but we
are unlikely to regard them as central to historical linguistics. However, the
recent sociolinguistic perspective in historical linguistics (see Chapter 9)
has produced an increasing awareness of these languages among historical
linguists; indeed, 'from being the special and the marginal case, pidginization and creolization have become, for some linguists, the test case for any
theory of change' (Traugott 1977: 70).

   There are various reasons why historical linguists might wish to study
pidgins and creoles, and more specifically pidginisation and creolisation.
First, and most trivially, these processes provide conclusive proof against
Bloomfield's view that it is methodologically impossible to observe
language change in progress: if we can actually see new languages being
born, and trace their subsequent development, then we are certainly
observing change! Change also seems to proceed more quickly during
pidginisation and creolisation than elsewhere, so that developments which
can only be suggested for the history of other languages can be directly
observed or at least recovered in pidgins and creoles, without resorting to
apparent-time studies; this may allow the confirmation of various
hypotheses on the nature and spread of change. However, the processes

found in pidginisation and creolisation are only likely to be relevant to general theories of change if they are of the same type as changes which affect other languages.

Trudgill (1983: Chapter 5) attempts to draw parallels between the changes characteristic of pidginisation and creolisation, and those found elsewhere. He suggests a general division of changes into two types, which he labels 'natural' and 'non-natural': 'natural' changes are those which are 'liable to occur in all linguistic systems, at all times, without external stimulus, because of the inherent nature of linguistic systems themselves', while 'non-natural' changes are generally the result of language contact. Trudgill proposes that 'natural' changes are likely to include grammaticalisation; sound changes traditionally ascribed to ease of articulation, such as assimilation; and increases in redundancy, such as the double marking of the definite article in Norwegian seen in *den store mannen*, literally 'the big man-the'. These processes involve a general move from analytic to synthetic structure. On the other hand, 'non-natural' changes include reductions in morphological marking for case, an increase in the use of prepositions, the reduction of conjugational classes for verbs and declensional classes for nouns, increased use of periphrasis and reduced use of inflected forms, and the development of fixed word order; all these involve a shift from synthetic to analytic structure.

Trudgill's central hypothesis is that languages which have undergone a good deal of linguistic contact will exhibit more change, faster change, and specifically more 'non-natural' changes than related languages which have not experienced such contact. For instance, Faroese is a more isolated language in sociolinguistic and geographical terms than its relative Norwegian, and Faroese is more conservative in its inflectional system: Faroese retains marking for three cases in nouns and pronouns, while Norwegian has only two cases and only for pronouns; Faroese has several verb conjugations which Norwegian has reduced to one; Faroese maintains three noun declensions per gender while Norwegian again has only one; and Faroese has eleven inflected verbal forms to Norwegian's five.

Trudgill goes on to propose that pidgins, as high-contact languages, exhibit predominantly 'non-natural' changes, while creoles show mainly 'natural' ones. This seems to be broadly borne out by the evidence in previous sections; pidgins do manifest a dramatic shift towards analytic structure, and a reduction to the point of complete loss of inflectional morphology, while creolisation is characterised by grammaticalisation and increased redundancy, which lead to a move back towards syntheticity. There are, however, some problems with Trudgill's proposals. One concerns the implied categorisation of creoles as non-contact languages; creoles do seem to borrow at least some of their novel structures from the superstrate and substrate languages of their ancestor pidgins, and are generally spoken in areas with many indigenous languages – indeed, this may promote the development of a creole as a lingua franca, as was the case for Tok Pisin in Papua New Guinea. Furthermore, Trudgill suggests that 'natural' change will tend to be slower than 'non-natural' change, but this is patently not the case in creolisation, which may take place, with all its attendant expansion and elaboration, in as little as a single generation – less time than some pidgins take to develop! Finally, it may not be so easy as Trudgill's dichotomy indicates to make a clear distinction of 'natural' and 'non-natural' changes, since a change which is already occurring in a language may be reinforced by a model in another language with which it is in contact; and it seems reasonable to suppose that a particular change may be the result of language-internal phenomena on one occasion, but motivated by contact on another. However, it seems less outlandish to refer to changes as sometimes internally and sometimes externally motivated, than to call the same process sometimes 'natural' and sometimes 'non-natural'; this may seem like quibbling about terminology, but terms like 'unnatural' in historical linguistics have often led to judgements of 'undesirable' or the like (see Chapter 12), and 'natural' and 'non-natural' are arguably just too close to 'natural' and 'unnatural' for comfort.

If we at least accept that certain types of processes are characteristic both of pidgins and high-contact languages, while others operate frequently in creoles and low-contact languages, we can regard pidginisation and creolisation 'not as different in kind from other processes of language change, but as extreme cases of the hybridization that goes on in language all the time' (Traugott 1977: 74). This sort of connection of pidginisation and creolisation with other cases of linguistic change has been interpreted in several ways. The most literal is the idea that pidginisation and creolisation themselves may have formed part of the history of languages which would not now be classified as pidgins or creoles. For instance, there is a view that Middle English, due to the extensive admixture of French into English during the period following the Norman Conquest, became a creole. Certainly Middle English shows a large number of 'non-natural' changes, involving the loss of inflectional morphology, but these were arguably already under way in late Old English, where scribes seem to become increasingly confused about the appropriate spelling for inflectional endings; in any case, such changes are more characteristic of pidginisation than creolisation. If Middle English were really a creole, then we would expect it to have developed not only a relatively fixed word order, and periphrastic constructions, which it has, but also grammaticalised inflections to replace the ones lost earlier, which it has not.

The problem is that claims for a creole stage in English, or in French and the other Romance languages between Vulgar Latin and the earliest Romance texts, are hard to prove, largely because appropriate data from the periods concerned tend to be lacking. Diagnostics of prior pidginisation and creolisation might be developed, for instance by taking a set of features like Bickerton's twelve characteristics of creole grammar reported in 10.3, and assessing which of these appear in certain modern or attested languages; languages with more than a certain number of these features would be classified as having creole ancestry. Romaine (1988) considers thirty pan-creole features, and discovers that Old Japanese has approximately one-third of these while Modern English has very few: however, we should be cautious before using such evidence to debunk the claim that Middle English was a creole while asserting that the ancestor of Old Japanese was one, since English may simply have undergone rapid change away from the creole state in the period since Middle English.

Some linguists have reacted to these difficulties by coining terms like creoloid, which, as Holm (1988–9: 10) suggests, 'has been used for so many different kinds of vaguely creole-like languages that its usefulness has become rather limited'. Holm himself uses the term for languages with some creole features, which nonetheless seem not to have actually undergone creolisation; while Trudgill (1983) applies it to languages like Middle English, Norwegian and Afrikaans, which have no pidgin in their history, but have undergone many contact-induced changes and are now relatively easy for adult second-language learners to acquire, compared to their linguistic ancestors. Unfortunately, creoloids and the like are rather hard to distinguish from so-called mixed languages, which have borrowed structures from other, often unrelated languages through linguistic contact; and since almost all languages have borrowed some features at some time or another, we are in danger of identifying almost all languages as having greater affinities with pidgins and creoles than they actually *do* have. The connection is simply the property of being languages used in situations involving communication between linguistic groups, which facilitate the leakage of linguistic features from one system to another. It seems doubtful whether we need more terms for this phenomenon than those, like contact and borrowing, which we have already. In short, pidginisation and creolisation share certain processes and features with other cases of language change, but that does not make those cases equivalent to pidginisation and creolisation; the sociolinguistic context and the output are clearly different.

Another claim of affinity between pidgins, creoles and other languages involves genetic relationship, and the traditional family tree representation of this. In fact, Schuchardt in the late nineteenth century first became interested in pidgins and creoles because he felt they represented a challenge to the genetic classification of languages and the doctrine of the regularity of sound change, both elements of Neogrammarian theory which he attempted to refute. Proponents of monogenesis might suggest a separate pidgin/creole family, descended from the proto-pidgin Sabir, but this tree will necessarily be too static to show the waves of contact and relexification which form a crucial part of the monogenetic hypothesis, and will also fail to show the influence of either the superstrate or the substrate languages. However, it is equally difficult to incorporate pidgins and creoles into established family trees, because of the indirect relationship between the superstrate, the substrates, and the resulting pidgins and creoles: should Haitian Creole be a daughter of French, or a sister, or an independent branch in the Romance tree? Similarly, is Tok Pisin Indo-European, like its superstrate, or Austronesian like its substrates? Faced with questions like these, the family tree model develops glaring inadequacies. One way of dealing with these is to extend the family metaphor, as Taylor (1956: 413) does when he asserts that 'languages originating in a pidgin or jargon, while genetically "orphans", may be said to have two "foster-parents": one that provides the basic morphological and/or syntactic pattern, and another from which the fundamental vocabulary is taken'. Setting aside the difficulty of including 'foster-parents' in the conventional family tree, this view incorporates the idea, now largely discredited, that the superstrate language is responsible only or primarily for pidgin and creole vocabulary, while the substrates supply grammar: it now seems that both superstrate and substrates donate lexical and grammatical structures, and often patterns from one will reinforce material from another.

An alternative strategy is adopted by Thomason and Kaufman (1988), who claim that pidgins and creoles are non-genetic languages; although their contributing ancestors generally belonged to some linguistic family, these languages themselves have arisen through a process of discontinuous transmission and can no longer be classified as members of any family group. Thomason and Kaufman extend this set of non-genetic languages to cover those which have undergone extensive structural borrowing, such as Mbugu or Ma'a, which has effectively ceased to be a Cushitic language due to the volume of borrowings from Bantu, but which cannot really be classified as a Bantu language either. However, again, it is hard to draw the line: is English, with its widespread lexical borrowing from Romance, or Rumanian, which has borrowed heavily from Slavic languages, non-genetic? As Holm (1988–9: 14–15) points out, French and Middle English do show clear signs of the effects of language contact relative to Latin and Old English, but there is no evidence of any major break in transmission;

generation-to-generation acquisition seems to have continued uninter-
rupted, with speakers believing that they spoke the same language as their
predecessors, whereas this is not the case for pidgins and creoles.

Finally, another productive line of research, though not one which has
been much pursued as yet, involves the search for similarities between
pidginisation and second language acquisition, and creolisation and first
language acquisition respectively. If, as Bickerton claims, pidginisation is
second language acquisition with restricted input, while creolisation is first
language acquisition with restricted input, then such similarities certainly
ought to exist; but one caveat should be imposed. Historical linguists have
so far had little success in assuming that children learning language initiate
language change, since there is very limited overlap between changes and
characteristics of child language (Drachmann 1978). Invoking the child
seems to make much more sense within particular linguistic theories, like
Andersen's work on abduction (see Chapter 4), or Lightfoot's on syntactic
change (see Chapter 5). How the child learns therefore seems more relevant
to the historical linguist than the performance errors she makes. With this
in mind, we can proceed to an ambitious, acquisition-based account of
creolisation, which recognises creoles as unique, but also as a key to
language change, language learning and linguistic evolution.

10.5   The Language Bioprogram Hypothesis

Bickerton (1977, 1981, 1984, 1990; Muysken and Bickerton 1988), the
originator of the Language Bioprogram Hypothesis, aims ultimately to
answer three questions, which he sees as intrinsically interconnected. First,
he is concerned to discover how creoles originate; then, how children
acquire language; and finally, how language evolved: and in his view, the
key to this whole ambitious enterprise is the study of creolisation.

Bickerton notes that creole languages tend to share particular features of
grammar; most notably, perhaps, almost all creoles have a system of three
preverbal particles which mark tense, mood and aspect distinctions (see
10.3 above). The typical expansions of creole structure, and especially this
TMA system, have often been ascribed to substrate influence or monogenesis. However, Bickerton claims that the similarities found across
creoles cannot be due entirely to these factors. For instance, he notes that
Caribbean creoles and Hawaiian Creole, which certainly do not share any
substrate, have much the same TMA system; to maintain a substratist
explanation, we would have to assume that all substrates had the same
features, and this is simply not the case. More specifically, substratists may
find a potential source for some creole feature in a particular African
language, but fail to demonstrate that the speakers of that language were

in the right place at the right time and in sufficient numbers to transmit the construction into the creole. For instance (Bickerton 1984), a possible source for the creole TMA system in some creoles is the language Fon, but the number of Fon speakers in, for instance, late-eighteenth-century Haiti was rather small, probably in the region of 0.2 per cent. Similarly, to uphold monogenesis, we would have to assume that the TMA system in, for instance, Hawaiian Creole was inherited from some previous contact proto-pidgin; but Bickerton claims that the relevant constructions do not occur in Hawaiian Pidgin.

The usual difficulty with claims of this sort is the sheer impossibility of substantiating them; once a language has creolised, it tends to die out as a pidgin, and it is therefore almost impossible to find both pidgin and creole speakers at the same time, unless the language is still undergoing creolisation. However, Bickerton (1984) notes that Hawaii is probably the latest site of European colonisation, with the original pidgin being formed during the period 1900–20, and creolisation occurring subsequently. He interviewed speakers aged around seventy to ninety, who had arrived in Hawaii in the period from 1907–30, and found that they predominantly spoke a rather rudimentary version of Hawaiian Pidgin, which shows little consistency in syntax and is often heavily influenced by the speaker's native language. Bickerton argues that, even if the language of these speakers has changed since the 1900–20 period, perhaps under the influence of subsequent generations of creole speakers, it is likely to have become more rather than less complex – which suggests that early Hawaiian Pidgin was even more rudimentary than the surviving pidgin, if anything. There seems little possibility that this extremely rudimentary system supplied patterns for the more complex constructions which later appear in the creole; and yet children born in Hawaii, who were exposed to the pidgin as linguistic input, seem to have developed structures like those in (9).

(9)a. *dei gon get naif pok you*
        'they will stab you with a knife'
        – speaker born 1896, showing verb serialisation
   b. *dei wen go ap dea in da mawning go plaen*
        'they went up there in the morning to plant (things)'
        – speaker born 1896
        pipl no laik tekam fo go wok
        'people don't want to have him go to work (for them)'
        – speaker born 1901
        Shows embedding, plus *go* for realised, *fo* for unrealised complements.
            (Bickerton 1984: 175)

It follows that speakers exposed to pidgin as children have acquired a more complex, creole system, while those learning as adults acquired only a very simple and restricted pidgin. Moreover, patterns for the new constructions which emerge in the creole often have no clear sources, in the superstrate, the substrates or the pidgin itself; and to support monogenesis we would have to argue that the importers of the proto-creole to Hawaii must have taught or otherwise transmitted it to all children born in Hawaii and no adults. We cannot therefore rely on monogenesis or substrate influence to account for creolisation fully, and must seek an alternative explanation in terms of language acquisition.

However, children with a pidgin as their primary linguistic input are faced with a task rather different from 'normal' acquisition: their model is impoverished, unstable, and inadequate. As Bickerton (1981: 5) puts it, 'children of pidgin-speaking parents have as input something which may be adequate for emergency use, but which is quite unfit to serve as anyone's primary tongue; which, by reason of its variability, does not present even the little it offers in a form which would permit anyone to learn it; and which the parent, with the best will in the world, cannot teach, since that parent knows no more of the language than the child (and will pretty soon know less)'. Bickerton's answer is to suppose that these pidgin-learning children can 'invent' structures for which there is no evidence in the speech of the previous generation; that is, 'there can be rules of language that are not derived from any linguistic input' (Bickerton 1977: 65). Once we understand this sort of innovation, we may also be closer to understanding 'normal' cases of language acquisition, since a single explanation should ideally cover both creole and non-creole learning; if we propose two separate strategies, the child would have to work out what sort of data she was receiving to decide which strategy to use.

It would, however, be equally unreasonable to expect very young children to invent such complex constructions without help; and in any case, if no guidance were available, we would logically expect different children, and different creoles, to come up with different strategies and structures. As we have seen, this is precisely what we do not find; instead, unrelated, geographically distant creoles exhibit strikingly similar patterns. Bickerton therefore proposes that children are provided with some assistance in 'inventing' new creole constructions, and that this help comes in the form of the bioprogram, a neurally encoded, genetically transmitted set of instructions which specify certain semantic and syntactic features. These, Bickerton argues, were the first features to develop in linguistic evolution, and are still the first to be given linguistic expression by *any* child learning language. Similar syntactic structures and semantic distinctions will therefore appear in the early language of all children whether their primary linguistic data is French, English, Japanese, Dyirbal or Hawaiian Pidgin. However, over centuries or millennia of linguistic change, older-established languages have often developed patterns of their own which fail to match, or directly contradict, those specified in the bioprogram. In such cases, children will first produce bioprogram features, but will subsequently, due to overt correction by adults or simply greater exposure to data, replace these with the structures and distinctions of their own languages. Only in creoles, where the preceding pidgin is likely to be too impoverished and restricted to contradict the bioprogram, will bioprogram features emerge and remain as an integral part of the resulting adult language; hence the importance of creoles in discovering the initial features of evolving language and child language. For instance, child English and German often lack inverted order in questions, a feature which all creoles retain. Similarly, the construction *a gon full Angela bucket* ('I'm going to fill Angela's bucket') (Bickerton 1984: 185), with an adjective used as a verb, is attested in child English but would have precisely the same form and meaning in Guyanese Creole. Finally, in the domain of semantics, Bickerton (1981) reports an experiment by Maratsos conducted to see whether English-speaking children could discern non-specific uses of the indefinite article (*I want a dog* – any dog) from specific instances (*I have a dog* – a particular dog). His findings were that three-year-olds were 90 per cent efficient in grasping this distinction, although English gives very few overt cues to the appropriate interpretation. As we have already seen, creoles tend to mark this distinction overtly, using the indefinite article for asserted specific noun phrases, but zero in non-specific cases. In short, (Bickerton 1984: 185), many apparent errors in child language 'would have been grammatical if the child had been learning a creole language'.

We shall return below to a specification of the contents of the bioprogram, but it should first be noted that not all creoles are equal when it comes to the expression of bioprogram features. In his earlier work, Bickerton defined creoles as languages arising out of a pidgin which had existed for no more than one generation, and developing in a population where no more than 20 per cent spoke the superstrate, with the remaining 80 per cent being speakers of various substrate languages: his idea here is to concentrate on cases where (Bickerton 1981: 4) 'the human linguistic capacity is stretched to the uttermost'. Aitchison (1983) suggests that this restriction represents a convenient excuse for Bickerton to concentrate on the two creoles which he knows best, namely Hawaiian Creole and Guyanese Creole, ignoring creoles like Tok Pisin which might provide counter-examples. This allegation may be slightly unfair, since it is obviously impossible to consider all creoles, and the particular restriction Bickerton adopts, emphasising the poverty of the input available to the child, is probably as valid as any; when he has stated his case, it is then the task of other linguists to confront him with conflicting data from other creoles. The fact that Bickerton's criteria include the two creoles with which he is most familiar might cause some faint unease, but he does not by any means restrict his data to these two languages; in his survey of features of creole grammar (Bickerton 1981: Chapter 2), for instance, Bickerton considers evidence from Guyanese Creole, Hawaiian Creole, Papiamentu, Seychelles Creole, Haitian Creole, Lesser Antillean Creole, Saramaccan, Sranan, Jamaican Creole, Mauritian Creole, Crioulo, Tok Pisin and various others; and although he has not done fieldwork on all of these himself, few of us can afford to be surprised or critical on that account. In more recent work (Bickerton 1984), Bickerton has in any case relaxed his original criteria for creole status, and instead sets up a scale of creoles, from those nearest to the bioprogram to those furthest away. Creoles are ordered on this hierarchy on linguistic and demographic grounds; broadly speaking, the more disruptive the circumstances of acquisition of the creole, the more bioprogram features it will display. The degree of disruption will depend on the amount of access which adults learning the pidgin have to the superstrate, which determines the degree of restriction of the pidgin, and the impoverishment of the data available to creole-acquiring children; and the amount of access to the superstrate in turn depends on the proportion of superstrate to substrate speakers in the community, the period between the start of immigration and the point at which substrate speakers outnumber superstrate speakers, and the rate of population increase thereafter, which all contribute to the dilution of the model. On this account, the creole nearest to the bioprogram should be Saramaccan, which was spoken initially by a group of escaped slaves, who had previously had little contact with the superstrate and who, after their escape, had access to neither the superstrate nor to any common native language. Sranan, which has English as its superstrate but had this withdrawn soon afterwards when Surinam was ceded to the Dutch, will be a little further from the bioprogram; and Haitian Creole, with its French superstrate withdrawn rather later in its history, will be further away still. Furthest away from the bioprogram will be creoles like Réunion Creole, which existed as a pidgin for a long period before the substrate population outstripped the superstrate speakers, and perhaps Tok Pisin.

So far, we have been discussing the bioprogram without explicitly specifying its contents. In fact, Bickerton argues that the bioprogram contains at least a restricted Phrase-Structure Grammar and four semantic distinctions. It is therefore unlike Chomsky's Universal Grammar, which is predominantly syntactic in nature. However, Chomsky's and Bickerton's approaches are not necessarily entirely incompatible: it might be, for instance, that Chomsky's Language Acquisition Device, which helps the child build a grammar of his native language, has as one component the bioprogram, which specifies the minimal structure required.

In terms of syntax, Bickerton (1984: 178) argues that 'creole similarities stem from a single substantive grammar consisting of a very restricted set of categories and processes, which ... constitute part, or all, of the human species-specific capacity for syntax'. Bickerton suggests the rudimentary syntax in (10). COMP is a complementiser, which is taken to be empty but may be filled optionally by question words; INFL is the home of auxiliaries; Det. is shorthand for Determiner, the class including articles; items in brackets are optional; and the commas in each rewrite rule indicate that the order is not fixed, so that either Adjective Noun or Noun Adjective might be grammatical.

(10) $S \longrightarrow$ COMP, S
        $S \longrightarrow N^3$, INFL, V^3
        $N^3 \longrightarrow \left\{ \begin{array}{c} S \\ (\text{Det.}), N^2 \end{array} \right\}$
        $N^2 \longrightarrow$ (Numeral), N^1
        $N^1 \longrightarrow$ (Adj.), N
        $V^3 \longrightarrow V^2$, (S)
        $V^2 \longrightarrow V^1$, (N^3)
        $V^1 \longrightarrow V$, (N^3)

In addition to this set of Phrase-Structure Rules, Bickerton suggests a single movement rule, which will allow N^3 or V to be moved to a vacant site; the vacant site really has to be COMP, and this strategy is used in fronting constituents for emphasis, a technique extremely common in creoles.

This simple syntax is unable to generate nonfinite clauses (such as English *To see Bill is impossible*), or Verb Phrases containing further Verb Phrases (like *They all persuaded Mary to leave*). However, it is very nearly able to generate the structures of Saramaccan, which lacks such complex constructions and which is reputedly the creole closest to the bioprogram. Two modifications will be required to generate Saramaccan adequately. First, the commas must be removed from the rules in (10), so that the orders SVO and Determiner – Numeral – Adjective – Noun become obligatory. Second, the bioprogram syntax does not mention prepositions, and Saramaccan has two, *a* and *ku*, so that the syntax slightly under-generates. However, as Bickerton (1984: 179) notes, the small number of prepositions characteristically found in creoles may explain the need for serial verbs in constructions like that in (11), where non-creole languages would tend to use a preposition. With these minor alterations, the suggested bioprogram syntax can generate Saramaccan; and it certainly captures the core constructions which seem to be found in other creoles.

(11)   Saramaccan
        dee   o-tei   faka tjoko unu
        'they MODAL-take knife stab you (pl.)'
           (Bickerton 1984: 179)

Although this syntactic component is rudimentary, it is rather specific, and this may be problematic, since not all linguists would be happy with the idea that a set of rules of this sort could be innately specified. Bickerton's more recent work may be more promising in this respect; he has proposed that, within the principles and parameters model (see Chapters 5 and 6 above), the syntactic component of the bioprogram might be interpreted as providing a default setting for each parameter. This would be overridden only if the child heard conflicting data in the linguistic input.

Bickerton (1981, 1984) claims that the bioprogram also includes the four semantic distinctions listed in (12).

(12)   1. Specific / non-specific
            – specific noun phrases marked by determiner; non-specific unmarked.
         2. Tense – [±anterior]
            – topic time unmarked; times prior to topic time marked by a preverbal particle.
         3. Mood – [±irrealis]
            – realised events unmarked; unrealised events marked by a preverbal particle.
         4. Aspect – [±punctual]
            – completed or one-off actions unmarked; habitual or progressive actions marked by a preverbal particle.

As we have already seen, creoles consistently tend to have such particles, when they co-occur, in the order TMA; and combinations of particles also tend to have consistent meanings across creoles. In terms of the syntax in (10), the three TMA particles will be generated as part of INFL.

In short, then, Bickerton proposes that all human beings have as part of their genetic inheritance a linguistic bioprogram, which contains basic syntactic and semantic information. The constructions and distinctions specified in the bioprogram are assumed to be those which developed first during human evolution of language (although here we are reduced, as Bickerton himself admits, to speculation). Furthermore, they will tend to surface during child language acquisition. However, children learning an established language will encounter novel constructions, built up during centuries of linguistic change, which may contradict bioprogram instructions; and they will tend to select the forms and distinctions they hear in the data around them. On the other hand, children having a pidgin as their primary linguistic input will have no access to features contradicting the bioprogram; on the contrary, they will hear no evidence at all for many syntactic and semantic features, and will have to rely on the bioprogram to help them build their grammar. 'In other words, the human species comes equipped ... with the capacity to reconstitute language itself should the normal generation-to-generation transmission of input data be interrupted or distorted by extralinguistic forces' (Muysken and Bickerton 1988: 282). Bioprogram features will therefore appear consistently in creoles, with most occurring when the preceding pidgin has been most impoverished and access to superstrate and substrate languages has been least available. Creoles consequently become central to linguistics, as the only reliable source of information on features which are crucial in linguistic evolution and acquisition.

It is scarcely surprising that a proposal as radical as Bickerton's should have become controversial, particularly since we cannot hope, at least at present, for conclusive evidence of the existence of the bioprogram, which is unobservable except by its alleged results. This gives the bioprogram much the same status as Chomsky's equally unobservable language faculty or Language Acquisition Device, and opens it to much the same set of criticisms: notably, Romaine (1988) accuses Bickerton of circularity in his claim that the TMA distinctions found in creoles are basic and part of the bioprogram, when the only evidence is their occurrence in creoles. Direct evidence on linguistic evolution seems unlikely to be forthcoming, and we are consequently stuck with what we can observe in current or attested systems, making such protests of circularity almost inevitable. However, one promising line of research might be to consider other areas of language acquisition where, as in creolisation, the normal method of transmission is impaired or interrupted. Romaine (1988: 297ff) reports on some work on the acquisition of sign language, where again there is weak adult-to-child transmission and the child's sign language is therefore an emerging system based on relatively little evidence. In fact, sign language does seem to share many characteristics with creoles; for instance, both lack copulas and passives, use adjectives as verbs, and have a distinctive pattern of article use. Such support for the notion of the bioprogram from a non-creole source might defuse accusations of circularity.

The main opponent of Bickerton's ideas, however, is Aitchison, who begins her review of his 1981 book with a quotation from the philosopher Whitehead, who asserts that 'It is more important that a proposition be interesting than that it be true' (Aitchison 1983: 83). We have already mentioned Aitchison's criticism of Bickerton's restricted definition of creoles and his use of data predominantly from Hawaiian and Guyanese Creole, although these points were partly answered above. Aitchison also criticises Bickerton's assertion that novel constructions found in Hawaiian Creole were 'invented' by children with help from the bioprogram. She holds that the changes involved, such as the reanalysis of main verbs as auxiliaries, are simply natural tendencies which could be found in any language, and which do not require special explanation. She also argues that, if Bickerton's data were more extensive, it might show traces of these allegedly new constructions in Hawaiian Pidgin. The second point is essentially uncontestable, since the variety really no longer exists; however, the answer to the former criticism might be that the bioprogram is implicated in linguistic change regardless of the language concerned – if it exists, it is, after all, common to all of us.

Aitchison's main criticism concerns Bickerton's evidence from child language acquisition. She argues that he makes use of rather limited experimental data, and does not take sufficient account of variation in child language or in child language theory, suggesting that 'Bickerton's pronouncements on child language show both naivety and wishful-thinking. His standard mode of argument is to take one or two well-known papers on a topic, and to assume that these represent the consensus of opinion in the field. If necessary, he reinterprets them to suit his purpose' (Aitchison 1983: 91). It is true that Bickerton is not an expert on language acquisition, and nor does he claim to be one; on the other hand, if we restricted inter-disciplinary work to those with acknowledged expertise in all the fields being investigated, there would be precious little of it around. Bickerton may not be fully up-to-date with acquisition studies, or fully aware of the controversies in the area; but this does not provide proof against the bioprogram. If anything, it provides an opportunity for someone who *does* have expertise in language acquisition to impartially re-examine Bickerton's claims. Finally, Bickerton may have recast some of the observations he found on child language in terms of the bioprogram, but it is dubious to suggest that he therefore reinterpreted results to suit himself: after all, he is hardly likely to have found mention of bioprogram phenomena or links with creoles in child language studies carried out before he had suggested the existence of a bioprogram.

Aitchison herself regards appeals to innateness as a last resort, arguing that 'an obsession with innateness can lead to a neglect of other possible reasons behind language universals' (Aitchison 1987: 14). She favours a commonsense approach, based on the idea that 'one fairly obvious observation about human life is that, for most problems, there are usually a finite number of possible solutions. And quite often, the same solution will be rediscovered by generation after generation' (Aitchison 1987: 17). Consequently, similarities among creoles may simply result from the fact that pidgins, as extremely restricted linguistic systems, have very few options for expansion; in extending their resources, they are therefore likely to select similar strategies. For instance, Aitchison notes that many creoles are SVO, but with leftward movement rules and a morphological marker distinguishing transitive from intransitive verbs. Tok Pisin, in its pidgin stage, was SVO; to focus a noun phrase, its speakers have various restricted options, such as changing the word order, repeating the constituent, coining some special particle, or using intonation. Both word order change and repetition will alter the fixed SVO order.

In creole Tok Pisin, the solution is to repeat the focussed noun phrase, but in a reduced form, as a pronoun, giving the order NP Pronoun V NP, or SSVO. This has subsequently been generalised to the Object Noun Phrase, which can also be fronted; and the repeated object pronoun has resulted in an -*im* suffix on transitive verbs. Finally, fronting has now been extended to adverbs, pronouns, *wh*-words, and other forms.

Aitchison argues that all these leftward movements of constituents produce the same sort of surface pattern, and that they all reinforce one another, leading to a proliferation of constructions of the same type. We therefore see a type of linguistic conspiracy, whereby one process produces a certain surface structure, which becomes the target for subsequent processes. A language in this situation is involved in a 'snowball' effect, where rules back one another up and push the language in a certain direction; and in the case of pidgins, where the starting point is so restricted, the options available will be few, so that 'different pidgins will be caught in more or less the same snowball, giving the impression that there is some preordained blueprint. In fact, the phenomenon may represent the rediscovery of the same type of rules, given certain basic parsing and memory abilities' (Aitchison 1987:26).

Aitchison (1989a) also uses this notion of preferred pathways to argue against Bickerton's notion that primitive, general categories tend to be generated in creole development, then subsequently differentiated. She considers the TMA system of Tok Pisin, and attempts to show why certain options were chosen and others rejected during the development of this system. Her data are from six young women, aged seventeen–twenty, who are first-generation creole speakers. These informants used *bin* as the particle marking pastness or [+ anterior], and *pinis* to mean 'after'. However, Aitchison claims that *bin* and *pinis* were formerly both possible markers of pastness, which have diverged and specialised in their meaning. Once *bin* was accepted as the pastness marker, it was used more frequently and redundantly, and located just before the main verb. Finally, it began to be combined with other particles, initially by one young, fluent, fast speaker who claimed not to know her parents' languages well. The habituality particle *sa* and the irrealis / future marker *bai* developed in a similar, gradual way. In all cases, the apparently neat creole pattern is the result of 'the gradual simplification of an originally highly variable and fairly messy situation' (Aitchison 1989a: 168). The eventual system is favoured by various principles: these include generality (the particles which 'win' are those which can be used most frequently); overlapping (each particle has a number of meanings); and elimination of pointless variety.

However, this account is not entirely explanatory since we do not know why these particular principles should exert such a strong influence on linguistic development. Aitchison (1987, 1989a) talks hopefully of 'general cognitive factors' and of eventually linking these principles with properties of the human mind. It is tempting to say that this brings her closer to Bickerton than she might like to be; after all, a bioprogram could well turn out to be principle-based, and if we need a name for some undefined something in the human mind which helps us in certain circumstances to select certain linguistic options, we might as well call it the bioprogram as anything else – so long as we do not think that having a name for it means no more investigation is needed.

The validity of Bickerton's Bioprogram Hypothesis must be left, for the moment, as an open question. However, it is worth stressing that the bioprogram is not intrinsically incompatible with other explanations of creole features, such as claims of substrate or superstrate influence – after all, the bioprogram may tell the child to make some semantic distinction or create some syntactic structure, but the child then needs to find linguistic material to clothe it in. Arguably, then, substratist, superstratist and universalist explanations are all compatible with one another. This sort of all-embracing attitude is symptomatic of a recent trend in creole studies, which may represent the next step forward. For instance, Thomason and Kaufman (1988: 164–65) argue that adults may well contribute something to an emerging creole as well as their children, in that linguistic material in the creole frequently comes from the pidgin or the adults' native languages. When structures in different substrates coincide, these will be especially likely to be introduced into the creole; the bioprogram is here seen as a last-resort explanation, to be invoked when the relevant substrate structures conflict or no evidence for a particular structure is available.

We should be careful, however, not to return by this route to a radically substratist approach. Of course, substrate influence can sometimes be observed in grammar and vocabulary (such as Tok Pisin *kaikai* 'food' which has no superstrate source). However, not all creole grammar is substrate-based; for instance, Crowley (1991) notes that Bislama, the creole language of Vanuatu and a relative of Tok Pisin, has certain structures which can be ascribed to various indigenous languages, but cautions against an over-enthusiastic interpretation of this information, arguing that 'substratum has very clearly not been the *only* factor involved in the evolution of Bislama. Modern Melanesian Pidgin is certainly not relexified Tolai, Kwaio, or Nakanamanga, by any stretch of the imagination' (Crowley 1991: 387).

It is also crucial that superstrate influence should be properly taken into account: but it cannot be demonstrated if we look only at the modern standard version of the superstrate language concerned – modern Standard British English, for instance, with an RP accent. Instead, we must try to ascertain when English speakers, for instance, arrived in the Caribbean or in New Guinea, which areas they came from, and therefore what dialects they are likely to have spoken. A recent study of this kind (Singh 1991) demonstrates the influence of Early Modern English dialects on Trinidadian Creole. For instance, the universal relative form in the creole is *that*, as shown in (13), just as it was in sixteenth and seventeenth century Scots varieties, and still is in modern non-standard Scots dialects.

(13)   Trinidadian Creole
        The man in the car that get bounce, he foot get break.
        I know the girl that did get shoot.
                (Singh 1991:22)

Early Modern English also had an uninflected genitive form, lacking final [s], for words ending in [s] or before words starting in [s], as shown in (14). This was extended into certain formations, such as *ladybird* (from *Our Lady's bird*) and *lady chapel* (from *Our Lady's chapel*). This tendency remains in the creole (see (15)).

(14)   *for conscience sake*
        for God sake

(15)   Trinidadian Creole
        Christmas Day is Our Lord day.
        The doctor son does come here plenty.
                (Singh 1991: 22)

Finally, Trinidadian Creole uses *does be* as a habitual marker, as shown in (16); this construction is reminiscent of structures like those in (17), which are found in modern Irish dialects, and (18), which were current in South Western England until at least 1898. Constructions like those in (19) are still very common in the varieties of English spoken in the South Welsh valleys (Mari Jones, personal communication).

(16)   Trinidadian Creole
        I does be there everyday.
        He does be playing the fool all the time.
        He does work on the estate.
                (Singh 1991: 18)

(17)   Irish dialects
        He does be late for dinner sometimes.
        They does be fighting among other.

(18)   *She do be strict with us gals.* (Oxfordshire)
        The childer do be laffen at me. (Cornwall)
                (from Rickford 1986)

(19)   *She do be quite good at that.*
        He do be less talkative since his wife died.

The *does be* habitual may have spread from Irish English into the creole, since many Irish indentured workers migrated from Barbados to Trinidad in the nineteenth century. However, the Irish at this period may well have spoken Gaelic rather than English, and may have learned English in the Caribbean, introducing features such as *does be* by analogy with similar constructions in their native Gaelic. This habitual construction may also have been reinforced by parallel forms in South Western English varieties, which were spoken by many of the Trinidadian overseers and land-owners. The Irish, as indentured servants, would have had contact with these superstrate speakers, and perhaps passed on the *does be* construction to the slaves, who were predominantly speakers of West African languages, many of which also have habitual markers. Singh (1991) is at pains to point out that the impetus for introducing a habitual marker into the creole at all may have come from the bioprogram, or some universal demand to have this distinction marked; but that this universal motivation for the category does not rule out the possibility that its expression comes from the superstrate (which would be English for the Irish, and Irish English for the Africans).

This view of mutual reinforcement is probably best represented by Crowley (1991: 387–8), who argues that 'the more potential sources a form or a construction can be construed as having, the more chance there is that this form or construction will be incorporated as part of the final product' - that is, the creole. For instance, in Bislama, a form *se* is being introduced as a complementiser and a copula, in examples like those in (20), and Crowley traces this form to both English *say* and French *c'est*, both languages which have been important in the formation of Bislama.

(20)   Bislama
        a. *Namba blong yu se 3093?*
           'Is your number 3093?'
        b. *Oli stanemap wan komiti se disasta komiti.*
           'A committee was formed as a disaster committee'
                    (Crowley 1991: 398)

Similarly, *be*, from colloquial French *mais* > *bais*, is becoming a subordinator and a copula in Bislama. However, some indigenous languages of Vanuatu have a very similar form as a copula, including North Ambrym *be* and Paama *ve*, leading here to a good case for mutually supporting superstrate and substrate influence.

Crowley's conclusion is that the bioprogram alone may be replaced by 'a consensus that what is most likely to 'survive' in a radically altered contact language is a set of features combining substratum and superstratum features, as well as other features that develop independently, for a variety of reasons, including universal pressures' (Crowley 1991: 385). Such harmonious consensus seems a distant hope at the present stage of creolistics, but may represent a goal towards which historical linguists as well as creolists can contribute, by collecting sound historical and linguistic data on creoles and creolisation, and attempting to include pidgins and creoles in our theories of language change. However, we must face the fact that no single, monolithic theory will easily cope with the complex phenomenon of creolisation; instead (Singh 1991: 4), 'the ultimate theory of creolisation ... may have to be as much of a creole as the language it describes'.

11 Language death

11.1 Introduction

> Language death occurs in unstable bilingual or multilingual speech communities as a result of language shift from a regressive minority language to a dominant majority language (Dressler 1988: 184)

Dressler's definition immediately allows us to link the special social context of language death with its linguistic consequences: as we shall see below, language death essentially involves 'normal' linguistic changes, but occurring at an accelerated rate for particular sociolinguistic reasons. Language death consequently resembles pidginisation and creolisation, which together contribute to language birth, in several respects: all these processes involve linguistic contact; all are partly motivated by social factors; all involve characteristic subsets of linguistic changes; and all, although our knowledge of them is still rather limited, seem to have important implications for linguistic theory, language acquisition, and language change.

Although the study of language death as a field in its own right is very recent (the first major study is probably Dorian 1981), people have been aware that languages disappear for much longer. For instance, Swadesh (1948) is one of the earliest commentators on language death, although he concentrates almost exclusively on the social context of disappearing languages, rather than on structural changes which might result. Some early comments on dying languages are also judgemental in tone, condemning the speech of residual informants: we shall reject this evaluative approach, especially since, as Swadesh (1948: 234–5) notes, it seems that ' ... the factors determining the obsolescence of languages are non-linguistic. There are no such things as inherently weak languages that are by nature incapable of surviving changed social conditions.' However, in Chapter 12 we shall review nineteenth-century theories of language change which saw certain language types as more suited for survival than others, and discuss the suitability of biological terms like language death for the description of linguistic changes.

The definition of language death we shall adopt essentially involves a transfer of allegiance of part of a population from a language which has been native in the area, to a more recently introduced language in which the indigenous population has become bilingual. The new language is generally spoken natively by more powerful speakers, who may also be more numerous, and is typically associated by speakers of the minority language with prestige, wealth and progress. The minority language is then effectively deserted by its speakers, becoming appropriate for use in fewer and fewer contexts, until it is entirely supplanted by the incoming language. Although terminology in this area is not yet settled, I shall call this sociolinguistic change language shift. However, there are also linguistic consequences for the dying minority language. Parents will typically stop passing this language on to their children, who will not use it enough to become fully fluent speakers; the minority language will therefore die over several generations, with items of vocabulary and constructions gradually falling out of use. I shall use the term linguistic obsolescence for these gradual changes which are the linguistic concomitant of language shift. It might be argued that obsolescence is not a particularly felicitous term, given the connotational connections of 'obsolete' with objects which are old-fashioned and out of date, and which have generally been replaced by better models. I have already said that I do not intend any categorisation of Language X as better or worse than Language Y; but it might be noted that the use of the term 'obsolete' in its less impartial sense accords well with native speakers' judgements of their obsolescing language, which they typically regard as being of little practical use in the modern world, and often of purely sentimental value.

It is not yet clear whether obsolescence can be arrested or even reversed once it has begun (see Fishman 1991), or whether eventual death will ultimately be predictable from signs of obsolescence. However, for present purposes, we might tentatively accept that language shift and linguistic obsolescence together entail eventual language death.

This preliminary definition of language death is, however, intended to be exclusive as well as inclusive. Most readers will probably have encountered the phrase 'dead languages' in connection with Latin or Ancient Greek (often as part of a query as to why one is studying them). However, what has happened to Greek or Latin is not death, but metamorphosis; the normal processes of linguistic change have affected these systems, transforming Ancient Greek into Modern Greek, and causing Latin to diversify into its present-day Romance descendants, including French, Catalan, Italian and Portuguese. Since modern forms of Latin and Greek are still in everyday use, the languages have not died.

Three further situations, involving the actual loss rather than change of a language, are to be excluded from our study of language death; these are described by Campbell and Muntzel (1989). The first is sudden death, which involves the loss of a language through the death of all its speakers, as happened following the European colonisation of Tasmania in the nineteenth century: the last speaker of Tasmanian died in 1876 (Swadesh 1948). The relative shortness of this period means that there was effectively no obsolescing stage. A similar situation is that of radical death, which is again rapid but is typically motivated by political oppression. For instance (Campbell and Muntzel 1989), an uprising of peasants in El Salvador in 1932 was put down by a massacre of at least 25,000 Indians. Speakers of Indian languages like Lenca and Cacaopera stopped using these as a form of self-defence, so that they would not be identified as Indians. Again, the rapidity of the death of these languages has stopped any gradual structural decay. Finally, we shall not be dealing with 'bottom-to-top death', which involves the loss of a language from casual contexts first, with retention longer in ritual contexts – the opposite of the norm in language death, where, as we shall see, minority languages tend to be retained longest in casual, intimate, in-group exchanges. Campbell and Muntzel (1989) describe various cases of 'bottom-to-top death': one involves a 'speaker' of Chiapanec who knew only a few residual words, plus a long religious text called an *alabanza*, or 'hymn of praise', which he had memorised to perform on ritual occasions, although he did not know what the text meant. Similarly, although less radically, Huffines (1989) notes that Pennsylvania German is now predominantly used only in church.

These special cases will not be discussed further here. Instead, we shall consider two commonly distinguished subtypes of gradual language death (see Aitchison 1981), which rejoice in the names of <u>language suicide</u> and <u>language murder</u>. Again, these terms are not altogether settled, although they appear fairly regularly in the literature; and in fact, they are arguably not entirely appropriate. As we shall see below, the criteria for distinguishing between the two types of language death have not been clearly established: they are largely based on the degree of relationship between the two languages involved, in that language suicide typically involves a creole and its superstrate, while in language murder the dying language and the new language need not be related at all. Obviously, this is not a rigid definition, and might in practice be rather hard to apply. Furthermore, the terms could be misleading if we take them to refer to the attitudes of the speakers of the dying language, since we might suppose that in a case of suicide the speakers voluntarily abandoned their language, while in murder they were forced to do so, despite resistance. In fact, this is not the case at all: as we shall see, one of the main factors involved in language murder is the marked reluctance of many dying language speakers to use their native variety, and their willingness to embrace the newer and more prestigious language in the community. Instead, suicide and murder must be construed as referring to the effect on the dying variety – in cases of suicide, it absorbs a considerable quantity of material from the more prestigious language, while in murder, it is simply ousted by the newcomer, without necessarily undergoing much borrowing.

In a new subfield, these preliminary terminological difficulties are inevitable; and in the rest of this chapter, I shall adopt the terms language suicide and language murder, but with the above caveats in mind. Language suicide will be discussed in 11.2, and four case-studies of the more common language murder in 11.3; and in 11.4 we shall attempt to isolate some common features of language death and compare these to pidginisation and creolisation.

11.2 Language suicide

In language suicide, the less prestigious of two closely-related languages co-existing in a community progressively borrows words and constructions from the more prestigious language, until the two eventually become almost indistinguishable. The less prestigious language consequently appears to commit suicide by absorbing more and more material from its socially superior neighbour. The few studies of language suicide which have appeared (see especially Aitchison 1981) have tended to concentrate on situations where a creole 'gets devoured by its parent' (Aitchison 1981: 210), to the extent that language suicide has become almost synonymous with decreolisation.

Decreolisation is apt to begin when a creole remains in contact with its superstrate language. The superstrate is often the medium of education, government, commerce and the professions, reinforcing an assignment of prestige: as Todd (1990) notes, decreolisation among the English-based creoles is furthest advanced in the West Indies, since English-medium education has been compulsory there for much longer than in West Africa or Papua New Guinea. Under these circumstances, there is a strong social motivation for creole speakers to learn the superstrate, and they will therefore tend to avoid particularly stereotyped features of the creole, and to introduce features of the superstrate into their speech.

However, the creole does not immediately disappear, leaving the superstrate as the sole language of the area. Instead, a creole continuum develops; in the speech community, a continuum of varieties will come into existence, with the superstrate, or acrolect, at one end, and the 'deep' creole, or basilect, at the other. In-between are a number of varieties, collectively known as the mesolect. The two end-points of the continuum are likely to be mutually unintelligible, and will not both be used by the same speaker; but each speaker will typically control various adjacent points along the continuum. Crucially, then, the creole continuum does not represent a model of a single speaker, but of language use in a speech community. It is also both synchronic and diachronic; for instance, Bickerton (quoted Romaine 1988: 165) reports on the basis of his work in Guyana that 'a synchronic cut across the Guyanese community is indistinguishable from a diachronic cut across a century and a half of linguistic development.' In other words, diachronic changes are preserved in synchronic structure. An example of a partial continuum is given in (1) below; the basilect is Guyanese Creole, while the acrolect is clearly a dialect of English.

(1)   Guyanese Creole: *mi gii am*
                             mi bin gii am
                             mi bin gii ii
                             mi bin gi ii
                             mi di gii ii
                             mi di gi hii
                             a di gi ii
                             a di gii ii
                             a did gi ii
                             a did giv ii
                             a did giv hii
                             a giv ii
                             a giv im
                             a giv him
                             a geev ii
                             a geev im
                             a geev him
         English: *I gave him*
              (Romaine 1989: 158–59)

Finally, early work assumed that the creole continuum resulted from random mixing of the acrolectal and basilectal grammars, giving rise to an unprincipled jumble of varieties in between. However, the continuum seems to be much more structured than this, and can be analysed and formally described using a technique known as implicational scaling. We need not pursue this in detail here (see Romaine 1988 for details), but the basic idea is that linguistic change from the basilect towards the acrolect will proceed in a particular order, with certain features changing before others in the community. Consequently, a synchronic scale can be created to show that, if a certain speaker uses a particular feature, he will also use certain others; while a feature located near the basilectal end of the scale will be incompatible with one close to the acrolect. A schematised implicational scale for six features is given in (2). If features A–F are all acrolectal, then speaker 1 uses the acrolect consistently, speaker 7 uses the basilect, and speakers 2–6 speak mesolectal varieties.

(2)   Feature

		A	B	C	D	E	F
	1	y	y	y	y	y	y
	2	y	y	y	y	y	n
Speaker	3	y	y	y	y	n	n
	4	y	y	y	n	n	n
	5	y	y	n	n	n	n
	6	y	n	n	n	n	n
	7	n	n	n	n	n	n

y = feature found; n = feature not found

The next question is how the superstrate influences the creole, or how acrolectal features are introduced into the basilect to produce the creole continuum. Aitchison (1981) makes some suggestions based on the decreolisation of Tok Pisin in urban areas of Papua New Guinea. Tok Pisin is one of the official languages of Papua New Guinea, but English is also widely used, for instance in commerce and as the medium of university education; contact with the superstrate is therefore maintained. Tok Pisin is the language of government and is used in parliament in Port Moresby, the capital; however, paradoxically, this official recognition provides the main motivation for the first step in decreolisation, since Tok Pisin lacks vocabulary for parliamentary topics. Many words in the creole already have English models, and consequently there is no particular difficulty about borrowing more: for instance, Aitchison (1981: 212) quotes a radio broadcast in which English-derived words and expressions like *oposisen* 'opposition', *palamen* 'parliament', *mosin ov nou konfidens* 'motion of no confidence', *praim minista* 'Prime Minister' and *konstitusin* 'constitution' are extremely prevalent and, despite their minor adaption to the creole spelling and sound systems, extremely obvious.

As we saw in Chapter 8, large-scale lexical borrowing may be the first stage in a far-reaching set of contact-induced changes, and this seems to be the case in Tok Pisin. Borrowing is now widespread for at least some urban creole speakers in other semantic fields; for instance, the system of temporal expressions in Tok Pisin is being replaced by English forms. Thus, the English-based phrase *de bihain long tumoro* 'day after tomorrow' is replacing the earlier pidgin *haptumora*, while expressions like *foa klok* 'four o'clock', *hapas tri* 'half-past three' are becoming common even in rural areas, instead of the pidgin terms which typically refer to the position of the sun or the amount of light so that 6 p.m. is *taim bilong san i godaun*. These temporals seem rather easy to borrow because the days of the week, and words like *wik* 'week', *yia* 'year' already have English models; and they bring with them the English plural affix -*s*, giving *tri des*, *wan an haf auas*, *wikends* and so on (Aitchison 1981: 214). Although we cannot predict this with any certainty, it seems likely that the -*s* affix will now spread to other constructions. Furthermore, the volume of English loans is also affecting the Tok Pisin sound system; for instance, the introduction of *after* and *afternoon* instead of pidgin *apinun* has legitimated the previously disallowed medial cluster [ft].

Two caveats must be borne in mind in connection with decreolisation. First, we should not automatically assume that all change in a creole system is in the direction of the superstrate; the basilect may also act as a model for change in some circumstances. This is the case in recreolisation, which Romaine (1988: 192) describes as a 'refocussing of norms in the direction of basilectal speech'. For instance, in London, young black British people descended from West Indian immigrants are now tending to use overtly creole forms in adolescence as a method of reinforcing and stating their identity. This does not involve simply an exaggerated use of the language of the parents – as is shown by the fact that Jamaican Creole forms are used even by speakers whose parents come from other islands – but rather a conscious choice of maximally basilectal forms. The resulting system, London Jamaican, is neither standard English nor Jamaican Creole; it relies predominantly on those forms which are most different from standard English, and is therefore to some extent stereotyped, lacking the usual range of stylistic options of the creole.

Secondly, the frequent association of language suicide with decreolisation should not lead us to assume that only creoles and their superstrates can be involved in this type of change. For instance, the characteristic continuum found in decreolisation is mirrored in the range of varieties which can be found in an area where a non-standard local dialect and a more prestigious standard variety are spoken: an example is given in (3), which shows a continuum of forms which might be found among Catholic speakers in Northern Ireland. The top, or basilectal end of the continuum shows rather strong Irish Gaelic influence, whereas the final, acrolectal example is indistinguishable from standard English, except for the colloquial *buyin'* form; and of course, in performance this would be produced with a Northern Irish accent.

(3)   *Yiz is buyin' bread that biz kyoch*
        Yiz is buyin' bread that diz be kyoch
        Yiz is buyin' bread that biz raw in the middle
        Yiz is buyin' bread that diz be raw in the middle
        Yiz are buyin' bread that does be raw in the middle
        Youse are buyin' bread that does be raw in the middle

You're buyin' bread that's usually uncooked in the middle
  (Romaine 1988: 160)

There might well be another parallel here, since non-standard dialects are characteristically evaluated as less prestigious and desirable than standard varieties, even by their own speakers; consequently, language suicide might be an appropriate description of the loss or reduction in use of a dialect in favour of a standard. Hoenigswald (1989) bemoans the lack of studies on dialect death; but this is now being partially remedied. For instance, Jones (1992) argues on the basis of extensive fieldwork in two Welsh communities that Welsh dialects are becoming increasingly mixed and standardised, to the extent that young Welsh speakers can no longer reliably identify features as belonging to their own as opposed to another dialect. Jones concludes that this dialect suicide may strengthen allegiance to standard Welsh and perhaps enable Welsh to combat the threat of murder by English; but if so, the language will survive at the cost of dialectal diversity.

11.3   Language murder: four case-studies

11.3.1   *Hungarian in Austria*: *Gal* (1979)

Although language suicide may be more common than has hitherto been thought, if standardisation and dialect loss are included under this heading as well as decreolisation, language murder arguably still represents a more typical pattern. In language murder, the two systems involved will not be so closely related as a creole and its superstrate, or a dialect and standard, and in fact need not be related at all; and the gradual loss of the less prestigious, minority language does not necessarily follow massive borrowing from the dominant language, or involve the formation of a continuum of structures. On the contrary, the majority of changes during obsolescence do not involve borrowing of dominant language structures, and may not even follow patterns in the dominant language; and to the extent that a continuum exists at all, it is a continuum of proficiency in the obsolescing language, rather than a scale of varieties linking the two polar systems. In this section, we shall consider four case-studies of language murder, before attempting a partial summary in 11.4.

Gal (1979) represents one of the earliest detailed studies of the social circumstances in which a language may be lost. In this case, the language is Hungarian, as spoken in the village of Oberwart (or Felsöör) in the Burgenland of eastern Austria. Of course, even if Hungarian should be entirely lost from Oberwart, and from Austria, it is likely to survive in Hungary as the national language; and even if it does not, its death there will be a separate matter from its 'murder' by German in Austria. However, the context and consequences of language shift and obsolescence seem much the same regardless of whether an entire language or a residual or immigrant variety outside the indigenous area is involved, so that we may refer to both as *language* death.

Oberwart is one of five Hungarian-speaking villages in the Burgenland; all were settled around 1,000 years ago as Hungarian guarding communities. An influx of German speakers between 1200 and 1600 has left the former guarding communities as 'speech islands' surrounded by German and not directly in contact with other Hungarian speakers. Oberwart itself has been a bilingual community for at least 400 years: however, in 1921, when the village was granted to Austria, 75 per cent of the population spoke Hungarian, whereas in 1971 only 25 per cent did, and these were all peasants or the children of peasants. Language shift is clearly well under way – the question is how and why this shift has happened.

Oberwart expanded greatly in the nineteenth century from a mainly Hungarian-speaking peasant community to a small city with an increased population and a thriving commercial centre. The newcomers were predominantly German-monolingual Lutherans, who became a new, richer class of merchants and artisans. However, a counterbalancing influx of Catholic, Hungarian-speaking professionals also entered the town in the later nineteenth century, leading to a policy of Magyarisation, whereby Hungarian increasingly became the language of the professional élite and of higher education, although German was retained in the Lutheran community. Magyarisation was effectively halted when Oberwart became part of Austria in 1921; the Hungarian élite mainly fled to Hungary, and those Hungarians left were almost exclusively peasants, who gradually became bilingual. Ties with Hungary were considerably loosened by the German Anschluss in 1938, and by the Communist regime in Hungary thereafter, meaning that Hungarian has gradually become less prestigious. This is especially true since Hungarian is strongly associated with peasant life, which is now seen as undesirable. More German monolinguals have settled in the community, and German is being used in progressively more contexts, while Hungarian speakers now tend to assert that you can't go very far, either geographically or socially, with Hungarian. Children are tending not to learn Hungarian unless both their parents are Hungarian speakers, while parents are proud if their children speak German with no Hungarian influence. In short, German is seen as the language of education and of the wage-earning future, while Hungarian is the language of the peasant community and of the past.

Since all Oberwart Hungarian speakers are now bilingual, it is also interesting to see when they tend to use Hungarian, and when German is favoured. Gal argues that the single most important factor in language choice is the speaker's age and peasant status; young people rarely speak Hungarian, sometimes leading to unreciprocal communication where parents or grandparents address a child or grandchild in Hungarian, but the child answers in German. The other crucial factor is the identity and status of the interlocutor. When a German monolingual is present, all Hungarian speakers will use German. German is also typically used to young people, government officials, and the doctor, while Hungarian is most frequently used when talking to God, grandparents, and black market clients; these are friends or acquaintances who visit the informant's house to have unlicensed carpentry, hairdressing or some similar service done.

However, identity of speaker and of interlocutor are not enough to predict language choice: we must also take account of each informant's social network (see Chapter 9). Gal assessed network structure by asking thirty-two informants, fourteen men and eighteen women, to give an account of their day-to-day contacts, then determined whether each informant's contacts were predominantly with peasants or non-peasants. Status as a peasant depended on eleven criteria: these included ownership of animals, especially cows or pigs; possession of an inside toilet; and wearing of traditional clothes, aprons for men and kerchiefs for women. In short (Gal 1979: 141), 'the statuses of the speaker's social contacts predicted language choice at least as powerfully as the speaker's own status'. For instance, Gal interviewed two men, János Vonatos and Sándor Acs, who were much the same age, were both workers, and were of the same 'degree of peasantness'. However, their social networks differed, and this correlated highly with the amount of Hungarian spoken. János Vonatos interacted mainly with non-peasants, and spoke Hungarian only to his grandparents, while Sándor Acs had most contacts with peasants, and spoke Hungarian to everyone except his children, to whom he spoke sometimes German and sometimes Hungarian.

Gal's investigation suggests that German is being introduced gradually into Oberwart, encroaching progressively on linguistic territory once occupied by Hungarian. Thus, although Oberwart peasants probably spoke little German before the 1920s or 1930s, all are now bilingual and typically use German to more categories of interlocutors in each generation. Hungarian is now a mark of peasant identity or peasant ancestry, and is used predominantly in in-group usage, among people with a high degree of peasantness. It is illuminating that Hungarian alone tended to be used in black market dealings, a risky business requiring trust from all parties; the use of a system affirming group membership would be particularly appropriate in such a context.

Gal's study concentrates on language shift; she does not comment in detail on any signs of linguistic obsolescence. There *is* a good deal of unidirectional lexical borrowing from German into Hungarian, although Gal's (1979: 81) comment that 'virtually any German word equipped with Hungarian suffixes and grammatical markers can appear in a Hungarian sentence' suggests that Hungarian grammar is not being affected. We shall now go on to look at another case of language shift, this time with more documentation on the linguistic changes involved.

11.3.2   *East Sutherland Gaelic: Dorian* (1981)

Nancy Dorian's pioneering fieldwork on Scottish Gaelic, reported in Dorian (1981) and in several papers (Dorian 1973, 1977a, 1977b, 1978), represents the first attempt to study intensively both the social motivation for language shift and the linguistic changes which follow in the dying language. Although Dorian concentrates on one dialect of Gaelic, namely that of East Sutherland, she still refers to her findings as indicating language death since East Sutherland Gaelic (ESG) is in fact under threat from a distinct language, English, rather than a related dialect. Furthermore, although Dorian investigates only this one variety, the fate of Scottish Gaelic in general is uncertain, and it is almost certainly dying as a whole, albeit at a rather slower rate than is the case for ESG.

Dorian has been carrying out fieldwork in the three villages of Brora, Golspie and Embo since the early 1960s, working with speakers from all areas of the proficiency continuum. There are now no Gaelic monolinguals in the area, rather an increasing number of English monolinguals, especially among the younger people; 100 out of 202 of Dorian's fluent Gaelic speakers died during the course of her fieldwork between 1963 and 1978, underlining the fact that it is now the language of the old. In Brora and Golspie, there are still some Gaelic-dominant bilinguals, all over seventy years of age. In Embo, a smaller and more isolated village, Gaelic has survived further down the age scale, and there are still some younger fluent speakers in their forties; 30.4 per cent of the population of Embo claimed to speak Gaelic in 1972, compared to 1.6 per cent in Brora and 3 per cent in Golspie. In all three communities, there are also semi-speakers, usually younger people who understand Gaelic well and speak it to a limited extent, but in a much-reduced form; Dorian was the first to identify this semi-speaker phenomenon, and we shall return to it below.

Gaelic was almost certainly spoken in East Sutherland before AD 900 (Dorian 1981). Sutherland was probably bilingual during the Viking period, but Gaelic regained the ascendancy in the thirteenth century. In common with most of the Scottish aristocracy of the time, the Earls of

Sutherland used Latin, French, English and Scots, but not Gaelic; and gradually Gaelic became confined to the poor, with English or Scots the prestigious language of the ruling class. From the eighteenth century, after the Act of Union joining Scotland and England, the Earls of Sutherland lived mostly in London, and attempted to discourage the use of Gaelic (and Scots) among their tenants by requiring such education as there was to be through the medium of English. Highland chiefs, attempting to live the expensive life of the Court, forcibly removed the peasants and small farmers from their land in the late eighteenth and nineteenth centuries in what have become known as the Highland Clearances, making way for intensive and profitable sheep-farming. The displaced tenants were frequently forced into emigration; in East Sutherland, they were also resettled on the coast, in communities like Brora, Golspie and Embo, and encouraged to take up fishing for a living; since they were typically given too little land to survive by farming, this opportunity was in the nature of Hobson's choice.

The arrival from around 1850 of numerous English-speaking sheep farmers, and of English-medium education, ended the centuries-old isolation of East Sutherland. Gaelic almost immediately began to decline rapidly. Dorian (1981: 51) argues that 'in terms of possible routes towards language death, it would seem that a language which has been demographically stable for several centuries may experience a sudden "tip", after which the demographic tide flows strongly in favour of some other language. In eastern Sutherland the end of a protective isolation precipitated this tip locally, exposing Gaelic speakers to the forces which had greatly favoured English nationally for several hundred years.' As English spread from the top of the social order downwards, Gaelic became restricted to the lowest members of the hierarchy; and these were the fishers.

It might be thought that the influx of cleared Gaelic speakers into the coastal settlements would strengthen the language, but in fact exactly the opposite happened. The newcomers, although Gaelic monolinguals, were looked down on by the existing inhabitants, partly because they were generally destitute, and partly because of their involvement with fishing which, although potentially lucrative, was seen as dirty and dangerous. The fishers in Brora, Golspie and Embo represented an isolated social group; each village has an area called 'Fishertown', and fishermen and their families only very rarely settled outside this area. Intermarriage among fishing families was the norm, with marriage outside the occupational group almost unheard of before the First World War. Furthermore, the fishers had gradually become linguistically isolated: they were the last group to become bilingual; their Gaelic remained free of influence from English longer than that of other groups; they retained imperfect, Gaelic-influenced English for longest; and they are now the last people in the villages Dorian studied to retain Gaelic at all.

All Dorian's informants agreed that the fishers were stigmatised as a social group: for instance, an English monolingual from Brora told her in 1978 that '"a 'fisher' was a term of abuse, there's no question about that"' (Dorian 1981: 61). Only the itinerant tinkers came lower on the social hierarchy. The children of fishers could not find work in shops or offices; even seating areas in church were segregated. Many emigrated, and even those remaining began to abandon Gaelic along with other fisher behaviours, adopting English as one route to greater prestige and better employment. Many of the children of fishers are now English monolinguals; and it goes almost without saying that all of Dorian's bilingual informants had been fishermen themselves, or had spent their childhood in a fishing household.

Other factors similarly militate against the survival of ESG, one of the most prominent being education: the Scottish Education Act of 1872 actually fails entirely to mention Gaelic. There is now some Gaelic-medium primary education in the Western Isles, and one secondary school, the Nicholson Institute in Stornoway, conducts some classes in Gaelic. Even here, there are enormous problems, since English has for centuries been preferred to Gaelic for the discussion of technical topics and Gaelic therefore lacks much of the necessary vocabulary. Thus, Thomson (1979: 19) reports that, although there is a good deal of literature in Gaelic, there is little art, music or literary criticism, largely because the relevant terms simply do not exist: 'equivalents for *stream of consciousness, empathy, counterpoint, ambiguity,* even *symbol,* do not leap to mind'. Thomson himself translated a biology textbook for use at the Nicholson Institute, and admits to wrestling with the question of whether to adopt English terminology, or to attempt to translate it into Gaelic, perhaps using semantically related Gaelic forms. In the end, he sometimes chose the first solution, as with *cromosom* 'chromosome', *gamait* 'gamete' and *haidrodean* 'hydrogen', which have only been altered to conform with Gaelic spelling, and sometimes the second, as with *cealla* 'cell', *searbhag* 'acid' and *ginteil* 'genetic'. Unfortunately, the hope of having the book adopted by schools in large enough numbers to make the experiment worth the publishers' while repeating for other subjects, seems a faint one. In any case, many parents and children are likely to favour secondary education in English, partly because no university education is available through the medium of Gaelic. Furthermore, the initiatives in the Western Isles (which, laudable though they are, may themselves be too little and too late) are of no help to ESG: outside the Western Isles Region, there is almost no provision for Gaelic-medium schooling, and very few schools even offer Gaelic as part of the curriculum. For many years, Gaelic was banned at school, and children speaking it, even in the playground, were likely to be punished. Dorian (1981) reports that Gaelic is now taught to a very limited extent in Embo, and there are also night-classes in the ESG area; however, few bilinguals persevere with these as the teachers almost invariably attempt to impose standard, textbook Gaelic and do not accept, or even actively denigrate, ESG. ESG is generally seen as a rather aberrant variety of Gaelic, an opinion shared by its own speakers; they feel that their Gaelic is inadequate and full of errors, complain that they have fewer 'words for things' than their grandparents, and sometimes argue that ESG is not a real language, partly because Gaelic literacy in the area is almost non-existent. They also claim not to be able to understand other dialects of Gaelic, so that even the small amount of Gaelic television and radio broadcasting which exists is inaccessible to them. Speakers of other Gaelic varieties can generally understand ESG, since it is reduced in comparison to their dialects, but are highly critical of it; one Hebridean speaker told Dorian (1981: 87) that hearing ESG 'made his teeth hurt'.

Despite these problems, many of the speakers of ESG interviewed by Dorian felt more at home in Gaelic than in English, and more emotionally involved with it; they also condemned other bilinguals as 'proud' if they refused to speak Gaelic. However, these attitudes only hold within the older age-group; it is considered quite acceptable not to teach Gaelic to one's children, and those of school-age are now usually passive bilinguals at best. Consequently, even older people now have fewer and fewer opportunities to use ESG, and it is appropriate in a decreasing number of contexts. Gaelic is used in the domains of home life and religion, if at all; and it is also characteristic of joke-telling, and used on shopping trips as a secret language, since shop-keepers tend to be English monolinguals. However, even a large group of bilinguals speaking Gaelic will defer linguistically to an English monolingual who joins the conversation by switching to English.

Let us turn now to the linguistic consequences of this social movement away from Gaelic. Dorian, using a mixture of techniques, including recording conversations, administering questionnaires, and asking informants to translate sentences from English to Gaelic, discovered a continuum of proficiency in the communities she studied, whereby older speakers might still be very fluent, but those younger people who spoke ESG at all tended to use a reduced, simplified variety (except, as we have seen, in Embo, where there was also a group of younger fluent speakers, in their forties). Dorian christened the youngest group, with their aberrant Gaelic, semi-speakers, and found that these had typically had too little exposure to

ESG as children to learn it perfectly. Semi-speakers typically speak more slowly than fluent speakers, and their grammar and phonology will be aberrant from the point of view of the fluent speakers' norms; they also characteristically use more loanwords from the dominant language. Some of the semi-speakers Dorian identified admitted to speaking some Gaelic, while others denied that they could do so. However, all could understand more than they could speak, and many had a passive competence almost equivalent to that of a full bilingual.

Dorian's information on semi-speaker usage comes mainly from translation exercises (Dorian 1977a, 1978, 1981); although she was well-integrated into the communities she worked in, and could therefore obtain good casual continuous speech from her older, more fluent informants, she discovered free conversation to be extremely stressful to semi-speakers, who found that the attempt to consistently speak Gaelic made strong demands on their weak linguistic resources. Semi-speakers generally use little Gaelic, liberally interspersed with English, so that translating individual sentences resembles their normal usage much more; an interesting point when so much sociolinguistic investigation centres around encouraging natural conversation to elicit the vernacular! Fluent speakers similarly enjoyed giving translations, sometimes commenting that they felt they were taking part in a quiz.

In general, semi-speakers displayed the same linguistic behaviour as fluent speakers, but taken to extremes; in other words, ESG is undergoing certain changes for all its speakers, but these are progressing much more quickly in the speech of the semi-speakers. We shall now consider a number of these ongoing changes.

Grammatical information in Scottish Gaelic, and in the other Celtic languages, is often expressed by suffixation, as it is in English; but the Celtic languages also have a system of initial mutations, whereby the initial consonant of a word is changed. These mutations were originally sound changes occurring in particular phonological environments, but as the conditioning sounds were gradually lost, they became fossilised, morphological markers. The two initial mutations of Scottish Gaelic are lenition, which broadly speaking involves a change of voiceless stops to fricatives, and fricatives either to /h/ or to zero; and nasalisation, which primarily replaces voiceless consonants with voiced ones. These mutations are extremely important in verbal morphology: the root /priʃ/ means 'break', and the unmutated root with a pronoun, /priʃ a/ is the imperative 'break it!' However, the same form with lenition, /vriʃ a/ expresses the past tense, 'it broke', while /briʃ a/, with nasalisation, is the interrogative future, meaning 'will it break?' These mutations are so common that it is hard to find a sentence without at least one; and any breakdown in the system of mutations would clearly have profound consequences for Gaelic grammar.

Dorian (1977a) attempted to assess the retention of lenition in ESG by asking 8 fluent speakers and 7 semi-speakers to translate the same 115 English sentences. She concentrated on four contexts in which lenition would normally be expected in Gaelic: the independent form of the past tense; the vocative case; a feminine nominative or accusative noun following the feminine definite article; and an adjective or noun following the common adverbs *glé* 'very' and *ro* 'too' or the numeral *dà* 'two'. The past and vocative are marked solely by lenition, while feminine nouns following the definite article <u>may</u> be identified as feminine only by lenition, although there may also be a feminine diminutive suffix or a feminine pronoun in the next clause to help, so that this instance of lenition is less grammatically salient; finally, lenition after the adverbs and *dà* has no grammatical function whatsoever.

Dorian's results are given in (4) below; the tables show the number of opportunities for use of these types of lenition in her experimental sentences, and the number and percentage of failures for fluent and semi-speakers.

(4)a. Fluent Speakers

Environment	Opportunities	Failures	%
1. Past	104	0	0
2. Feminine	80	1	1.25
3. Adv./Num.	104	2	2
4. Vocative	59	10	17

b. Semi-speakers

Environment	Opportunities	Failures	%
1. Past	85	9	10.5
2. Feminine	91	42	46
3. Adv./Num.	70	34	48
4. Vocative	50	37	72

(after Dorian 1977a: 99)

As the percentage figures show, lenition is gradually falling out of use for both the fluent and the semi-speakers, and is following the same pattern in both cases, with strongest retention in the past tense, and weakest in the vocative. However, the loss is much more advanced for the semi-speakers; they retain lenition in feminines and after *dà*, *ro*, *glé* only at around chance level, and fail to mark over 70 per cent of vocatives. It might be expected that decay would be faster after the adverbs than in the vocative, since in the former case the mutation carries no grammatical information; however, Dorian notes that the leniting adverbs and *dà* are extremely common, and that failure to lenite forms following these has the status of a stereotype in the communities she studied, which might promote retention. On the other hand, although lenition is the only segmental marker of the vocative, there is also suprasegmental marking, involving a change in intonation pattern, which is becoming the sole marker of the vocative for younger semi-speakers. Dorian notes that the presence or absence of marked grammatical categories in English may influence the retention of lenition in Gaelic. For instance, English has a grammatically marked past tense, and this is the context in which lenition is most consistently retained in ESG; however, English has no marking of the vocative case, unless we count an intonation pattern particular to terms of address – and it is in the vocative that the use of lenition has decayed most comprehensively, being replaced by a suprasegmental signal in ESG. However, the influence of the dominant language is insufficient to explain the developing hierarchy of mutation loss or retention, and language internal factors must also be invoked: for instance, Dressler (1988) suggests that lenition (this time a process of voicing) survives best of the three initial mutations operative in Breton because it applies in the greatest number of contexts, affects most consonants, and is a rather natural phonological process.

Dorian (1978) has also tested for loss or retention of morphological marking in the plural of nouns, which, as (5) shows, can be formed in eleven ways. Plurals also have the advantage of occurring very frequently, and hence of being easy to elicit. Again, Dorian asked speakers to translate sentences; this time, four were older fluent speakers, four younger fluent speakers, and between five and eight were semi-speakers – some of these could only cope with relatively simple test material.

(5)   Noun Plurals

		singular	plural	
1.	suffixation	/preːg/	/preːgən/	'lies'
2.	final mutation	/pʰũːntʰ/	/pʰũːntʃʰ/	'pounds'
3.	suppletion	/tʰɛ/	/tʰroːr/	'houses'
4.	quantity change +suffixation	/pʰyuːr/	/pʰyuriçɛn/	'sisters'
5.	final mutation +suffixation	/seːx/	/seːçɛn/	'dishes'
6.	vowel alternation	/makʰ/	/mikʰ/	'sons'
7.	vowel alternation +final mutation	/tʰəuɫ/	/tʰwiːlʲ/	'holes'
8.	vowel alternation +suffixation	/kʰuː/	/kʰɔnʲ/	'dogs'
9.	vowel alternation +final mutation +suffixation	/yax/	/yəiçu/	'horses'
10.	vowel alternation +syncope +suffixation	/tarəs/	/tɔrsin/	'doors'

11. quantity change   /in'an/   /in'an:/   'onions'
                    (after Dorian 1978: 595)

Fluent speakers employ suffixation and various quantity changes most
frequently, with vowel alternations affecting few but common nouns.
However, the semi-speakers use predominantly suffixation, which is now
the only productive strategy with loans or new analogical forms.
Furthermore, semi-speakers use one suffix, /-ən/, far more frequently than
any other, although in Dorian's data nine different suffixes were produced
by fluent speakers, and more certainly exist. In fact, use of /-ən/ increases
by 17 per cent between the older fluent speakers and the semi-speakers.
Finally, semi-speakers relatively frequently fail to mark plurals in any way;
zero plurals are unknown to older fluent speakers and occur in only 0.5 per
cent of cases for younger fluent speakers, but account for 9 per cent of semi-
speaker plurals.

The strategies which seem to be disappearing most rapidly involve
lengthening of final consonants, and vowel alternation with final mutation,
and semi-speakers seem disinclined to use either vowel alternation or final
mutation at all, whether alone or with other pluralising devices; however,
these and other minority strategies do remain at a very low level even for
the semi-speakers.

Part of the motivation for these developments may again come from
English; semi-speakers do not tend to use phonemes which have no
English equivalent, and are therefore losing distinctive consonant length, a
feature of Gaelic but not of English. Similarly, semi-speakers are
weakening the ESG vowel length distinction; and here it should be
remembered (see Chapter 3) that Scots and Scottish English are unique
among varieties of English in lacking contrastive vowel length. Furthermore, English tends to mark plurals by suffixation, and favours the
single suffix /-s/; and although this morphological marker is not itself
borrowed into ESG, the pattern of marking plurals in a unified way with
a single suffix does seem to influence semi-speaker usage.

Dorian found similar results in a parallel experiment on gerund
formation, where fluent speakers also tend to use zero rather frequently;
suffixation is also relatively common, particularly involving /-u/, while
suppletion affects few, but common verbs. Here again, semi-speakers are
turning to simple suffixation, and again one suffix, this time /-al/, has
become very productive for them, moving from 9 per cent for older fluent
speakers and 10 per cent for younger fluent speakers to 25.5 per cent for
semi-speakers. Zero formations also increase, but only slightly, while final
mutation and vowel alternation drop sharply. Again, this reflects to some
extent the situation in English, where the gerund is formed consistently
with /-ıŋ/; however, most strategies are again retained, albeit at a very low

level, even by the semi-speakers. As Dorian (1978: 608) puts it, 'ESG might be said to be dying, at least with regard to noun plurals and gerunds, with its morphological boots on'.

Dorian (1973, 1977a, 1977b, 1978, 1981) provides data on many other decaying features of the ESG grammar. For instance, semi-speakers are beginning to fail to mark gender accurately; Gaelic has two grammatical genders, masculine and feminine, and semi-speakers are beginning to generalise the masculine pronoun /a/ to all inanimates, and losing feminine /i/. They also tend to use nasalisation, the mutation formerly appropriate to masculine nouns, after the definite article, rather than lenition for feminines and nasalisation for masculines; but they are generalising the feminine diminutive suffix to all nouns. Consequently, contradictory gender signals are appearing in sentences, and the gender system is breaking down. In terms of cases, the nominative / accusative and the dative are surviving reasonably well, but the vocative, as we have seen, is now signalled only by suprasegmentals for semi-speakers, and the genitive is moribund: Dorian found no genitive plurals from any of her informants, and very few genitive singulars, with all groups preferring to use a prepositional phrase instead. In the verb, the past tense is generally still preserved, although methods of marking it are changing; but semi-speakers no longer control the conditional well, and only five out of ten of Dorian's semi-speakers produced any recognisable conditionals at all. Of two passive constructions in ESG, only one is used by semi-speakers, and two out of seven semi-speakers actually used no correct passives. Finally, Dorian asked her informants for the ESG equivalents of 220 English words; fluent speakers succeeded in translating a minimum of 193 words, and often missed items which they were later heard using in conversation, while semi-speakers failed to produce between 29 and 70 words from the list.

In general, then, Dorian's data seem to suggest that the changes we find in this dying language at least are very like those found in 'normal' language change: for instance, cases are lost and replaced by prepositional phrases, and analogical levelling takes place. However, these changes occur much more rapidly in an obsolescing language, and often strategies for morphological marking are being lost and not replaced; in 'healthy' languages, reduction is often followed by reanalysis or grammaticalisation which produce a new marker. Although the changes found are not exclusive to linguistic obsolescence, then, the rate and the sociolinguistic context of these changes are unique. The swiftness of these changes also means that we should be very cautious in interpreting semi-speaker data; it is, of course, easy to recognise semi-speakers if fluent speakers are still available for comparison, but since semi-speakers often come from a younger generation than the last fluent speakers, they are likely to be the last, residual speakers of a dying language, and data from them may consequently be used to reconstruct the lost system. However, in interviewing only semi-speakers, we may not know what we are missing; for instance, Dorian (1977b) reports that one semi-speaker from Embo, I. F., has almost entirely lost the mutation of nasalisation, so that if she were the last remaining speaker of ESG, and we had no written records or related languages or dialects to compare, we might not reconstruct such a mutation at all. Of course, this is a slightly far-fetched scenario, but the message is clear: 'It should probably be assumed, wherever a grammar is written or a proto-language reconstructed on the basis of materials gathered from a few last remaining speakers, that the stage of the language represented by those speakers is markedly deviant even in terms of the recent history of the language' (Dorian 1973: 438).

11.3.3   Irish Gaelic: Hindley (1990)

Dorian's work on ESG can profitably be compared with Hindley's socio-geographical research on Irish Gaelic, a closely related language facing many of the same problems and threatened from precisely the same direction. Like Gal, Hindley concentrates on the issues of language shift rather than linguistic obsolescence.

Hindley (1990) argues that no single factor can be identified as promoting a sudden 'tip' towards English and away from Irish in Ireland, but rather that the introduction of more prestigious English meant that Irish was gradually felt to be superfluous. English has been spoken in Ireland to some extent since 1170, and there have been occasional large-scale settlements of English speakers in the subsequent centuries. Bilingualism in the Irish people began in the north and east, and by 1800 monoglot Irish speakers were becoming increasingly rare in all areas: the people began to realise that English was the key to new opportunities, and parents encouraged their children to learn English and not to use their Irish. In the 1851 census, 1.5 million out of a total Irish population of 6.5 million people claimed to speak Irish, with approximately 300,000 being monoglots. The discouragement of Irish was helped by the devastating famines of 1845–9 and by subsequent emigration, which together halved the population by 1900.

In 1922, Ireland was divided into the southern Irish Free State, or Eire, and Northern Ireland. In the north, Irish is mainly used in the Catholic community, but it is no longer a native language on a significant scale. Irish is not compulsory at school, and is only relatively rarely an option; and even when offered, it is not overwhelmingly popular: in 1967–70, only about 25 per cent of pupils in the minority of schools offering Irish actually took it. Under the National Curriculum currently being introduced, children will have to choose one foreign language from French, German, Spanish, Italian and Irish, and the number studying the language therefore seems set to fall.

In southern Ireland, Irish speakers are now concentrated in the west and the south, in the Gaeltachtai, or official Irish-speaking areas, established in 1926. Even here, it is becoming increasingly difficult to find habitual speakers of Irish. All Southern Irish children now learn some Irish at school, and it was for some time necessary to pass an examination in Irish to gain the School Leaving Certificate, but this requirement was abolished in 1973–4. In the Gaeltachtai, teaching through the medium of Irish is also provided.

The compulsory teaching of Irish at school means that Irish has an odd age-profile of speakers for a dying language. Whereas in most obsolescing languages speaker numbers fall gradually with age, in Ireland the percentage of school-age children claiming to know Irish is higher even than for the over-60s. For instance, in the 1981 census, 50.8 per cent of 10- to 14-year-olds are declared as Irish speakers, but only 25.6 per cent of 45- to 64-year-olds. However, this high percentage rapidly tails off as school Irish is forgotten; and the rather artificial nature of these inflated figures is apparent since only 4.9 per cent of 3- to 4-year-olds in the same census are listed as Irish speakers, indicating clearly that Irish is no longer acquired at home, but taught at school.

An additional problem in interpreting census returns is that they involve self-declaration. The inevitable possibility of error is strengthened by the fact that children in the Gaeltachtai who can demonstrate by their fluency in Irish that Irish is the language of their home can qualify for a small grant, the *deontas*. Furthermore, families can claim large housing grants if all their school-age children have earned the *deontas*, and since the Gaeltachtai are frequently rather deprived areas economically, there is an obvious motivation for exaggerating the amount of Irish spoken. Although the *deontas* scheme is intended to encourage the use of Irish, Hindley (1990) argues that it is in fact rather divisive, since people in relatively strongly Irish-speaking areas see grants being awarded in other regions where Irish is almost exclusively taught at school, and may then feel that it is not worth trying to pass on the language to their own children. Furthermore, the Irish learned at school is only rarely kept up afterwards, especially among those who leave the Gaeltachtai. It seems that neither making Irish a compulsory school subject, nor allowing for choice, has significantly helped preserve it: in short, 'the voluntarism of the North is as much a failure as compulsion proved in the South and there is no point in either...hoping to recoup its own disasters by emulating the failed policies of the other' (Hindley 1990: 160).

Irish nowadays seems to be supported by a wish to assert an Irish identity; the remoteness of the Gaeltachtai has been another major factor in the retention of Irish. The compulsory teaching of Irish, Irish-medium teaching in the Gaeltachtai, and the various grants based on Irish proficiency, have also played some part in maintaining the language. However, there is a much longer list of adverse factors. For instance, speakers of Irish tend to identify strongly with their own dialect, and not with standard Irish, so that the limited amount of Irish radio broadcasting may not be accessible to them; there are also relatively few textbooks for native speakers, most being designed for learners of the standard language. The isolation and poverty of the Gaeltachtai has led to an association of Irish with deprivation, and inhabitants often speak English to distance themselves from this. Men from the Gaeltachtai have also tended to move to other areas of Ireland or to Britain to take seasonal jobs, requiring English. As the population becomes more mobile, people leave the Gaeltachtai to live in the towns, and speak English on return visits. Industrialisation has also introduced monoglot English speakers into the Gaeltachtai, and intermarriage is becoming more common; and given the sparse population of these areas, a relatively small number of incomers could easily swamp the language. The Gaeltachtai are also fragmented, so that each Gaeltacht has closer links with adjacent anglicised areas than with other Gaeltachtai; and the omnipresence of English on television reinforces the message that English is needed for contact outside the Gaeltacht, and for mobility in world terms. In short, the prospects for Irish are not good: 'Large numbers of teachers and officials expect it to "see them out" but longer perspectives and expectations are rare' (Hindley 1990: 214).

11.3.4   *Dyirbal*: *Schmidt* (1985)

Of 200 or so languages spoken in Australia before the coming of the Europeans, Schmidt (1985) estimates that 50 are now dead and 50 in the process of obsolescing (see also Dixon 1980). The topic of her study is Dyirbal, which was once spoken over around 8000km² of the rainforest area of North Queensland, but is now confined to a few communities near Murray Upper. Schmidt worked in the closed aboriginal community of Jambun, which has around 100 inhabitants, who mix with outsiders only irregularly. Even in Jambun, however, Dyirbal is being progressively replaced by English; and Schmidt's intention was to investigate the usage of young people aged between fifteen and thirty-nine, who were generally semi-speakers and often criticised their own Dyirbal, and to compare their Dyirbal with an existing account of the Traditional Dyirbal still spoken by older people.

Dyirbal has progressively become associated with poverty and lack of education, and with an older way of life which tends to be stigmatised increasingly by both white and aboriginal society. English-medium education is compulsory, and the now ubiquitous television broadcasts only in English; there is also no literature in Dyirbal. Parents keen for their children to succeed at school discourage them from speaking Dyirbal, and English is fast becoming the language of primary socialisation in the home. No inhabitant of Jambun is monolingual in Dyirbal, and those aged under fifteen speak a few words of Dyirbal at best, although they may understand a limited amount.

Bilinguals tend to defer to white English monolinguals by switching to English in their presence, so that again the interlocutor factor is important in determining when Dyirbal is spoken. However, whereas normally an obsolescing language will be used more in vertical than in horizontal communication (that is, mostly to older people rather than to one's peers), Dyirbal is not typically used by younger, semi-speakers to their elders. Schmidt (1985) suggests that this is because, unusually in a dying language, older Dyirbal speakers still correct semi-speakers when they deviate from the grammatical norms of Traditional Dyirbal, and especially when they use English loanwords; since semi-speakers are already critical of their own Dyirbal, the fear of being corrected and even ridiculed by their elders seems to discourage them from using the language when older people are present. Consequently, parents often address their children in Traditional Dyirbal, but the children answer in English. Young People's Dyirbal has become an important medium of in-group communication among the 15- to 39-year-olds, but tends to be governed by peer-group norms rather than by those of Traditional Dyirbal, and includes 'morphological simplification and intrusion of English and pidgin-type forms' (Schmidt 1985: 131).

Traditional Dyirbal has a split-ergative system of inflection, so that nouns and their modifiers which are the subject of an intransitive verb or the object of a transitive verb appear in a case known as the absolutive, while subjects of transitive verbs appear in the ergative. The absolutive is unmarked in Traditional Dyirbal, while the ergative has the suffix -ngu and a wide range of other allomorphs. In Young People's Dyirbal, however, the better semi-speakers maintain the single suffix -gu, while others have lost the ergative – absolutive distinction completely and rely on an English-type system with the word order identifying subject and object; this is quite alien to Traditional Dyirbal, which has exceptionally free word order.

Marking for the locative case is also being lost for young speakers, who are instead introducing English prepositions like *in*, *on* to precede the Dyirbal noun phrase. Among the verbs, Traditional Dyirbal marks futures with the suffix *-ny*, and non-futures with *-nyu* / *-u*, but in Young People's Dyirbal either *-ny* alone is kept, with non-futures unmarked, or increasingly, *-ny* and *-nyu* are used interchangeably and a word like [ŋulga] 'tomorrow' must be introduced to signal futures. Irregular verbs like [yanu] 'go' have also been reformed analogically by semi-speakers. Finally, although the singular-dual-plural distinction is retained by speakers of Young People's Dyirbal, some 'pidgin-type pronoun forms' (Schmidt 1985: 88) are also being introduced: these include *wi-fela*, *yu-fela*, *alugeda* for first, second and third person plural. The first two of these forms also include [f], which has been borrowed from English; Traditional Dyirbal has no fricatives. Semi-speakers are also beginning to use *bin* to mark the past tense, another pidgin-like development.

Young People's Dyirbal has also decayed semantically and lexically with respect to Traditional Dyirbal. In Traditional Dyirbal, there are four classes of nouns: Class I contains human masculines and other animates; Class II has human feminines and nouns relating to water, fire and fighting; Class III has the names of edible fruits and vegetables; and Class IV contains the residue. However, nouns may turn up in an unexpected class for three reasons. If Noun B is mythologically connected with Noun A, it will fall into the same class as Noun A, so that birds ought to be Class I, but are thought to be the spirits of dead women, so that they belong in Class II instead. Secondly, class membership is ruled by concept formation, so that 'fish spear' falls into Class I since it is related to 'fish'. Thirdly, nouns denoting harmful things are placed in a separate class; thus, 'fish' is Class I, but 'stonefish', a dangerous variety, is placed in Class II to mark its harmfulness. In Young People's Dyirbal, less-fluent speakers have reorganised this system so that it is based only on animacy and sex. Classes III and IV are collapsed, using the markers from Class III, and the single resulting class contains nouns denoting inanimates; Class I is for masculine animates, and Class II for feminine animates. The rules for transferring nouns between classes have been lost entirely.

Finally, there is a great deal of lexical borrowing from English into Young People's Dyirbal. While older speakers object to this, and attempt to supply the appropriate Traditional Dyirbal forms, among young people 'there is little resistance to the intrusion of English forms ... This indicates that, in the terminal phase of a language, the speakers come to rely on the linguistic resources of the replacing language' (Schmidt 1985: 189).

11.4   Language death, pidginisation and creolisation

We can now conclude that certain changes are consistently found in obsolescing languages (although many more case-studies are required before we can identify any change as an essential part of all language death situations). Prominent among these changes are the loss of irregularities and reduction of allomorphy, usually by analogy, and a movement from synthetic to analytic structures: for instance, morphological marking of nouns and modifiers as ergative or absolutive in Dyirbal is replaced by the use of word order to signal subject versus object, while the genitive case in East Sutherland Gaelic is being gradually replaced by prepositional constructions.

Some of these changes are motivated by the dominant language, but not all represent direct borrowing. The amount of lexical borrowing from the dominant into the dying language varies widely; there is a great deal in Young People's Dyirbal, but relatively little in dying ESG. Furthermore, it is often the patterns existing in the dominant language which exert influence on the dying language, rather than lexical material which is directly copied. For instance, the use of a single affix -s for the vast majority of English plurals may well be a factor in the increased incidence of a single plural suffix among semi-speakers of ESG; but the suffix is Gaelic -en, not English -s. Similarly, the ESG vocative is retained better than the genitive for Dorian's informants, although English has a genitive and lacks a morphologically marked vocative.

Language murder also has its own specific sociological context. Typically, a new language will be introduced into an area, entering into competition with an established, indigenous language. The speakers of the incoming language will tend to be more powerful socially and economically, and often more numerous, leading to an association of their language with wealth and power. Speakers of the indigenous language will become bilingual, and begin to absorb these judgements and denigrate their own language. Seeing the dominant language as a passport to greater prestige, parents will stop passing the minority language on to their children, who will become semi-speakers at best. There is also typically a lack of institutions to support or determine a norm for the minority language; it is often unwritten, as with Dyirbal and ESG (although other varieties of Gaelic are written) and is frequently banned or at best discouraged in the schools. Gradually, over several generations, the dying language will become associated with older people and an old-fashioned, vanishing way of life, and with poverty and lack of opportunities, eventually surviving only in in-group usage. This rejection seems to accelerate the rate of change in the dying language, which is subject to reductions without compensation in other areas of the grammar, making it ultimately inflexible and monostylistic. Thus, 'the reduction and adaption of linguistic structures are signs of threatening language death. But they also hasten language death, as an undermined, reduced and alienated language may seem to its speakers less worthy of being spoken, and is thus even less likely to be preserved' (Dressler and Wodak-Leodolter 1977: 9). The attitude of native speakers that their language is unsuitable for the modern world and in some sense dysfunctional and deficient therefore becomes a self-fulfilling prophecy.

Furthermore, as the dying language loses its own resources, speakers turn increasingly to the dominant language. In Young People's Dyirbal (Schmidt 1985), large numbers of English loans are habitually used; in Oberwart Hungarian (Gal 1979) almost any German word, equipped with Hungarian affixes, is acceptable; and in Mexican Nahuatl, Hill and Hill (1977) recorded up to 40 per cent Spanish loans, including nouns, verbs, hesitation forms like *este, a ver* and common items such as *entonces* 'then', *pues* 'well', *para que* 'so that' and *porque* 'because'. Many of Hill and Hill's informants were proud of Nahuatl and of their Indian identity (as one man put it (Hill and Hill 1977: 60) '"after all, to whom did the Holy Virgin of Guadalupe appear? Not to some gringo, not to some millionaire, but to a Mexicano-speaking Indian like ourselves."') However, they also felt that genuine Nahuatl, which they might have been motivated to preserve, is gone; the language which remains is regarded as *revuelta* 'topsy-turvy' and *mezclada* 'mixed', and they reject it.

Despite this distinctive sociolinguistic context, the changes involved in linguistic obsolescence are reminiscent of those found in other language contact situations. Comparisons of language death with pidginisation and creolisation are therefore inevitable. It has also been suggested that language death bears certain similarities to deacquisition (Giacolone Ramat 1983, Menn 1989); however, too little work has been done comparing obsolescence with normal acquisition or with language loss in aphasic or dysphasic patients, for instance, to substantiate this. Moreover, language loss typically takes place within an individual speaker, whereas in language death an entire community and a far longer time-span are involved. In view of these inclarities, we shall concentrate here on the claims that linguistic obsolescence is equivalent to pidginisation (Dressler and Wodak-Leodolter 1977) or to 'creolization in reverse' (Trudgill 1976).

Dressler and Wodak-Leodolter (1977: 8) argue that, in situations of language death, 'the non-dominant language often pidginizes in its last stages of existence'. Unquestionably, some similarities do exist between pidginisation and obsolescence: notably, both pidgins and dying languages have a limited vocabulary, relatively little morphology, simple syntax characterised by a lack of subordination, and a general prevalence of analytic over synthetic structures. Both tend to have a single, rigid word order, and are simple, reduced systems (where simplification means increasing regularity, and reduction means the loss of some part of a language, along with some expressive capacity). Pidgin-like forms, such as *bin* and *wi-fela* in Young People's Dyirbal, may appear in dying languages. Both pidgins and obsolescing languages are also monostylistic, and are, or become, inadequate for use as the sole language of a speech community. Finally, in both cases, a large number of analogically regularised forms tend to appear. Romaine (1988: 372–3) attributes the retention of such forms to the amount of variability and uncertainty shown by adult speakers, and to the consequent lack of a corrective mechanism applied by adults to children, arguing that 'in normal communities the expectation is that adults act as brakes on the innovations produced by children so that analogical and other deviant forms like *foots* get corrected and do not persist. In the case of dying and pidgin languages it may be that children have greater scope to act as norm-makers due to the fact that a great deal of variability exists among the adult community.' This may seem to be refuted by the clear existence of a corrective mechanism for Dyirbal (Schmidt 1985); but it should be remembered that in this case young people, not wishing to expose themselves to the embarrassment of being corrected, have ceased to use Dyirbal in vertical communication with their elders and now reserve it for in-group communication with their peers, where the norms are largely English-based and the biggest sin is to speak in a way that is 'too flash' or too close to Traditional Dyirbal. Thus, both the presence and the absence of corrective mechanisms seem to contribute to linguistic obsolescence.

Not all the linguistic features of pidginisation are mirrored in language murder. For instance, areas of morphological complexity tend to remain in obsolescing languages: in ESG, the majority of the eleven pluralisation strategies attested by Dorian for fluent speakers were also found, albeit on fewer occasions, for semi-speakers; and derivational affixes, and suffixes showing aspect tended to be retained in Young People's Dyirbal. The same goes for syntax: thus, although semi-speakers knew only one of the two passive constructions of ESG, they could nonetheless produce this fairly reliably, whereas the category of passive is rarely expressed in pidgins, and only reconstituted at the subsequent creole stage. However, the main differences between language death and pidginisation concern the socio-cultural situations in which these processes occur. For example, a pidgin is the first stage in the development of a language, while language shift and obsolescence represent the last. Furthermore, 'pidgins typically begin in formal situations between strangers for purposes that often relate to commerce and trade. In contrast, dying Dyirbal is spoken in informal situations between people sharing close personal ties' (Schmidt 1985: 217). Schmidt's assessment of Dyirbal can be extended to the other dying languages we have examined; and in general, it seems that the primary function of pidgins is communication, while that of a dying language is the assertion of in-group identity. The mode of acquisition of pidgins and dying languages also seems to be different (Dressler 1988). Typically, younger speakers of dying languages will have contact with more fluent older speakers, whereas the first generation of pidgin speakers will be the only users of the language. Language death occurs in bilingual situations, but pidginisation in trilingual or multilingual communities. Finally, while obsolescing languages have native speakers (albeit bilingual ones), a pidgin is not a native language at all.

In view of all these discrepancies, the similarities between pidginisation and language death seem to reduce to the occurrence of a few linguistic changes which are characteristic of languages in contact. Since pidgins arise and languages obsolesce only in contact situations, this is not altogether surprising; and, given the multitude of phenomena which can be described as contact-induced, it is certainly an insufficient basis on which to identify the two processes. If we equate language death with pidginisation, we are simply creating a vast category into which any contact-induced change can be placed, regardless of its individual context or characteristics; and such categories rapidly become meaningless.

Let us now turn to Trudgill's (1976) description of language death as 'creolization in reverse'. Trudgill seems to be considering primarily language murder; language suicide does indeed seem to be the reverse of creolisation in a limited sense, since it involves a movement away from a creole language towards its original superstrate. Trudgill considers the case of Arvanitika, a language descended from Albanian which has been spoken in villages around Athens for several centuries and which is now under threat from Greek. He argues that there is a case for considering the obsolescence of Arvanitika (and, by extension, that of other dying languages like Dyirbal, Gaelic and Irish) as creolisation in reverse. First, the sociolinguistic situation is a neat inverse; while creolisation involves the acquisition of native speakers by a language, language death is characterised by the loss or abandonment of a language by its native speakers. The proficiency continuum which develops in obsolescing languages can also be compared to the creole continuum which appears during decreolisation (Romaine 1988), provided that we do not take this comparison too far and equate the deep creole with the decaying, deviant performance of semi-speakers.

Trudgill also argues for language death as the linguistic reverse of creolisation, on the grounds that creoles tend to be simplified (relative to their superstrate) but not reduced, and not restricted, since they can be used in any context; dying languages, on the other hand, are restricted and reduced but not, according to Trudgill, simplified. However, Trudgill is unable to justify this opposition fully: he certainly finds cases of straightforward reduction, such as the loss of the past definite versus imperfect tense distinction, in Arvanitika; but he also finds phenomena which could well be analysed as simplificatory. For instance, the conditional tense markers are being lost from Arvanitika, but are being replaced by periphrastic forms; since the meaning of the conditional can still be expressed, this is not reduction, but as analytic, periphrastic forms seem easier for language users than synthetic ones, it may involve simplification in the morphology, albeit with some cost in the syntax. Cases of loss of redundancy are also clearly simplificatory. Consequently, 'even if "creolization in reverse" is an accurate term sociolinguistically, it is much less so linguistically, since the parallels are by no means complete' (Trudgill 1976: 49).

Our tentative conclusion, then, is that the equation of language death with pidginisation is partly appropriate from a linguistic point of view but quite misleading in social terms; while its description as creolisation in reverse is appropriate sociolinguistically, but not linguistically. However, it should be noted that this is an interim assessment, not the end of the story: we need more studies of language death, and better comparisons with pidginisation, creolisation, other contact phenomena, first and second language acquisition and individual language loss before we can say with any certainty where language death fits in. For example, Romaine (1988: 370) notes that 'in some cases, a language may exist in pidginized or creolized form, in several immigrant varieties with differing degrees of vitality, as well as in its full form with social and regional variation. Spanish, French and Arabic are such cases.' A comparative study of the varieties of such a language, including obsolescing ones, would be of enormous value to the study of language death.

We are also unable at present to predict language death: reports of death may be greatly exaggerated for any or all of the languages considered here, and they may yet recover and surprise us all; Hindley (1990), recognising this possibility, subtitles his book on Irish 'a qualified obituary'. Hoenigswald (1989: 353) resignedly notes that 'demise can be predicted, it seems, only at the terminal stage, where it is obvious, what with a last speaker surviving in California or on some Dalmatian island'. The low prestige of a language alone does not guarantee its death (Giacolone Ramat 1983); rapid growth in the prestige of the dominant language is also a prerequisite. This is often the result of economic changes, and leads to the sociolinguistic 'tip' (Dorian 1981) which accelerates shift and obsolescence. It is also unclear, in the absence of further individual and comparative studies, whether certain changes are invariably associated with language death, and can 'be taken as harbingers of impending language shift' (Woolard 1989: 356). Dressler (1988: 190), for instance, claims that 'there are inherent principles of language change that affect the way that languages decay and die, partially irrespective of the structures ... of the dominant language': we must hope that further research will help us find them.

12 Linguistic evolution?

12.1 Introduction

One of the most controversial issues in current historical linguistics (if not all linguistics) is the question of whether metaphors borrowed from biology should be applied to language. Some intimidatingly famous names have objected strongly to the introduction of metaphors and analogies into linguistics: Saussure, for instance, declares himself 'firmly convinced that anybody who sets foot in the realm of language may consider himself abandoned by all the analogies of heaven and earth' (quoted Percival 1987: 3). In fact, biological models and concepts were very frequently invoked by linguists and philologists during the nineteenth century, and have only in this century been seen as inappropriate and even distasteful. Evolution, in particular, has become a 'dirty word' in modern linguistic theory.

There are good reasons for the fact that 'serious use of biological metaphors is common among professional linguists through the early nineteenth century, but after that is confined mostly to amateurs' (Wells 1987: 42). For metaphors to be successful, the borrowers of concepts from other fields must know what they are borrowing, not merely in outline but in detail. Otherwise, 'such borrowings often turn from theoretical claims into sloppy metaphors, leading to varieties of "vulgar X-ism", the result of overenthusiastic appropriation with insufficient sense of the subtlety or precise applicability of the originals' (Lass 1990: 79). As we shall see, this is precisely what happened in the case of nineteenth-century extensions of evolutionary concepts to linguistics.

However, the unfortunate history of biological metaphor in linguistics need not discourage present-day linguists from seeking parallels with other disciplines; their task is rather to examine potential analogies carefully, to make sure they understand both sides of the equation, and not to overstate their case: 'we should be neither misled by metaphors nor afraid of them' (Wells 1987: 42). There is a good deal of terminological intermarriage among the sciences, and if the terms are understood, there seems no reason why linguistics should not also participate. There is always the argument that linguistics is not a science; but it does at least share a number of characteristics with scientific disciplines, including the collection and observation of data, and the formulation and testing of (ideally falsifiable) hypotheses. I am inclined to agree that

the use of advances in one science to stimulate advances in another has been one of the most important factors in the establishment of science as a valid and consistent system for describing the whole human environment. The important thing is that the differences and similarities between language and other objects of study be clearly understood, so that the paradigms may be applied correctly, without drawing unjustified conclusions about language on the basis of an imperfect analogy. (Gilman 1987: 8–9)

In fact, there is currently a resurgence in the use of biological metaphor, specifically in historical linguistics – we have already found uses of language death and language birth. In the final section of this chapter, we shall see that linguistic evolution can also be a profitable metaphor in the study of language change, provided that evolution is understood in its current (post-)Darwinian biological sense and not, as in nineteenth-century linguistic work, used with a pre-Darwinian meaning.

Finally, the evolution of a language should not be confused with the origin of language, which I will not be discussing here (although the topic will arise briefly in connection with Schleicher's ideas, in 12.2 below). Given our current state of knowledge, I do not believe that the origin question is answerable; this has not stopped people trying, and the result is several centuries' worth of sometimes amusing but generally un-productive speculation: it was for good reasons that the Société Linguis-tique de Paris banned discussion of the topic from its meetings in 1866. Insofar as there are interesting things to be said about the origin of language, they should in any case be said in connection with linguistic reconstruction rather than language change.

We can now proceed to our consideration of the term evolution. The three sections below deal with three definitions of the word (from Webster's *Third New International Dictionary*) – the nineteenth-century sense, the teleological sense, and the current biological meaning.

12.2   Evolution 1

a process of continuous change from a lower, simpler, or worse condition to a higher, more complex, or better state: progressive development.

Nineteenth-century linguists and philologists tended to see language change in terms of progress or decay, with decay the majority view; as

Hodge says (1970: 2) of nineteenth-century writings, 'the odour of decay is almost as real as the musty smell of the books themselves; it is all too frequent a metaphor'. Nineteenth-century linguists certainly use biological terminology: Bopp, for instance, regards languages as organisms which can be dissected and classified, and is clearly influenced here by the development of comparative anatomy (Nerlich 1989). However, these linguists, including Schleicher, who has often subsequently been described as a Darwinian, were using the notion of evolution in the pre-Darwinian sense quoted above. That is, to look ahead, they adopted the idea of transformism, rejecting creationism and the doctrine of the fixity of species, but they did not understand or adopt the essentially Darwinian notion that evolution proceeds via mutation, variation and natural selection. Thus, while Darwinian evolutionary theory excludes any notion of progress or advance, the nineteenth-century linguists invoked the idea of the life-cycle; organisms, and therefore languages, were seen as entities which were born, underwent progressive development from a primitive state to some notional prime, then decayed and ultimately died.

We must, then, begin by considering the evolution of the term <u>evolution</u>. I shall introduce both major components of the Darwinian sense of evolution here, although the second will not really become relevant until 12.4.

The first element of evolutionary theory, which was certainly adopted by nineteenth-century linguists, is the notion of transformism of species, which holds that biological species may change into other species over time. This notion arose via the development of taxonomy in the eighteenth century by Linnaeus, who classified biological organisms into phyla, orders, genera and species, as shown in (1).

However, for Linnaeus this was a synchronic taxonomy only; naturalists of the time still accepted that organisms had been created in their present-day forms, and that, once created, the characteristics of a species were fixed and immutable. A creationist scenario, involving fixity of species, also existed for language in the form of the Biblical Tower of Babel story:

And the whole earth was of one language, and of one speech ... And the [people] said, Go to, let us build us a city and a tower, whose top may reach unto heaven; and let us make us a name, lest we be scattered abroad upon the face of the whole earth. And the Lord came down to see the city and the tower, which the children of men builded. And the Lord said, Behold, the people is one, and they have all one language, and this they begin to do; and now nothing will be restrained from them, which they have imagined to do. Go to, let us go down, and there confound their language, that they may not understand one another's speech. So the Lord scattered them abroad upon the face of all the earth: and they left off to build the city. Therefore is the name of it called Babel; because the Lord did there confound the language of all the earth: and from thence did the Lord scatter them abroad upon the face of all the earth. (Genesis 11: 1, 5–9)

(1)   Linnaean taxonomy

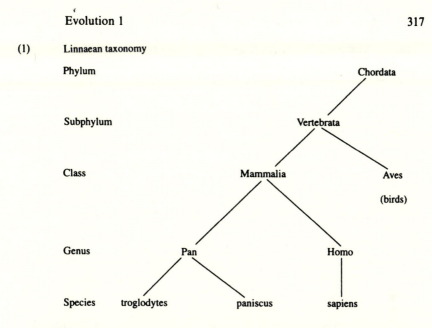

In biology, Lamarck in the early nineteenth century reinterpreted Linnaeus' static taxonomy in evolutionary terms, maintaining that species were not fixed, but could be transformed over time. In this one case of the rejection of creationism, and acceptance of the transformism of species, linguists actually had a head start over biologists, in that Sir William Jones had already suggested, in 1786, that Sanskrit, Greek, Latin and at least Gothic and the Celtic languages, belonged to a single language family and were descended from a common proto-language which no longer existed. Jones' speculations provided the basis for the grouping together of the languages we know as the Indo-European family, and for the reconstruction of Proto-Indo-European; and similar groupings had been proposed even earlier for the Semitic and Finno-Ugric families. It is possible that transformism was accepted earlier in linguistics than in biology because the process of change is so much faster in language than in biological species, and is therefore much more readily observable: for instance, older people may remember linguistic features which are now obsolete, and the existence of written records provides documentation of the history of some languages, including the metamorphosis of Latin into French, or Old English into Modern English. It might be noted in passing, however, that these written records suffer from fundamentally the same deficiencies as the fossil record in biology: they are selected by circumstances beyond our control, and suffer from gaps and difficulties of interpretation.

Having established that languages and species change, and accepted transformism rather than creationism, we turn now to the mechanism of transformism, which takes us to the second crucial element of Darwinian evolution.

The idea of heredity, or genetic inheritance, was first proposed by Lamarck in the early nineteenth century. Lamarck suggested a division of the genetic material, now known as the DNA, from the somatic or body material. The DNA carries information to be passed on to the next generation, while the somatic material is partly an expression of instructions in the DNA, but also displays acquired characteristics of the individual organism. The notion of heredity is therefore essentially pre-Darwinian (although, as we shall see in 12.4, Lamarck was not quite right in all respects). Darwin's real contribution was to flesh out the mechanisms by which transformism or speciation proceeds.

Darwin's first idea is that random genetic mutations arise spontaneously in organisms. The term <u>mutation</u> has now acquired some rather unfortunate connotations, but mutations need not produce alien-like creatures with three heads; they can cause simple, minor alterations, perhaps producing creatures with slightly longer legs, or a different shade of coat. The same mutation will not arise in all the organisms of a species, but perhaps only in one or two; this leads to variation in the species, since some organisms will show the mutated characteristics, while others will not.

The next step depends on the environment. The varieties which have developed may simply co-exist. On the other hand, natural selection may step in and favour one variety, which happens to be advantageous given the environment. For instance, in an environment with lots of vegetation growing on tall trees, a mutation producing longer-legged herbivores is likely to give its bearers some advantage. The long-legged beasts will then be successful and will reproduce; a certain percentage of their offspring will inherit the long-legged characteristic, and this may then spread, ultimately becoming a feature of the whole species. However, since mutation is random, changes are not always beneficial to organisms; they may equally arise in environments where they are detrimental, and will then die out. In addition, an initially beneficial mutation may become detrimental due to some change in the environment. Mutations cannot therefore be seen as definitively advantageous or problematic, and Darwin's theory contains no notion of progress. Indeed, since mutation is random, it is impossible to see natural selection as some grand design manipulating species along a route of eternal self-improvement. It is instead a rather negative process – variations arise, those which do not fit into the immediate environment die out, and what's left carries on. Final evidence that evolution does not always operate in a beneficial direction exists in the form of extremely badly-adapted organisms or species. For instance, the giant panda is completely unsuited to its environment and its diet; its physiology marks it out as a carnivore, but it is found only in a small, restricted geographical area, and eats bamboo since this is the most nutritious food in its environment. Miraculously, the giant panda has not died out. Its survival may be partly due to mutation and natural selection, however; these cannot solve all the panda's problems, but have, through the process of evolution, provided it with a false thumb especially adapted for stripping bamboo. It seems that nature (as Lightfoot 1979a says of language; see Chapter 5) practises therapy and not prophylaxis, or cure rather than prevention.

This second component of Darwinian evolution will be more extensively explored in 12.4. For the moment, however, we must return to the nineteenth-century linguists. Although they generally accepted the idea of transformism, that languages change and moreover change into other languages, there is no use of the mutation – variation – natural selection pathway as a suggested mechanism for transformism. Instead, we find claims that languages are either decaying or improving; these linguists are still caught up in the notion of advance versus deterioration characteristic of pre-Darwinian thought.

I shall concentrate here on August Schleicher who, despite assertions that he was profoundly influenced by Darwin, is in fact a proponent of the view that evolution involves the attainment of perfection, and is followed by degeneration. We shall then briefly consider Jespersen's opposing view that more recent stages of languages are an improvement on previous ones, and that language is therefore undergoing a gradual advance rather than a progressive decline.

August Schleicher certainly adopted the doctrine of transformism in his writings on language, and made use of biological terminology; his family tree of the Indo-European languages is obviously the forerunner of trees like that in Chapter 1 above, but is written sideways, with PIE (Schleicher's 'Indo-German') on the left and the modern daughters on the right. Schleicher's tree is clearly influenced by Linnaeus' taxonomy, and Schleicher explicitly equates language families with genera, languages with species, dialects with races, and idiolects with individual organisms (Schleicher 1863 in Koerner 1983: 31–2). In fact, the first biologist to translate Linnaeus' taxonomic tables into diagrammatic trees was Schleicher's friend, the German naturalist Ernst Haeckel. Schleicher's Indo-European tree resembles these distinctly, although it is more schematic: Haeckel's trees are *real* trees, bark and all.

Philosophically, however, Schleicher was a nineteenth-century German Romantic progressivist, influenced more by Hegel than by Darwin.

Schleicher did know Darwin's work – his friend Haeckel sent him a copy of the German translation of the *Origin of Species* in 1860 (a year after its publication in Britain) because of Schleicher's interest in 'amateur gardening and botanizing' (Schleicher 1863 in Koerner 1983: 14). In response to this work, Schleicher published a pamphlet, *The Darwinian Theory and the Science of Language*, in 1863, and a further paper, 'On the significance of language for the natural history of man', in 1864. However, the views Schleicher expresses in these works match those of his earlier, pre-Darwinian writings, supporting the view that 'Schleicher's evolutionism was whole and entire before he had ever heard the name of Charles Darwin' (Maher in Koerner 1983: xix). That is, Schleicher's idea of Darwinism was extremely selective; he adopted transformism, but not Darwin's theories on the mechanism of transformism, instead using Darwin to support his own notions of language development and decay.

For Schleicher, the evolution of language is inextricably involved with the evolution of man, since language is the factor which sets men apart from the animals. The development of mankind to date therefore falls into three stages, shown in (2).

(2)a.   The physical evolution of man.
   b.   The evolution of language.
   c.   History.

This division of evolution from history follows from Hegel's view 'that History cannot begin till the human spirit becomes conscious of its own freedom; and this consciousness is only possible after the complete development of language' (Jespersen 1922: 77). Once evolution, the progressive development of simple forms to complex ones, is complete, the period of history is entered; in history, nothing new can be created, and the only possibility is decay, <u>Verfall</u>. The life of languages therefore also has three stages: growth or advance, a brief moment of glorious evolutionary perfection, and irrevocable decline.

Schleicher gives a rather vague account of the origin of language, assuming that many primitive languages arose, each consisting of simplex, unmodifiable roots: 'the oldest material of language was sounds designating objects and concepts. There was as yet no expression of relations, nor differentiation of word classes, nor declension, nor conjugation' (Schleicher 1863 in Koerner 1983: 80). Many of these languages died out, but those surviving began the long evolutionary climb towards perfection.

The obvious question at this point is how one measures progress in linguistic terms; and the usual nineteenth-century answer was that greater complexity, specifically in the morphology, signalled a more advanced and highly valued language. Schleicher borrowed from A. W. Schlegel and von

Humboldt, among others, a typology of languages as isolating, agglutinating or inflecting (although these terms themselves are more recent). These language types are schematised in (3).

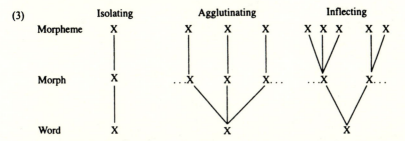

(3)

In isolating languages like Chinese or Vietnamese, each morpheme, or lexical or grammatical unit of information, is signalled by a single morph, or piece of linguistic material. The morph also corresponds to the word (and generally to the syllable). In agglutinating languages like Turkish or Swahili, the word generally consists of several morphs, each expressing one morpheme, as shown in (4).

(4)   Turkish
          Morpheme   {HOUSE} {plural}   {HOUSE} {possessive}
          Morph   ev   ler   ev   i
          Word   evler   evi
          Gloss   'houses'   'his/her house'

          Morpheme   {HOUSE} {plural}   {possessive}
          Morph   ev   ler   i
          Word   evleri
          Gloss   'his/her houses, their house(s)'

Finally, in inflecting languages, like Latin or Greek, single morphs may express whole strings of morphemes – for instance, in the Latin verbal form *amō* 'I love', *am-* is the stem, but *-ō* tells us that the form is first person, singular, present tense, active and indicative – at least five pieces of grammatical information. Of course, languages do not belong uniformly with one type; English, for instance, has agglutinating characteristics (*cat* + *s* = CAT + plural) and inflecting ones (*feet* = FOOT + plural). However, many languages show a predominance of forms of one type, which makes a rough classification possible.

Schleicher interprets this isolating – agglutinating – inflecting classification, not as a static typology, but as an evolutionary scale, alleging that languages proceeded, during the period of evolution, from the isolating or analytic type, to the synthetic types, first agglutinating, then inflecting. This hypothesis makes languages like Latin, Greek and Sanskrit, with highly complex systems of inflectional morphology, the high-point of linguistic evolution.

Not all languages participated in this evolutionary progress to the same extent; Chinese, for instance, did not reach the inflecting ideal. However, once some languages attained this state, evolution ended and history began, signalling the start of a progressive decline back from synthetic towards analytic structures. Again, the process of decay does not operate at the same speed for all languages; Schleicher correlates the rate of decay with the extent to which the speakers of a language participate in 'historical life' or civilisation. Decay is therefore negatively valued from a linguistic point of view, but is positively valued societally, since faster and greater decay indicates an active, civilised people. From this correlation follows Schleicher's apparently self-contradictory remark (Schleicher 1864 in Koerner 1983: 82) that 'certain peoples, such as the North American Indian tribes, are unfitted for historical life because of their endlessly complicated languages, bristling with overabundant forms; they can only undergo retrogression, even extinction'. It seems that this assertion is based on warped reasoning: if decaying languages decay because their speakers are 'involved in history', then decay signals civilisation; and if the Amerind languages haven't decayed, this must mean their speakers aren't civilised, and are therefore unsuited to historical life; they will therefore inevitably die out. Paradoxically, a language which lingers too long at the inflecting apex of evolution may signal its own and its speakers' extinction.

It is clear now that languages die because of socio-political factors, not inherent defects, as can be seen from the cases of language death reported in Chapter 11. In fact, the Darwinian theory of biological evolution applies only to individual variation and change within a species, and at present has nothing to say about competition between species; we therefore should not seek to apply our evolutionary metaphor to cases where languages are in competition. It is true that speakers of dying languages may describe their language as inferior or deficient, but we must accept this as a reaction to socio-political values and the relative prestige of the competing languages in the speech community, and not to the language itself. This is probably one of the few cases where we should adopt Bloomfield's dictum: 'Accept everything a native speaker says in his language, and nothing he says about it.'

Although Schleicher represents the majority view of nineteenth-century linguists and philologists in asserting that modern languages are the result of a period of cumulative decay, there were critics of this position. The best-known of these is probably Jespersen, who proposes the converse: modern European languages, which have lost the majority of their inflections, are 'better' than their predecessors of the highly inflecting type, because they allow maximum communicative efficiency with minimum effort. In Jespersen's opinion, 'that language ranks highest which goes furthest in the art of accomplishing much with little means, or, in other words, which is able to express the greatest amount of meaning with the simplest mechanism' (1922: 324). Analytic languages are therefore seen as more efficient and flexible than the rigid synthetic type. Jespersen justifies his claim that the most recent stages of languages are superior to earlier ones by noting that modern forms are shorter, saving on muscular exertion and time; there are none of the 'clumsy repetitions' found in systems of agreement; 'a clear and unambiguous understanding is secured through a regular word-order' (1922: 364); and forms are fewer and more regular.

Jespersen claims that this progressive development from synthetic to analytic structure is characteristic of all languages, but in fact his data are heavily weighted towards Indo-European. It is hard to say what Jespersen would have made of the case of Tok Pisin, for instance, a partially Indo-European-based pidgin which seems to be working its way back from Jespersen's ideal analytic type towards greater synthesis, via grammaticalisation (see Chapter 10). In fact, both Schleicher's scale and Jespersen's have many clear exceptions; languages seem to change both from analytic to synthetic and vice versa, or may develop in one direction in one area of the grammar, and in the opposite way elsewhere. This, plus the possibility of arguing, as Schleicher and Jespersen respectively do, for the same changes as indicative of decay and degeneration or progress and advance, illustrates the absurdity of seeing the morphological classification of languages as isolating, agglutinating and inflecting as an evolutionary ladder at all, rather than as a synchronic means of typological classification.

Jespersen's view that languages are constantly improving, and Schleicher's notion of evolution in opposition to history, have died out alone and do not require further attention here. However, Schleicher's contention that languages are currently decaying is more dangerous, since it builds on a long and continuing tradition which sees linguistic change as an essentially retrograde process which should, if possible, be stopped: as Dr Johnson says in the Preface to his Dictionary, 'Tongues, like governments, have a natural tendency to degeneration.' This view is part and parcel of human nostalgia, the belief in a Golden Age which is always just beyond living memory, and manifests itself in a view that current languages and states of languages are profoundly degenerate compared with what went before. It must be emphasised that there is no reason for such a view, beyond an inherent traditionalism, and perhaps, in the West, a connection of the civilisation and influence of the Greeks and Romans with their languages, and a feeling that the influx of Barbarians which signalled the Dark Ages had not a little to do with their barbarous (and relatively inflectionless) languages.

Jespersen points out that it is natural for the nineteenth-century linguists, themselves trained in the Classical languages, to have believed that these represented some prime in linguistic history. As for other varieties, 'such poor languages as had either lost much of their original richness in grammatical forms (e.g. French, English or Danish), or had never had any, so far as one knew (e.g. Chinese), were naturally looked upon with something of the pity bestowed on relatives in reduced circumstances, or the contempt felt for foreign paupers' (Jespersen 1922: 321). However, there is no need for us to be seduced by equations of 'older' or 'more complex' with 'better'. Indeed, this sentimentalist view is increasingly criticised in linguistics as nineteenth-century prescriptivism gives way to twentieth-century descriptivism, with the idea that languages should be described in their own terms and regarded as equal. As Sapir puts it, 'a linguist that insists on talking about the Latin type of morphology as though it were necessarily the high-water mark of linguistic development is like the zoologist that sees in the organic world a huge conspiracy to evolve the race-horse or the Jersey cow' (1921: 131).

The modern view, at least of historical linguists if not the general public, is simply that languages change; we may try to describe and explain the processes of change, and we may set up a complementary typology which will include a classification of languages as isolating, agglutinating or inflecting; but this morphological typology has no special status and certainly does not represent an evolutionary scale. In general, we have no right to attack change as decay or to exalt it as progress. It is true, as we have seen elsewhere in this book, that individual changes may aid or impair communication to a limited extent, but there is no justification for seeing change as cumulative progress or decline: modern languages, attested extinct ones, and even reconstructed ones are all at much the same level of structural complexity or communicative efficiency. We cannot argue that some languages, or stages of languages, are better than others; instead, 'if we wish to understand language … we must disabuse our minds of preferred "values" and accustom ourselves to look upon English and Hottentot with the same cool, yet interested, detachment' (Sapir 1921: 131–2).

Finally, and perhaps most importantly, we have no business at all indulging in the Canute-like activity of trying to stop language change. The futility of such attempts can readily be illustrated, for instance, by the constant battle of the Académie Française against English loanwords of the *le weekend, les teenagers* type. Even more successful forays, like Louth's attempt to eradicate the unLatinate (and therefore illogical) multiple negative from English, are small-scale victories, won only in writing and sometimes in the spoken standard language; multiple negation persists in much spoken English. It is unlikely that we shall entirely defeat the attitude that 'the English language is going to the dogs', but this certainly *will* persist if linguists continue to see language change as indicative of deterioration. The sense of evolution as cumulative progress, and its converse notion of progressive historical decay, are therefore ideas that historical linguistics can well do without.

12.3   Evolution 2

A series of related changes in a certain direction.

In the last section, we examined cases of evolution seen as gradual advance, as well as the opposing 'anti-evolution' of progressive linguistic decay. In 12.4, we shall consider more closely some parallels of modern historical linguistics with current Darwinian evolutionary theory; first, however, we must dispense with a second less useful use of <u>evolution</u>. This is the teleological sense of change as cumulative and directed towards some goal, although this goal need not be advantageous – teleological changes may have adaptive, neutral or maladaptive results. As Lass says, in cases of teleology, 'effects precede (in time) their final causes' (1974: 312).

The notion of teleology is best introduced by a slightly circuitous route, via a problem in phonological theory. In Generative Phonology, there are two recognised relations between phonological rules: one is ordering (rule A precedes rule B), and the second is formal relatedness, which is indicated by the collapsability of two rules into a single schema. Such schemata are highly valued in Generative Phonology because they allow one rule to do the job of two or more, saving on features and satisfying economy, one of the main objectives of the Standard Generative theory. An example of two formally related rules is given in (5).

(5)   Rule A: $X \longrightarrow Y$ / --- VC#
         Rule B: $X \longrightarrow Y$ / --- VCC

         Schema: $X \longrightarrow Y$ / --- $VC \begin{Bmatrix} \# \\ C \end{Bmatrix}$

However, there are arguments for recognising a third relationship, one of function rather than form. For instance, the two Yawelmani rules in (6a) and (6b) (from Kenstowicz and Kisseberth 1979) are clearly not formally related; in fact, one deletes vowels while the other inserts them, so that superficially they have opposing effects.

(6)a. $\begin{bmatrix} V \\ -long \end{bmatrix} \longrightarrow \phi$ / VC ——— CV $\begin{Bmatrix} \# \\ C \end{Bmatrix}$

  b. $\phi \longrightarrow V$ / C ——— C

  c.   CCV   **CC#   **CCC

If we consider the permitted and outlawed combinations of consonants and vowels in Yawelmani in (6c), however, a connection between these rules becomes apparent. Rule (6a) operates only in the environment VC -- CV, where it creates the permitted sequence CCV. If it operated in any other context, such as C -- C# or CC -- C, it would create the ill-formed sequences **CC# or **CCC. This rule therefore applies only where it does not contravene the phonotactics. As for rule (6b), this inserts a vowel in precisely those sequences which would otherwise surface with the prohibited sequences **CC# or **CCC. These two rules seem to owe their form to the same surface phonetic constraint, and to work together, or conspire, to produce a particular output or stop certain potential outputs from surfacing. Such functionally related rules, or rule conspiracies, clearly involve common motivation, and are therefore teleological; the goal, or the end result, determines the form of the rules.

This outline is relevant to us because it has been suggested (Lass 1974) that we should recognise not only synchronic conspiracies, but also historical ones. These will involve a series of changes, operating over some variable length of time, which look unrelated and individually unmotivated, but which, when taken together, can be interpreted as conspiring together to produce an eventual goal. It is in such situations, where the effects of successive changes cumulatively create some output situation, that we might consider a cause (the goal) to follow its effects chronologically.

This notion of final causes as explanations introduces a new type of potential explanation into historical linguistics. In general, we deal in causal explanations, which argue that Y happens because of X. In teleological explanations, this scenario is inverted, and we say that X happens in order that Y will be the case. Many traditional accounts of sound change, for instance, can be reinterpreted teleologically. For example, if a language at Time 1 has clusters [mb], [md], [mg], [nb], [nd], [ng], [ŋb], [ŋd], [ŋg] but at some later Time 2 has only homorganic clusters [mb], [nd], [ŋg], we can attempt an explanation in two ways. In a causal framework, homorganicity develops because of assimilation. In a teleological model, however, the clusters become homorganic in order to ease the effort of articulation.

Arguments for and against teleology have swung back and forth through the history of ideas. For Aristotle, it was inconceivable for the universe to be non-teleological, whereas for Darwinians, teleology is anathema, or 'at the very least weak-minded, romantic or obscurantist' (Lass 1980). The same discrepant attitudes appear in the history of linguistics. Bloomfield, for instance, says that 'teleology cuts off investigation by providing a ready-made answer to any question we may ask' (quoted Vincent 1978: 409). Jakobson, however, takes the opposite view, arguing that every change in a phonological system is necessarily purposeful; and from Jakobson's ideas arise the notions of functional load, economy of systems and the essentially Praguian concept of therapeutic change, whereby one change disturbs the equilibrium of a system, which must be restored by further change. In Generative Phonology, little attention is ostensibly paid to teleology, although the notion of maximal simplicity or economy may well be teleological.

Before considering the philosophical issues raised by teleology, we should look in some detail at an example of a historical conspiracy. Perhaps the clearest of these is from Lass (1974), and involves changes affecting vowel length in the history of English.

In Chapter 3 we encountered the vowel system of Scottish Standard English, and the Scottish Vowel Length Rule; rough statements of the historical and synchronic versions of this process are given in (7) and (8) below.

(7)   Historical SVLR (Scots: sixteenth century)

a. V: > V except before $\left\{ \begin{array}{l} r \\ v\ z\ 3\ ð \\ \text{word-final} \end{array} \right\}$

b. V > V: before $\left\{ \begin{array}{l} r \\ v\ z\ 3\ ð \\ \text{word-final} \end{array} \right\}$

(8)   Synchronic SVLR

V ⟶ V: / —— $\left\{ \begin{array}{l} r \\ v\ z\ 3\ ð \\ \text{word/morpheme final} \end{array} \right\}$

(not /ɪ ɛ ʌ/)

The Scottish Vowel Length Rule has neutralised the phonological distinction of long and short vowels in Scottish Standard English and Scots dialects. Whereas in other varieties of English, vowels are contrastively long or short, giving oppositions of short /ɪ/ in *bit* versus long /iː/ in *beat*, in Scots/SSE such a length distinction no longer appears. There are phonetic differences of length, but these are entirely predictable given the rule in (8) above; some examples appear in (9). In modern Scots/SSE, then, to use Generative terminology, all vowels are underlyingly short, but they all (except /ɪ ɛ ʌ/) become long in the environments listed in (8).

(9)   [i]   beat   leaf   bead   eel
        /i/
            [iː]   beer   leave   bee   bees

The question to address here is whether SVLR is an isolated historical development, or connected to other changes in the history of English. Lass

(1974) chooses the second option, and claims that SVLR is part of an orthogenetic or teleological pattern, 'the (nearly) last step in a series of directed changes stretching back to proto-West Germanic' (1974: 326). The other changes in this supposed sequence are given in (10) – (16).

(10)   West Germanic Final Lengthening

$$\emptyset > V \ / \ \begin{bmatrix} V \\ + \text{accented} \end{bmatrix} \text{---} \#$$

(11)   Pre-Cluster Shortening I
(OE: sixth-seventh century)

$$V > \emptyset \ / \ V \text{---} CCC$$

*g/o:/dspell > g/o/dspell; *br/æ:/mblas >br/æ/mblas

(12)   Trisyllabic Shortening
(OE: sixth-seventh century)

$$V > \emptyset / \ V \text{---} CCVCVC_0\#$$

s/a/mcucu 'half-alive' < *s/a:/m;

/e/nlefan 'eleven' < /æ:/n

(13)   Pre-Cluster Lengthening
(OE: Late ninth century)

$$\emptyset > V \ / \ V \text{---} \begin{bmatrix} - \text{obstruent} \\ + \text{continuant} \\ \alpha \ \text{place} \end{bmatrix} \begin{bmatrix} + \text{obstruent} \\ - \text{continuant} \\ \alpha \ \text{place} \end{bmatrix}$$

c/i/ld > c/i:/ld;   f/i/ndan > f/i:/nden

(14)   Pre-Cluster Shortening II
(ME: generalisation of (11))

$$V > \emptyset / V \text{---} CC$$

c/e:/pte > k/e/pte;   m/e:/tte > m/e/tte

(15)   Trisyllabic Shortening II
(ME: generalisation of (12))

$$V > \emptyset \ / \ V \text{---} CVCVC_0\#$$

s/u:/ðerne > s/u/therne; h/æ:/ligdæg > h/a/lidai

(16)   Middle English Open Syllable Lengthening
(twelfth century North, thirteenth century South)

These sound changes operated, if we exclude for the moment the rather later SVLR, over about 800 years, from proto-West Germanic to the thirteenth century. Some shorten vowels while others lengthen them, and two later changes can be seen formally as generalisations of earlier ones; but apart from these rather tenuous links, they are not obviously connected: it simply seems that vowel length must have been unstable in early English. Lass, however, criticises this approach as defeatist, and claims that this situation is precisely the kind to conceal teleology: we have a collection of events that seem irrational and unconnected, but if we examine them closely we find a common goal, and the changes are then interpretable as steps towards it. The changes implement a particular synchronic state which we wish to explain; and the existence of that state explains the changes.

So, to recap, we have a set of apparently unrelated sound changes, operating over a long period in the history of a language. The language at the completion of these changes is different in some typological feature from the situation prior to these changes. We can then argue that our sound changes are the cumulative source of this typological change, so that the individual changes are part of a historical conspiracy, either aiming at the present, new typology, or on the way via this stage to some other eventual goal.

The next task is to identify the goal of our particular conspiracy. Lass notes that, before any of the changes in (10)-(16) applied, vowel length in English was completely free; that is, both long and short vowels could appear in all possible contexts. However, each of these changes reduced the number of environments where vowel length is idiosyncratic, and increased the contexts where it is predictable. Each change is a quantity-neutralising rule, and part of what Lass calls 'the Great English Length Conspiracy'. After MEOSL (16), quantity remained free only in stressed syllables closed by a final consonant. By this stage, free length is becoming the exception rather than the rule, and the contrast of V: versus V is largely dissolved. The time seems to be approaching when, although length and shortness still appear, their distribution is predictable by rule; and this, of course, is precisely the situation which SVLR has effected in Scots/SSE, by taking another step in the same direction, making all vowel length predictable and all vowels underlyingly short.

According to Lass (1974), then, teleology involves the rise of mutations, with cumulative effects, which cause change in some predetermined direction. Lass proposes the existence of a metarule; so, the individual changes in the Great English Length Conspiracy all implement some superordinate instruction to increase the predictability of vowel length. Lass asserts that, in circumstances where we have structure, relatedness and direction, as he claims is the case for these vowel-length rules, we must assume that this is non-random. If our best guess at present is that these changes are related by teleology, then we must make that guess, even if it ultimately turns out to be wrong, because the only other option is to assume a massive coincidence. Explanations, in this view, are 'coincidence-avoiders'; any attempt at explanation is better than none, as Lass rather weakly concludes, because at least it demonstrates that the data in question belong together.

This kind of 'how else?' argument is attacked by Vincent (1978), and later by Lass himself (1980: Chapter 3). I shall now consider some of the objections raised in their work.

The first major objection relates generally to the problem of using some state in the future to explain ongoing or past events, and specifically to the distinction between teleology of function and teleology of purpose. Teleology of purpose is the more powerful and controversial of the two, since it includes, at least by implication, some notion of (conscious) intent. Such a notion of intentionally directed change is relatively unproblematic if the instigator is a speaker or group of speakers, since humans are rational beings and can be ascribed motivation and purpose. Conscious decisions by speakers are apparent in the development of taboos and euphemisms, and in instances of prescriptivism ('It's not "John and me went", it's "John and I"', or 'say [bʌtə], not [bʌʔə]'). However, these cases are generally minor, affecting vocabulary and the occasional structural feature, but more often having no effect at all; and they are almost always aimed at stopping a change which is already under way, not starting a new one. Intervention by individual speakers cannot, then, be solely responsible for our historical conspiracy. In any case, no single speaker was around for the whole millenium it took the English length conspiracy to reach its current state. Our only option, if we are to maintain teleology of purpose, is therefore to ascribe some kind of superordinate rational directionality to the language, personifying it in some way and allowing it to determine changes in its own structure, which would not otherwise know which direction to take. This, I would argue, is another extremely dubious use of biological metaphor, which should be rejected. This does not mean that linguistic changes have no reality outside the individual speaker, nor that patterns across the length of a language's history cannot be observed; but the observation of patterns need not signify predestination or the presence of any guiding hand. Instead, I suggest that patterns arise partly from the human predilection for seeing patterns, and partly from the operation of mutation and natural selection, random processes which may produce perceived directionality in biology and language, as will be shown in 12.4.

Further problems arise from teleology of purpose. If changes can be cumulative and achieve some goal, then questions are obliquely raised of the usefulness of such goals, plunging us back into the muddy waters of assessing some languages as better than others. Lass (1974) explicitly

denies that teleological developments are necessarily adaptive or therapeutic, claiming that English would gain no clear advantage from losing
contrastive vowel length. Vincent (1978), however, finds it rather peculiar
that languages can select goals to aim at, but neglect to choose useful ones.
A related problem is the identification of the goals themselves: Lass does
indeed observe a line of sound changes, but 'the observation of a line says
nothing about its direction' (Vincent 1978: 426). That is, the end-point
may not be significant; in Vincent's view, the starting-point may be more
relevant, in that one sound change operates, and subsequent changes will
tend to proceed in more or less the same direction (see also the discussion
of Aitchison 1987 and 1989a in the last chapter). There need be no goal;
however, at some stage phonotactic restrictions are likely to develop, and
these will act as filters, reinforcing changes which fit in with current
possibilities. The elimination of vowel length contrasts, once begun, could
be reinforced in this way. Lass (1980) attacks the proposition of goals even
more strongly, alleging that we may see some situation as a goal when it is
only a terminus, or the fortuitous outcome of a certain sequence of events.
In other words, we need more evidence for the goalhood of a supposed goal
than the fact that a certain number of changes produce it.

Even if we rule out teleology of purpose, teleology of function presents
problems of its own, since functional explanations are notoriously
particularistic. That is, such explanations work in some cases but not in all,
and tend to be invoked in circumstances where they are useful, but not
mentioned elsewhere. This means that potential counterexamples are
ignored, and that teleology of function cannot be a strong, empirical
explanation; if functional explanations are simply said not to be applicable
in problematic areas, they can never in principle be falsified. In any case,
functional explanations can generally be replaced by other, non-teleological explanations; we shall now look at three such cases.

1   *Humboldt's Universal*

Humboldt's Universal is an instruction to maximise iconicity and
minimise allomorphy, and is often said to be the motivation and/or
explanation for the analogical levelling of allomorphs. Lass (1980)
considered the history of the English verb *tell*, to see whether sound
changes and analogy do tend to reduce allomorphy. Of ten changes
affecting the verb, one did decrease the number of allomorphs, but two
increased it, while the remaining seven kept the number constant. So, out
of ten cases where Humboldt's Universal might be invoked, it operated
precisely once. We must then ask whether an explanatory principle which
can apparently be randomly implemented or ignored is truly explanatory
even in this case.

2   *Morphological conditioning of sound change.*

In Ancient Greek, /s/ deletes intervocalically. After the operation of this sound change, [s] continued to surface in the future tense forms of certain verbs, but only when it constituted the sole marker of futurity; thus, *lúō* 'loosen' has the future form *lúsō*, while *menō* 'remain' becomes *menéō*, where the *é* indicates the future tense, rather than **menésō. Either a teleological or a non-teleological explanation can be invoked here. According to the teleological one, the sound change is blocked in the case of *lúsō* because the future and present would be formally identical if the /s/ were lost. The non-teleological account proposes that /s/ was in fact lost in all cases, but was later reintroduced into *lúsō*, by analogy with futures like *trépsō* 'turn' (where /s/ is not intervocálic and had therefore been retained), since this reintroduced the formal present-future distinction. In one case, we have genuine teleology, but in the other, wreckage and repair: as Vincent (1978: 416) puts it, 'Whereas speakers, *qua* human beings, have the power to assess the future consequences of their actions, linguistic or otherwise, and modify their behaviour accordingly, sound change can only proceed remorselessly on, leaving the speaker to do the best he can to mend any pieces of language that get broken in the process.'

3   *Homonymic clash*

We have already encountered Gilliéron's famous example of homonymic clash, whereby Latin *cattus* and *gallus* should have merged by normal phonological developments in Gascon; however, the output [gat] is retained only for 'cat', and a variety of new forms, including *faisan*, *vicaire* are found for 'cockerel'. Vincent again argues that this is not teleological – or rather, that speakers <u>are</u> teleological (because this sound change, having operated, causes problems, and speakers find ways of remedying them), but that languages are not (otherwise, the sound changes creating [gat] should have failed to operate in the 'cockerel' word). We shall end this section by considering another case of homonymic clash, or the avoidance of inconvenient ambiguity, from Lass (1980).

Old English /y/ regularly develops as shown in (17).

(17)

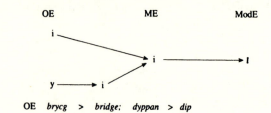

OE   *brycg* > *bridge;* *dyppan* > *dip*

However, some lexical items fail to show this majority development; instead, they undergo the change in (18).

(18)   OE   ME   ModE

                        y ——————————→ u - ——————————→ ʌ

    OE *rysc* > *rush*   'sedge'; *crycc* > *crutch*

    Anglo-Norman *ruser* (<u> = /y/) > *rush* 'hurry';

    also *just, study*. . .

One lexical item which does develop as in (18) is OE *scyttan* 'shut' (< Gmc. *skutjan), which becomes ModE *shut*. Had it developed regularly, it would have ended up as *shit* – precisely the sort of pernicious homophony speakers might want to avoid. The teleological argument is therefore that OE *scyttan* has backing rather than unrounding in order to avoid this homophony.

Lass (1980) argues that this case, like Gilliéron's, is non-teleological, and offers five counter-arguments.

a. One record of precisely this merger exists (in an Elizabethan scriptural dictionary!). This could be an error, but provides at least tenuous evidence (see (19)).

(19)   'Conclusus: Thrust bak. Shit vp.'
            (William Patton: *The Calendar of Scripture* 1575, f183).

b. The same sporadic change which is responsible for *shut* has produced other homophonous pairs, like the two *rush* words in (18).

c. Since there is no principled limit on the amount of homophony permissible in languages, such explanations are necessarily *ad hoc*.

d. The teleological argument suffers from flawed logic; as (20) shows, this is technically a case of the fallacy of affirming the consequent, where the premises do not support the conclusion.

(20)   There is some function x.
            Implementation of x would cause y.   p q
            y happened.   q
            Therefore x must have been implemented.   p

e. Finally, Lass (1980) argues even against Vincent's (1978) position that changes are not teleological but speakers are, in that they can recognise a 'broken' piece of language and mend it after a change has caused difficulties. As Lass says, if a speaker produced *shit* after the change had operated, how could she know that the /i/ is from OE /y/, making /u/ the etymologically appropriate alternative? This last comment may, however, follow from too much attention to the speaker and not enough to the speech community; we can assume a period of variation, during which some speakers would have said *shut* and others *shit*. Speakers hearing *shit* but not wishing to say it would be able to choose *shut*, the other current alternative.

There is a useful verdict of Not Proven in the Scottish courts, and this seems the best judgement on teleology. We cannot prove teleological explanations wrong (although this in itself may be an indictment, in a discipline where many regard potentially falsifiable hypotheses as the only valid ones), but nor can we prove them right; they rest on faith in predestination and the omniscient guiding hand. More pragmatically, alleged cases of teleology tend to have equally plausible alternative explanations, and there are valid arguments against the teleological position. Even the weaker teleology of function is flawed because of the numerous cases where it simply does not seem to be applicable. However, this rejection does not make the concept of conspiracy, synchronic or diachronic, any less intriguing, or the perception of directionality, to which we shall return in 12.4, any less real. And there certainly are an awful lot of vowel length changes in the history of English.

12.4   Evolution 3

> the development of a race, species or other group ... : the process by which through a series of changes or steps any living organism or group of organisms has acquired the morphological and physiological characters which distinguish it: the theory that the various types of animals and plants have their origin in other preexisting types, the distinguishable differences being due to modifications in successive generations.

In the two previous sections, we have consulted two interpretations of the term evolution, both of which, I have argued, should be rejected. The problems arising from these misleading metaphors might be thought to justify Stevick's remark that 'bad luck with biological models has left historical linguistics with such a heritage of confusion and specious explanations as to condition linguists to reject or ignore all putative parallels between languages and living organisms' (1963: 159). However, these problems generally developed, not because of any inherent inappropriateness of biological metaphors, but because linguists frequently have not fully understood the terms they borrow, or have taken comparisons too literally, interpreting languages as organisms and ascribing them features, like life-cycles or (conscious) rationality, which are only characteristic of such organisms. These unsuccessful experiments with metaphor need not deter us, but should warn us to lay out the basis of comparison carefully, and that we need not equate to compare.

In this section, we shall consider the Darwinian theory of biological evolution, which, as outlined in 12.2 above, rests on the random generation of mutation, and the operation of natural selection on the resulting variation, favouring variants which fit well into the current environment and allowing these to be passed on to subsequent generations in a species. We shall see that enlightening comparisons exist between Darwinian evolutionary theory and language change. In the nineteenth century, the emphasis on corruption and decay and the prevalence of prescriptivism in language study did not permit such comparisons; even the Neo-grammarians, although they reintroduced the notion of order in linguistic history by proposing the regularity of sound change, took little interest in linguistic variation. In current twentieth century historical linguistics, however, descriptivism has succeeded prescriptivism, and languages are described as equals on their own terms; it is recognised that social factors are involved in change, which is not purely mechanical; and individual speakers are seen as producers of variation and therefore promoters of change. This link of variation with change allows Darwinian evolutionary theory to be borrowed from biology into linguistics.

Historical linguistics and historical biology can be recognised as two specific areas of a general theory of evolution, in that 'they are particular developments of the general model of persistence with modification of complex systems' (Stevick 1963: 169). Languages and species are both systems which exist and continue through time, changing as they do so. This notion of persistence-with-change gives us the doctrine of trans-formism of species and languages, which translates visually into taxonomic family trees for both languages and species. We saw in 12.2 that the transformist view, and the classification of languages into families as biological organisms are classified into orders, phyla, genera and species, was already successful in nineteenth-century linguistics. This comparison need not be rejected, only disentangled from nineteenth-century ideas of progress and decay.

Languages and biological populations have two further characteristics in common: structures can be transmitted from generation to generation; and varieties which are isolated from one another tend to develop differently. In biology, the genetic mechanism of heredity allows charac-teristics to be passed from parent to child, while genetic divergence, often exacerbated by geographical isolation, leads ultimately to mutual sterility between varieties, which are then recognised as distinct species. Language is also transmitted from parents to children (although at present we understand the mechanisms involved only imperfectly, and do not know to what extent they are genetic and to what extent environmental), and isolation of varieties due to geographical distance and/or socio-political boundaries leads to the development of locally different varieties which may eventually become distinct languages.

Again, we are not equating language with biological species; there are also differences between them. For instance, 'physical characteristics acquired by the parent cannot be genetically transmitted to the offspring of animals or plants' (Gilman 1987: 4). Only those characters specified in the genetic material can be inherited by children; so, if I have grey eyes, my children have a quantifiable chance of inheriting grey eyes, but if I acquire a suntan and then have a child, she will not be born with tanned skin. Language, however, has no comparable distinction of use and transmission, and any language may acquire any material from any other, which need not be areally, genetically or typologically related. Furthermore, changes operating in one speaker's lifetime can easily be passed on to her children; if I, in common with a fair proportion of the English speaking world, borrow the word *perestroika* from Russian, my children might certainly acquire it (whether from me or not). It follows that the spaces between the branches in species trees are uncrossable because mutual sterility cannot be reversed; in linguistic trees, however, they can be crossed due to social and political changes, borrowing and other contact phenomena, and so on. In fact, the question of the inheritance of acquired characteristics is the subject of a controversy in the history of evolutionary theory. As we have seen, current evolutionary theory assumes that such characters cannot be inherited by genetic transmission; this hypothesis is appropriate for biological organisms, but not for languages. However, Lamarck, writing in the early nineteenth century before Darwin, at first proposed that acquired characters may be inherited by offspring. For instance, a Lamarckian explanation of the giraffe's long neck would assume that an early giraffe stretched its neck muscles slightly in trying to reach tall trees; its offspring would inherit slightly elongated necks, would stretch their necks further in turn, and so on, until we reach the current generation of giraffes with suitably long necks. The Lamarckian position has been criticised and even ridiculed; its *reductio ad absurdum* can be found in the assumption that, if I break my leg, I will then bear children with broken legs. However, although the revised, Darwinian model is clearly more appropriate for biological populations, it seems we must allow languages to display the Lamarckian type of inheritance.

To return from differences to similarities, 'both disciplines distinguish variation and change: variation consists in differences viewed without respect to time, change consists in differences viewed as occurring in temporal succession. The two are found to be interdependent' (Stevick 1963: 164). This connection of variation and change is characteristic of much recent work in historical linguistics, especially that of Labov and others using similar sociolinguistic methods (see Chapter 9). Furthermore, it is impossible to predict the occurrence of change in linguistics or biology, since change results from random, chance mutations. In this matter, however, biology is far ahead of linguistics, since biologists have been interested in variation for much longer; nineteenth century linguists were not much concerned with dialectal or idiolectal variation, so that 'by the time regularity of sound change was established ... historical biologists not only understood regularity in evolutionary change, together with chance variation, but had formulated some of its conditions as well' (Stevick 1963: 165).

Our biological model here raises questions for historical linguistics, but may also help solve a vexing problem. If we accept that variation arises randomly, how can it be that change is predominantly regular, and successive stages of languages are ordered and systematic? We may be able to account for this apparent paradox by borrowing a further idea from biology, since '"Chance in combination with selection produces order" is one of the axioms of evolutionary methodology' (Stevick 1963: 165).

This axiom would help us solve our problem of perceived directionality, for which teleological explanations have previously been proposed. Perceived directionality is accepted in current evolutionary theory as resulting from random variation and natural selection, which combine to produce order with no necessary external direction: an accumulation of historical accidents may still look like a conspiracy. Again, we need not assume conscious movement towards a goal. Speakers do change languages by their actions; they may for instance, consciously or subconsciously, select a particular variant to indicate allegiance to a particular social group. But these actions are not goal-directed beyond the immediate situation; instead, they have 'the unintended effect of changing the language gradually by a process of variation and selection' (Nerlich 1989: 105). To borrow another metaphor from evolutionary theory, speakers of a language are 'blind watchmakers', fitting pieces into a pattern they cannot see.

Many questions remain if we are to make full use of our evolutionary terminology in historical linguistics. We do not know which units selection might operate on in language history; are they words, rules, speakers, or languages themselves? We do not know whether linguistic evolution is governed only by general, universal tendencies, or whether these can be overridden by language-specific factors. And we have yet to formulate the conditions under which variation and selection might conspire to produce regularity.

One possible way of addressing such questions might lie in investigating Aitchison's hypothesis, discussed in Chapter 10, that 'when languages are faced with a "spaghetti junction" of possible options, a variety of converging factors often guide them down certain recurrent routes' (Aitchison 1989a: 151). The options available depend in part on the language's existing structure and on the options chosen previously, and in part on social phenomena, general cognitive factors, computational ability and memory limitations. Aitchison proposes that languages may be caught in a 'snowball' of factors promoting a particular pathway; presence of all promoting factors makes the change overwhelmingly likely. If we can identify such clusters of phenomena, and therefore potential conspiracies, 'prediction of the normal "unmarked" development of a language may be within our grasp' (Aitchison 1987: 29).

We have no space here to consider further potential answers to the questions raised by our biological parallels. However, I do feel that such parallels are useful, and that the adoption of evolutionary theories and terms can be demonstrated to be enlightening when applied to language – provided that the theories are understood and the terms properly construed. As Lass says, 'given ANY population of individuals that show some variation (aspects of style, constructions, genetic constitutions), and some (unspecified) conditions that prevent all of them from surviving and predispose to the survival of certain individuals or types, the 'Darwinian' mode of talking becomes an appropriate one' (1990: 96).

Having accepted the outline of evolutionary theory as an appropriate model of certain aspects of language change, we are free to consider whether further recent developments in the study of biological evolution might provide enlightening analyses or explanations of how and why linguistic evolution takes place. I shall conclude by mentioning one such case, Lass's (1990) discussion of exaptation.

The notion of exaptation is a relatively new aspect of evolutionary theory, introduced by Gould and Vrba (1982). Previously, theorists had concentrated on adaptations, which involve features evolving in a particular role. However, structures may evolve to fulfil one function, or indeed develop with no apparent purpose at all, and may then take on some quite different role; these cases of evolutionary recycling are exaptations. For instance, much of our genetic material is 'junk' DNA, apparently functionless duplicates of functional genes. Gould and Vrba suggest that this unemployed DNA may be exapted, providing a locus for evolutionary change. Organisms can therefore be seen, not as structures with a place for everything and everything in its place, but rather as 'bundles of historical accidents, not perfect and predictable machines' (Gould, quoted Lass 1990: 81).

Lass (1990) suggests that languages are also characterised by exaptations; like organisms, they 'are to some extent jury-rigged or cobbled together, and the remnants of old structures can be recobbled into new ones' (1990: 81). Lass provides two case histories of linguistic exaptation, one of which we shall consider below; both involve languages with some distinction marked morphologically, where the distinction is lost but the morphological signal remains. The language then has three options: it can lose the 'junk' morphology; keep it with no function; or use it for some other purpose. The last strategy involves exaptation.

Lass's second case-study involves the Afrikaans adjectival ending -e. Seventeenth-century Dutch, the source of Afrikaans, retains a reduced inflectional system relative to common Germanic, with two genders, common or neuter, a few residual genitive and dative markings, and otherwise two patterns, Adj-Ø and Adj-e, which are inherited by Afrikaans. The presence or absence of -e is controlled, in seventeenth-century Dutch and early Afrikaans, by syntactic factors. All predicative adjectives (*the house is red*) are endingless; among attributive adjectives (*the red house*), the main determining factor is the gender of the head noun: as shown in (21), neuter nouns tend to take endingless adjectives, while common nouns take Adj-*e*, although the -*e* ending tends to appear with plurals of both genders.

(21)   Common singular: *in een lang-e ry* 'in a long row'
        Neuter singular: *een zwart mantelken* 'a little black cloak'

        Plural: *de groot-e huizen* 'the big houses' (neuter)
                 onduitsch-e termen 'un-Dutch terms' (common)
        (after Lass 1990: 90)

By around 1750, however, the inherited Dutch system had collapsed in Afrikaans, since the distinction of common and neuter gender was lost, removing the main conditioning factor for the adjective ending. The distribution of -*e* was random for a time, and the ending, which was now functionless, might have been expected to drop completely. However, 'Afrikaans not only did not lose the -*e*/Ø contrast, it restabilized it and redeployed it in a new and complex (and more rigid) system' (Lass 1990: 91). That is, in modern Afrikaans the possession of the -*e* ending is no longer determined by the syntax, but by the adjective itself. Morphologically complex adjectives (except comparatives) and morphophonemically complex adjectives with more than one stem allomorph tend to be categorically inflecting, appearing with -*e* in all attributive contexts, while other adjectives are categorically non-inflecting.

This Afrikaans example parallels the situation in Middle English, although the outcome is different. Adjectival -*e* in ME lost its previous function as a marker of case, gender and the definiteness/ indefiniteness contrast, and was exapted as a plural marker, but in the fifteenth century final /ə/ -*e* was lost, leaving the English adjective invariable. In this respect, English is 'wasteful' and Afrikaans, which recycles its inflection, 'conservationist'; to borrow another current metaphor, some languages may be 'greener' than others.

In this chapter, then, we have seen that interpretations of the term evolution as meaning progressive advancement or goal-directed activity are badly motivated and should not be borrowed into linguistics. However, the Darwinian theory of biological evolution, with its interplay of mutation, variation and natural selection, has clear parallels in historical linguistics, and may be used to provide enlightening accounts of linguistic change. Having borrowed the core elements of evolutionary theory, we may then also explore novel concepts from biology, such as exaptation, and assess their relevance for linguistic change. Indeed, the establishment of parallels with historical biology may provide one of the most profitable future directions for historical linguistics. Those interested in reciprocity as well as parallels might also note that the 1991 Reith Lectures on genetics, given by Dr Steve Jones, were entitled 'The Language of the Genes', and partook liberally of analogies from language in explaining genetic and evolutionary theory. In view of all this, I am inclined to agree at least in part with Sampson, who says: 'I venture to predict... that as the linguistics of the immediate past has been psychological linguistics, so the linguistics of the near future will be biological linguistics' (1980: 242).

Bibliography

Aarsleff, Hans, Louis G. Kelly and Hans-Josef Niederehe (eds.) (1987) *Papers in the History of Linguistics*. Benjamins: Amsterdam.

Aitchison, Jean (1979) 'The order of word order change.' *Transactions of the Philological Society*: 43–65.

(1980) Review of Lightfoot (1979a). *Linguistics 18*: 137–46.

(1983) 'On roots of language.' *Language and Communication 3*: 83–97.

(1987) 'The language lifegame: prediction, explanation and linguistic change.' In Koopman, van der Leek, Fischer and Eaton (eds.) (1987): 11–32.

(1989a) 'Spaghetti junctions and recurrent routes: some preferred pathways in language evolution.' *Lingua 77*: 151–71.

(1989b) 'Tok Pisin and how it got its Aux.' Talk given at University of Cambridge, Michaelmas Term.

(1991) *Language Change: Progress or Decay*? Cambridge University Press.

Aitken, A. J. and Tom McArthur (eds.) (1979) *Languages of Scotland*. Chambers: Edinburgh.

Allen, W. Sidney (1961) Review of Brosnahan (1961). *The Cambridge Review*, 25 November: 152.

Andersen, Henning (1973) 'Abductive and deductive change.' *Language 49*: 765–93.

Anderson, John M. and Charles Jones (eds.) (1974) *Historical Linguistics. Volume 1: Syntax, Morphology, Internal and Comparative Reconstruction. Volume 2: Theory and Description in Phonology*. North Holland: Amsterdam.

Anderson, Stephen R. (1992) *A-Morphous Morphology*. Cambridge University Press.

Anttila, Raimo (1972) *An Introduction to Historical and Comparative Linguistics*. Macmillan: New York.

(1977) *Analogy*. Mouton: The Hague.

Aronoff, Mark (1976) *Word Formation in Generative Grammar*. MIT Press: Cambridge, Mass.

Ashby, William (1981) 'The loss of the negative particle *ne* in French: a syntactic change in progress.' *Language 57*: 674–87.

Bailey, Richard W. and Manfred Görlach (eds.) (1984) *English as a World Language*. Cambridge University Press.

Baldi, Philip and Ronald N. Werth (eds.) (1978) *Readings in Historical Phonology*. Pennsylvania State University Press: University Park Philadelphia.

Bauer, Laurie (1983) *English Word-Formation*. Cambridge University Press.

(1988) *Introducing Linguistic Morphology*. Edinburgh University Press.

Bennett, Paul (1979) 'Observations on the transparency principle.' *Linguistics 17*: 843–61.

Bever, T. G. and D. T. Langendoen (1971) 'A dynamic model of the evolution of language.' *Linguistic Inquiry 2*: 433–60.

(1972) 'The interaction of speech perception and grammatical structure in the evolution of language.' In Stockwell and Macaulay (eds.) (1972): 32–95.

Bickerton, Derek (1977) 'Pidginization and creolization: language acquisition and language universals.' In Valdman (ed.) (1977): 49–69.

(1981) *Roots of Language*. Karoma: Ann Arbor.

(1984) 'The language bioprogram hypothesis.' *The Behavioral and Brain Sciences 7.2*: 173–222.

(1990) *Language and Species*. Chicago University Press.

Bloomfield, Leonard (1935) *Language*. George Allen & Unwin: London.

Bosworth, Joseph and T. Northcote Toller (1972; original edition 1898) *An Anglo-Saxon Dictionary*. Oxford University Press.

Bréal, Michel (1964) *Semantics: Studies in the Science of Meaning*. Translated by Nina Cust. Dover Publications Inc: New York.

Brosnahan, L. F. (1961) *The Sounds of Language: An Inquiry into the Role of Genetic Factors in the Development of Sound Systems*. Heffer: Cambridge.

Brown, Gillian (1972) *Phonological Rules and Dialect Variation*. Cambridge University Press.

Burton-Roberts, Noel (1986) *Analysing Sentences*. Longman: London.

Bybee, Joan (1985) 'Diagrammatic iconicity in stem-inflection relations.' In Haiman (ed.) (1985): 11–47.

Bynon, Theodora (1977) *Historical Linguistics*. Cambridge University Press.

Campbell, Lyle and Martha C. Muntzel (1989) 'The structural consequences of language death.' In Dorian (ed.) (1989): 181–96.

Chambers, J. K. and P. Trudgill (1980) *Dialectology*. Cambridge University Press.

Chen, Matthew (1977) 'The time dimension: contribution towards a theory of sound change.' In Wang (ed.) (1977): 197–251.

Chen, Matthew and Hsin-I. Hsieh (1971) 'The time variable in phonological change.' *Journal of Linguistics 7*: 1–13.

Chen, Matthew and William Wang (1975) 'Sound change: actuation and implementation.' *Language 51*: 255–81.

Chomsky, Noam (1957) *Syntactic Structures*. Mouton: The Hague.

(1965) *Aspects of the Theory of Syntax*. MIT Press: Cambridge, Mass.

(1981a) *Lectures on Government and Binding*. Foris: Dordrecht.

(1981b) 'Principles and parameters in syntactic theory.' In Hornstein and Lightfoot (eds.) (1981): 32–75.

(1986) *Knowledge of Language*. Praeger: New York.

Chomsky, Noam and Morris Halle (1968) *The Sound Pattern of English*. Harper & Row: New York.

Christie, William (ed.) (1976) *Current Progress in Historical Linguistics*. North Holland: Amsterdam.

Coates, Richard (1987) 'Pragmatic sources of analogical reformation.' *Journal of Linguistics 23*: 319–40.

Comrie, Bernard (1981) *Language Universals and Linguistic Typology.* Blackwells: Oxford.

Croft, William (1990) *Typology and Universals.* Cambridge University Press.

Crowley, Terry (1991) *Beach-La-Mar to Bislama.* Oxford University Press.

Crystal, David (ed.) (1987) *The Cambridge Encyclopedia of Language.* Cambridge University Press.

Culler, Jonathan (1976) *Saussure.* Fontana: London.

Dixon, R. M. W. (1980) *The Languages of Australia.* Cambridge University Press.

Dorian, Nancy C. (1973) 'Grammatical change in a dying dialect.' *Language 49*: 413–38.

(1977a) 'A hierarchy of morphophonemic decay in Scottish Gaelic language death: the differential failure of lenition.' *Word 28*: 96–109.

(1977b) 'The problem of the semi-speaker in language death.' *Linguistics 191* (= *International Journal of the Sociology of Language* 12): 23–32.

(1978) 'The fate of morphological complexity in language death.' *Language 54*: 590–609.

(1981) *Language Death: The Life Cycle of a Scottish Gaelic Dialect.* University of Pennsylvania Press: Philadelphia.

Dorian, Nancy C. (ed.) (1989) *Investigating Obsolescence: Studies in Language Contraction and Death.* Cambridge University Press.

Drachmann, G. (1978) 'Child language and language change: a conjecture and some refutations.' In Fisiak (ed.) (1978): 123–144.

Dressler, Wolfgang U. (1972) 'On the phonology of language death.' *Papers of the Chicago Linguistics Society 8*: 448–57.

(1981) 'Language shift and language death: a Protean challenge for the linguist.' *Forum Linguisticum 1981*: 5–28.

(1985) 'On the predictiveness of Natural Morphology.' *Journal of Linguistics 21*: 321–37.

(1988) 'Language death.' In Newmeyer (ed.) (1988), Volume IV: 184–192.

Dressler, Wolfgang U., H. C. Luschützky, O. E. Pfeiffer and J. Rennison (eds.) (1987) *Phonologica 1984.* Cambridge University Press.

Dressler, Wolfgang U. and Ruth Wodak-Leodolter (eds.) (1977) Special issue on language death, with introduction. *Linguistics 191* (= *International Journal of the Sociology of Language* 12).

Emeneau, M. B. (1956) 'India as a linguistic area.' *Linguistics 32*: 3–16.

Ernout, A. and A. Meillet (1939) *Dictionnaire Etymologique de la Langue Latine.* Klincksieck: Paris.

Fischer, Olga C. M. and Frederike C. van der Leek (1981) Review of Lightfoot (1979a). *Lingua 55*: 301–49.

Fishman, Joshua (1991) *Reversing Language Shift.* Multilingual Matters: Clevedon.

Fisiak, Jacek (ed.) (1978) *Recent Developments in Historical Phonology.* Mouton: The Hague.

(ed.) (1980) *Historical Morphology.* Mouton: The Hague.

(ed.) (1984) *Historical Syntax.* Mouton: The Hague.

Foley, W. A. (1988) 'Language birth: the processes of pidginisation and creolisation.' in Newmeyer (ed.) (1988), Volume IV: 162–183.

Gal, Susan (1979) *Language Shift.* Academic Press: New York.

Giacolone Ramat, Anna (1983) 'Language shift and language death.' *Folia Linguistica 17*: 495–507.

Gilman, Charles (1987) 'Stolen paradigms: Stammbaum to black box.' In Aarsleff, Kelly and Niederehe (eds.) (1987): 3–11.

Givón, Talmy (1971) 'Historical syntax and synchronic morphology: an archaeologist's field trip.' *Chicago Linguistic Society Papers 7*: 394–415.

(1979) *On Understanding Grammar*. Academic Press: New York.

Gould, S. J. and E. S. Vrba (1982) 'Exaptation – a missing term in the science of form.' *Paleobiology 8*: 4–15.

Greenberg, Joseph H. (1957a) 'Language and evolutionary theory.' In Greenberg (1957b): 56–65.

(1957b) *Essays in Linguistics*. University of Chicago Press.

(1959) 'Language and evolution.' In Meggers (ed.) (1959): 61–75.

(1963a) 'Some universals of grammar with particular reference to the order of meaningful elements.' In Greenberg (ed.) (1963b): 73–113.

Greenberg, Joseph H. (ed.) (1963b) *Universals of Language*. MIT Press: Cambridge, Mass.

Greenberg, Joseph H. (1979) 'Rethinking linguistics diachronically.' *Language 55*: 275–90.

Grimm, Jakob (1848) *Geschichte der deutschen Sprache. Volume I*. Weidmannische Buchhandlung: Leipzig.

Guilbert, Louis (1975) *La Créativité Lexicale*. Larousse: Paris.

Gumperz, John J. and R. Wilson (1971) 'Convergence and creolization: a case from the Indo-Aryan / Dravidian border.' In Hymes (ed.) (1971): 151–68.

Haiman, John (1980) 'The iconicity of grammar: isomorphism and motivation.' *Language 56*: 515–40.

Haiman, John (ed.) (1985) *Iconicity in Syntax*. Benjamins: Amsterdam.

Hale, Kenneth (1973) 'Deep-surface canonical disparities in relation to analysis and change: an Australian example.' In Sebeok (ed.) (1973): 401–458.

Halle, Morris (1959) *The Sound Pattern of Russian*. Mouton: The Hague.

Hancock, Ian (1980) 'Lexical expansion in creole languages.' In Valdman and Highfield (eds.) (1980): 63–88.

Harris, John (1986) 'Phonetic constraints on sociolinguistic variation.' *Sheffield Working Papers in Language and Linguistics 3*: 120–43.

Harris, Martin (1976) *Romance Syntax*. University of Salford.

(1978) *The Evolution of French Syntax: a Comparative Approach*. Longman: London.

(1984a) 'On the causes of word order change.' *Lingua 63*: 175–204.

(1984b) 'On the strengths and weaknesses of a typological approach to historical syntax.' In Fisiak (ed.) (1984): 183–97.

Hashimoto, M. J. (1981) Review of Wang (1977). *Language 57*: 183–91.

Haugen, Einar (1950) 'The analysis of linguistic borrowing.' *Language 26*: 210–31.

Hawkins, John (1979) 'Implicational universals as predictors of word order change.' *Language 55*: 618–48.

(1980) 'On implicational and distributional universals of word order.' *Journal of Linguistics 16*: 193–235.

(1983) *Word Order Universals*. Academic Press: New York.

Hawkins, John (ed.) (1988) *Explaining Language Universals*. Blackwell: Oxford.

Heath, J. G. (1984) 'Language contact and language change.' *Annual Review of Anthropology 13*: 367–84.

Hill, Jane and Kenneth Hill (1977) 'Language death and relexification in Tlaxcalan Nahuatl.' *Linguistics 191* (= *International Journal of the Sociology of Language 12*): 55–69.

Hindley, R. (1990) *The Death of the Irish Language: A Qualified Obituary.* Routledge: London.

Hock, Hans H. (1986) *Principles of Historical Linguistics.* Mouton de Gruyter: Amsterdam.

Hockett, Charles F. (1965) 'Sound change.' *Language 41*: 185–204.

(1973) *Man's Place in Nature.* McGraw-Hill: New York.

Hodge, Carleton T. (1970) 'The linguistic cycle.' *Language Sciences 13*: 1–7.

Hoenigswald, Henry M. (1960) *Language Change and Linguistic Reconstruction.* University of Chicago Press.

(1989) 'Language obsolescence and language history: matters of linearity, leveling, loss and the like.' In Dorian (ed.) (1989): 347–54.

Hoenigswald, Henry M. and Linda F. Wiener (eds.) (1987) *Biological Metaphor and Cladistic Classification.* Frances Pinter: London.

Holm, J. (1988–9) *Pidgins and Creoles.* 2 Volumes. Cambridge University Press.

Holmes, Janet (1992) *An Introduction to Sociolinguistics.* Longman: London.

Holthausen, F. (1934) *Altenglisches Etymologisches Wörterbuch.* Carl Winter: Heidelberg.

Hornstein, Norbert and David Lightfoot (eds.) (1981) *Explanation in Linguistics: The Logical Problem of Language Acquisition.* Longman: London.

Hudson, Richard A. (1980) *Sociolinguistics.* Cambridge University Press.

Huffines, Marion L. (1989) 'Case usage among the Pennsylvania German sectarians and nonsectarians.' In Dorian (ed.) (1989): 211–226.

Hughes, Geoffrey (1988) *Words in Time: A Social History of the English Vocabulary.* Blackwell: Oxford.

Hyman, Larry M. (1975) 'On the change from SOV to SVO: evidence from Niger-Congo.' In Li (ed.) (1975): 113–47.

Hymes, Dell (ed.) (1971) *Pidginization and Creolization of Languages.* Cambridge University Press.

Jakobson, Roman (1963) 'Implications of language universals for linguistics.' In Greenberg (ed.) (1963b): 263–78.

(1972) 'On the theory of phonological associations among languages.' In Keiler (ed.) (1972): 241–52.

(1978) 'Principles of historical phonology.' In Baldi and Werth (eds.) (1978): 103–20.

Jeffers, Robert J. and Ilse Lehiste (1979) *Principles and Methods for Historical Linguistics.* MIT Press: Cambridge, Mass.

Jespersen, Otto (1922) *Language: Its Nature, Development and Origin.* George Allen and Unwin Ltd: London.

(1946) *Mankind, Nation and Individual from a Linguistic Point of View.* George Allen and Unwin: London.

Jones, Mari C. (1992) *Language and Dialect Death in Contemporary Wales.* PhD thesis, University of Cambridge.

Jones, Sir William (1786) 'The third anniversary discourse, on the Hindus.'
Published 1788, *Asiatick Researches I.*

Joos, Martin (1957) *Readings in Linguistics I.* University of Chicago Press.

Joseph, B. (1980) 'Language universals and syntactic change.' *Language 56:*
345–70.

Joseph, Brian D. (1983) *The Synchrony and Diachrony of the Balkan Infinitive.*
Cambridge University Press.

Kaisse, Ellen and Patricia D. Shaw (1985) 'On the theory of lexical phonology.'
Phonology Yearbook 2: 1–30.

Katamba, Francis (1989) *An Introduction to Phonology.* Longman: London.

Kay, Billy (1988) *Scots: The Mither Tongue.* Grafton: London.

Keiler, Alan R. (1972) *A Reader in Historical and Comparative Linguistics.* Holt,
Rinehart and Winston: New York.

Kenstowicz, Michael and Charles Kisseberth (1979) *Generative Phonology.*
Academic Press: New York.

King, Robert D. (1967) 'Functional load and sound change.' *Language 43:*
831–52.

(1969a) *Historical Linguistics and Generative Grammar.* Prentice-Hall: Engle-
wood Cliffs, New Jersey.

(1969b) 'Push chains and drag chains.' *Glossa 3.1:* 3–21.

Kiparsky, Paul (1974) 'Remarks on analogical change.' In Anderson and Jones
(eds.) (1974): 257–75.

(1978) 'Rule reordering.' In Baldi and Werth (eds.) (1978): 218–235.

Kisseberth, Charles W. (1970) 'On the functional unity of phonological rules.'
Linguistic Inquiry 1: 291–306.

Klima, E. S. (1964) 'Relatedness between grammatical systems.' *Language 40:*
1–20.

Koerner, Konrad (ed.) (1983) *Linguistics and Evolutionary Theory: Three Essays by
August Schleicher, Ernst Haeckel and Wilhelm Bleek.* With Introduction by J.
Peter Maher. Benjamins: Amsterdam.

Kolin, Philip (1979) 'The pseudo-suffix -oholic.' *American Speech 54:* 74–6.

Koopman, Willem, Frederike van der Leek, Olga Fischer and Roger Eaton (eds.)
(1987) *Explanation and Language Change.* Benjamins: Amsterdam.

Krishnamurti, B. (1978) 'Areal and lexical diffusion of sound change: evidence
from Dravidian.' *Language 54:* 1–20.

Kuno, S. (1974) 'The position of relative clauses and conjunctions.' *Linguistic
Inquiry 5:* 117–36.

Kuryłowicz, Jerzy (1949) 'La nature des procès dits "analogiques".' *Acta
Linguistica 5:* 15–37.

(1965) 'The evolution of grammatical categories.' *Diogenes 51:* 55–71.

Labov, William (1972) *Sociolinguistic Patterns.* University of Pennsylvania Press:
Philadelphia.

(1981) 'Resolving the Neogrammarian controversy.' *Language 57:* 267–308.

Ladefoged, Peter (1982) *A Course in Phonetics.* Harcourt, Brace, Jovanovich: New
York.

Lakoff, Robin (1972) 'Another look at drift.' In Stockwell and Macaulay (eds.)
(1972): 172–98.

Lambert, W. E., R. C. Hodgson, R. C. Gardener and S. Fillenbaum (1960)

'Evaluation reactions to spoken language.' *Journal of Abnormal and Social Psychology 60*: 44–51.

Lass, Roger (1974) 'Linguistic orthogenesis? Scots vowel length and the English length conspiracy.' In Anderson and Jones (eds.) (1974): 311–43.

(1976) 'Variation studies and historical linguistics.' *Language in Society 5*: 219–29.

(1980) *On Explaining Language Change*. Cambridge University Press.

(1987) 'Language, speakers, history and drift.' In Koopman, van der Leek, Fischer and Eaton (eds.) (1987): 151–76.

(1990) 'How to do things with junk: exaptation in language evolution.' *Journal of Linguistics 26*: 79–102.

Lehiste, Ilse (1988) *Lectures on Language Contact*. MIT Press: Cambridge, Mass.

Lehmann, Christian (1985) 'Grammaticalization: synchronic variation and diachronic change.' *Lingua e stile 20.3*: 303–18.

Lehmann, Winfred P. (1973a) *Historical Linguistics: An Introduction* (2nd edition). Holt, Rinehart and Winston: New York.

(1973b) 'A structural principle of language and its implications.' *Language 49*: 47–66.

Lehmann, Winfred P. (ed.) (1978) *Syntactic Typology: Studies in the Phenomenology of Language*. The Harvester Press: Hassocks, Sussex.

Lehmann, Winfred P. and Yakov Malkiel (eds.) (1968) *Directions for Historical Linguistics*. University of Texas Press: Austin.

(eds.) (1982) *Perspectives on Historical Linguistics*. Benjamins: Amsterdam.

Leigh Fermor, Patrick (1986) *Between the Woods and the Water*. Penguin: London.

Lepschy, Giulio (1970) *A Survey of Structural Linguistics*. Faber: London.

Li, Charles N. (ed.) (1975) *Word Order and Word Order Change*. University of Texas Press: Austin.

(ed.) (1977) *Mechanisms of Syntactic Change*. University of Texas Press: Austin.

Lightfoot, David (1979a) *Principles of Diachronic Syntax*. Cambridge University Press.

(1979b) Review of Li (1977). *Language 55*: 381–95.

(1981a) 'Explaining syntactic change.' In Hornstein and Lightfoot (eds.) (1981): 209–40.

(1981b) 'A reply to some critics.' *Lingua 55*: 351–68.

(1988) 'Syntactic change.' In Newmeyer (ed.) (1988) Volume I: 303–23.

(1991) *How to Set Parameters: Arguments from Language Change*. MIT Press: Cambridge, Mass.

Lyons, John (1977) *Semantics. Volume 2*. Cambridge University Press.

(1981) *Language and Linguistics*. Cambridge University Press.

Malkiel, Yakov (1981) 'Drift, slope and slant: background of, and variations upon, a Sapirian theme.' *Language 57*: 535–70.

Mańczak, Witold (1958) 'Tendences générales des changements analogiques.' *Lingua 7*: 298–325, 387–420.

(1980) 'Laws of analogy.' In Fisiak (ed.) (1980): 283–8.

Marchand, Hans (1969) *The Categories and Types of Present-Day English Word-Formation*. Beck: Munich.

Martinet, A. (1952) 'Function, structure, and sound change.' *Word 8*: 1–32.

(1955) *Économie des changements phonétiques*. A. Francke: Bern.

Masek, C. S., R. A. Hendrick and M. F. Miller (eds.) (1981) *Papers from the Parasession on Language and Behavior*. Chicago Linguistic Society.

Matthews, Peter H. (1981) 'Do languages obey general laws?' Inaugural lecture of the University of Cambridge: Cambridge University Press.

(1991) *Morphology*. (2nd edition). Cambridge University Press.

McMahon, April M. S. (1991) 'Lexical phonology and sound change: the case of the Scottish Vowel Length Rule.' *Journal of Linguistics 27*: 29–53.

Meggers, Betty J. (ed.) (1959) *Evolution and Anthropology: a Centennial Appraisal*. Anthropological Society of Washington.

Meillet, Antoine (1912) 'L'évolution des formes grammaticales.' In Meillet, *Linguistique Historique et Linguistique Générale*: 131–48. Champion: Paris.

Mencken, H. L. (1936) *The American Language*. New York.

Menn, Lise (1989) 'Some people who don't talk right: universal and particular in child language, aphasia, and language obsolescence.' In Dorian (ed.) (1989): 335–46.

Mermin, N. David (1990) 'E pluribus boojum.' *English Today 24*: 7–16.

Meyer, Heinrich (1901) 'Über den Ursprung der Germanischen Lautverschiebung.' *Zeitschrift für deutsches Altertum und deutsches Litteratur 45*: 101–28.

Milroy, James (1990) 'A social model for the interpretation of language change.' Paper presented at the 6th International Conference on English Historical Linguistics, Helsinki.

(1992) *Linguistic Variation and Change*. Blackwell: Oxford.

Milroy, Lesley (1980) *Language and Social Networks*. Blackwell: Oxford.

(1987) *Observing and Analysing Natural Language*. Blackwell: Oxford.

Milroy, James and Lesley Milroy (1985) 'Linguistic change, social network and speaker innovation.' *Journal of Linguistics 21*: 339–84.

Moroney, M. J. (1951) *Facts from Figures*. Pelican: London.

Moulton, W. G. (1960) 'The short vowel system of Northern Switzerland: a study in structural dialectology.' *Word 16*: 155–82.

Mühlhaüsler, Peter (1980) 'Structural expansion and the process of creolization.' In Valdman and Highfield (eds.) (1980): 19–55.

(1986) *Pidgin and Creole Linguistics*. Blackwell: Oxford.

Muysken, Peter and Derek Bickerton (1988) 'The linguistic status of creole languages: two perspectives.' In Newmeyer (ed.) (1988), Volume II: 267–306.

Naro, Anthony J. (1978) 'A study on the origins of pidginization.' *Language 54*: 314–47.

Nerlich, Brigitte (1989) 'The evolution of the concept of "linguistic evolution" in the 19th and 20th century.' *Lingua 77*: 101–12.

Newmeyer, F. J. (ed.) (1988) *Linguistics: The Cambridge Survey. Volume I – Linguistic Theory: Foundations. Volume II – Linguistic Theory: Extensions and Implications. Volume IV – The Socio-Cultural Context*. Cambridge University Press.

Newton, B. (1972) *The Generative Interpretation of Dialect*. Cambridge University Press.

Ohala, John J. (1981) 'The listener as a source of sound change.' In Masek, Hendrick and Miller (eds.) (1981): 178–203.

(1987) 'Explanation in phonology: opinions and examples.' In Dressler, Luschützky, Pfeiffer and Rennison (eds.) (1987): 215–25.

Paul, Hermann (1978) 'On sound change.' Reissued in Baldi and Werth (eds.) (1978): 3–22.

Percival, W. Keith (1987) 'Biological analogy in the study of languages before the advent of comparative grammar.' In Hoenigswald and Wiener (eds.) (1987): 3–38.

Posner, Rebecca (1985) 'Post-verbal negation in non-standard French: a historical and comparative view.' *Romance Philology 39*: 170–97.

Postal, Paul (1968) *Aspects of Phonological Theory*. Harper & Row: New York.

Price, Glanville (1984) *The French Language: Present and Past*. Grant and Cutler: London.

Radford, Andrew (1981) *Transformational Syntax*. Cambridge University Press.

Ramat, Paulo (ed.) (1980) *Linguistic Reconstruction and Indo-European Syntax*. Benjamins: Amsterdam.

Rickford, John R. (1986) 'Social contact and linguistic diffusion: Hiberno-English and New World Black English.' *Language 62*: 245–89.

Robertson, J. S. (1983) 'From symbol to icon.' *Language 59*: 529–40.

Romaine, Suzanne (1981) 'The transparency principle: what it is and why it doesn't work.' *Lingua 55*: 277–300.

(1988) *Pidgin and Creole Languages*. Longman: London.

(1989) 'Pidgins, creoles, immigrant, and dying languages.' In Dorian (ed.) (1989): 369–84.

Rubin, Joan and Björn H. Jernudd (eds.) (1971) *Can Language be Planned?* University Press of Hawaii: Honolulu.

Ruhlen, Merritt (1991) *A Guide to the World's Languages. Volume 1: Classification*. Edward Arnold: London.

Sampson, Geoffrey (1980) *Schools of Linguistics: Competition and Evolution*. Hutchinson: London.

Sandfeld, Kristian (1930) *Linguistique Balkanique: Problèmes et Résultats*. Champion: Paris.

Sankoff, Gillian and Penelope Brown (1976) 'The origins of syntax in discourse.' *Language 52*: 631–66.

Sankoff, Gillian and Suzanne Laberge (1974) 'On the acquisition of native speakers by a language.' *Kivung 6*: 32–47.

Sapir, Edward (1921) *Language*. Harcourt, Brace and Co.: New York.

Saporta, Sol (1965) 'Ordered rules, dialect differences, and historical processes.' *Language 41*: 218–24.

Saussure, Ferdinand de (1974) *Course in General Linguistics*. Translated C. Baltaxe. Fontana: London.

Schmidt, Annette (1985) *Young People's Dyirbal: An Example of Language Death from Australia*. Cambridge University Press.

Sebeok, Thomas A. (ed.) (1973) *Current Trends in Linguistics. Volume 11: Diachronic, Areal and Typological Linguistics*. Mouton: The Hague.

Singh, Ishtla A. S. (1991) *The Influence of Early Modern English on the Trinidadian English-Based Creole*. M.Phil. Dissertation, University of Cambridge.

Smith, Neil V. (1981) 'Consistency, markedness and language change: on the notion "consistent language".' *Journal of Linguistics 17*: 39–54.

(1989) *The Twitter Machine*. Blackwell: Oxford.

Sommerfelt, Alf (1962) *Diachronic and Synchronic Aspects of Language*. Mouton: The Hague.

Soudek, Lev I. (1978) 'The relation of blending to English word-formation: theory, structure and typological attempts.' *Proceedings of the 12th International Congress of Linguists.*

Southworth, F. (1964) 'Family tree diagrams.' *Language 40*: 557–65.

Stampe, David (1972) *How I Spent my Summer Vacation*. Ph.D. thesis, Ohio State University.

Stevick, R. D. (1963) 'The biological model and historical linguistics.' *Language 39*: 159–69.

Stockwell, Robert P. and Ronald K. S. Macaulay (eds.) (1972) *Linguistic Change and Generative Theory*. Indiana University Press: Bloomington.

Sturtevant, Edward H. (1917) *Linguistic Change*. University of Chicago Press.

Swadesh, Morris (1948) 'Sociologic notes on obsolescent languages.' *International Journal of American Linguistics 14*: 226–35.

Taylor, Douglas R. (1956) 'Language contacts in the West Indies.' *Word 13*: 399–414.

Thomas, Alan R. (1967) 'Generative phonology in dialectology.' *Transactions of the Philological Society*: 179–203.

Thomason, Sarah G. (1976) 'Analogic change as grammar complication.' In Christie (ed.) (1976): 401–9.

Thomason, Sarah G. and Terrence Kaufman (1988) *Language Contact, Creolization and Genetic Linguistics*. University of California Press: Berkeley.

Thomson, Derick S. (1979) 'Gaelic: its range of uses.' In Aitken and McArthur (eds.) (1979): 14–25.

Todd, Loreto (1990) *Pidgins and Creoles* (2nd edition). Routledge: London.

Traugott, Elizabeth C. (1972) 'Diachronic syntax and generative grammar.' In Keiler (ed.) (1972): 201–16.

(1977) 'Pidginization, creolization and language change.' In Valdman (ed.) (1977): 70–98.

(1982) 'From propositional to textual and expressive meanings: some semantic-pragmatic aspects of grammaticalization.' In Lehmann and Malkiel (eds.) (1982): 245–71.

(1985) 'Conditional markers.' In Haiman (ed.) (1985): 289–307.

(1989) 'On the rise of epistemic meanings in English: an example of sub-jectification in semantic change.' *Language 65*: 31–55.

Trudgill, Peter (1974) *The Social Differentiation of English in Norwich*. Cambridge University Press.

(1976) 'Creolization in reverse: reduction and simplification in the Albanian dialects of Greece.' *Transactions of the Philological Society*: 32–50.

(1983) *On Dialect*. Blackwell: Oxford.

Ullmann, Stephen (1957) *Principles of Semantics*. University of Glasgow Press.

(1962) *Semantics: An Introduction to the Science of Meaning*. Blackwell: Oxford.

Valdman, A. (ed.) (1977) *Pidgin and Creole Linguistics*. University of Indiana Press: Bloomington.

Valdman, A. and A. Highfield (eds.) (1980) *Theoretical Orientations in Creole Studies*. Academic Press: New York.

Vennemann, Theo (1972) 'Rule inversion.' *Lingua 29*: 209–42.
  (1974) 'Topics, subjects and word order: from SXV to SVX via TVX.' In Anderson and Jones (eds.) (1974): 339–76.
  (1975) 'An explanation of drift.' In Li (ed.) (1975): 269–305.
  (1978) 'Phonetic and conceptual analogy.' In Baldi and Werth (eds.) (1978): 258–74.
Verner, Karl (1978) 'An exception to Grimm's Law.' In Baldi and Werth (eds.) (1978): 32–63.
Vincent, Nigel (1974) 'Analogy reconsidered.' In Anderson and Jones (eds.) (1974): 427–45.
  (1976) 'Perceptual factors and word order change in Latin.' In Harris (ed.) (1976): 54–68.
  (1978) 'Is sound change teleological?' In Fisiak (ed.) (1978): 409–29.
  (1980) 'Iconic and symbolic aspects of syntax: prospects for reconstruction.' In Ramat (ed.) (1980): 47–65.
Voorhoeve, Jan (1973) 'Historical and linguistic evidence in favour of the relexification theory in the formation of creoles.' *Language in Society 2*: 133–45.
Walde, A. and J. B. Hofmann (1938/1954) *Lateinisches Etymologisches Wörterbuch*. 2 Volumes. Carl Winter: Heidelberg.
Waldron, R. A. (1967) *Sense and Sense Development*. Deutsch: London.
Wang, William (1969) 'Competing changes as a cause of residue.' *Language 45*: 9–25.
Wang, William (ed.) (1977) *The Lexicon in Phonological Change*. Mouton: The Hague.
Warner, Anthony (1983) Review of Lightfoot (1979a). *Journal of Linguistics 19*: 187–209.
Watkins, Calvert (1976) 'Towards Proto-Indo-European syntax: problems and pseudo-problems.' *Papers from the Parasession on Diachronic Syntax*: 305–26. Chicago Linguistic Society.
Weinreich, Uriel (1953) *Languages in Contact: Findings and Problems*. Mouton: The Hague.
  (1954) 'Is a structural dialectology possible?' *Word 10*: 388–400.
Weinreich, Uriel, William Labov and Marvin I. Herzog (1968) 'Empirical foundations for a theory of language change.' In Lehmann and Malkiel (eds.) (1968): 95–195.
Wells, John C. (1982) *Accents of English*. 3 volumes. Cambridge University Press.
Wells, Rulon S. (1987) 'The life and growth of language: metaphors in biology and linguistics.' In Hoenigswald and Wiener (eds.) (1987): 39–80.
Wescott, Roger W. (1971) 'Linguistic iconism.' *Language 47*: 416–28.
Wexler, K. and P. W. Culicover (1980) *Formal Principles of Language Acquisition*. MIT Press: Cambridge, Mass.
Whitely, R. (1967) 'Swahili nominal classes and English loan-words: a preliminary survey.' In *La classification nominale dans les langues négro-africaines*. Centre National de la Recherche Scientifique: Paris.
Williamson, Robert C. and John A. Van Eerde (eds.) (1980) *Language Maintenance and Language Shift*. Special issue, *International Journal of the Sociology of Language 25*.

Winter, Werner (1973) 'Areal linguistics: some general considerations.' In Sebeok
    (ed.) (1973): 135–48.
Woolard, Kathryn A. (1989) 'Language convergence and language death as social
    processes.' In Dorian (ed.) (1989): 355–68.
Wurzel, Wolfgang U. (1989) *Inflectional Morphology and Naturalness*. Kluwer:
    Dordrecht.
Yule, George (1988) *The Study of Language*. Cambridge University Press.

Index

Printed in the United Kingdom
by Lightning Source UK Ltd.